VOICES OF AFRICAN WOMEN

VOICES OF AFRICAN WOMEN

WOMEN'S RIGHTS IN GHANA, UGANDA, AND TANZANIA

Johanna Bond

CAROLINA ACADEMIC PRESS
Durham, North Carolina

Library of Congress Cataloging-in-Publication Data

Bond, Johanna.
    Voices of African women : women's rights in Ghana, Uganda, and
Tanzania / by Johanna Bond.
        p. cm.
    ISBN 0-89089-124-9
    1. Women's rights--Ghana. 2. Women's rights--Uganda. 3. Women's
rights--Tanzania. I. Title.

    HQ1236.5.G4B66 2004
    305.42'096--dc22

                                                            2004020559

Carolina Academic Press
700 Kent Street
Durham, NC 27701
Telephone (919) 489-7486
Fax (919) 493-5668
www.cap-press.com

Printed in the United States of America
Cover Design by Erin M. Ehman

*This book is dedicated to my parents, Richard and Judy Bond,
and to my husband, J.D. King.*

CONTENTS

PREFACE

With two exceptions, the authors in this volume have all participated in a fellowship program called the Leadership and Advocacy for Women in Africa (LAWA) Program. The LAWA Program brings accomplished women's rights lawyers to Washington, D.C. for a sixteen-month fellowship program in which the lawyers pursue an LL.M. degree at Georgetown University Law Center and work at a Washington-based non-profit organization for six months. As part of their degree program, each of the LAWA lawyers authored a graduate thesis concerning some aspect of women's rights law in her home country. Those graduate papers formed the basis of the essays included in this volume. For this compilation, the papers have been excerpted and in many cases updated to reflect developments in the law.

Although the geographic reach of the LAWA program has expanded in recent years, the program began as a pilot project focused on Ghana, Tanzania, and Uganda. As a result, the essays in this compilation address women's rights concerns in those countries. As of 2003, the LAWA program has included thirty-nine participants from Botswana, Ghana, Sierra Leone, South Africa, Swaziland, Uganda, Tanzania, and Zimbabwe.[1]

The LAWA program is part of a larger women's rights fellowship program called the Women's Law and Public Policy Fellowship Program (WLPPF), which has been housed at Georgetown University Law Center since its inception in 1983. As a complement to the LAWA program, the WLPPF program brings women's rights lawyers from across the United States to Washington, D.C. for a one-year fellowship, during which the fellows work for non-profit organizations dedicated to protecting and improving women's rights. The WLPPF program is not merely a way to funnel talented attorneys into women's rights organizations. The program, which convenes bi-weekly, substantive seminars that the LAWA and WLPPF fellows attend, invests in developing the leadership and professional capacity of each of the fellows. The two programs enjoy a symbiotic relationship; the interaction between the U.S. fellows and the LAWA fellows enriches both groups in innumerable ways.

Not surprisingly, the LAWA program attracts an applicant pool that is unsurpassed both in its credentials and its collective passion for women's rights

---

1. The LAWA Program also included a fellow from Afghanistan in 2002.

activism—all of which makes the program fertile ground for a collection of women's rights essays. Although the authors share some attributes, such as a deep commitment to women's rights advocacy, they differ in significant ways as well. Although each is a lawyer, their human rights careers include a range of diverse experiences. The group includes a Member of Parliament, a law professor, a Labor Commissioner, a legal expert for the United Nations High Commissioner for Human Rights, and directors of non-governmental organizations, to name just a few.

The research these lawyers accomplished while they were pursuing an LL.M. degree at Georgetown reflects not only their scholarly research but also their years of activism fighting for gender justice in their own countries. As such, many of these essays include pragmatic strategies born of years of activism in the trenches. Some of the strategies are transferable across borders and will interest like-minded activists in other countries. Many of the essays include broader theoretical questions, such as the role of judicial activism in the quest for social justice. Despite the range of topics and strategies, however, the authors share a steadfast commitment to gender equality. This book is intended to share their expertise and, in so doing, contribute to the global effort to promote and protect women's human rights.

ACKNOWLEDGMENTS

First and foremost, I am grateful to the authors contributing to this volume. Their extensive knowledge about and dedication to women's rights was the inspiration for the book. It has been a privilege to work with them through the Leadership and Advocacy for Women in Africa (LAWA) Program, and I continue to learn from them on a daily basis.

I am deeply indebted to Mary Hartnett, Susan Deller Ross, and Wendy Webster Williams for their early and unrelenting support of this project. A number of people at Georgetown University Law Center contributed their talent and expertise to ensure successful completion of the project, including Tracey Bridgman, Tony Crossed, Jermaine Cruz, Marci Hoffman, Christopher Knott, and Zinta Saulkalns. Two people in particular, Anna Selden and John Showalter, proved themselves to be indispensable throughout the project. My research assistants, Rachel Brauner Vogelstein, Todd Schneider, and Nicole Smith performed invaluable research.

I am grateful to the Fulbright Program for providing the support necessary to collaborate with the authors and conduct the research to update the essays. In particular, I owe a special thanks to Ann Martin at the U.S. Department of State, Bureau of Educational and Cultural Affairs and to Debra Egan at the Council for International Exchange of Scholars (CIES). They recognized the value of the authors' research and supported the idea of sharing it with other activists and academics in the form of a compilation. I am thankful for their vision.

Introduction

Overview of History and Legal Systems: Ghana, Tanzania, and Uganda

Anne Daugherty Leiter

Plural Legal Systems

Ghana, Tanzania, and Uganda each have a plural legal system in which statutory law, customary, and religious law operate simultaneously. The interplay between statutory and African customary law stems from colonial occupation during which the colonial powers, chiefly Great Britain in the case of these three nations, sought to import British common law to govern certain areas of law. The colonial powers retained African customary law for certain areas, most notably family law disputes between African litigants. As a result of this decision, family law, which covers such important and potentially contentious areas as inheritance, marriage, and divorce, remains largely governed by African customary or religious law, except where statutory law specifically overrides it.[1]

Although the colonial powers purportedly left family law within the purview of traditional leaders, the colonial administrators affected the community's perception of women and, by extension, the community's interpretation of customary law. As Sylvia Tamale observed, "Colonialists worked hand

---

1. Center for Reproductive Law and Policy, Women of the World: Laws and Policies Affecting Their Reproductive Lives: Anglophone Africa 10 (1997).

xvi OVERVIEW OF HISTORY AND LEGAL SYSTEMS

in hand with the African patriarchs to develop inflexible customary laws, which evolved into new structures and forms of domination [of women]."[2] Although it is difficult to generalize across many different communities, customary and religious law often offer women less protection of their rights than statutory law.

The impact of multiple and, at times, conflicting legal systems has led to what one commentator described as a "legal cocktail ... [in which] judges empowered to administer these systems had to determine the proper law applicable to a given transaction."[3] Indeed, the national court systems of Ghana, Tanzania, and Uganda must determine if and when to apply customary law in a given case. In many African countries with significant Muslim populations, Islamic law forms yet another part of the plural legal systems. In plural legal systems such as Tanzania's, courts have formulated particular tests for determining which system of law applies. These tests attempt to discern whether the relevant parties lived in accordance with traditional customs or religious tenets. In all three nations, judicial determinations about which legal system applies have serious implications for women because the specific legal rights that women enjoy vary within the different legal systems.

The United Republic of Ghana

The modern nation of Ghana was the first Black African country to achieve independence from a colonial power.[4] Although English is the nation's official language, Ghana has several ethno-linguistic groups within its ten administrative regions.[5] The largest of these groups are the Akans, who traditionally reside along the coast, the Guans, from the plains of the Volta River, the Ga and Ewe speaking peoples from the south and southeast, and the Moshi-Dagomba-speaking groups that traditionally live in the northern regions.[6]

---

2. Sylvia Tamale, When Hens Begin to Crow: Gender and Parliamentary Politics in Uganda 9 (1999).

3. *Id.*

4. United States Central Intelligence Agency, *Ghana, in* The World Factbook 2002 198 (2002), *available at* http://www.cia.gov/cia/publications/factbook/print/gh.html.

5. *See* U.S. Department of State, Background Note: Ghana (2003), *available at* http://www.state.gov/r/pa/ei/bgn/2860pf.htm [hereinafter Ghana Background Note].

6. The population speaks the following languages: Akan (49%), Mole-Dagbani (16%), Ewe (13%), Ga-Adangbe (8%), Guan (4%), others (10%). Ghana Background Note,

Sixty-nine percent of Ghana's population identifies as Christian, 16 percent identify as Muslim,[7] and the remaining 21 percent are either non-practicing or practice traditional or indigenous religion.[8] Like many neighboring nations, agriculture is the dominant industry in Ghana, employing over half of its estimated 19.7 million inhabitants.[9] Education is mandatory until the end of junior secondary school, and 72.6 percent of the population is literate.[10]

Historical Considerations

Portugal was the first European nation to colonize the Gold Coast region, which together with British Togoland comprises much of modern day Ghana.[11] It was, however, the British who formally declared the creation of the British Crown Colony of the Gold Coast in 1874.[12] Despite British control, the impact of two powerful native empires, the Asante and Fante, continued to influence the population throughout the colonial period.[13] Popular support for nationalism and independence grew in the 1940s and early 1950s, culminating in a 1956 request from the Ghanaian government for independence from the British Commonwealth.[14] The British granted this request, and the Gold Coast became the independent nation of Ghana on March 6, 1957.[15]

The years following independence, however, were marked by military coup d'etats and abrogated constitutions. Dr. Kwame Nkrumah, who fought for independence from the British, served both as Ghana's first Prime Minister upon independence and, when the nation became a republic in 1960, as Ghana's first President.[16] He ruled until the Ghanaian army and police force overthrew

---

supra note 5.

7. See Ghana Background Note, *supra* note 5.

8. *Id.*

9. *Id.*

10. *Id.*

11. *See id.* Ghana borders the nations of Burkina Faso to the north, Togo to the east, and Cote d'Ivoire to the west; its southern coastline, which is the most densely populated and financially stable area in the nation, overlooks the Atlantic Ocean. *See id.*

12. *See History, at* http://www.ghana.gov.gh/visiting/ghana/history.php (last visited Dec. 4, 2003).

13. *Id.*

14. GHANA: A COUNTRY STUDY 30 (LaVerle Berry, ed., Library of Congress, 1995).

15. *Id.*

16. *Id.* at 33.

him on February 24, 1966, claiming that his "flagrant abuse of individual rights and liberties, his regime's corrupt, oppressive, and dictatorial practices, and the rapidly deteriorating economy" necessitated his immediate removal from power.[17] The military leaders who espoused an eventual return to democratic rule established the National Liberation Council (NLC). The NLC ruled Ghana in preparation for the nation's return to a constitutionally bound, civilian government.[18] In all, in the almost thirty-six years between Ghana's independence in March 1957 and the establishment of the current government in January 1993, a total of four military governments and three civilian governments held power.[19]

In this climate of ever-changing administrations, Flt. Lt. Jerry John Rawlings instigated two separate regime changes and was able to remain in the forefront of Ghanaian politics for over two decades. Rawlings initially came to power after a 1979 revolt in which the Armed Forces Revolutionary Council (AFRC) overthrew the previous military regime.[20] He was only in power for three months when general elections brought an opposition party, the People's National Party, to power. In 1981, Rawlings overthrew the People's National Party, after which he became Chairman of the Provisional National Defence Ruling Council (PNDC), a group of military and civilian officials charged with running the country.[21]

Rawlings' early years in power did not reflect the multiparty democracy over which he eventually presided. On the contrary, the PNDC initially exercised unchecked control over Ghanaian society, suspending the 1979 Constitution, outlawing opposition political parties, and disbanding the parliament.[22] The only structure maintained was the judiciary, but the PNDC supplemented the existing judicial structure with its own legal system, the National Investigation Committee (NIC). By 1984, Rawlings' government was under pressure, both from within Ghana and from abroad, to transition from his paramilitary government towards a democratic, civilian State.[23] Rawlings complied and remained in power during the drafting and the adoption of the

---

17. GHANA BACKGROUND NOTE, *supra* note 5.

18. *Id.*

19. *See* http://www.ghana.gov.gh/visiting/ghana/history.php for a thorough overview of each of these governments.

20. GHANA: A COUNTRY STUDY, *supra* note 14, at 46.

21. *See id.* at 48–49.

22. GHANA BACKGROUND NOTE, *supra* note 5.

23. *See id.*

1992 Constitution, a document that, as noted below, established a constitutional democracy and outlined numerous guarantees of human rights. The 1992 Constitution paved the way for the January 7, 1993 creation of the Fourth Republic.[24] Rawlings was sworn in as President, a position he retained until term limits forced him to retire in 2000. The current President, John Agyekum Kufuor, won the 2000 election to succeed Rawlings.[25]

Implications of the 1992 Constitution

Constitutional Guarantees

The 1992 Constitution established the Fourth Republic of Ghana, thereby officially restoring multiparty, participatory democracy after almost twelve years of paramilitary control by the PNDC.[26] Chapter Five of the Constitution, entitled "Fundamental Human Rights and Freedoms,"[27] mandates that "[e]very person in Ghana, whatever his race, place of origin, political opinion, color, religion, creed or gender shall be entitled to the fundamental human rights and freedoms of the individual contained in this Chapter but subject to respect for the rights and freedoms of others and for the public interest."[28] Chapter Five also prohibits discrimination, defined as affording "different treatment to different persons attributable only or mainly to their respective descriptions by race, place of origin, political opinions, color, gender, occupation, religion or creed, whereby persons of one description are subjected to disabilities or restrictions to which persons of another description are not made subject or are granted privileges or advantages which are not granted to persons of another description."[29]

---

24. *See History, at* http://www.ghana.gov.gh/visiting/ghana/history.php (last visited Dec. 4, 2003).

25. *See id.*

26. *See* GHANA: A COUNTRY STUDY, *supra* note 14, at 216–19.

27. In addition to explicitly mandating gender equality, Chapter Five includes strong anti-discrimination guarantees for children and for the disabled.

28. GHANA CONST. art. 12 (2) (1992).

29. *Id.* art. 17 (1)-(5) ("(1) All persons shall be equal before the law. (2) A person shall not be discriminated against on grounds of gender, race, colour, ethnic origin, religion, creed or social or economic status.... (4) Nothing in this article shall prevent Parliament from enacting laws that are reasonably necessary to provide

(a) for matters relating to adoption, marriage, divorce, burial, devolution of property on death or other matters of personal law;

(b) for the imposition of restrictions on the acquisition of land by persons who are not cit-

The Constitution contains specific mandates for equal treatment, such as the requirement that guarantees women "equal rights to training and promotion without any impediments from any person." [30] It likewise includes provisions, such as the explicit allowance of affirmative action policies[31] and the requirement that mothers get special protection,[32] designed to protect women's interests and promote their upward mobility.

Political Structure

Ghana is a constitutional democracy. The President is elected for a four-year term.[33] The Constitution provides for a Council of State, a body explicitly charged with advising the President in the performance of his duties.[34] The Constitution also establishes a unicameral Parliament that is charged with all legislative responsibilities, including the promulgation of national statutory law.[35] All Members of Parliament (MPs) represent the constituencies that elected them.[36] At the current time, the 200 member Parliament has representatives from four political parties, in addition to 4 independent candi-

---

izens of Ghana or on the political and economic activities of such persons and for other matters relating to such persons; or

(c) for making different provisions for different communities having regard to their special circumstances not being provision which is inconsistent with the spirit of this Constitution.

(5) Nothing shall be taken to be inconsistent with this article which is allowed to be done under any provision of this Chapter.").

30. *Id.* art. 27(3).

31. *See id.* art. 24 (4) ("Nothing in this article shall prevent Parliament from enacting laws that are reasonably necessary to provide - (a) for the implementation of policies and programmes aimed at redressing social, economic or educational imbalance in the Ghanaian society.").

32. *See id.* art. 27 ("(1) Special care shall be accorded to mothers during a reasonable period before and after child-birth; and during those periods, working mothers shall be accorded paid leave. (2) Facilities shall be provided for the care of children below school-going age to enable women, who have the traditional care for children, realise their full potential.").

33. *Ghana, in* THE WORLD FACTBOOK 2002, *supra* note 4, at 199.

34. GHANA CONST. art. 89(1) (1992).

35. *See id.* art. 93(2). *See also* art. 106(1) ("The power of Parliament to make laws shall be exercised by bills passed by parliament and assented to by the President.").

36. *See id.* art. 47 (1) ("Ghana shall be divided into as many constituencies for the purpose of election of members of parliament as the Electoral Commission may prescribe, and each constituency shall be represented by one member of Parliament."). The universality of Ghana's direct election stands in contrast to the situation in Tanzania, where the Con-

dates.[37] The New Patriotic Party (NPP), commands the majority, having won 100 seats.[38]

Judicial Systems

Although the Constitution allows for multiple sources of law, the Constitution's supremacy clause mitigates the power of these alternate sources, declaring them void if they are "…found to be inconsistent with any provision of this Constitution."[39] Alternate sources of law, such as customary law, are further constrained by Article 26 of the Constitution which states that "every person is entitled to enjoy, practise, profess, maintain and promote any culture, language, tradition or religion subject to the provisions of this Constitution." [40] Article 26 also prohibits "[a]ll customary practices which dehumanise or are injurious to the physical and mental well-being of a person.…"[41]

The United Republic of Tanzania

While 80 percent of the population engages in agriculture,[42] an alarming 36 percent of the population lives below the poverty line.[43] In July 2003, the government estimated that Tanzania's population was 35, 922, 454.[44] Ninety-five percent of Tanzanians are *Bantu*, a delineation that encompasses more than 130 tribes native to Africa.[45] On mainland Tanzania, approximately 30 percent of the population is Christian, 35 percent is Muslim, and 35 percent adhere to indigenous beliefs. Zanzibar's Muslim population, in contrast, con-

---

stitution requires the reservation of certain numbers of seats for women and for members of Zanzibar's party.

37. *Ghana, in* THE WORLD FACTBOOK 2002, *supra* note 4, at 199.

38. *Id.*

39. GHANA CONST. art. 1 (2) (1992) ("The Constitution shall be the supreme law of Ghana and any other law found to be inconsistent with any provision of this Constitution shall, to the extent of the inconsistency, be void.").

40. *See* GHANA CONST., art. 26 (1992).

41. 41 *See id.* art. 26(1)-(2).

42. *See* UNITED STATES CENTRAL INTELLIGENCE AGENCY, *Tanzania, in* THE WORLD FACTBOOK 2002 504 (2002), *available at* www.cia.gov/cia/publications/factbook/print/tz.html (last visited Dec. 4, 2003).

43. *Id.* (based on 2002 estimate).

44. *Id.*

45. *Id.*

stitutes 99 percent of the island's population.[46] Despite this diversity of religions and tribal affiliations, Tanzania has been spared the political turmoil and civil wars suffered by some of its neighbors, including Uganda. Tanzania has, in fact, absorbed into its population significant numbers of displaced persons from neighboring countries devastated by internal conflict.[47]

Historical Considerations

Germany's colonization of Tanzania in the mid-nineteenth century led to a series of violent uprisings that cost the lives of thousands of Africans.[48] The uprisings, the most famous of which was the Maji Maji rebellion of 1905–1907, were the indigenous population's response to repressive German policies, and their existence signaled the beginning of Tanzania's nationalist movement.[49] Germany's control over Tanzania ended with their defeat in World War I, after which the League of Nations ceded control of the region to the United Kingdom.[50]

The British, unlike their German predecessors, permitted the use of customary law and allowed native Tanzanians to participate in the provincial administration. After World War II, when the power of colonial governments was decreasing throughout Africa, Tanzania became a trust territory of the United Nations.[51] The Tanganyika African National Union (TANU)[52] mounted a multitiered effort to convince the British, the United Nations, and Tanzanians themselves, that Tanzania was ready for home rule. The success of TANU-backed candidates accelerated Tanzania's progression from trust territory to independent nation on December 9, 1961.[53]

Julius Nyerere, President of TANU, became the first Head of State. The new nation had serious socioeconomic problems, including a lack of industrial-

---

46. *Id.*

47. *See, e.g.,* Beth Elise Whitaker, *Refugees in Western Tanzania: The Distribution of Benefits and Burdens Among Local Hosts,* 15 J. REFUGEE STUD. 339 (2002).

48. *See* U.S. DEPARTMENT OF STATE, BACKGROUND NOTE: TANZANIA (2003), *available at* http://www.state.gov/r/pa/ei/bgn/2843pf.htm [hereinafter TANZANIA BACKGROUND NOTE].

49. *Id.*

50. *Id.*

51. *See Tanzania,* THE WORLD FACTBOOK 2002, *supra* note 42, at 503.

52. Formerly the Tanganyika African Association (TAA).

53. *See* TANZANIA BACKGROUND NOTE, *supra* note 48, at *History; see also* PBS, *Commanding Heights: Tanzania, at* http://www.pbs.org/wgbh/commandingheights/lo/countries/tz/tz_full.html.

ization, high infant mortality rates, and no tradition of widespread school attendance. In addressing these problems, Nyerere and TANU embraced *Ujamaa*, an Afrocentric form of socialism.[54] Nyerere's government likewise embraced a one-party system, under which TANU was the only legally recognized
political party.

For much of the nineteenth century, Sultan Seyyid Said, the Arab ruler of
Zanzibar, informally increased Zanzibar's dependence on Great Britain. On
June 14, 1890, the Sultan formalized this relationship, officially making Zanzibar a British Protectorate.[55] The British created and implemented most of the
important political and economic decisions during this period. The British
Empire was in decline by 1963 and, rather than risk violent insurrections by
its subjects in Zanzibar, Britain agreed to grant Zanzibar independence, which
it did on December 19, 1963.[56]

The governments of Tanganyika and Zanzibar united their countries on
April 26, 1964, the date that they signed the Article of Union.[57] TANU and
ASP were the official parties of Tanzania and Zanzibar, and they had unchal-
lenged authority to create national policy. In 1967, the government, under
President Nyerere, built upon Ujamaa and promulgated the Arusha Declaration. This new policy reorganized Tanzanian society by attempting to create a
command economy. To further this goal, the government nationalized the
banking industry and forced peasants to resettle in communal villages.[58] In
1977, TANU and ASP united to form the Chama Cha Mapinduzi (CCM). This
combined party, which would remain the only legal party in Tanzania for more
than fifteen years, continued the nation's commitment to African socialism.

President Nyerere retired in 1985 and Alu Hassan Mwinyi, then the President of Zanzibar, assumed leadership of Tanzania.[59] In 1992, the Tanzanian

---

54. "The true African socialist does not look on one class of men as his brethren and
another as his natural enemies. He does not form an alliance with the 'brethren' for the ex-
termination of the 'non-brethren.' He rather regards all men as his brethren—as members
of his ever extending family.... '*Ujamaa*,' then, or 'familyhood,' describes our socialism."
Julis Kambarage Nyerere, *Ujamaa: The Basic of African Socialism, at* http://www.nathaniel-
turner.com/ujamaanyerere.htm (last visited Dec. 5, 2003). *See* PBS, *supra* note 53.

55. Fauz Twaib, The Legal Profession in Tanzania 302 (1997).

56. *See* Tanzania Background Note, *supra* note 48, at *History*.

57. *See id.* The creation of CCM did not, of course, signal the complete integration of
mainland Tanzania and Zanzibar. For example, Zanzibar retains its own House of Representatives, to deal with internal affairs. *Tanzania*, The World Factbook 2002, *supra* note
42, at 504.

58. *See* PBS, *supra* note 53.

government ratified the Eighth Amendment to the 1977 Constitution, thereafter permitting multiparty politics.[60] By the 1995 election cycle, the first for
which the amendment was effective, thirteen political parties had duly registered to challenge candidates from CCM. CCM candidates won the important
national posts, including Benjamin William Mkapa, who was elected President of Tanzania.

Representatives of other parties, however, were able to claim seats in the
Bunge and in Zanzibar's House of Representatives. Reserved seats for women
in both of these Houses enabled women from opposition parties to run for
office for the first time;[61] additionally, the number of females elected to represent constituencies increased from two to eight.[62] The issue of reserved seats
for women remains controversial among Tanzanian women's rights organizations. Some activists believe that the quota system sends the message that
women cannot and should not compete with men for constituency seats and
should be satisfied with the seats allotted to them; other activists believe that
a quota system remains necessary because, in its absence, gender bias would
prevent many women from being elected.[63]

Implications of the 1977 Constitution and the 1984 Bill of Rights

Constitutional Guarantees

Tanzania's Interim Constitution, enacted in 1965, established the new nation
as a one-party system and lacked a Bill of Rights enumerating the rights and protections afforded the citizenry.[64] The second constitution, the Constitution of the
United Republic of Tanzania, enacted in1977, likewise did not include a Bill of

---

59. *See* Harrison George Mwakyembe, Tanzania's Eighth Constitutional
Amendment and its Implications on Constitutionalism, Democracy and the
Union Question 187 (1995).

60. *See id.* at 160–62. The Political Parties Bill, passed that same year, dictated the
terms and procedures for registering political parties. *See id.* at 162 (citing Political Parties
Act, no. 5 of 1992 (1992) (Tanzania)).

61. Bookie Kethusegile, Beyond Inequalities: Women in Southern Africa 36
(2000).

62. *Id.*

63. Jennifer L. Rakstad et. al, *The Progress of Tanzanian Women in the Law: Women in
Legal Education, Legal Employment and Legal Reform*, 10 S. Cal. Rev. L. & Women's Stud.
35, 108–12 (2000).

64. Beyond Inequalities, *supra* note 61, at 36.

Rights. Widespread calls for a Bill of Rights surfaced in 1982, when a legal conference brought the issue back to national prominence.[65] As a result of the political pressure exerted by conference attendees, the government promulgated the Tanzanian Bill of Rights, enacted an addendum to the 1977 Constitution in 1984.

Unfortunately, Article 13(5), which delineates protected categories for non-discrimination, includes only race, place of origin, political opinion, color, occupation, and creed.[66] Gender and sex was conspicuously absent from this list. Article 13(5), however, was amended in 2000 to specifically include gender as a category of prohibited discrimination.

Political System

The Constitution established the legislative branch, called the National Assembly or *Bunge*, to promulgate statutes applicable both to the entire nation and to mainland Tanzania only. The *Bunge* consists of 274 members, 232 of whom are popularly elected from Tanzania's 26 administrative regions.[67] The remaining forty-two seats are reserved by Constitutional mandate; of these seats, women are allotted thirty-seven seats and members of the Zanzibar House of Representatives, a body that promulgates laws effective within Zanzibar alone, are guaranteed five seats.[68]

The *Bunge's* laws are automatically applicable to the mainland, but they must meet specific criteria to apply to Zanzibar.[69] Zanzibar retains its own House of Representatives, responsible for laws affecting only Zanzibar. This body has fifty members whom the people of Zanzibar directly elect.[70]

Judicial System

After unification, the Tanzanian government attempted to standardize the new nation's judicial structure and to integrate specific portions of statutory,

---

65. *Id.* at 40.

66. TANZ. CONST., art. 13(5) (1982).

67. *See* TANZANIA BACKGROUND NOTE, *supra* note 48, at *Government*; *Tanzania, in* THE WORLD FACTBOOK 2002, *supra* note 42, at 503.

68. *Tanzania, in* THE WORLD FACTBOOK 2002, *supra* note 42, at 504.

69. Specifically, the legislation must be "expressed to extend to Zanzibar or expressly amend, modify, revoke or repeal a law of Zanzibar; or [the legislation must] amend, modify, revoke, or repeal a law of Tanganyika which was extended to Zanzibar by Presidential Decree under the Act of Union, or an Act which is expressed to extend to Zanzibar." *See* TWAIB, *supra* note 55, at 307 (citing Article 64 of the 1977 Constitution).

70. *Tanzania, in* THE WORLD FACTBOOK 2002 *supra* note 42, at 504.

customary, and Islamic law. In 1984, the government enacted a revised Magistrates Courts Act, which established that the judiciary consists of the Court of Appeal of the United Republic of Tanzania, the High Court of Tanzania, the High Court of Zanzibar, Magistrates Courts, and Primary Courts. [71]

The Tanzanian government did not establish a unified code of law to apply in their integrated court system. Instead, the government made limited attempts to streamline the judicial process and assist with choice of law questions. Towards this end, the government mandated that the Tanzanian Penal Code and Criminal Procedure Code govern all criminal matters, removing criminal matters from the purview of customary and Islamic law.[72] The government also designed the Law of Marriage Act (LMA), enacted in 1971, to standardize the basic rights accorded married couples across legal systems. Although the LMA permits marriage under customary and religious law, the LMA preempts customary and religious law when there is a conflict between those laws and the LMA.[73] In practice, the LMA dictates the legal rights and responsibilities of spouses, both during marriage and upon divorce, even though couples are free to solemnize their marriage according to customary or Islamic law.

Some of these innovations have improved women's legal rights. Courts have, for example, cited the LMA when striking down the application of discriminatory customary and Islamic laws.[74] Indeed, one appellate judge noted that "where there is clear statutory law governing a point, and such law is more in line with equity than some other law on the same point, such as customary or Islamic law, then statutory law should prevail."[75]

The LMA does not apply to inheritance, meaning that there is no statutory law that automatically supersedes customary law in this arena. Although the Indian Succession Act of 1865 creates statutory rules governing the allocation of land, money, and property after death, it presumes that native Tanzanians

---

71. *See Government: Judiciary*, *at* http://www.udsm.ac.tz/tanzania/indexE.html (Official Website for Tanzania's government) (last visited Dec. 5, 2003).

72. Hilliard v. Castilla, *How Leaders, Ideology and Organizations Effect Nation-Building: A Look at the Role of Julius Nyerere, Ujamaa and TANU in Shaping Tanzania's Law and Legal System* 6A.130.13, *in* 6A THE MODERN LEGAL SYSTEMS CYCLOPEDIA (Kenneth Robert Redden ed., 1984 & 1995 rev.)

73. WOMEN OF THE WORLD, *supra* note 1, at 122.

74. *See* Bart Rwezaura, *Tanzania: Building a New Family Law Out of a Plural Legal System*, 33 U. LOUISVILLE J. FAM. L. 523, 533 (citing *Asha Mbulayambele v. William Shibungi*, High Court Civil Appeal No. 56 of 1986).

75. *Id.*

would prefer that customary law govern their affairs unless there is express proof to the contrary.[76]

Courts attempting to determine whether customary or statutory law applies in a case involving, for example, intestate succession will use a "mode of life test." For statutory law to apply to African Christians, the test requires proof that "the deceased had in his lifetime abandoned his customary way of life 'in favour of what may be called Christian and non-traditional.'"[77] This is a difficult standard to meet. A Tanzanian man, for example, may participate nominally in traditional activities, such as community ceremonies, even though he does not conduct his daily life according to traditional custom. In an inheritance dispute, however, the man's participation in traditional ceremonies may constitute evidence that he lived in accordance with customary practices, rendering his heirs ineligible for protection from statutory inheritance law. Because it is difficult to prove that a person abandoned a customary way of life, customary law still governs most inheritance issues in Tanzania.

The sizeable Muslim population in Tanzania necessitates the existence of a third legal system, namely Islamic Law. Like customary law, Islamic law governs some family law matters. The LMA supersedes Islamic law in cases concerning most aspects of marriage and divorce but, as it does not apply to inheritance, Islamic law retains jurisdiction in inheritance matters involving Muslim litigants.

The Republic of Uganda

As of 2003, Uganda's population was approximately 24,699,073.[78] Uganda is a landlocked country, bordering Sudan in the north, Rwanda and Tanzania in the south, the Republic of Congo in the west, and Kenya in the east.[79] Uganda's primary export is coffee, although it also exports cotton. A large number of the

---

76. WOMEN OF THE WORLD, *supra* note 1, at 124.

77. Magdalena Kamugisha Rwebangira, *Some Aspects of Women and the Courts in Tanzania: The Case of Inheritance, in* PROCEEDINGS OF A NATIONAL WORKSHOP ON WOMEN AND LAW IN EASTERN AFRICA 30 (M.K. Rwebangira ed., 1993).

78. *See* UNITED STATES CENTRAL INTELLIGENCE AGENCY, *Uganda, in* THE WORLD FACTBOOK 2002 529 (2002), *available at* www.cia.gov/cia/publications/factbook/print/ug.html (last visited Dec. 4, 2003).

79. *Id.* at 528.

country's inhabitants rely on agriculture for their livelihoods and the majority of the nation's women engage solely in subsistence agriculture.[80]

Historical Considerations

Like many of its neighbors, Uganda has survived colonization, civil war, and more than one military coup. Great Britain eventually consolidated its control over Uganda and ruled the country as a British protectorate from 1860 until Ugandan independence in 1962.[81] Britain adopted a system of "indirect rule" in which it utilized local chiefs and kinship structures to implement the Empire's laws under the supervision of a Colonial Governor.[82] Many Ugandans were not content with this system, but widespread support for independence did not materialize until after World War II.[83] From then on, however, Ugandans utilized demonstrations, strikes, boycotts and, eventually, riots, to convey nationalist sentiments to the British. The Uganda National Congress (UNC) was the first political party, and several other parties whose members desired self-rule followed.[84]

Organized efforts to improve women's status reached the national level, ironically, during colonial rule; the 1947 establishment of the Ugandan National Council of Women was an important first step towards changing women's roles. In the 1960s, the Ugandan National Council of Women continued to be active, distributing, for example, informational pamphlets designed to educate women about the need for increased educational opportunities, better medical services, and fewer laws that discriminated according to gender.[85]

Uganda achieved independence in 1961, and Milton Obote was the first Head of State.[86] General Idi Amin staged a military coup on January 25, 1971, in which he ousted Obote from power and installed himself as Uganda's Head of State.[87] Sadly, the many Ugandans who celebrated Amin's victory had no way of knowing that his eight-year reign would leave countless people dead

---

80. Chip Lowe, *The Legal System of Uganda* 6A.150.7, *in* 6A THE MODERN LEGAL SYSTEMS CYCLOPEDIA (Kenneth Robert Redden ed., 1984 & 1995).

81. *See id.* at 6A.150.9.

82. *See* UGANDA: A COUNTRY STUDY 13 (Rita M. Byrnes, ed., Library of Congress, 1992).

83. THOMAS P. OFCANSKY, UGANDA: TARNISHED PEARL OF AFRICA 33 (1996).

84. *Id.* at 36.

85. *See* THOMAS P. OFCANSKY, UGANDA: TARNISHED PEARL OF AFRICA 87 (1996).

86. *Id.* at 38.

87. *Id.* at 42.

and the infrastructure of Uganda gutted. As one commentator noted, "[u]nlike the brutal methods used by many tyrannical governments to achieve political goals, the violent tactics employed by the Amin regime often had no purpose other than to terrorize the Ugandan population."[88]

Amin's promise to "Africanize" Uganda's economy appealed to some of his citizens' xenophobic tendencies and kept many citizens from criticizing his regime. In 1972, Amin used the Asian population of Uganda as a scapegoat for some of the nation's economic troubles. He expelled all Asians from Uganda and claimed their property for friends and supporters of his regime.[89]

Amin's reign also had devastating consequences for women. His administration banned all women's organizations and perpetuated the stereotype of unmarried women as social deviants.[90] Amin's government ordered the removal of all single women, whom the government publicly decried as prostitutes, from the nation's cities and towns.[91] Amin followed this forced removal with a campaign to force all Ugandan women to marry.[92] When combined with the decreased employment opportunities characteristic of Amin's reign, many women had no choice but to live a "traditional" lifestyle focused on pleasing their husbands, catering to their children, and providing family meals through subsistence agriculture.[93]

Amin's brutality ended when the Uganda National Liberation Front (UNLF), a group formed by Ugandan exiles and aided by Tanzania, forced him from power in 1979.[94] In the year after Amin's reign, Uganda saw the brief tenures of two UNLF leaders, Y.K. Lule and Binsana. In 1980, however, former Head of State Milton Obote won Uganda's national election, thus beginning his second term as President.

Future President Yoweri Kaguta Museveni spent the next five years engaged in a guerrilla war against the regimes of Obote and his successor, Tito Okello.[95] Okello, who ousted Obote in yet another military coup, attempted to negoti-

---

88. *Id.* at 43.

89. *Id.* at 44; UGANDA: A COUNTRY STUDY, *supra* note 82, at 28.

90. *See* OFCANSKY, *supra* note 85, at 87.

91. *Id.* at 88.

92. *Id.*

93. *Id.* at 87.

94. Lowe, *supra* note 80, at 6A.150.10.

95. *See State House, Republic of Uganda: The President, at* http://www.statehouse.go.ug/president.php.

ate with Museveni and his forces, but these talks broke down amidst continued fighting. On January 29, 1986, shortly after Kampala fell to Museveni's
forces, Museveni became Uganda's Head of State.[96]

President Museveni, who represents the National Resistance Movement
(NRM), won re-election in March 2001. Under the "Movement" system, approved in a June 2000 referendum, candidates must campaign independently
and not as representatives of political parties.[97] This structure remains controversial, however, as proponents of multipartyism assert that the ban on political activities, in essence, creates a one-party state and violates international
human rights, including the freedom of association.[98]

Opponents of the Movement system are not the only dissenting voices in
modern day Ugandan politics. Indeed, the Lord's Resistance Army (LRA) continues its military operations in northern and western Uganda. The LRA's
forced enlistment of male and female child-soldiers has garnered international
attention in recent years, leading to widespread condemnation of this human
rights abuse.[99]

Impact of the 1995 Constitution

Constitutional Guarantees

The 1995 Constitution contains many provisions that are particularly important for women's rights activists. Specifically, it provides that all people are
equal before the law and that discrimination based on sex, race, social or economic standing, or disability is prohibited.[100] Furthermore, it notes that
"women shall be accorded full and equal dignity with men."[101]

---

96. *See id.*

97. *See* AMNESTY INTERNATIONAL, *Annual Report 2000: Uganda, available at* http://www.
amnesty.org.

98. Amy Lippincott, *Is Uganda's "No-Party" System Discriminatory Against Women and
a Violation of International Law,* 27 BROOK. J. INT'L L. 1137, 1142 (2002).

99. *See* AMNESTY INTERNATIONAL, *Uganda: The Full Picture. Uncovering HR Violations
By Government Forces in the Northern War* (1999), *at* http://web.amnesty.org/library/
Index/ENGAFR590051999?open&of=ENG-369 ("The organization has documented scores
of killings of unarmed civilians—including of children—dozens of rapes and hundreds
of beatings by government forces over the last three years. While some soldiers have been
arrested for these crimes, few have been brought to court as weaknesses in the criminal justice system delay trials of soldiers almost indefinitely.").

100. UGANDA CONST., art. 21(2) (1995).

101. *Id.* art. 33(1).

The Constitution makes the Ugandan government responsible for taking affirmative action "in favor of marginalized groups on basis of gender, age, disability or any other reason created by history, tradition or custom for purposes of redressing the imbalance."[102] Other express guarantees for minorities include the promise that "minorities have a right to participate in the decision-making process in order to articulate their interests"[103] and the provision that, "every person has a right to participate in affairs of government individually or through representatives."[104]

Political System

The political structure of Uganda has achieved increased stability in the wake of the 1995 Constitution, Uganda's fourth since its independence in 1962.[105] The Constitution provides for Executive, Judicial, and Legislative branches, as well as an extensive administrative structure that is beholden to the Executive branch.

The national Legislative branch is comprised of a unicameral Ugandan Parliament that includes reserved seats for minority groups, such as women and the disabled.[106] The Parliament promulgates constitutional amendments and statutory law.[107] On the local level, Uganda is divided into districts, each of which maintains their own District Councils. These districts are subdivided into smaller units, called Municipal Councils, Town Councils, or Parish Councils, depending upon the region.[108]

---

102. *Id.* art. 32(1).

103. *Id.* art. 36.

104. *Id.* art. 38(1).

105. 105 Lippincott, *supra* note 98, at 1140.

106. UGANDA CONST. art. 78(1) (1995):

Composition of Parliament (1) Parliament shall consist of-

(a) members directly elected to represent constituencies;

(b) one woman representative for every district;

(c) such numbers of representatives of the army, youth, workers, persons with disabilities and other groups as Parliament may determine; and

(d) the Vice-President and Ministers, who, if not already elected members of Parliament, shall be ex-official members of Parliament without the right to vote on any issue requiring a vote in Parliament.

107. Members introduce bills, amendments, or motions which, if seconded, are read twice and then referred to an appropriate committee. The Committee may change the bill if they see fit, before sending it back to the Parliament for a third reading and vote. *See Rules of Procedure for the Parliament of Uganda,* at http://www.parliament.go.ug/rules_procedure_session2.htm.

108. *See generally,* MARY KADDU, WOMEN EMERGING IN UGANDA'S DEMOCRACY: A

Judicial Structure

The 1995 Constitution also delineates the structure of Uganda's judiciary. The Constitution specifies that there must be the Supreme Court of Uganda; the Court of Appeal of Uganda; the High Court of Uganda; and "such subordinate courts as Parliament may by law establish...."[109] In accordance with this mandate, the Ugandan Parliament established 27 Chief Magistrates' Courts, 52 Magistrates' Courts, and 428 Grade II Magistrates' Courts.[110] These inferior courts are located throughout the country, thereby increasing judicial access to citizens living in rural areas. The High Court of Uganda has unlimited original jurisdiction in all matters and appellate jurisdiction over decisions made by inferior courts, such as the Magistrates' Court.[111] The Court of Appeal of Uganda hears appeals from the High Court, and the Supreme Court of Uganda, the highest court in the land, is the final avenue of appeal.

Uganda's formal judicial system coexists with its system of customary law. Because of the multiplicity of ethnic groups in Uganda, customary law varies among the regions and people. The 1995 Constitution, however, explicitly holds that, "[I]f any other law or any custom is inconsistent with any of the provisions of this Constitution, the Constitution shall prevail, and that other law or custom shall, to the extent of the inconsistency, be void."[112] The fact that the Constitution explicitly states that "[l]aws and traditions abusing women's rights are proscribed" further indicates the supremacy of constitutional over customary law.[113]

DOCUMENTATION OF WOMEN'S EXPERIENCES IN UGANDA'S LOCAL COUNCIL AND LOCAL GOVERNMENT ELECTIONS, 1998 (Sheila Kawamara ed., 1998). The Local Government Act of 1997 details the structure and function of these local political bodies. The Local Government Act, Act 1 of 1997 [Uganda].

109. *See* UGANDA CONST., art. 129(d). This provision provides for the existence of "Qadhis' courts for marriage, divorce, inheritance of property and guardianship, as may be prescribed by Parliament." Qadhis' courts apply to the nation's Islamic minority, and provide a religious forum in which Muslims may deal with cases relating to marriage, divorce and succession.

110. *See The Republic of Uganda: Courts of Judicature,* at http://www.judicature.go.ug/magistrate_court.html.

111. UGANDA CONST., art. 139(1).

112. *See id.* art. 2(2).

113. *See id.* art. 33(6).

Voices of African Women

CHAPTER ONE

WOMEN'S RIGHT TO PARTICIPATE IN PUBLIC LIFE

Chapter Introduction, *Johanna Bond*

In the aftermath of World War II, countries around the world formed the United Nations in an effort to protect fundamental human rights and prevent future atrocities like the Nazi genocide.[1] The United Nations adopted the Universal Declaration of Human Rights (UDHR) in 1948, establishing what would become the core human rights principles accepted around the world. Building on the UDHR, the United Nations General Assembly adopted two international treaties that entered into force in 1976, one focusing on civil and political rights and the other on economic, social, and cultural rights.[2]

Historically, the International Covenant on Civil and Political Rights (ICCPR) has enjoyed privileged status over the International Covenant on Economic, Social and Cultural Rights (ICESCR). The ICCPR has strong enforcement mechanisms and carries an expectation that states parties will immediately refrain from activity that contravenes the provisions of the treaty, such as custodial torture of political prisoners. The ICESCR, on the other hand, requires that a state party "take steps...to the maximum of its available resources, with a view to achieving progressively the full realization of the

---

1. PAUL GORDON LAUREN, THE EVOLUTION OF INTERNATIONAL HUMAN RIGHTS 145 (1998) (providing a detailed history of the development of human rights principles and the affect of World War II on the process).
2. *Id.* at 258–59.

rights recognized in the...Covenant.[3] The perceived primacy of civil and political rights and the weaker enforcement mechanisms of the ICESCR have created a de facto hierarchy of rights. Civil and political rights have traditionally been characterized as "first generation" rights, while economic, social, and cultural rights have been dubbed "second generation" rights.

In the 1990s, however, activists began to link civil and political rights to economic, social, and cultural rights, recognizing the interconnections between the two types of rights. The notion that all rights are interdependent and indivisible has gained widespread acceptance in the international human rights community. Activists now recognize, for example, that the right to education—which was traditionally considered an economic, social, and cultural right—is integrally linked to the right to hold political office—which has traditionally been understood as a civil and political right. Moreover, effectively eliminating barriers to women's access to education requires that women be part of the policy making process, although as Jane Magigita's essay demonstrates, not all women are feminist policy makers.

This chapter brings together women's political rights and women's right to education as critical components of the broader right to participate in the public life of a community. Dora Byamukama and Mande Limbu examine the impediments to women's access to higher education in Uganda and Tanzania, respectively. Magigita assesses the effectiveness of Tanzania's affirmative action system, which is designed to increase women's representation in Parliament. Jacqueline Asiimwe explores why the Ugandan women's movement has made progress in achieving greater equality for women in the public sphere but not in the private sphere. Finally, Regina Rweyemamu discusses women's use of the Tanzanian court system to improve their legal status and describes the importance of activist judges in that struggle.

Barriers to Politics and Higher Education

Gender Stereotypes and Cultural Values

Women all over the world encounter sexist stereotypes in politics. Such stereotypes, often inculcated in young children, may "teach" that girls do not have the intellectual capacity for politics or that they simply do not belong in

---

3. International Covenant on Economic, Social and Cultural Rights, Jan. 3, 1976, art. 2, para. 1, 993 U.N.T.S. 3, 5 [hereinafter ICESCR].

the public realm. Similar stereotypes about girls' abilities often influence their educational opportunities; parents who do not believe that girls are capable of success in education will not spend scarce family resources on the education of their daughters.

When girls and women overcome these stereotypes and enter politics or higher education, they face further limitations on their success. In politics, they may be perceived as qualified only with respect to issues traditionally associated with the family or the private sphere. Within institutions of higher education, women may be channeled into courses or professions typically associated with women or "women's work," such as the humanities or nursing. As Byamukama from Uganda and Limbu from Tanzania describe in this chapter, gender stereotypes also contribute to widespread sexual harassment of female students at the university level, creating yet another impediment to women's educational success. These stereotypes unfairly restrict women's options, limiting their ability to distinguish themselves in politics and higher education.

Poverty and Domestic Work

Women often do not consider politics an option because most of their energy is concentrated on simply meeting basic needs such as food, clothing, and shelter for themselves and their families. Women produce 80 percent of Africa's food[4] and spend a disproportionate number of hours each day meeting the subsistence needs of the community. In Uganda, for example, the average number of hours women work per week is twice that of men.[5] Men's refusal to share the burden of domestic work contributes to women's inability to engage in the political life of the community.

Moreover, launching a campaign for political office requires significant resources. Women often simply do not have the finances to run an effective campaign. Because women face discrimination in the formal labor market and often lack the collateral to obtain credit, they face financial constraints that may prevent them from seeking elective office.

When poverty forces families to prioritize the educational needs of their children, daughters often lose out. Despite the existence of free primary education in many countries, families must often pay for school uniforms and

---

4. *The African Woman Food Farmer: The Status of Women*, available at: http:/www.thp.org/prize/99/status_women.htm. (Last visited Oct. 10, 2003).

5. On average, women in Uganda work fifty hours per week while men average twenty-three hours per week. *Id.*

textbooks—costs that make education prohibitively expensive, particularly for girls. As described by Byamukama in this chapter, traditional practices such as brideprice sometimes lead parents to marry daughters off early, interrupting their education, in order to receive the brideprice from the family of the prospective groom. Early marriage, in general, is also an impediment to women's education and is often directly linked to a family's poverty and inability to feed its children. Adolescent pregnancy also results in increased dropout rates for young girls.

Efforts to Increase Women's Representation in Politics and Higher Education

As described by Asiimwe and Magigita, Uganda and Tanzania have implemented affirmative action programs to increase women's representation in politics. Although the specific details of these programs vary by country, they share some similarities, including their controversial impact. Although a proponent of affirmative action, Magigita describes many of the problems associated with Tanzania's current affirmative action policy, including the misplaced loyalty that some women in reserved seats feel toward their political parties. Asiimwe describes a similar phenomenon in Uganda and cautiously observes that women's increased representation in national politics is the result of political expediency by the ruling National Resistance Movement government rather than the result of a genuine commitment to gender equality.

Uganda and Tanzania have also attempted to increase women's representation in tertiary educational institutions. Byamukama describes the importance of higher education for Ugandan women, details the affirmative action efforts at Makerere University, and makes recommendations for expanding affirmative action measures and generating alternative sources of funding for women's education. Similarly, Limbu examines Tanzania's affirmative action program for women in higher education and makes recommendations for expanding the reach of the program and for combating the rampant sexual harassment that exists within that country's tertiary educational institutions.

Women in Public Life: The Role of the Activist Judge

Also in this chapter, Rweyemamu cogently argues that activist judges have a role to play in improving women's legal and social status. By vigorously enforcing women's human rights, the activist judge helps to ensure that women have a legitimate role to play in the public life of their communities. Although Rweyemamu's essay does not focus on women's participation in public life per se, she underscores the importance of the judiciary in safeguarding women's rights and helping to eliminate the stereotypes that often keep women confined to the "private" sphere of the home and family.

Brief Overview of International Human Rights Law Relevant to Women's Political Participation and Higher Education

Women's Right to Political Participation

The ICCPR, which Ghana, Tanzania, and Uganda have ratified, protects the right of every citizen to "take part in the conduct of public affairs, directly or through freely chosen representatives; [t]o vote and to be elected…; [and] [t]o have access, on general terms of equality, to public service in his [or her] country.[6] The ICCPR also contains a strong, freestanding nondiscrimination clause in article 26, which underscores that all people are equal before the law.[7]

In an effort to provide states parties with guidance in interpreting the ICCPR, the Human Rights Committee, which is the body that oversees implementation of that covenant, has issued a number of "general comments." In General Comment No. 28, the Human Rights Committee explains the right to gender equality as it relates to the other provisions of the treaty, including the government's obligation to ensure the right to participate in public affairs. The Human Rights Committee underscores that "States parties must ensure that the law guarantees to women the rights contained in article 25 on equal terms with men and take effective and positive measures to promote and en-

---

6. International Covenant on Civil and Political Rights, Mar. 23, 1976, art. 25, 999 U.N.T.S. 171, 179 [hereinafter ICCPR].

7. Article 3 of the ICCPR guarantees women the right not to be discriminated against with respect to the rights enumerated in the covenant. *Id.* at 174. Article 26, on the other hand, is not explicitly tied to the rights listed in the ICCPR. Instead, its broad language states: "All persons are equal before the law and are entitled without any discrimination to the equal protection of the law. In this respect, the law shall prohibit any discrimination and guarantee to all persons equal and effective protection against discrimination on any ground such as race, colour, sex, language, religion, political or other opinion, national or social origin, property, birth or other status." *Id.* at 176.

sure women's participation in the conduct of public affairs and in public office, including appropriate affirmative action.[8]

The Convention on the Elimination of All Forms of Discrimination Against Women (CEDAW) also includes a broad right to participate in public life. Article 7 of CEDAW unequivocally states: "States Parties shall take all appropriate measures to eliminate discrimination against women in the political and public life of the country and, in particular, shall ensure to women, on equal terms with men, the right: (a) To vote in all elections and public referenda and to be eligible for election to all publicly elected bodies....[9] Like the Human Rights Committee, the CEDAW Committee also issued general recommendations to aid in the interpretation of CEDAW. The CEDAW Committee's General Recommendation No. 23 defines the reach of article 7 broadly, recognizes that women have been harmed through their relegation to the private sphere, recommends that states take positive action to combat negative stereotypes about women, and encourages temporary special measures, such as affirmative action, to remedy the historical exclusion of women from political life.[10]

Article 4 of CEDAW allows states parties to establish affirmative action programs, or "temporary special measures," designed to achieve de facto equality between the sexes. Although CEDAW does not mandate such programs, it does specify that "temporary special measures" do not contravene the nondiscrimination principles enshrined in the convention.[11] Additionally, the Convention on the Political Rights of Women protects a more limited range of women's rights within the political arena.[12]

---

8. *Report of the Human Rights Committee on the Covenant on Civil and Political Rights, CCPR General Comment No. 28: Equality of Rights Between Men and Women,* U.N. GAOR, 55th Sess., Supp. No. 40, at 138, U.N. Doc. A/55/40 (Vol. 1) (2000). The Human Rights Committee has also issued a general comment related to the right to participate in public life as articulated in article 25 of the ICCPR. For a more detailed description of the scope of article 25, *see Report of the Human Rights Committee on the Covenant on Civil and Political Rights, CCPR General Comment No. 25: The Right to Participate in Public Affairs, Voting Rights and the Right of Equal Access to Public Service,* U.N. GAOR, 51st Sess., Supp. No. 40, at 98, U.N. Doc. A/51/40 (Vol. 1) (1996).

9. *Convention on the Elimination of All Forms of Discrimination Against Women,* G.A. Res. 180, U.N. GAOR, 34th Sess., Supp. No. 46, at 195, U.N. Doc. A/34/46 (1979) [hereinafter CEDAW].

10. *Report of the Committee on the Elimination of All Forms of Discrimination Against Women, CEDAW General Recommendation 23 (16th Sess.): Political and Public Life,* U.N. GAOR, 52nd Sess., Supp. No. 38, at 61, U.N. Doc. A/52/38/Rev.1 (1997).

11. CEDAW, *supra* note 8, at 195.

12. Convention on the Political Rights of Women, July 7, 1954, 193 U.N.T.S. 135.

The African (Banjul) Charter on Human and Peoples' Rights provides yet another source of protection for women's right to participate in public life. Article 13 of the African Charter states, "Every citizen shall have the right to participate freely in the government of his [or her] country, either directly or through freely chosen representatives in accordance with the provisions of the law.[13] Although not yet in force, the Protocol to the African Charter on Human and Peoples' Rights on the Rights of Women in Africa requires states parties to take action to promote women's equal participation in the "political life of their countries.[14]

Women's Right to Higher Education

Because education is one of the most promising avenues for escaping intractable poverty, it is the fulcrum for the enjoyment of many related rights. An individual's higher education, for example, may lead to formal employment, which may, in turn, create options for housing or health care that did not previously exist. The right to education has been recognized as a critical component of a human being's economic, social, and cultural rights. As such, it was included as part of the UDHR, one of the foundational human rights documents.[15]

The ICESCR also protects the right to education. Article 13 of the ICESCR states that "[h]igher education shall be made equally accessible to all, on the basis of capacity, by every appropriate means, and in particular by the progressive introduction of free education.[16] When this provision is combined with the nondiscrimination provision in article 3 of the ICESCR, it is clear that states parties have an obligation to make higher education accessible and to do so without discriminating against women.

The Committee on Economic, Social and Cultural Rights has also provided guidance to states parties in the form of general comments. General Comment No. 13 specifically advises that affirmative action measures in education do not violate the ICESCR's nondiscrimination clause as long as they do not create "separate standards for different groups" and do not continue after they

---

13. *African [Banjul] Charter on Human and Peoples' Rights*, OAU Doc. CAB/LEG/67/3 rev. 5, Oct. 21, 1986, art. 13, 21 I.L.M. 58 [hereinafter *African Charter*]. Article 13 also states, "(2) Every citizen shall have the right of equal access to the public service of his country."

14. *Protocol to the African Charter on Human and Peoples' Rights on the Rights of Women in Africa, adopted* July 11, 2003, African Union, Art. 9.

15. Universal Declaration of Human Rights, G.A. Res. 217A, U.N. Doc. A/810, at 76 (1948).

16. ICESCR, *supra* note 3, at 8.

are no longer needed.[17] The General Comment also recognizes that "education has a vital role in empowering women.[18] It encourages states parties to combat stereotypes that detrimentally affect girls' and women's access to education.[19]

CEDAW also protects women's right to education. Article 10 of CEDAW requires states parties to "take all appropriate measures to eliminate discrimination against women…in the field of education….[20] This obligation includes a duty to eliminate stereotypes about the "roles of men and women" in education. Article 5 of CEDAW provides further support for the State's obligation to eliminate negative stereotypes about women that may interfere with their enjoyment of the right to education and other human rights.[21]

The African Charter provides that "every individual shall have the right to education.[22] The Charter also stipulates that everyone shall enjoy the rights guaranteed in the Charter "without distinction of any kind such as…sex…."[23] Taken together, these provisions impose an obligation on the state to ensure the enjoyment of the right to education without any form of discrimination against women. This broad protection of women's right to education encompasses not only issues of access but also issues of equality in the enjoyment of the right, including protection against sexual harassment, a form of gender-based inequality that interferes with the enjoyment of the right to education— as described by Limbu in this chapter.

Conclusion

In the past decade, human rights activists have successfully begun to break down the de facto hierarchy of rights that once privileged civil and political

---

17. *Implementation of the International Covenant on Economic, Social and Cultural Rights, General Comment No. 13: The Right to Education,* Committee on Economic, Social and Cultural Rights, 21st Sess., ¶32, E/C.12/1999/10 (1999).

18. *Id.* at ¶1.

19. *Id.* at ¶55.

20. CEDAW, *supra* note 8, at 195.

21. *Id.* at 195. Article 5 states, "States Parties shall take all appropriate measures: (a)To modify the social and cultural patterns of conduct of men and women, with a view to achieving the elimination of prejudices and customary and all other practices which are based on the idea of the inferiority or the superiority of either of the sexes or on stereotyped roles for men and women."

22. African Charter, *supra* note 12, at art. 17.

23. *Id.* at art. 2.

rights over economic, social, and cultural rights. Human rights, such as the right to political participation and the right to education, are now seen as inextricable and interdependent. Together, these rights offer women a world of opportunities and the ability to assert control over their personal and professional lives.

Legal Strategies to Increase Ugandan Women's Access to Higher Education

Dora Kanabahita Byamukama

Discrimination against women in access to higher education,[1] as well as in other aspects of Ugandan life, limits women's opportunities and theoretically deprives Uganda of half of its creative talent. Research indicates that investment in the education of girls and women may provide the highest return of any investment in developing countries.[2] A country can reduce poverty, raise productivity, lower population pressures, and offer subsequent generations a better future by properly educating women.[3] Despite this, Uganda has paid little attention to women's higher education, and wide differences in male and female education persist.[4]

---

1. Formal education in Uganda covers three main levels: the primary school cycle, lasting seven years; the secondary school cycle, lasting six years; and tertiary education, which on an average lasts three years (although courses like medicine take five years to complete). Higher education for purposes of this paper is considered in a wide sense to include universities as well as all other advanced post-secondary educational institutions (or their equivalent), which offer advanced diplomas, certificates, or degree courses. Sometimes these institutions are collectively grouped as third level or tertiary level education. Higher education typically is attained by persons of 18 years and above.

2. The World Bank, Priorities and Strategies for Education: A World Bank Review 28–31 (1995) [hereinafter Priorities].

3. The World Bank, Uganda Growing Out of Poverty 110–11 (1993) [hereinafter Growing Out of Poverty].

4. Priorities, *supra* note 2, at 43–45.

The Status of Women's Education in Uganda

A Historical Perspective on Education in Uganda

Uganda's educational system was once the best in East and Central Africa.[5] Makerere University produced professionals not only for Uganda, but for the entire region as well. In 1971, however, the country entered two decades of civil unrest that disrupted this educational center.[6] Idi Amin's regime, which started in 1971, "radically reversed the economic and social progress that Uganda had attained since independence [from Britain in 1962], and the ensuing civil strife resulted in a tremendous loss of human life."[7] Access to education at this point in time was particularly difficult for women, who had to contend with both new hardships and the cultural, economic, financial, social, and legal constraints that predated the political turmoil.

The Status of Women in Education in Recent Times

Although famine and civil unrest continue to some extent, Ugandans have made progress since the National Resistance Movement came to power in 1986.[8] The number of schools in Uganda has more than doubled in the last decade, mainly as a result of community action. Parents contribute significantly to the salaries and welfare of teachers through Parents and Teachers Associations.[9] The government is spending more money on education. For example, spending for primary education increased 130 percent from 1988 to 1992, while spending for tertiary education increased 170 percent during that same time period.[10]

In 1987, however, the National Resistance Movement signed agreements with the International Monetary Fund and World Bank, committing the coun-

---

5. *See* WILLIAM SAINT, UNIVERSITIES IN AFRICA: STRATEGIES FOR STABILIZATION AND REVITALIZATION (1992).

6. *Id.*

7. GROWING OUT OF POVERTY, *supra* note 3, at xi. It is estimated that as many as 500,000 Ugandans lost their lives during Amin's eight year dictatorship and as many as one million were internally displaced from their homes and farms. A 1985 estimate by the U.S. Committee for Refugees concluded that in that year one out of every fourteen Ugandans was either a refugee or was displaced; it was estimated that as many as 200,000 Ugandans had fled the country and were living in exile. *Id.* at 3.

8. GROWING OUT OF POVERTY, *supra* note 3, at 39.

9. UNICEF, CHILDREN AND WOMEN IN UGANDA: A SITUATION ANALYSIS 61–62 (1989).

10. GROWING OUT OF POVERTY, *supra* note 3, at 111.

try to economic structural adjustment programs.[11] Resulting cuts in social services put more pressure on the government to decrease expenditures on education. As a result, cost sharing in education has been instituted and education at the university level is less subsidized than in previous times.

The current Ugandan government clearly recognizes women's role in both economic and social development and the critical need to raise women's status.[12] The government's efforts to alleviate the plight of women is evident in its recent active engagement in revising the constitution, which now contains numerous provisions that are very progressive with respect to women's rights.[13] In 1989, the government introduced an affirmative action program for women candidates to Makerere University. This program allows women to be admitted despite having slightly lower grades than their male counterparts. As a result, 658 women entered University in 1990–91, compared to 407 in 1987–90.[14] Although increased numbers of women students are a welcome change, women still constitute a minority, as the total intake was 2205 in 1990–91.[15]

In an effort to advance the goals of the 1998 Education Strategic Investment Plan and Uganda Vision 2035, the Ministry of Education and Sports, with significant input from local NGOs, promulgated the National Strategy for Girls' Education in Uganda, identifying eighteen barriers to girls' education and proposing a plan of action.[16]

The Importance of Ensuring Increased Access to Higher Education for Women

Investment in women's access to higher education provides the type of economic and social benefits that serve as indicators of any country's develop-

---

11. *Id.* at 42.

12. *Id.* at 39.

13. *See, e.g.,* Uganda Const. art. 33(2) (providing that the State will create opportunities to enable women to realize their full potential); *id.* art. 33(6) (prohibiting laws or customs that are against the welfare and dignity of women).

14. Obbo, *Affirmative Action at Makerere,* The Weekly Topic (Uganda), Sept. 28, 1990, at 4.

15. *Id.*

16. Min. of Educ. & Sports, Nat'l Strategy for Girls' Education in Uganda [1998] [hereinafter National Strategy].

ment, including increased productivity and wages of female workers, increased participation in politics and decision-making, reduction in child bearing rates, and reduction in maternal and child mortality rates. [17]

Investment in women's higher education contributes to the stability of the economy and the reduction of poverty.[18] Educated women tend to marry later and often choose to have fewer children, enabling them to spend more time and effort on the health and development of each child.[19] Educational opportunity is closely linked to economic security and advancement for individual women and their families.[20] Education leads to better health and nutrition, improving the quality of people's lives. Women's earnings are not merely "supplemental" but critical to their families' incomes.[21] Economically secure women help to end the cycle of poverty, illiteracy, and women's limited access to higher education.[22]

Uganda suffers major economic and social losses by failing to effectively utilize women's potential contribution.[23] The role of education in increasing economic productivity has been well documented.[24] Although basic education enables women to carry out routine activities, higher education has a major impact on the production of appropriate human resources for the various sectors of the economy.[25] They obtain skills in decision making, managing others, and working independently as professionals.[26] When women move into non-traditional fields, employers have a larger and more diverse labor pool from which to draw their workforce; this enhances productivity and per-

---

17. Joy C. Kwesiga, Gender Issues in Higher Education and Issues of Development Management in Sub-Saharan Africa: An Overview (June 1992) (a paper prepared for A Brainstorming Session on Building Technical Capacity and Gender Advocacy of Young Professional African Women, Nairobi, Kenya) [on file with author].

18. GROWING OUT OF POVERTY, *supra* note 3, at 38.

19. *Id.*

20. *Id.* at 110–11.

21. *Id.*

22. For example, because educated women know the economic returns derived from higher education, they make sure that their daughters not only go to school but stay in school. GROWING OUT OF POVERTY, *supra* note 3, at 38–40.

23. *See* GROWING OUT OF POVERTY, *supra* note 3, at 38.

24. *See, e.g.,* WORLD BANK, PRIMARY EDUCATION: A WORLD BANK POLICY PAPER (1990); LAWRENCE SUMMERS, INVESTING IN ALL THE PEOPLE: EDUCATING WOMEN IN DEVELOPING COUNTRIES (1994).

25. GROWING OUT OF POVERTY, *supra* note 3, at 26–27.

26. Kwesiga, *supra* note 17.

formance in the changing market place.[27] In addition, women tend to pay attention to issues concerning women's welfare so, for example, the increased number of women working in the criminal justice system is likely to coincide with improved handling of domestic violence cases, which benefits families and society as a whole.[28]

Barriers to Women's Access to Higher Education

While continuing civil unrest in the northern parts of the country and the HIV/AIDS pandemic present significant barriers to education and rightfully occupy many news headlines, perhaps more pervasive are social, cultural, economic, and legal factors that have created significant barriers to women's access to higher education.

Social and Cultural Barriers

Cultural and traditional biases against women often prevent them from accessing higher education.[29] These gender biases manifest themselves in pressure on women to be passive, to perform time-consuming domestic work, to assume all family responsibilities, to succumb to the practice of bride price, to accept society's negative attitude towards women's education, and many other forms of sex discrimination. Gender-based stereotypes teach women to have little ambition or motivation to pursue their education or to enter into male-dominated areas of higher education.

One does not require a host of statistics to prove that Ugandan society preferences male children both in duration and quality of education. To most who grew up in Uganda, comments such as "girls do not need education as much as boys" or "she will just go off and get married" are very familiar.[30] Parents encourage boys to continue with higher education while they advise girls to get married early and "settle down." It is even more difficult for a woman to continue with education after she marries because of the heavy family re-

---

27. GROWING OUT OF POVERTY, *supra* note 3, at 26–27.

28. *Id.*

29. NATIONAL STRATEGY, *supra* note 16, at 5, 23; *see also* GOVERNMENT WHITE PAPER: EDUCATION FOR NATIONAL INTEGRATION AND DEVELOPMENT 163 (Kampala, Uganda 1992) [hereinafter WHITE PAPER].

30. GROWING OUT OF POVERTY, *supra* note 3, at 38.

sponsibilities women are expected to assume upon marriage.[31] Similarly, the practice of bride price leads needy or greedy parents to marry off daughters as soon as possible to get bride wealth.[32] In some families, the discrimination against girl children may be the result of a lack of adequate social welfare facilities, pensions, and retirement benefits. Families allocating sparse family resources may look to the education of sons more than daughters as an investment in their own long-term security.[33]

Barriers in the Educational System

The schooling system itself perpetuates discrimination against women. Structural barriers to women's higher education include sexism at the elementary level,[34] inequality in vocational and athletic programs,[35] overt sexism

---

31. The Kampala Education Declaration (1996) recognizes that women and girls have barriers to education that men do not face, including community expectations of "heavy domestic chores and responsibilities" and the general "lack of a supportive environment within communities that allows women the necessary time to attend classes." The Education Declaration was the culminating document from the African Conference on Functional Literacy and Education of the Girl-Child, arranged by the OAU and hosted by Uganda. Shelia Kawamara, *The Kampala Education Declaration to Enhance Women's Status*, 1 E. AFR. INITIATIVES 8 (1997).

32. When a man marries a woman in Ugandan society, he gives her family valuable goods such as livestock to compensate them for the loss of her labor and mark her new status as a member of his family. This is the payment of bride price. This custom has been distorted and has now outlived its usefulness. As part of the constitutional reform process, the Ministry of Gender and Development, with Danida (Danish Agency for Development Assistance) support, organized seminars throughout the country aimed at giving women the opportunity to voice their opinion about the reform and to influence the framing of the new constitution. Between November 1990 and May 1991, 113 county-level seminars were held in 25 districts of the country, and more than 4,000 women had participated in the Consultations. I was one of the resource persons in one district in the south-western part of Uganda called Rukungiri, when the issue of bride wealth came up there was divided opinion—to my surprise many women wanted the custom to continue!

33. Julie Stewart et al., *The Legal Situation of Women in Zimbabwe*, in THE LEGAL SITUATION OF WOMEN IN SOUTHERN AFRICA 201 (Julie Stewart & Alice Armstrong eds., 1993).

34. Girls receive significantly less attention in class than do boys. For this and other reasons girls' self-esteem and self-confidence often plummet as they reach adolescence. The low esteem, negative body image, and depression that begin early in adolescence often do not disappear as girls mature. *See* Anne Peterson et al., *Adolescent Depression: Why More Girls?* 20 J. YOUTH & ADOLESCENCE 247, 247–71 (1991).

35. Today, it is widely understood that participation in athletics has a positive impact on the educational development of young women, just as it does for their male counter-

and harassment against women who choose non-traditional areas of study,[36] rigid examination systems, biased admission procedures, limited educational facilities,[37] and teenage pregnancy.[38]

Of particular concern, sexual harassment has become part of school culture, further alienating girls and young women from the educational system in Uganda. Sexual harassment causes girls to lose interest in school and diminishes their academic performance. Sexual harassment is found at every level of the educational system, from elementary school to postgraduate programs, yet Ugandan schools have failed to respond with appropriate meas-

---

parts. Athletics helps them develop self-confidence and critical leadership skills. *See* NATIONAL STRATEGY, *supra* note 16, at 29.

36. Young women face overt sexism and harassment when they choose a non-traditional course of study, which causes many of them to abandon such courses and thereby to lose the opportunities the courses offer for greater earning power. Girls are not encouraged, particularly in co-educational schools, to take science subjects and are often directed to take those courses that are seen as training for the traditional female-supportive role occupations (the "pink collar" sector) such as nursing rather than the more traditionally male-oriented professions such as engineering. Thus, even for today's educated women, the persistence of sex segregation contributes to entrenchment of the wage gap, as women remain in fields of lower-paying jobs. *See* NATIONAL STRATEGY, *supra* note 16, at 30–31; *see also* WHITE PAPER, *supra* note 29, at 163.

37. For example, limited facilities are prevalent at Makerere University in newly introduced areas like Dental Surgery, Pharmacy, Food Sciences, and Mass Communication. There is a dire need to expand educational facilities, beginning with increasing the number of women's halls of residence at Makerere University. *See also* WHITE PAPER, *supra* note 29, at 164.

38. For information on the teenage birthrate in Uganda, see Doris M. Toolanen, *Uganda and Adolescent Health: A Country Case Study*, World Bank Training Workshop (Jan. 2002), at:

http://wbln0018.worldbank.org/HDNet/HDdocs.nsf/c840b59b6982d2498525670c004de
f60/9b4307418f94daec85256c09005a5ac9/$FILE/ARH%20in%20Uganda%20dec.pdf

(last visited July 18, 2003). For a more general discussion on the impact of teenage pregnancy on education in the United States (which, from the author's observations, is highly relevant to Uganda), see Verna L. Williams, *In Search of a Vision: Gender Equity in Education in the Clinton Administration, in* NEW CHALLENGES: THE CIVIL RIGHTS RECORD OF THE CLINTON ADMINISTRATION MIDTERM 131 (Corrine M. Yu & William L. Taylor eds., 1995). The authors explain, "With the odds already stacked against them, pregnant and parenting teens seeking to complete their schooling frequently face additional obstacles from school administrators." They are often seen as a "bad influence" or "lost cause." Because these excluded students are prevented from obtaining the skills necessary to support themselves and their families, removing the impediments to education of pregnant and parenting teens is essential, *id.* at 135.

ures.[39] Although Uganda spearheaded the effort to create the Kampala Education Declaration, which recognized that sexual abuse and harassment of girls impedes their educational opportunities,[40] the Government needs to do more to prevent sexual harassment. It is not surprising that girls and young women are reluctant to report harassment when the only consequence of their taking a stand is likely to be retaliation against them and even more harassment, especially in cases where the harasser is the student's lecturer.

Economic Barriers

Economic barriers to women's access to higher education are central because education in Uganda is not free.[41] Because most Ugandan families cannot afford to educate all of their children, and because most parents expect girls to get married and move away, often parents view investment in their daughters' education as a waste of money.[42] With parents unable or unwilling to pay for girls' education, limitations on financial assistance also foreclose educational opportunities for women in higher education. The government's adherence to structural adjustment mandates further exacerbates financial pressures. Before the 1990s, when children reached the tertiary level of education they were able to obtain free education; since 1987, Uganda has been committed to an economic structural adjustment program that mandates cuts in government spending, severely reducing social expenditure on education. This makes women's access to higher education even more difficult because greater economic pressures on parents leads to greater discrimination against girls in education.

Legal Barriers

Although the Ministry of Education has taken an important step by creating the National Strategy for Girls' Education in Uganda, the government must follow up with concrete actions, adequate funding, and active enforce-

---

39. Sexual harassment and defilement of girl students by male teachers is a commonly reported problem, and one that has seldom resulted into discipline of teachers. UNICEF, *supra* note 9 at 82.

40. Shelia Kawamara, *The Kampala Education Declaration to Enhance Women's Status*, 1 E. AFR. INITIATIVES 8 (1997).

41. NATIONAL STRATEGY, *supra* note 16, at 43.

42. GROWING OUT OF POVERTY, *supra* note 3, at 38–39.

ment. With no specific statute relating to women in education, customary law continues to govern the factors that encumber women's educational rights.

In the majority of cases, customary law[43] undermines the status of women in society in at least two ways. First, customary law in Uganda does not reflect current realities. Customary law has not, for example, created new ways to address barriers, such as pregnancy, that continue to impede women's access to higher education.[44] Second, there has been no effort to date to document the customary laws of the various tribes of Uganda. In Uganda, more than thirty-five distinct sets of customary law exist, and these customs are peculiar to each tribe. Uganda's customary law is not recorded; it exists in the minds and behavior of the people it governs.[45] In most cases, men make and interpret customary law because of the patrilineal nature of the Ugandan societies. Judges, who primarily are men, control the substantive content of customary law by choosing who to consult on the content of customary law (invariably male court assessors), which textbooks and anthropological works to consult (written by white men after consulting with African men), and by manipulating judicial precedents. Through this process sexist values have been indelibly imprinted on the customary law. Judges and community leaders use this constructed, static, corrupted version of customary law to oppress, subordinate, and discriminate against women.[46] The government and other groups have ignored or resisted calls to change the aspects of customary law that discriminate against women on several grounds, including the need to preserve African culture and values. Ugandan society has conditioned women to think that they are inferior to men to such an extent that they do not relate to laws that give them equal status with men. Because customary law perpetuates the subordination of women and negative stereotypes about women's capacities, it plays a role in obstructing women's access to higher education.

---

43. Customary law is a blend of African customs, imported colonial common and civil law notions, and religious concepts from Christianity, Islam, and African traditional religions. Fitnat Naa-Adjeley Adjetey, *Reclaiming The African Woman's Individuality: The Struggle Between Women's Reproductive Autonomy And African Society And Culture*, 44 Am. U. L. Rev. 1380 (1995).

44. *See id.*

45. *Id.*

46. *See* Alice Armstrong et al., *Uncovering Reality: Excavating Women's Rights in African Family Law*, 7 Int'l J. L. & Fam. 314, 330 (1993).

Economic and cultural constraints make the courts, at worst, completely inaccessible to women. At best, the courts reflect the discriminatory legacy of male-dominated legal systems and judiciaries.[47] In Uganda, women's relative poverty, lack of education and knowledge of their rights, and their discriminatory socialization frequently prevent them from asserting their claim for legal rights.[48] Proceedings in traditional courts are simpler, cheaper, and more informal than in the Magistrate's courts and High court. Consequently, when women want to institute legal proceedings, they usually find themselves in the traditional courts, which are permeated with sexism, nepotism, and corruption.[49] Local people, who often are not conversant with the law, preside over traditional courts; so the "justice" these courts deliver generally reflects male dominance over women. For example, when sexual harassment cases come up, traditional courts approach them from with a male bias because, although there are some women on the traditional courts, women are still to a large extent in the minority.

The magistrates, High Court, and Supreme Court levels are inaccessible to women because of the exorbitant filing and lawyers' fees. Even if a woman can access these courts, procedure is very technical, and this delays resolution of cases and therefore denies justice. Although the statutory law usually provides women with significant rights, the structure of the court system and women's general socioeconomic condition dictate that customary law, which may be prejudiced against women, will still govern most women's rights.[50] Most women do not have the confidence to present their cases in court because of the way they are treated in courts. For example, when barriers to women's higher education, such as sexual harassment, are brought up in court, lawyers and the courts put the reputation and credibility of the woman on trial. Rather than focusing on sexual harassment, the court's attention shifts to the woman's reputation. This discourages most women from presenting their cases, because the issue becomes a public affair. More generally, in Uganda, as in most countries worldwide, judges and court personnel frequently operate on the basis of biased assumptions about women's roles and capabilities and treat women with less respect than they show men.[51]

---

47. Marsha A. Freeman, Women's Rights In The Family: Issues and Recommendations for Implementation 9 (1993).

48. *Id.* at 10.

49. *Id.*

50. Julie Stewart et al., *The Legal Situation of Women in Zimbabwe, in* The Legal Situation of Women in Southern Africa 168 (Julie Stewart & Alice Armstrong eds., 1990).

51. *Id.* at 9.

Proposals for Reform

The proposals for reform discussed below aim to overcome the social, cultural, structural, economic, and legal barriers discussed in this essay. I advocate four proposals: (1) both community and governmental loan projects available exclusively for women for a period of time; (2) a reformed affirmative action program at Makerere University; (3) re-articulation of customary law based on notions of equality and adoption of customary "living law," which reflects the real life experiences of people on a day-to-day basis; and (4) litigation and use of international legal instruments to further increase women's access to higher education. These proposals, in conjunction with free basic education, will increase women's access to higher education. These proposals ensure educational opportunities for women, as guaranteed by the Uganda Constitution, that will enable them to realize their full potential and advancement.[52] The proposals accord women full dignity with men because higher education helps enable access to equal opportunities in political, economic, and social activities.[53]

Education Loans

As explained above, often parents determine whether girls will have access to higher education. Because most parents prefer to educate boys, lack of finances presents a major barrier to women's access to higher education. Parents' preference to educate boys has over time created an imbalance in women's access to higher education, which can, to some extent, be redressed by giving financial assistance exclusively to women for a period of time.

Families, parents, teachers associations, and local government should create a forum in which the community may discuss the barriers women face in accessing higher education and propose community-oriented solutions. The community might decide to fund, for example, five girls to enable them access to higher education. Communities should give preference to those who pursue non-traditional areas of study and those that benefit society as a whole, such as medicine. The community should require girls who receive education loans to serve the community for a number of years after they have completed their studies. Alternatively, the community should require recipients of education loans to sponsor the higher education of another girl in turn.[54]

---

52. UGANDA CONST. art. 33(2).

53. *Id.* art. 33(4).

54. This project has been tried in the Ho area of Ghana where it has been successful.

Community-level action that supports increased access to higher education for women is premised on the constitutional right to development, with a focus on self-reliance.[55] The Constitution requires the state to take all necessary steps to involve the people in the formulation and implementation of development programs that affect them.[56] Objective XIV(b) of the Constitution further provides that the state shall endeavor to fulfill fundamental rights of all Ugandans and, in particular, the right to education.[57] Community-based education loans promote self-reliance by requiring the recipients to serve the community for a period of time after they have completed their studies. This proposal involves people in the programs that affect them.

Government, non-governmental organizations, and the donor community should also give women education loans, grants, and scholarships to facilitate increased access to higher education.[58] Article 21(4) of the Constitution supports programs such as this which aim to redress economic and educational imbalance in Ugandan society.[59] These education loans, grants, and scholarships should be confined to women's higher education for a limited period of time, until the inequality due to gender discrimination has been eradicated. The Ugandan Constitution mandates laws such as this to give full affect to affirmative action.[60] The Constitution specifically provides that its equality provisions shall not preclude laws aimed at redressing educational imbalance in society. Under the Constitution, the state must take steps to enhance women's welfare and to enable them to realize their full potential and advancement. The Constitution, therefore, supports this proposal to give women financial assistance to facilitate their access to higher education for a period of time.[61]

Discussion with Hilary Gbedemah, Fellow, Leadership and Advocacy for Women in Africa (March 1996).

55. UGANDA CONST. obj. IX (stating the state shall encourage private initiative and self-reliance in order to facilitate rapid and equitable development).

56. *Id.* obj. X.

57. *See also id.* obj. XVIII(ii) ("[T]he state shall take appropriate measures to afford every citizen equal opportunity to attain the highest education standard possible.").

58. For a discussion on how student loan schemes can assist in increasing access to higher education, see Maureen Woodhall, *Financing Higher Education: The Potential Contribution of Fees and Student Loans*, Center for Int'l Higher Educ. (2001), *at* http://www.bc.edu/bc_org/avp/soe/cihe/newsletter/News22/text008.htm (last visited July 18, 2003).

59. UGANDA CONST. art. 21(4).

60. *Id.* art. 32(2).

61. *Id.*

Review and Reform of the 1.5 Affirmative Action Program at Makerere University

As explained above, the Constitution provides for affirmative action in favor of marginalized groups for the purpose of addressing existing imbalances. In 1989, the Government initiated the existing affirmative action program at Makerere University. This program is confined to Makerere University, a government-funded institution, and it automatically awards all female entrants 1.5 points over and above male students, allowing women to be admitted despite having slightly lower grades than their male counterparts. The government should conduct research to find out whether this program has achieved its goals. Review of the affirmative action program also should outline specific goals, schedules, and timetables as to when the desired increase in women's access to higher education shall be achieved. The Ugandan Constitution offers strong support for this proposal.[62]

New laws must expand this affirmative program to all tertiary institutions and increase the points allowed women, if the 1.5 points have not insufficiently increased women's access to higher education. Because Ugandans recognize that women have been discriminated against in the past and continue to be discriminated against and because the Constitution encourages affirmative action, a strengthened affirmative action program is clearly warranted. Increased access to women's higher education is crucial if women are to realize their full potential. Confining the program to Makerere University is insufficient to increase women's access to higher education.

Re-Articulation of Customary Law

Statute books still contain legal rules and principles that legitimate the subordination of women. The structure and administration of Ugandan laws, socioeconomic realities, and pervasive patriarchal ideology often prevent the transition of abstract rights into real, substantive rights. In order to transition the right to higher education into something substantive, it is necessary to study and analyze the existing laws and the socioeconomic realities of Ugan-

---

62. *Id.* art. 32(2) (requiring the establishment of an equal opportunities commission for the purpose of giving full effect to affirmative action programs). *See also id.* art. 21(4) (providing that nothing in the Article which provides for equality and freedom shall prevent Parliament from enacting laws that are necessary for implementing policies and programs aimed at redressing social, economic, and educational imbalance).

dan society. In addition to analyzing and reforming statutory laws, women's rights lawyers must begin to re-envision and re-articulate customary law so as to make it more responsive to the day-to-day lives of the people it affects.

New interpretations and empirical research are needed to make customary laws more relevant and responsive to increasing women's access to higher education. Women's rights lawyers and other activists must begin to re-orient people's thinking by embracing customary "living law" that reflects real life experiences. Customary "living law" would be rich, varied, and flexible; it would change in response to changing conditions in society. As society increasingly recognizes women's rights, for example, dynamic customary law would reflect that progress. This dynamic nature of customary "living law" can be used to increase women's access to higher education.[63]

The Constitution protects women's rights, but these rights as articulated by the Constitution are merely abstract. Transition of the abstract rights into specific rights (like women's right to higher education) must take into account the de facto position of women.[64] A gender-neutral implementation of these rights will, therefore, be inadequate. Uganda must go a step further and enact particular laws that provide for women's increased access to higher education while providing for the different experiences of men and women.

The Preamble of the Uganda Constitution provides that the people of Uganda are committed to building a better future by establishing a socioeconomic and political order on principles of equality.[65] Uganda may secure this equality if all persons are equal before the law in all spheres of political, economic, social, and cultural life and if all persons enjoy equal protection of the law.[66] The Constitution prohibits discrimination on the basis of sex[67] and requires Parliament to enact laws necessary for the implementation of policies

---

63. *Id.* at 1.

64. Stewart et al., *supra* note 50, at 165. "Discrimination can result even where rules seem to be sex neutral, because in spite of its apparent neutrality, the law in question either does not specify that women have the same rights as men or fails to make provision for different experiences of men and women. This often works against the interests of women because it is often assumed that women are adequately protected by the existing law." *Id.*

65. UGANDA CONST. art. 28(1).

66. *Id.* art. 21.

67. *Id.* art. 21 (3), defines discrimination as to means to give different treatment to different persons attributable only to or mainly to their respective descriptions by sex, race, color, ethnic origin, tribe, birth, creed or religion, or social or economic standing, political opinion, or disability.

and programs aimed at redressing educational imbalance in society.[68] A new law to enable women to overcome barriers to higher education fulfills the state's obligation to take appropriate measures to afford every citizen equal opportunity to attain the highest education standard possible.[69] A specific law that prohibits gender discrimination in programs and activities receiving government financial assistance could read as follows: "No person in Uganda, shall on the basis of sex, be excluded from participation in, be denied benefits of, or be subjected to discrimination under any education program or activity receiving government assistance, except where this law is not consistent with religious tenets of the institution or where traditionally and continually from its establishment the institution has had a policy of admitting only students of one sex."[70]

Existing law should be "construed with such adaptations, qualifications, and exceptions as may be necessary to bring it into conformity with [the new] constitution."[71] There is a need to review all laws to determine those that are discriminatory against women. Uganda must then develop and execute a plan to remedy discrimination within the law and determine how to modify discriminatory customs so that gender equity becomes a cultural value and not just an unrealized legal right.

Litigation and International Legal Instruments

A right that exists only in theory is of little, if any, practical use. New laws are ineffective if women cannot effectively use them to overcome barriers in accessing higher education. Legal education, strategic litigation, and use of international law present some strategies that can be used to make new law effective.

---

68. *Id.* art. 21 (4).

69. UGANDA CONST. obj. XVIII.

70. The proposed language for Uganda's new sex discrimination law could be modeled on the United States' Title IX of the Education Amendments of 1972 Act (usually referred to as Title IX). 20 U.S.C. §§ 1681 et seq. Title IX is the most far-reaching law in education in the United States. It forbids discrimination in public and private schools receiving federal money, which helps provide important protection to women in academia. *See* SUSAN DELLER ROSS ET AL., THE RIGHTS OF WOMEN: THE BASIC ACLU GUIDE TO WOMEN'S RIGHTS 248–78 (3rd ed. 1993). Title IX should be altered to suit Uganda's circumstances. For example, in Uganda, it is imperative that the law allows single sex programs, especially in cases where parents may be apprehensive about co-educational institutions.

71. UGANDA CONST. art. 273(1).

Legal education is crucial because women have to be educated on statutory and customary laws in order to effectively use both to their advantage. The government and non-governmental organizations should conduct legal education to make the Ugandan population aware of new laws and to end conflict with customary law. Women's awareness of their rights will increase their confidence enough to assert their rights and become full participants in eliminating barriers to higher education.

The courts may be sympathetic to women's rights and the law on the books may be very positive, but the law will be useless if women are not prepared to challenge the preconceptions of society. Women's rights lawyers should use strategic litigation to bring the new laws into effect and to challenge discriminatory stereotypes. Specifically, women's rights activists should use test cases and amicus curie procedures to challenge barriers to women's access to higher education. Women should argue that international human rights conventions that support women's education and to which Uganda is a party should be of persuasive effect in local courts.

Conclusion

To experience long-term, sustainable development, Uganda needs to remove social, cultural, structural, and legal barriers to women's access to higher education. Uganda's history, colored by civil unrest and compounded by discriminatory social, cultural, and economic practices, has made higher education increasingly inaccessible to women. Gender equity in Uganda's higher education system is not the stuff of headlines and television specials. The long-term impact of the denial of women's right to higher education, however, could be even greater than the ravages of drought and civil wars, which have become the daily fare of not only Ugandan but also world news. Unless Uganda's women are given the opportunity to access higher education and develop their full potential, the nation is destined to permanent second-class status in the world arena, and the crisis we see today will pale in comparison with what is to come.

WOMEN AND HIGHER EDUCATION IN TANZANIA

Mande Limbu

Introduction

The right to education is enshrined in the Constitution of Tanzania.[1] Since attaining independence, Tanzania has worked to correct the imbalance between male and female students at all levels of education. Unlike the improvements in primary and secondary education, however, very little progress has been made in improving women's access to the university level. Women are vastly underrepresented in terms of enrollment and they are usually concentrated in gender-stereotyped subjects. The low participation of women in university level education and their lack of preparation for critical fields such as mathematics, physics, and engineering negatively affects their capacity to move into a wide range of occupations in the labor market.[2]

There is no doubt that the status of women can be improved if more women have access to higher levels of education. This essay will examine women's right to education as a liberating force behind their struggle for equality and economic independence. Only a partnership among lawmakers, policymakers, higher education institutions, and local communities can alleviate the current situation that deprives women of educational opportunities on an equal basis with men.

---

1. TANZ. CONST. § 11(2), (3) (1977) states: "Every person has the right to self education and every citizen shall be free to pursue education in a field of his choice up to the highest level according to his merits and ability; The Government shall endeavor to ensure that there are equal and adequate opportunities to all persons to enable them to acquire education and vocational training at all levels of schools and other institutions of learning."

2. MARJORIE MBILINYI AND PATRICIA MBUGHUNI, EDUCATION IN TANZANIA WITH A GENDER PERSPECTIVE (1991) [hereinafter GENDER PERSPECTIVE].

Women and Higher Education

There are six universities in Tanzania. University of Dar es salaam (UDSM) is the largest publicly owned university, which was re-inaugurated after the break up of the University of East Africa. Tanzania has five other universities, including the Sokoine University of Agriculture (SUA), the Open University of Tanzania (OUT), the Hubert Kairuki Memorial University, Tumaini University, and the University in Bukoba. All of these universities constitute what is known as the first tier of higher learning institutions.

Female enrollment at the university level has fluctuated in response to different policies and economic conditions. Poor examination results at the high school level and the growth of alternative second tier education opportunities has led to low female enrollment. Since admission requirements for second tier colleges are lower and training is shorter, women often opt for such training. Statistics show that in 1987 there were more than twice as many first year enrollments in the diploma courses offered at the Institute of Finance Management, Institute of Development Management, UCLAS, and Technical Colleges than at first-tier universities.[3]

Between 1974 and 1984, the Tanganyika African National Union (TANU), the major political party at the time, barred secondary school graduates from direct entry to university.[4] The policy required applicants to have two years of work experience and to obtain positive recommendations from TANU and the applicant's employer. This directive had a greater negative effect on women, as there were very few women in the working world with the required academic qualifications.[5]

Even when women are enrolled in a university, they are underrepresented in programs that require a strong mathematics and physics background. This is partially due to the fact that there are not many female applicants in science fields, because many girls either do not take science or perform poorly in those subjects in secondary schools.[6] Also, female students are afraid to enroll in science classes because of a belief that these courses are difficult and present a threat of failure.[7] The underrepresentation of women in science fields can also

---

3. *Id.* at 53.

4. George A. Malekela, *Access and Equity in University Education in Tanzania*, 15(1) J. SOC'Y FOR EDUC. RES. AND DEV. 39 (1999).

5. *Id.*

6. GENDER PERSPECTIVE, *supra* note 2, at 60–66.

7. *Id.*

be attributed to the structure of the curricula. In many African countries, including Tanzania, schools still structure curricula to reinforce societal perceptions of women's role in family life, creating the perception that science will be irrelevant to women, who are confined largely to the domestic sphere.[8] There is clearly a need to abandon these social stereotypes, and teachers should encourage more women to pursue science subjects.

Affirmative Action

Preferential Admissions and the Pre-entry Program

Equal educational opportunity for women requires compensatory measures to make up for past discrimination and to bring the class discriminated against up to the level of competitive advantage that the favored class enjoys.[9] As applied in the higher education context, the term affirmative action may mean taking "positive action to overcome the effects of systematic institutional forms of exclusion and discrimination."[10] Preferential admission to women at UDSM is one form of affirmative action. Affirmative action may also include financial assistance earmarked for women. In 2001, a one-million-dollar grant paid for tuition, books, and living stipends for approximately 150 qualified women.[11] This grant, in part, also funded initiatives to recruit, admit, and retain women students.[12] Another type of affirmative action practiced at the UDSM is the Pre-entry Program. The Pre-entry Program is a remedial course for the admission of female candidates in Science and Engineering Faculties that aims to increase the number of female students in sciences. According to the progress report for 2000, the proportion of female students in the Faculty of Science is expected to increase from about 15 percent in 1996–97 to about 30 percent in 2003. At the Sokoine University of Agriculture (SUA), there is a similar pre-entry science program for female students. SUA plans to attain enrollment of 40 percent female students by the year 2005. The long-term target is to correct the gender imbalance and to attain a 50-50 level.[13]

---

8. *Id.*

9. Kathryn Swanson, Affirmative Action and Preferential Admissions in Higher Education (1981).

10. *Id.* at v.

11. Henry Lyimo, *UDSM Receives Grant for Women Scholarships*, The Guardian (Tanzania), Aug. 4, 2001.

12. *Id.*

In addition to the preferential admissions and pre-entry programs, special support systems, including female-oriented scholarships, are also encouraged to overcome sex discrimination in postgraduate education. A number of women have received scholarships from various governments and private foundations as a result.

Critics

Affirmative action revolves around conflicting interpretations of the meaning and nature of justice and equality. Many opponents criticize the fact that female students are being welcomed even when they are not as qualified as male applicants. It is clear that some admitted female students' scores are lower than those of some rejected male applicants.[14] Moreover, some academicians have argued that special treatment destroys the idea of being judged on the basis of individual merit, violates the constitutional guarantee of equal protection under the laws, and undermines the democratic concept of equality of opportunity.[15] These opponents view affirmative action as "reverse discrimination." Some feminist scholars also argue that instead of reducing stereotypes of women, preferential treatment reinforces the image that women cannot "make it on their own" and need governmental sanctions to succeed.[16]

Nevertheless, there are many reasons that affirmative action programs, like those introduced by UDSM, should be encouraged and continued. First, affirmative action is not a long-term strategy and can be stopped when the goal of equality of opportunity has been achieved. Second, affirmative action for women does not undermine the democratic standard of equality of opportunity because Tanzanian women do not currently experience this equality; rather, they are affected by the social, economic, and societal constraints that men are not. Moreover, the argument that affirmative action indicates that women cannot compete or "make it on their own" is not convincing because these programs do not admit women who are wholly unqualified but, rather,

---

13. Interview with Dr. A. Kihupi, Sokoine University of Agriculture.

14. Author's personal observations.

15. *See* Michael K. Brasswell et al., *Affirmative Action: An Assessment of Its Continuing Role in Employment Discrimination Policy*, 57 ALB. L. REV. 365, 410–11 (1993).

16. *See* Madeline E. Heilman et al., *Intentionally Favored, Unintentionally Harmed? Impact of Sex-Based Preferential Selection on Self- Perceptions and Self-Evaluations*, 72 J. APPLIED PSYCHOL. 62, 67–68 (1987).

admit women who are otherwise deserving of entry but are just shy of the cut-off point for admission.[17]

Inhospitable Educational Environment for Women on Campus

Sexual Harassment

Sexual harassment on campus is a problem for female university students and contributes to women's academic failure and psychological problems. Although there is some protection against sexual harassment, many cases go unreported for a number of reasons; some female students do not know their legal rights, and those who do are afraid of being ridiculed or disbelieved in the judicial and administrative system.[18]

Legal Interpretation of Sexual Harassment

Sexual harassment is illegal under the Sexual Offenses Special Provision Act, 1998, which broadly defines the proscribed conduct as any assault, criminal force, or words or actions used to cause "sexual annoyance or harassment" or that intentionally insults "the modesty of any woman" by word, gesture, sound, or exhibition of objects or any body part. Such conduct may include using sexist terms or making comments about body parts.[19] Female students are far more likely to be sexually harassed at school than male students.[20]

---

17. Author's personal observations.

18. Author's personal observations.

19. Sexual Offenses (Special Provisions) Act 1998 [Tanz.], pt. II, §138(d)(1), (2). Sexual harassment has also been defined in the United States to include sexual innuendos, comments or bantering; asking or commenting about a person's sexuality; humor or jokes about sex of females in general; persistent sexual attention, especially when it continues after a clear indication that it is unwanted; touching a person including patting, pinching, stroking, squeezing, hugging or brushing against his or her body; calling women names such as "bitch"; using sexual ridicule or to insult a person; direct or indirect threats or bribes for sexual activity; attempted or actual sexual assault or abuse. Bernice R. Sandler & Robert J. Shoop, *What is Sexual Harassment, in* SEXUAL HARASSMENT ON CAMPUS: A GUIDE FOR ADMINISTRATORS, FACULTY, AND STUDENTS 1, 6 (Bernice R. Sandler & Robert J. Shoop eds., 1997).

20. ROBERT SHOOP & DEBRA EDWARDS, HOW TO STOP SEXUAL HARASSMENT IN OUR SCHOOLS: A HANDBOOK AND CURRICULUM GUIDE FOR ADMINISTRATORS AND TEACHERS 14 (1994).

Sexual Harassment by Teachers

The Sexual Offenses Act explicitly states that "unwelcome sexual advances by words or actions used by a person in authority" constitutes sexual harassment.[21] A teacher's abuse of authority either in a quid pro quo situation or in the context of an allegedly consensual relationship with a student may be illegal sexual harassment and, even if unrecognized by law, is detrimental to the student.

Quid Pro Quo

Quid pro quo is a Latin term often used in law, meaning "do something for me and I will do something for you." In the context of sexual harassment by a teacher, quid pro quo may include an offer of special treatment, such as awarding a better grade, in return for sexual favors. More commonly, a teacher threatens to lower a grade or refuses to write a letter of recommendation because a student rejects a sexual request. Many female students do not report these incidents simply because they do not want to draw attention to themselves.[22]

Consensual Relationships

Most consensual relationships between faculty members and female students are problematic. Consensual relationships raise conflict of interest issues because it is difficult for a professor to fairly evaluate someone with whom they are engaging in a sexual relationship.[23] The situation may worsen when a student no longer wants the relationship, and the teacher uses his power to try to maintain it. It is at this point that the relationship becomes sexual harassment.[24]

Rape

The Penal Code of Tanzania defines rape as having carnal knowledge of a woman without her consent.[25] Rape, together with attempted rape and indecent assault, are among the problems that women face on campus because of their gender. Society often blames a woman victim for sexual assault, accus-

---

21. Sexual Offenses (Special Provisions) Act 1998 [Tanz.], pt. II, §138(d)(3).
22. Sandler & Shoop, *supra* note 19, at 8.
23. *Id.* at 17.
24. *Id.* It is important to note that sexual harassment is not limited to teacher-student relationships; students (mostly male) also subject fellow female students to sexual harassment.
25. Penal Code, Cap 16 [Tanz.] §130.

ing her of provocative dress, alleging she enjoyed the assault, or using a pre-existing relationship with her attacker as an excuse to discount her claims. As a result, many cases of rape go unreported.

Physical Attack

Other instances of physical violence against women are equally discounted; one egregious example involved DARUSO, the Dar es Salaam University Students Organization. DARUSO is responsible for demanding student's rights from the government and it has staged regular class boycotts and campus disturbances. There are times when student leaders decide to boycott and female students refuse to participate. The women then become the targets of physical violence. One incident involved male DARUSO members attacking females at their halls of residence to force them to go to a planned meeting. Some women were beaten; some took refuge under their beds; and some doors and windows were broken. One female student said that the men broke into her room and forced her to dress quickly while they waited for her to make sure she would attend the meeting. Although these frightening occurrences made front pages in local newspapers, many others do not.[26]

Harassment

Peer harassment can interfere with not only a woman's education, but also her mental health. One example of peer harassment is "Punch." When a student is "punched," she is publicly humiliated by pictures and derogatory materials, often including comments about a woman's personal life and sexuality, displayed on the "Punch wall," a public bulletin board.[27] Victims of Punch are frequently women. This particular form of wall literature has assumed formidable powers, acting as a censor of social and moral conduct, especially for female students.[28] These tactics are used to "keep women in their place." For example, the first woman to run for the DARUSO vice presidency in 1997 was "punched" because male students wanted to monopolize the student body and did not want a female vice president. Another female student committed sui-

---

26. Experience of the author, a first-year UDSM student at the time.

27. Jennifer Rakstad et al., *The Progress of Tanzanian Women in the Law: Women in Legal Education, Legal Employment and Legal Reform,* 10 REV. OF L. AND WOMEN'S STUD. 35, 51 (2000).

28. *Id.*

cide after a Punch episode. After her death, the University of Dar es Salaam worked to prevent "punching" by patrolling the wall often used for posting. If University officials catch a student "punching," the prosecutor may charge the student with libel under the Penal Code, but prosecutors typically drop such cases.[29]

Consequences of Sexual Harassment

It is clear that sexual harassment has academic effects because it not only discourages classroom participation, but also forces women to avoid classes. This impedes the academic development of female students and destroys their relationship with the faculty, a relationship that is crucial for their future professional development.[30] Sexual harassment also has physical consequences; it causes physical injury and it may cause health problems such as unwanted pregnancy, HIV/AIDS, headaches, and ulcers.[31] Psychologically, many women are ashamed and embarrassed and are reluctant to talk about what has happened or is happening to them. A woman's self esteem may suffer badly, resulting in feelings of helplessness, lack of control, shame, guilt, depression, inability to concentrate, and difficulty in handling day to day tasks at school.[32] In extreme cases, this leads to suicide. The following anecdote illustrates the potential damage to a victim's mental health.

The Death of Revina Mukasa[33]

Revina was admitted to the UDSM in 1989. When she attended the Freshers' Ball with her boyfriend, they had a fight because she talked to another man. A few days later, someone posted Revina's registration number with the caption "Wanton Fresher coming soon." Revina saw this, became very depressed, and did not attend classes the following day. Male students often approached her, suggesting that if she agreed to have sex with them, they would influence the "Punch" for her; attempts to ward them off were not taken seriously, Revina began to question whether something was seriously wrong with her. Once, while lying in

---

29. *Id.* at 53.
30. Sandler & Shoop, *supra* note 19, at 15.
31. *Id.* at 16.
32. *Id.* at 60–63.
33. The following is the summary of what happened to the late student Revina Mukasa.

bed, Revina's door was unlocked with another key by a male student who inflicted pain on her breast and jaw; she only managed to free herself after digging her teeth into his arm. Revina reported the incident, but the administration did not give her problem prompt attention. On 7th Feb. 1990, Revina's roommate noticed that Revina's eyes were closed but her mouth was open; she was rushed to the hospital where the doctor pronounced Revina dead soon after arrival.[34]

It is clear that the Punch poster and other incidents related to it caused Revina to take her life. Although Revina's suicide is the only case that has been officially reported, there are other suicides that have occurred but are not as easily traced to sexual harassment.

University Regulations on Sexual Harassment

The University supplies all UDSM students with a copy of university regulations, which prohibit force or violence against a fellow student; use of slanderous, abusive, obscene, or threatening language against another student; sexual harassment, whether physical or psychological in nature; and rape or indecent assault. [35] The Disciplinary Authority arbitrates violations of these regulations.[36] Upon breach of any of the disciplinary offenses specified, the authority may impose penalties including warning, reprimand, fine, compensation, exclusion from Halls of Residents, suspension, rustication, and expulsion.[37]

Although the university administrators know that sexual harassment is pervasive, they are not doing enough to prevent it from occurring. Administrators wait for students to complain instead of making efforts to reduce the problem through an active program of anticipation and prevention. In addition, the administrative staff in the halls of residence to whom students turn for help in case of problems are often unaware of university regulations. It was noted in a recent report that the Dean of Student Administration has a tendency to settle quarrels between students without recourse to established rules.[38]

---

34. UDSM, Report of The Committee of Enquiry on The Death of Student Revina Mukasa (1990).

35. *Id.* §31.

36. *Id.* §13.1.

37. *Id.* pt. V.

38. *Id.*

Recommendations

Higher Education Institutions

Universities must make efforts to increase the level of awareness of gender issues within their communities through comprehensive mandatory gender sensitization programs. Universities must also train employees to respond appropriately to harassment. The government should require an institution to provide other services such as counseling to students in the event of harassment in order to address its effects. Finally, universities need a clear, well-publicized policy prohibiting sexual harassment so students will know how to report harassment and administrators will be held accountable for enforcing it.

The quota system, preferential admissions, and other forms of affirmative action should continue. Institutions and faculties should follow the Faculty of Science model by establishing pre-entry programs to enhance the enrollment of female students. Universities should create tutoring, mentoring, and outreach programs encouraging women to apply for university admission, as well as programs designed to promote women's pursuit of careers in science.

Non-Governmental Organizations (NGOs) and the Private Sector

NGOs and the private sector should create an education fund for women to provide scholarships to female students. The fund should give students talented in science and technology courses high priority. The community should also create financial aid programs for female students, such as grants or work-study loans, to help them pay for tuition and other costs.

Women's organizations must continue to pressure the government to fulfill its obligations under the international human rights treaties it has ratified by preparing shadow reports[39] on education issues and submitting them to

---

39. The UN Convention on the Elimination of All Forms of Discrimination Against Women (CEDAW) requires state parties to eliminate discrimination against women in the field of education. Discrimination is defined in terms of effects or purpose, so that even when it is not possible to establish discriminatory intent, a state party might be responsible for a breach of CEDAW by virtue of practices that have a discriminatory effect. LOUIS HENKIN ET AL., HUMAN RIGHTS 361–66 (1999).

the Committee on the Elimination of All Forms of Discrimination Against Women (CEDAW Committee) and other relevant human rights committees and by bringing cases to court on the basis of constitutional violations of women's equal right to education. Women's organizations should also continue to work in policy bodies, national and international agencies, and at the grassroots level, in order to influence government action.

Government

Women's human rights issues are usually a low priority for the government.[40] The government should instead take into consideration the important link between promoting education for women and girls and economic development more generally. Tanzania must develop and apply a national policy that will promote equality of opportunity and of treatment in education and repeal all discriminatory laws. The government must enforce national laws prohibiting sexual harassment in an effort to protect women from sexual violence. In addition, Parliament must amend the definition of rape to include other forms of sexual assault, which are now characterized as indecent assault and receive lighter sentences.

The government should support women's access to higher education by funding women's scholarships for under- and post-graduate studies within Tanzanian institutions and abroad. The government should encourage and support private universities because competition among universities in the country will allow more women access to university education. Religious educational institutions might also offer financial aid for women through monetary assistance from sister churches abroad.

Community

The community must encourage girls and women to compete with boys and men through the development of their confidence,[41] frequent supervision of teachers, and social support. Also, qualified school counselors should provide career advice to girls, especially at the secondary school level, where girls are in a position to make important future decisions. The community in gen-

---

40. Margaret E. Galey, *Women and Education*, in 1 WOMEN & INT'L HUM. RTS. L. 403, 439 (Kelly Askin & Dorean Koenig eds., 1999).

41. This includes promoting women's understanding of their conditions as a group being oppressed by a patriarchal system.

eral, particularly parents, teachers, elected local officials, and other leaders should help change "culturally defined" stereotypes of women. Information and awareness-raising campaigns should also encourage women to register for school and promote local education projects.

Conclusion

Improving women's status through increased access to higher education would benefit both Tanzania as a country and women individually. To reap this benefit, Tanzania must eliminate inequality in its educational system. By creating a strong coalition between the government, private sector, educational institutions, and the local community, Tanzania can increase female enrollment in universities—a significant step forward in the long-term development of both women and Tanzania.

Implementation of Affirmative Action in Tanzania's Parliament: An Assessment of the Reserved Seats for Women

Jane Magigita

Introduction

Although women constitute the majority of voters in Tanzania, their participation in political life has been very low. Affirmative action in Parliament was implemented in order to rectify political gender imbalances that have existed since the nation's founding and to bring the voices and concerns of the country's women into the national political consciousness. In practice, however, women parliamentarians elected under the reserved seat system often strictly adhere to political party ideology, characterized by structural gender inequalities and male dominance, rather than advocate for women's issues. Unless the government addresses the obstacles encountered by newly elected women parliamentarians in bringing women's issues to the fore, reserved seats will act as a ceiling rather than a floor in achieving true equal participation in parliamentary politics.

Women in Parliament: Current Status Under Reserved Seat Laws

When Tanzania earned independence in 1961, only 6 women were elected to Parliament, or 7.5 percent of the total members.[1] After the 1995 general

---

1. Tanzania Ministry of Community Development, Women Affairs, and Children, Tanzania Women: Country Report to the 4th World Conference on Women,

election, Parliament had a total of 275 members and 45 (16.5 percent) were women.[2] The slight increase of women in Parliament was a result of legislation in 1992 intended to strengthen women's representation by allocating 15 percent of the total number of constituency seats to women legislators.[3] In 1995, there were 37 seats reserved for women,[4] and an additional 8 women won constituency elections, bringing the total number of women parliamentarians that year to 45. In 2000, the percentage of women-only seats was increased to 20 percent by the Thirteenth Amendment to the Constitution.[5] This cap is expected to increase to 30 percent by 2005.[6] The reserved seat system has raised the total number of women in Parliament from 11 percent in 1990[7] to 16.5 percent in 1995[8] and 22 percent in the 2000 general elections.[9]

Each party elects women according to its own procedures. Usually, women's sections are involved in the initial nomination of women candidates, but final nomination is left to the party's upper body. Although many have doubts about the fairness of party procedures used to elect women, there is a broad consensus that women need reserved seats in order to achieve political equality in Parliament.

The Strengths and Weaknesses of the Current System

Why Reserved Seats are Important

Reserved seats for women not only provide exposure and experience in the political arena, but also afford women confidence to run in open electoral con-

---

BEIJING SEPTEMBER 1995, at 56 (1994).

2. MAXIMILIAN MMUYA, GOVERNMENT AND POLITICAL PARTIES IN TANZANIA (AFTER THE 1995 GENERAL ELECTIONS): FACTS AND FIGURES 25–27 (1997).

3. Act No. 4 of 1992, § 4 (Tanz.) (amending art. 66 of THE CONST. OF THE UNITED REPUBLIC OF TANZANIA OF 1977).

4. MMUYA, *supra* note 2, at 27.

5. Act No. 3 of 2000, § 4 (Tanz.) (amending art. 66 of THE CONST. OF THE UNITED REPUBLIC OF TANZANIA of 1977).

6. THE UNITED REPUBLIC OF TANZANIA, WOMEN POLITICAL EMPOWERMENT AND DECISION MAKING, *at* http://www.tanzania.go.tz/issuesf.html (last visited June 30, 2003).

7. TANZANIA REPORT TO THE BEIJING CONFERENCE, *supra* note 1, at 56.

8. MMUYA, *supra* note 2, at 27.

9. INTER-PARLIAMENTARY UNION, WOMEN IN NATIONAL PARLIAMENTS, *at* http://www.ipu.org/wmn-e/classif.htm (last visited June 30, 2003).

tests. In addition, parliamentary membership functions as a prerequisite for cabinet positions. The small number of women in Parliament following Tanzania's independence narrowed the possibility of female appointees to the cabinet; now that affirmative action has increased the number of women parliamentarians, the government has no excuse for excluding females from ministry appointments.

The proportional system of representation that is applied in allocating the number of reserved seats for each party also allows women from minor political parties to participate in Parliament. Different ideological positions among women Members of Parliament (MPs) are likely to create a healthy debate in Parliament and consequently advance women's rights.

Finally, reserving seats for women in Parliament is important because cultural patterns that are embedded in Tanzanian society have created barriers to women's participation in politics. A critical mass of women in Parliament provides symbolic representation of women as active members of society and offers young women role models that may encourage them to enter politics.[10] Bringing women into Parliament also ushers in new perspectives on issues pertaining to the family, such as land, health, and child protection, which previously did not receive special attention. Some literature suggests that women have a "different set of values, experience, and expertise than men," and, therefore, their inclusion in political life creates a "more caring, compassionate society."[11]

Weaknesses of the Current System

Critics of the affirmative action program offer differing views on how to improve the performance of women legislators. Some advocate for further increases in the number of female parliamentarians, contending that women's right to equal representation will only be realized once women occupy an equal number of seats. By expanding women's presence in politics, they argue, the political culture will itself be transformed.[12] Others assert that problems women face in trying to get elected to Parliament persist once they enter the domain of power, and that, therefore, it is necessary to enhance the quality and effectiveness of women politicians.[13] These critics caution that "we need

---

10. SUE THOMAS, HOW WOMEN LEGISLATE 56 (1994).
11. ANNE PHILLIP, ENGENDERING DEMOCRACY 63 (1991).
12. THOMAS, *supra* note 10, at 85–104.
13. *See, e.g.,* INTERNATIONAL IDEA, WOMEN IN PARLIAMENT: BEYOND NUMBERS, OBSTACLES TO WOMEN'S PARTICIPATION IN PARLIAMENT, *at* http://www.idea.int/women/

to know the behavior of women politicians before deciding whether…we want to increase their numbers."[14] Despite differences over strategy, these critics of affirmative action agree that Tanzania needs to increase both the quantity and quality of women parliamentarians.

Quantity of Women Legislators

Even with reserved seats in Parliament, the number of women legislators is still lower than men. After the 2000 parliamentary elections, there were only 61 women out of a total of 274 MPs.[15] This minority makes it difficult to pass gender sensitive legislation. Additionally, the vast majority of women parliamentarians belong to one party, which further limits the diversity of views among advocates for women's rights.

Furthermore, the affirmative action program has caused fewer women to run in general constituent elections. Women are often discouraged from running for a general seat, because of the perception that they would either lose or, if they won, take the seat away from a man. Reserved seats should supplement, rather than substitute for, traditional ways of getting women involved in Parliament. Although historically women lose general elections, records show that a small number of women do manage to get elected. Following the introduction of reserved seats, however, even women who were previously successful through constituent elections have opted to compete through the affirmative action program. Because women are not fully exercising their political options, the number of women in Parliament remains low.

Finally, women are underrepresented in Parliament because female candidates find it hard to win acceptance from electorates who believe males are "naturally fitter to command than female[s]."[16] While reserved seats enable women to enter Parliament without competing with men, problems facing women in constituent elections remain unattended. Unless obstacles such as discriminatory customs, economic disempowerment of women, biased gender roles, and lack of women in party leadership positions are addressed, women will continue to be discouraged from participation in parliamentary

---

parl/ch2a.htm (last visited June 30, 2003).

14. VICKY RANDALL, WOMEN IN POLITICS: AN INTERNATIONAL PERSPECTIVE 151 (2d. ed. 1987)

15. INTER-PARLIAMENTARY UNION, *supra* note 9.

16. WALTER S. KOHN, WOMEN IN NATIONAL LEGISLATURES: A COMPARATIVE STUDY OF SIX COUNTRIES 234 (1980) (quoting Aristotle).

politics, thus preventing women parliamentarians from gaining equal numbers with men.

Who are Women MPs Representing?[17]

There are several ways of thinking about what constitutes "representation." In my assessment, I will apply two types of representation: (1) "standing for" representation[18] and (2) "acting for" representation.[19] While "standing for" representation implies symbolic representation, "acting for" representation connotes substantive action.

"Standing for" Representation

The provision for reserved seats is enshrined in article 66 of the Constitution of Tanzania, which states that women must comprise at least 20 percent of parliamentarians and requires fulfillment of this mandate by political party elections.[20] The election of women through the political parties leads to an understanding that parties have a stake in women's Parliament seats. Political parties claim authority because, as candidates, women use the party's label to get elected within their parties, and are addressed through party affiliation while in Parliament.

Although women rely on their party label in Parliament, it would be unfair to conclude that women parliamentarians elected through affirmative action stand only for political parties. Instead, an assessment of the party procedures used to select women candidates reveals that they are initially chosen by their fellow women through elections that were organized by party "women's wings." The qualifications for these female party candidates include a commitment to advancing women's causes, active membership in "women's wings," and a tradition of accessibility to women. The party factions involved during the election, such as "women's wings," regional women executive com-

---

17. "Representing here means acting in the interest of the represented, in a manner responsive to them. The representative must act independently; he [she]...must also be capable of independent action and judgment...And, despite the resulting potential for conflict between representative and represented about what is to be done, that conflict must normally take place...or if it occurs an explanation is called for." HANNA PITKIN, THE CONCEPT OF REPRESENTATION 209 (1967).

18. See SYLVIA TAMALE, WHEN HENS BEGINS TO CROW: GENDER AND PARLIAMENTARY POLITICS IN UGANDA 72–76 (1999).

19. See id. at 76–86.

20. TANZ. CONST., art. 66 (1977) (as amended in 2000).

mittees, and the National Women's Council indicate that party women are highly involved in the nomination process. Despite the party's role in enabling women candidates to serve in Parliament, these women are elected to stand not only for their parties but also for women in general.

"Acting for" Representation

Apart from the symbolic representation of women, "acting for" representation is necessary to make representation politically meaningful.[21] The idea that women representatives will alter the *status quo* is based on the notion that women approach issues differently than men, largely because of their family-centric role and also because of their inexperience in the public arena.[22] Many hope these differences mean that women will give priority to women's issues such as childcare, domestic violence, property ownership, and social security, thereby driving these problems into the public sphere.

Nevertheless, efforts by the government to include more women in Parliament do not necessarily mean that women MPs represent the interests and concerns of women. As one study has shown, not all women members of Parliament who have been elected to reserved seats "feel obliged to defend women's issues in the legislature."[23] Party politics still influence the legislative process, and many MPs are not sensitive to gender dynamics while discussing or passing laws.

Women and the Legislative Process

One way of assessing the performance of women legislators is to understand how legislators approached and met their goals through various activities in the Assembly.[24] In reviewing this progress, it is important to determine whether legislative activity in Tanzania is structured to accommodate women and to ensure their full participation in parliamentary politics.

Women and Session Floor

A study of parliamentary sessions conducted between 1986 and 1992 showed that women do not impose a commanding presence on the session

---

21. TAMALE, *supra* note 18, at 76.

22. THOMAS, *supra* note 10, at 62.

23. GENDER, DEMOCRACY AND DEVELOPMENT: POST BEIJING CHALLENGES FOR WOMEN'S EMPOWERMENT IN EAST AFRICA 37 (Reuben E. Ruhongole ed., 1996).

24. THOMAS, *supra* note 10, at 38.

floor.[25] In every session, an average of five to eight women MPs actually asked questions and gave comments. This number represents only 20 percent to 25 percent of the total number of women parliamentarians, while 75 percent of male MPs asked questions and gave comments.[26] Surprisingly, 50 percent of the comments by women constituted seconding motions; only 5 percent gave constructive criticism to the government and only 2 percent challenged the government, while a full 33 percent of the comments were silent expressions.[27] Furthermore, since independence, there has never been a women Speaker of the House.

Women parliamentarians elected to reserved seats have enjoyed moderate success in passing legislation aimed at promoting women's rights, namely the Sexual Offences Act of 1998[28] and the Land Acts of 1999,[29] which sought to protect women and children against sexual abuse and to improve women's access to land ownership. The passage of these two laws was not an easy task and required the efforts of women legislators, women's activists, and human rights organizations.[30]

Parliamentary Committees

Because of the low participation of women in plenary sessions, women legislators are expected to actively take advantage of Committees where members can debate and exchange ideas more freely with one another.[31] This venue works well for women who are more familiar with the unofficial, casual interaction characterizing committee sessions than the formal conduct of the

---

25. Kate Kamba, Women and Parliamentary Politics in Tanzania 34 (1997) (unpublished Masters of Arts Dissertation, University of Dar-es-Salaam, Tanzania, on file with the University of Dar-es-Salaam Faculty of Arts and Social Sciences).

26. *Id.* The survey covered both women legislators for reserved seats and those under Constituent seats. However women elected through reserved seats were 50 percent more likely to be silent than those elected by constituents.

27. *Id.* at 34.

28. The Sexual Offences (Special Provisions) Act 1998 (Act No. 4 of 1998) (Tanz.).

29. The Land Act 1999 (Act No. 4 of 1999) (Tanz.); the Village Land Act 1999 (Act No. 5 of 1999) (Tanz.).

30. *See generally* RESEARCH AND TEACHING ON HUMAN RIGHTS, GENDER AND DEMOCRACY ISSUES IN SOUTHERN AFRICA, TANZANIA COUNTRY PROFILE, *at* http://www.hrdc.unam.na/tanzania.htm (last visited July 7, 2003).

31. SOUTH AFRICA: DESIGNING NEW POLITICAL INSTITUTIONS 256 (Murray Faure & Jan-Erik Lane eds., 1996).

plenary.[32] The presence of women in all Committees is likely to influence work during the legislative process and ensure that Committees take gender dynamics into consideration when they discuss bills.

Male domination of Committees affects the outcome of bills, as gender issues are not accorded respect within Committee discussions. Only two women currently hold chairmanship positions in any Committees, and overall participation of women in parliamentary Committees remains low.[33] But unlike 1990 when only 34 percent of women legislators participated in Committees, in 2001 all 49 women legislators under reserved seats were serving in parliamentary Committees.[34] However, women parliamentarians are often channeled into Committees in accordance with stereotypes about the female role; therefore, more women legislators serve on committees concerning issues such as social development and environment rather than on those dealing with constitutional, defense, and security issues, which are crucial for assessing the impact of laws on women and other marginalized groups.

Recommendations

Government

The Executive

Constitution and Law Reform

Affirmative action programs are necessary, and the Constitution must protect reserved seats for women from attacks based on misplaced equality rhetoric or arbitrary abolition before the intended program results can be achieved. Parliament should amend the Constitution to establish affirmative action as a process necessary to pursue the realization of equal human rights,

---

32. TAMALE, *supra* note 18, at 146.

33. As of July 2003, the Hon. Sophia Simba (CCM) was Chairperson of the Social Welfare and Community Development Committee and the Hon. Anne S. Makinda (CCM) was Chairperson of the Natural Resources and Environment Committee. *See* PARLIAMENT OF TANZANIA, PARLIAMENTARY COMMITTEES: COMPOSITION, *at* http://www.parliament.go.tz/bunge/bunge.asp?Menu=32 (last visited July 7, 2003).

34. Between 1985–90, six women were Committee members in the Socio-Cultural Committee while for the same period only one was in the Constitution and Law Committee. Information obtained from Office of the Speaker of the National Assembly.

including women's rights.[35] Such an amendment should mandate 50 percent representation of women at all levels of decision making. Additionally, Parliament and the Cabinet members must be accountable to civil society via removal mechanisms.[36] The Constitution should further obligate the parties to promote and conform to democratic principles and ensure that women members enjoy equal status with men in the design and implementation of party programs.[37]

Special Program to Improve Constituents' Elections for Women

The government should adopt specific measures to ensure that women participate equally with men as candidates in parliamentary elections. The government must also address the problems encountered by women during constituent elections, such as sexist stereotypes, in an effort to create a favorable environment so that women who have acquired political experience in reserved seats have the capacity to compete with men for constituents' seats. Women's participation in constituent elections will leave space for other women to occupy reserved seats, and thus, acquire the necessary experience.

Accountability

Women in reserved seats should be assigned to geographical constituencies as representatives for women in those constituencies. This allocation is likely to ensure that their mandate derives from women to whom they are accountable and that they are subject to evaluation by the women they represent.

Women Ministers

Women's participation in the government should be established as a rule of democracy. Women legislators should be appointed to hold ministerial positions in equal numbers with men.

---

35. TANZANIA GENDER NETWORKING PROGRAMME (TGNP), INCLUSION OF WOMEN'S RIGHTS IN THE CONSTITUTION OF TANZANIA, Scenario 1(d), *at* http://www.eastafrican-law.com/LawArticle/inclusion_of_TZ_women.htm (last visited June 30, 2003).

36. *Id.* at Scenario 1(e).

37. Political parties are specifically mentioned in the German Constitution by Article 21 which reads: "(1) The political parties shall participate in the forming of the political will of the people. They may be freely established. Their internal organization must conform to democratic principles." ANNA PETERS, WOMEN, QUOTAS AND CONSTITUTIONS: A COMPARATIVE STUDY OF THE AFFIRMATIVE ACTION FOR WOMEN UNDER AMERICAN, GERMAN, EUROPEAN COMMUNITY AND INTERNATIONAL LAW 221–22 (1990).

Parliament
Legislative Action

The government should create a parliamentary committee to review issues relating to the status of women. This Gender Committee would ensure that Parliament assesses all bills for gender implications and that Parliament considers all relevant recommendations for changes or additions before bills become law. Gender expertise and sensitivity should be the primary criteria for membership in this committee.

Transforming Parliamentary Procedure and Changing the Rules

The Westminster model of parliamentary procedure needs to be reviewed to create a better environment for women's participation and for multiparty democracy. Changes in procedure should encourage women legislators to speak during parliamentary sessions and to make constructive remarks. Also, Parliament should introduce rules that promote proportional distribution of responsibility between men and women.

Women Parliamentary Empowerment Unit

Since women under reserved seats have less experience than their male counterparts, the government should create an "Empowerment Unit" to help women build their legislative capacity and to provide technical support. This Empowerment Unit would offer legal assistance in interpretation of bills and collaborate with the Women's Caucus in identifying issues for lobbying and planning strategies to ensure women's issues are part of every legislative agenda.

Women Caucus

Despite their diverse ideologies and priorities, women MPs need to set goals and benchmarks to ensure women's rights are systematically taken into consideration.

Political Parties
Introducing Party Quota

Parties that have committed in their election manifestos to end discrimination against women should adopt quota systems as temporary measures designed to overcome the imbalances that exist between men and women in party politics. The party quota will enhance women's representation in internal party bodies at all levels by guaranteeing that women will occupy a certain percentage of seats. Parties also need to introduce a quota system for the party list of candidates for parliamentary and local council elections. The party list will help to ensure that constituent's seats are not traded off with the reserved seats and that women participate fully in constituents' elections.

Political Parties' Programs

Parties should pay special attention to the principle of equality between men and women. Programs should be geared towards cooperation and partnership between men and women. Party committee membership should include both men and women in an effort to sensitize men to women's issues and to erode the stereotype that only women should be concerned with "women's issues."

Women's Sections of the Political Parties

Within political parties, women's sections should set clear goals for women legislators and create a feedback mechanism that will monitor successes and failures for women advocating for a "women's agenda" in Parliament. Women should urge their parties to compose equitable rules for candidate selection. Women will benefit if parties have fair, clear procedures for selecting candidates rather than a system based on loyalty to those in power.[38]

Media

Change of Women's Image

Mass media is an effective tool to change discriminatory images of women in the society and negative attitudes towards women as leaders. Sensitization of society will empower women, expanding their roles from mothers and caretakers to equal partners in politics.

Educate the Public

Media should ensure parliamentary proceedings are heard, and if possible, televised for the public. The media should give priority not only to televising

---

38. INTERNATIONAL IDEA, WOMEN IN PARLIAMENT: BEYOND NUMBERS, LESSONS FOR EXPANDING WOMEN REPRESENTATION, *at* http://www.idea.int/women/parl/ch3d.htm (last visited June 30, 2003).

parliamentary floor sessions but televising the Committees as well. This will enable the public to understand the work of their representatives and at the same time learn how to use Parliament to publicize their views.

Conclusion

Affirmative action is an important tool for improving the status of women and ensuring that women's issues are part of the national agenda. Unless reserved seats open doors for women legislators to participate equally in parliamentary politics, however, the Tanzanian government cannot legitimately claim to promote democracy or equality.

One Step Forward, Two Steps Back: The Women's Movement and Law Reform in Uganda from 1985–2000

Jacqueline Asiimwe

Introduction

Uganda's women's movement has enjoyed a marked increase in activism from 1985 to 2000. Globally, events such as the U.N. World Conference on Women,[1] the establishment of the Women's Convention,[2] and international proclamations of women's rights as human rights[3] have propelled the movement. Within Uganda, the movement was reborn on the heels of the present National Resistance Movement (NRM) government, providing a receptive political atmosphere for the growth of the movement. With the promulgation of the new constitution in 1995, which gives explicit recognition to women's rights, the movement has been able to make legitimate claims for the protection and promotion of the rights of women.

Nevertheless, although the women's movement has made considerable progress in the area of women's public rights, the same cannot be said of women's personal rights. Progress has been slow in this area, often taking the women's movement two steps back for each step forward. The fact that women

---

1. LOUIS HENKIN ET AL., HUMAN RIGHTS 358 (1999).
2. The Convention on the Elimination of All Forms of Discrimination Against Women, opened for signature Mar. 1, 1980, art. X, 1249 U.N.T.S. 13, X, 19 I.L.M. 33, X.
3. Particularly the 1993 UN World Conference on Human Rights in Vienna. *See* LOUIS HENKIN, *supra* note 1, at 359.

have not made progress in women's property rights and rights in the home continues to be a thorn in the flesh of the Ugandan women's movement.

This essay posits that although the movement's progress in securing public rights is positive,[4] the present discrimination of women in the home undermines the very rights gained outside the home. In order to make the achievements of the women's movement in the public sphere meaningful, society must also recognize women's rights in the private sphere.[5] The women's movement must make women's personal rights a political issue in order to reform the laws that presently discriminate against women in the private sphere.

The Gains of the Women's Movement

Women's Participation in Constitutional Reform

One example of the success of the women's movement in the public sphere is women's participation in the promulgation of the 1995 constitution. Women's participation in constitutional reform is important not only because women comprise more than half of the population (53 percent), but because they produce the greater percentage of the nation's wealth (80 percent).[6] The Ministry of Women in Development, Culture and Youth, with the assistance of The Danish International Development Agency (DANIDA) and some national women's organizations, embarked on a comprehensive education campaign for women on the constitution-making process. This campaign was un-

---

4. *See* Susan B. Boyd, Challenging the Public/Private Divide: Feminism, Law and Public Policy 8–10 (1997). Boyd notes:

> The public/private divide denotes the ideological division of life into apparently opposing spheres of public and private activities, and public and private responsibilities...Considerable feminist energy has been directed to the deconstruction of...the public/private divide...The...rallying cry "the personal is political" exemplifies this type of initiative. Social relations that were hitherto viewed as personal or private were to be politicized, analyzed, exposed to scrutiny and rendered an appropriate arena for regulation by the state and law...

5. By stating that we have made gains in women's political rights I do not in any way intend to paint a picture that we have "arrived." Indeed, we are far from the finish line in terms of women and politics; however, when compared to women's personal rights, women appear to have made leaps and bounds in politics.

6. Ministry of Women in Development, Recommendations by the Women of Uganda to the Constitutional Commission 2 (1991).

dertaken to complement the efforts of the Constitutional Commission and it achieved tremendous results.[7]

Some of the important provisions for women in the new constitution include equal protection under the law,[8] an express prohibition against discrimination on the basis of sex,[9] equality of the rights of married women and men both during marriage and at its dissolution,[10] and provisions granting widows the right to inherit the property of deceased spouses.[11] The constitution further provides for affirmative action in favor of groups marginalized by gender[12] and calls for the establishment of an "equal opportunities commission"[13] to ensure implementation of this program. The constitution also prohibits laws, customs, and traditions that are against the dignity, welfare, or interest of women or undermine their status.[14]

---

7. For example:
During the constitutional seminars conducted by the Ministry of Women in Development, Culture and Youth, women discussed a wide range of issues including a national language, citizenship, participatory democracy, electoral systems, the judiciary, land and fundamental rights and freedoms. The women emphasized among other things that the new Constitution should protect women against husbands who make it their right to decide whether or not their wives should work for a payment. They recommended that all discriminatory laws be repealed and be replaced with more up-to-date legislation. The areas of law identified included marriage laws, divorce laws, inheritance and property rights and employment regulations. Women also requested that with the present scourge of HIV/AIDS in the country, polygamous unions be outlawed by the Constitution. Women noted that there is a lot of suffering in polygamous homes because the man cannot love his wives equally and usually he does not have enough to provide sufficient support to his wives and numerous children, which then leaves the heavy burden on women to support the family. Further, they suggested that customary marriages, which confer unequal marriage status to the parties involved, be discouraged. Women called for the abolition of bride wealth, the treatment of women as equal partners with men in divorce proceedings, abolition widow inheritance and the outlawing of all customary practices that deprive women of their right to acquire property such as land and other fixed assets. *Id.* at 13–18.
8. Uganda Const. art. 21 cl.1.
9. Uganda Const. art. 21 cl.1.
10. Uganda Const. art. 31 cl. 1.
11. Uganda Const. art. 31 cl. 2.
12. Uganda Const. art. 32 cl. 1.
13. Uganda Const. art. 32 cl. 2.
14. Uganda Const. art. 33 cl. 6.

Women in Decision Making

Another example of the movement's achievements in the public sphere is the increased presence of women in government. In the 1989 National Resistance Council elections, the NRM government brought significant improvement to women's political participation. Thirty-four seats were reserved for women; two women won their seats in open contests against male candidates; the President nominated three women; and two women were historical members, appointed because of their participation in the guerrilla war led by the National Resistance Army. Through affirmative action, women made considerable headway in Parliament. When asked about the changes to women's status after the 1986 NRM takeover, women overwhelmingly responded that the biggest changes related to women's participation in politics, standing for office, becoming public and government leaders, and being able to express themselves publicly to a greater degree than in the past.[15]

Reasons for the Gains in the Public Sphere

Although Ugandan women have made strides in the public sphere, an examination of some of the underlying reasons demonstrates that the picture is not as promising as it may appear. The increase in the number of seats for women in the National Resistance Council (NRC) came at a time when the government of the day was looking for legitimacy beyond its borders. Indeed, in several countries, the fate of women in politics remains vulnerable to the "shifting needs of different regimes for legitimacy," because the government's agenda is "much less a response to domestic female constituencies than to international pressures…[and] domestic concerns to demonstrate a commitment to democracy.…"[16] Increasing the number of women in politics proves even more rewarding given aid agencies' recent emphasis on "gender indicators" and "gender profile" of a country in making funding decisions.[17] It is

---

15. Alice Emasu, *Ugandan Women in Top Decision Making*, THE NEW VISION, Mar 11, 2001.

16. ANNE MARIE GOETZ, THE POLITICS OF INTEGRATING GENDER TO STATE DEVELOPMENT PROCESSES: TRENDS, OPPORTUNITIES AND CONSTRAINTS IN BANGLADESH, CHILE, JAMAICA, MALI, MOROCCO, AND UGANDA 14 (1995).

17. Candace R. Jackson, Cutting the Coat According to the Cloth: Gender, Democracy, and Debate in Uganda 36 (2000) (Unpublished B.A. Thesis, Princeton University, on file with author).

more plausible to describe the NRM's leadership on gender issues as a product of political pragmatism than an ideological commitment to women's human rights. The NRM has exhibited a fixation with attaining and maintaining state power.[18] In fact, the NRM has never ascribed to any ideology or policy that did not strengthen its hold on state power.

In the 1996 Ugandan presidential and Parliamentary elections, women figured prominently in the NRM government's political calculation. "Indeed, it appears that the NRM has struck a kind of political deal with Ugandan women: In exchange for women's political support, the NRM is boosting women's presence in formal politics."[19] The latest evidence of gender politics in the NRM is President Museveni's appointment of a female vice president. Vice President Kazibwe was, at the time of her appointment, the highest-ranking female politician in Africa. Like the NRM affirmative action policy, the Kazibwe appointment appears to be a political move intended to position the NRM for exploitation of gender issues—and thus the women's vote—in future elections.

"Aside from electoral strategies, the low political and economic costs of the NRM's gender policies serve as an incentive to the NRM to maintain gender-sensitive positions. Symbolic gestures do not break budgets."[20] The practical effects of gender policies on the day-to-day lives of the majority of Ugandan women, however, are limited. The NRM has courted women for their votes,[21] "…but women's increased stature in politics has not resulted in significant policy initiatives.…The NRM…has not given priority to issues of special concern to women such as improvements in rural health, provision of small-scale loans, and programs that would ensure [the full implementation of the equality guarantees in the new constitution]."[22]

---

18. Dan Ottemoeller, *Gender Politics in Uganda: Symbolism in the Service of Pragmatism*, 42 Afr. Stud. Rev. 87, 94 (1999).

19. *Id.*

20. *Id.* at 95.

21. According to one person whom Jackson quoted, sometimes women are not even courted for their votes. "You have to understand the culture here. The NRM treats women like husbands treat wives. Women are always reminded that they should be grateful because the NRM brought us to the table. They don't court our vote, they just remind us where we used to be." Jackson, *supra* note 17, at 4.

22. Ottemoeller, *supra* note 18, at 95.

The Setbacks in Women's Private Rights

Despite success in the public sphere, the women's movement has failed to obtain legal reform in the private sphere. An examination of family law and land rights for women reveals the lack of progress in women's personal rights.

The Domestic Relations Bill (DRB)

The women's movement has made several attempts to pressure the government into changing the domestic relations laws that remain largely discriminatory against women. The move to change this law did not begin during the NRM government, but has been an ongoing concern of the movement since the early 1960s. One of the landmarks of the domestic relations reform process was the 1964 Report of the Commission on Marriage and Divorce, popularly known as the Kalema Report,[23] which offered recommendations for improving marriage, divorce, and property rights within marriage. Yet in the almost four decades since the issuance of the Kalema Report, Parliament has never amended the law to meet the changing times or to conform to the newly promulgated Constitution, which recognizes women's equal rights both during marriage and at its dissolution.[24]

The Co-ownership Clause

In the area of property rights, the women's movement lobbied for a co-ownership clause during the debate of the Land Bill in 1998. The purpose of the clause was to give wives greater control over family land. Parliament discussed and passed the clause, but it did not appear in the Land Act. The movement immediately lobbied for an amendment to the Land Act that would include the co-ownership clause. Finally, in February of 2000, the Minister of State for Lands introduced the co-ownership amendment to the Cabinet for debate.[25] The Cabinet rejected the clause outright and only decided to insert

---

23. W. W. Kalema, Report of the Commission on Marriage, Divorce and the Status of Women (1965).

24. Uganda Const. art. 31, cl.1.

25. In Uganda, Amendments to laws are introduced for debate by the Ministers responsible for the subject matter of the Amendment first to Cabinet (the body composed of Ministers of Government) and then in Parliament (the equivalent of the United States House of Representatives).

it in the Domestic Relations Bill as a last minute attempt to "save face" so that women's rights activists would not accuse the government of being anti-women.[26] Since then, the women's movement has lobbied to have the co-own-ership amendment reinstated in the Land Act where they feel it rightly be-longs. There is, however, a great deal of resistance to the co-ownership clause by men and some women who believe the clause will disrupt the family.[27]

Challenges Faced by the Women's Movement in Advocating for Women's Personal Rights

There are several reasons for the slow progress of the women's movement in securing legal reform in women's personal rights. First, women's family and property rights advocated in the co-ownership clause or the Domestic Rela-tions Bill are seen as problematic because these rights go to the root of op-pression and discrimination against women. Men often exercise unilateral power over their wives, and women are generally subordinate to their husbands in the home. Women's subordinate position is manifested through their low level of participation in decisions affecting their bodies, such as whether and when to have sex, the number and spacing of children, and contraceptive use. Women also do not generally make decisions about or own family property, and they are often unable to contribute monetarily to property. Women are subject to domestic violence and can be sent away from their homes at any time by their husbands. If a husband finds it hard to send his wife away, he will walk out of the marriage, leaving the wife and children destitute. The resilience of such patriarchal forms of control and discrimination stand in the way of gen-der equality and greater respect for women's private rights in Uganda.

Opponents of women's personal rights often embrace cultural relativism to challenge so-called Western feminist ideals and to remind women's activists what "true" African values are.[28] Calls to culture, African-ness, and religion

---

26. Aili Mari Tripp, *The Politics of Women's Rights and Cultural Diversity in Uganda*, in GENDER JUSTICE, DEVELOPMENT, AND RIGHTS 424 (Maxine Molyneux & Shahra Razavi eds., 2002).

27. *Id.* at 423.

28. "Regarding the situation of women in particular, relativists seek to retain the dom-inance of patriarchal structures of social ordering and to resist what would amount to a diminution of traditionally exercised power and control within the family, and its attendant implications to the community and the state." Joe Oloka Onyango, *Human Rights and Sus-tainable Development in Contemporary Africa: A New Dawn, or Retreating Horizons?* 6 BUFF. HUM. RTS. L. REV. 39, 50 (2000).

are often heeded and take precedence over the more urgent issue of freeing over half the population from the shackles of discrimination. The women's movement's recognition of women's autonomy and individuality also creates a tension that hinders the recognition of women's personal rights. The notion of individuality goes against the grain of communitarianism in African society, which emphasizes duties rather than rights and mutual obligations rather than individual advancement. Traditionalists accuse the women's movement of elevating women over and above family or society. Because the family is central to the structure of African society, traditionalists are likely to violently resist any proposed changes.

Uganda's ban on political parties also hampers the women's movement.[29] Unlike women's advocates in many pluralist societies, Ugandan women have not been able to use the competitive dynamic of a pluralist system in order to build leverage around their political demands.[30] The "no-party" system grants the Movement constitutional status as the country's political system and allows it to enjoy the privileges of a monopoly on state power.[31] The lack of pluralism and internal party democracy in Uganda means that women are dangerously dependent on presidential patronage for promoting gender equality. Although the role of the President is to lead women's emancipation in Uganda, President Museveni is, to say the least, ambivalent about women's rights. When speaking on the issue of the co-ownership clause, Museveni remarked: "When I learnt that the Bill was empowering the newly-married women to share the properties of the husbands, I smelt a disaster and advised for slow and careful analysis of the property sharing issue."[32] Although he was considered an ally of the women's movement in the early years (1986–90), as his statements on co-ownership show, he is fast becoming an obstacle to the attainment of women's personal rights.

In addition, politics and the political machinery in Uganda remains a male domain. As a result, government agencies responsible for law reform do not seriously entertain "revolutionary" proposals aimed at combating age-old cus-

---

29. Anne Marie Goetz and Shireen Hassim, *In and Against the Party: Women's Representation and Constituency-Building in Uganda and South Africa, in* GENDER JUSTICE, DEVELOPMENT AND RIGHTS, *supra* note 26, at 324–25.

30. *Id.* at 325.

31. *Id.* at 328–31.

32. Aili Mari Tripp, *The Politics of Autonomy and Cooptation in Africa: The Case of the Ugandan Women's Movement*, 39 J. OF MODERN AFR. STUD. 101, 120 (2001) (quoting President Museveni).

toms premised on men's superiority.[33] The ability of male lawmakers to deliberately stall the debate on the DRB without fearing effective reprisal by women points not only to the power of male interests, but also to the gender lobby's lack of political leverage. The state's strategic interests have also blocked the progress of the DRB. Many ministers consider the DRB divisive and do not wish to risk the support of key constituents by sending the Bill forward. For example, a number of policymakers feel that the provisions related to polygamy antagonize Muslims, many of whom practice polygamy.[34] The government fears rocking the cultural boat and would rather sacrifice women at the altar of archaic and discriminatory laws.

Most women in Ugandan politics do not come from the women's movement and do not share a gender equality agenda.[35] Feminists in civil society complain that most women MPs lack any interest in or conceptual grasp of gender issues.[36] Indeed, a number of women Parliamentarians who occupy seats reserved for women carefully distance themselves from a feminist legislative agenda.[37] The Movement system also elicits a powerful sense of loyalty from the women politicians who have benefited from it. Most women MPs view the affirmative action policy that put them in office as a favor (as opposed to a right) and are loath to challenge the NRM leadership in pursuit of gender equality.[38] This sense of obligation limits the ability of women to challenge the system and further women's personal rights.

Interventions for Change: Some Considerations

Many challenges face the women's movement at the turn of a new century, but these challenges are not insurmountable. A comprehensive strategy is needed to deal with the complex nature of women's subordination. One possible way to change the present state of affairs is to change the advocacy methods the women's movement has used, and fashion new and better approaches to these ever-changing problems.

---

33. Goetz, *supra* note 29, at 331–33.

34. *See* Elizabeth Kameo, *Don't Hold Your Breath*, Afr. Woman, Nov. 2002, http://www.africawoman.net/files/20nov02/AW7P06.pdf. (last visited June 15th, 2003).

35. Goetz, *supra* note 29, at 334.

36. *Id.* at 335.

37. Sylvia Tamale, When Hens Begin To Crow: Gender and Parliamentary Politics in Uganda 80–81 (1999).

38. *Id.*

First, the women's movement must actively engage in the democracy debate. It must consistently and conscientiously make its demands political because that is the language the government hears and understands. Issues that affect democratic development also affect the women's movement. Women need to engage in the public discourse on democratization. In doing so, women will forge stronger links between gender and democracy as a concept and as a practice and reaffirm their role as participants in decision-making. Women's new democratic skills will lay a foundation for challenging both the power of the Movement system and the patriarchal values embedded therein. Women's rights activists should also combat the system by seeking out gender-sensitive women with political potential and encouraging them to stand for elective office.

The support and participation of rural women is critical to the success of the women's movement. With increased diversity, the leaders of the movement will be able to quell accusations that they are elitist and out of touch with the rest of Ugandan women. Also, inclusion of rural women will extend the scope of the women's movement so that advocacy takes place not only at the Parliament in Kampala, but at all levels of government throughout the country. Effective advocacy requires regular consultation between the women's movement at the national and the grassroots level in order to identify policy needs based on real, as opposed to assumed, needs. The women's movement needs to build its capacity and expertise in lobbying and advocacy by creating a cadre of activists to press for solutions to these problems in Parliament. Advocates could also provide information to decision-makers on a variety of women's issues through position papers or issue briefs.

The women's movement should make use of information technology to network and advocate for rights both internationally and within the region. In order to maximize the limited resources, women's rights leaders should plan a national lobby week, mobilizing civil society both in rural and urban areas to bring pressure to bear on members of Parliament. This would inculcate a culture of accountability for women's rights among decision-makers and raise publicity for women's rights. By getting to know legislators on a one-to-one basis, women's rights activists would know who supported their agenda and who did not and would be better equipped to lobby the appropriate legislators.

The domestic legal system is another critical sphere for advocacy of women's personal rights. Many women's rights provisions lie dormant in the much-lauded gender-sensitive constitution; one way to resurrect them is to take constitutional cases to court and to promote women's personal rights through test case litigation. Taking these cases to court makes these ideas public; media coverage can open women's personal rights to debate and scrutiny and lead to a re-evaluation of Uganda's values as a nation.

Conclusion

In order to make the gains of the women's movement in the public sphere meaningful, Uganda must recognize women's personal rights have to be recognized as well. The personal is and must be political. Despite the many challenges it faces, the Uganda women's movement has not and should not surrender the fight for women's personal rights. Indeed, whatever obstacles are mounted against the march towards equality, the Uganda women's movement must walk on, taking two steps forward, because no one can ever take from them the justness of their cause.

Judicial Activism and Gender Rights in Tanzania: The Task Ahead

Regina M. Rweyemamu

Introduction

"The courts have to bridge the yawning gaps between the letter of the law and reality in the field of law."

Mwalusanya J.[1]

Discriminatory laws emerge as actual disputes between individuals for which courts must render a just decision. To reach a just decision between competing interests, the court interprets—or decides—the present law. An activist court can provide a vision for change using real facts to demonstrate the injustice of a discriminatory law. In this essay, judicial activism refers to a philosophy of judging that seeks to interpret law in light of social reality and consistent with overriding principles of justice and fairness,[2] as opposed to judicial restraint, in which the judge applies rules formally and consistently, "unconcerned with the larger issues of social justice."[3]

---

1. Palamagambo John Kabudi, *The Judiciary and Human Rights in Tanzania: Domestic Applications of International Human Rights Norms*, 24 Law and Politics in Africa, Asia & Latin America 271, 275 (1991).

2. This represents a realist philosophy of law. Under realist philosophy, the process of judging is basically an exercise in law making. "Until a court has given judgement on the facts no law on the subject is yet in existence. Before the decision the only law available is a lawyer's opinion. That opinion is not actually law but only a guess as to what the court will decide." C.M. Peter and M.K.B. Wambali, *Independence of the Judiciary in Tanzania: A Critique*, 21 Law and Politics in Africa, Asia & Latin America 72, 73 (1988) (quoting Judge Jerome Frank in J. Frank, Law and the Modern Mind (1935)).

Admittedly, change of laws by legislative or judicial action alone cannot improve the status of women in Tanzania, or elsewhere, because women's inferior status is a phenomenon rooted in the socioeconomic system that laws enforce and reinforce.[4] Progressive judicial action can supplement and sometimes prompt economic, social, and political efforts. The court, if it adopts a progressive activist position, offers one way to improve the status of women, a way that is sometimes more effective than legislation.[5]

This essay discusses how judges may use judicial activism to improve the status of women. It examines the legitimacy and limitations of judicial activism, offers some thoughts on possible activist steps necessary to achieve more justice for women, and suggests mechanisms to support and encourage such activism.

The Basis of Legitimacy of Judicial Activism

Activism is a legitimate process of judicial decision making. First, the role of an independent judiciary is to render just legal decisions. Not only does the legislative process sometimes take too long, but there are instances when the

---

3. Radhika Coomaraswamy, *Toward an Engaged Judiciary, in* THE ROLE OF THE JUDICIARY IN PLURAL SOCIETIES 1,10 (Neelan Tiruchelvam et al. eds. 1987) [Hereinafter *Engaged Judiciary*].

4. *See generally* FRIEDRICH ENGELS, THE ORIGIN OF THE FAMILY PRIVATE PROPERTY AND THE STATE (1971) (In Marxist parlance, the economic base gives expression to each society's superstructure, the political, social, cultural systems, and values. While Marxist economic determinism theory has its limits, it is valid in certain respects. For example, in parts of Africa where ownership of property follows the mother line (matrilineal societies), women enjoy a relatively superior position. Second, in western societies the subordination of women was held in place by use of oppressive laws e.g., under the system of covertures.).

5. The court can change laws which are discriminatory on their face, like customary laws which remain in place despite changes in the socioeconomic conditions upon which they were based. These laws were founded in a communal economy based on communal ownership and values which has now been replaced or mixed with the capitalist cash economy built around individualism. It can also invalidate protective labor laws, e.g., the Employment Ordinance, Cap 366 section 83 (1) (Tanz.) (prevents employment of women in Industrial undertaking between the hours of 10 p.m. and 6 a.m.) and section 86 (prevents female employment in underground mine works). For a critique of these provisions, *see* Legal and Human Rights Centre, General Observations and Recommendations on Reform of Labour Law Regime in Tanzania (Report Dec. 2002). www.humanrightstz.org/humanrights/Labour%20Law%20Recommendation-8%20Aug, 02.htm. (last visited June 10, 2003).

legislature simply fails to act. The legislature may refuse to act in areas in which the court already faces a dispute. In those cases, judicial activism is unavoidable.

Second, legal scholars, realists and positivists alike, generally accept that both liberal and conservative judges make law and that the judicial function is a "dynamic one."[6] Those who argue that the judge applies the will of the legislature and interprets law as the legislature intended merely mask reality. Ascertaining the will of the legislature at the point of legislation is neither an easy task nor a necessarily desirable one.[7] Both the activist and conservative judges interpret legislative intent in light of their own ideologies and use what it considers to be society's conscience as a guide. In the process, they help to form and modify that societal consciousness. The real debate should concern what kind of law judges make, that which supports the status quo[8] or that which promotes change for women.

Third, even in mature western democracies, legislative will generally means the will of the majority or powerful interests groups.[9] According to this theory, "Constitutional Law appropriately exists for those situations where representative government cannot be trusted."[10] Women cannot rely solely on the legislature as the latter's "preoccupation with 'expediency' and 'majority interests'" often prevents it from effectively protecting the rights and interests of politically powerless groups.[11] The assumption that the enacted law represents the will of the majority is sometimes a fallacy, especially in the socio-political environment of a country like Tanzania, where the majority is illiterate and does not follow modern politics. Moreover, the country has "no tradition

---

6. 6 WILLIAM ESKRIDGE, DYNAMIC STATUTORY INTERPRETATION 5 (1994).

7. Eskridge notes that "as distance between enactment and interpretation increases, a pure originalist inquiry becomes impossible and/or irrelevant." *Id.* at 6. He further notes that "the original intent of the legislature has less relevance for figuring out how the statute should apply in unforeseen circumstances...." *Id.* at 10.

8. *See* Upendra Baxi, *On the Shame of Not Being an Activist: Thoughts on Judicial Activism, in* THE ROLE OF THE JUDICIARY IN PLURAL SOCIETIES, *supra* note 3, at 171 (Baxi notes that between judicial restraint and the support of the status quo, there is a very thin line of difference, particularly in the third world.).

9. One of the proponents of this theory, John Ely, sees no conflict between democracy and judicial review so long as courts act only where there is a defect in the legislative process which prevents minority rights from being protected. JOHN HART ELY, DEMOCRACY AND DISTRUST: A THEORY OF JUDICIAL REVIEW 102–3 (1980).

10. *Engaged Judiciary, supra* note 3, at 3.

11. *Id.*

of public debates on proposed bills."[12] Lacking education and democratic traditions, the public is "effectively marginalized from the affairs of the state."[13]

Fourth, liberal democratic theory, which embraces the notion that the judiciary should adhere to rigid rules applied to facts elicited in an adversarial system, is far removed from the popular understanding of a system of justice. Scholars have noted that the pre-colonial African system of justice, from which customary laws derive, was process-oriented rather than rule-oriented.[14] It focused more on peaceful resolutions of disputes than on adherence to rules. It sought to achieve solutions considered just and fair—to deliver substantive justice. Scholars note that "[t]he very process of feeding customary law into the colonial court system led to the construction of customary law that sharply contrasted with African systems...."[15] This customary law is applied today, in a context that is different than the one in which it evolved. Delivering substantive justice, unconstrained by rigid adherence to rules, is closer to the Tanzanian majority's understanding of the role of courts and is not "antithetical to the adherence to rule of law... [where the latter is seen as] predicated upon a conception of social justice."[16] This necessarily imposes a duty on the court to make "substantive choices among competing values and indeed among inevitably controverted political, social, and moral conceptions."[17] It requires that the judge be aware of the needs of the society and the ramifications of the decision in that society.[18] In a nutshell, substantive justice requires a judge to be an activist.

---

12. LEGAL AID COMMITTEE, FACULTY OF LAW, UNIVERSITY OF DAR-ES-SALAAM, ESSAYS ON LAW AND SOCIETY 8 (1985). The Committee notes that Bills may not be published in time, not to mention that some important legislation may be rushed through the Assembly under a certificate of urgency. Also, if Bills are published at all, they are not available and if available, the public may not have a critical forum in which to air their views. Of course, there is also the problem of lack of a literate public and critical intelligentsia, whose interaction is a necessary basis for an informed and meaningful debate on proposed and existing laws. *Id.*

13. *Id.* at 9.

14. ALICE ARMSTRONG ET AL., UNCOVERING REALITY: EXCAVATING WOMEN'S RIGHTS IN AFRICAN FAMILY LAW 14 (1992).

15. *Id.*

16. Tracy B. Fitzpatrick, *Justice Thurgood Marshall and Capital Punishment: Social Justice and the Rule of Law*, 32 AM. CRIM. L. REV. 1065, 1083–84 (1995).

17. *Engaged Judiciary, supra* note 3, at 10 (quoting Professor Lawrence Tribe).

18. President Nyerere makes a similar observation that,

Justice demands many things.... [I]t demands an understanding by the judiciary of the people, and the people of the judiciary... [And that independence of

Fifth, as Justice Kisanga,[19] a judge on the Tanzania Court of Appeal, notes, a common feature in most developing countries is that justice is available to only a few. The majority of people possess rights they cannot enforce. The costs of litigation are beyond their reach. The situation is worse for women, most of whom do not possess the level of literacy and consciousness about their rights that would allow them to access the courts.[20] Women also have to contend with attitudes derived from a male dominated society.[21] Furthermore, studies indicate that Tanzanian women who do litigate in court are linguistically disadvantaged.[22] Despite these obstacles, some women still manage to access the courts and assert their rights. An activist decision, especially one from the Court of Appeal, would help develop the law and define the position of other women similarly situated but unable to access the court.

Finally, the judiciary has long defined the status of women through judge-made law based on the courts' interpretation of statutes and customary law. Precedent is generally followed, allowing these interpretations to continue. The court may easily change these prior interpretations without resorting to the legislature.

Limitations of Judicial Activism

Activism does have its limitations. An activist court must proceed with caution or risk rendering socially unacceptable decisions. Such decisions can invite conflict between the judiciary and other branches of government, a situ-

---

the judiciary] must not lead to the belief that a judge can be, or should, be "neutral" on the basic issues of our society. The fact that judges interpret the law makes it vital that they should be part of the society.... Their interpretation must be made in light of assumptions and aspirations of the society in which they live. Otherwise...[it] may lead the whole concept of law being held in contempt by the people.

ROBERT MARTIN, PERSONAL FREEDOM AND THE LAW IN TANZANIA 66 (1974).

19. R. H. Kisanga, *The Legal Profession, Pluralism and Public Interest Litigation in Tanzania, in* THE ROLE OF THE JUDICIARY IN PLURAL SOCIETIES, *supra* note 3, at 146.

20. Ulrike Wanitzek, *Legally Unrepresented Women Petitioners in the Lower Courts of Tanzania: A Case of Justice Denied?*, 30–31 J. OF LEGAL PLURALISM & UNOFFICIAL L. 255, 263 (1990–91).

21. *See, e.g.,* MONICA MHOJA ET AL., EXPOSED TO SOCIAL INSECURITY: VULNERABLE WOMEN AND GIRLS IN TANZANIA, (1995) (includes first-hand accounts of women who have contended with such difficulties).

22. Ulrike Wanitzek, *The Power of Language in the Discourse on Women's Rights: Some Examples from Tanzania*, 49 AFR. TODAY 3, 9–10 (2002).

ation not conducive to the rule of law or the independence of the judiciary.[23] This is especially true in the area of women's rights, where courts can easily be branded as tools of cultural imperialism.[24] The need for caution means the success of judicial activism depends on well-reasoned judgment, in which the socioeconomic ramifications of a case are reflected in the court's decision.

Second, activism does not mean limitless freedom for the courts to make law.[25] Courts must operate within the law, which requires operating according to accepted rules of law and legal processes. The court may only proceed when there is a legal dispute, and it must apply the relevant law to the facts of the dispute, thereby creating some degree of certainty that the courts will decide like cases alike. Established rules on procedure, evidence, and interpretation must guide the court.

Third, because the court cannot render decisions on unpleaded issues, the parties to the suit must present claims in a manner that will elicit the court's activism. The parties play a central role, as they help apprise the court on the socioeconomic aspects of the case. Judicial activism cannot succeed without help of enlightened litigants and advocates.

---

23. *See, e.g.,* Radhika Coomaraswamy, *Women, Ethnicity, and the Discourse of Rights, in* HUMAN RIGHTS OF WOMEN: NATIONAL AND INTERNATIONAL PERSPECTIVES 53–54 (Rebecca J. Cook ed., 1994) (Coomaraswamy discusses the *Shah Bano* case, which involved a husband's duty to provide maintenance after a divorce. The Supreme Court of India found no conflict with Muslim personal law, which does not impose a duty of maintenance, and the Criminal Code that requires maintenance to prevent destitution. However, the Prime Minister subsequently passed legislation that overruled the decision in order to appease the minority Muslim community.).

24. *See* Abdullahi Ahmed An-Na'im, *State Responsibility Under International Human Rights Law to Change Religious and Customary Laws, in* HUMAN RIGHTS OF WOMEN, *supra* note 24, at 171–75 (contains a detailed discussion of the cultural relativism debate in the area of women's equality). *See also* ARMSTRONG, *supra* note 14, at 11 (Bart Rwezaura comments on the role of customs in the post colonial African state as a symbol of reassertion of cultural identity—an extension of nationalist politics which were necessary for decolonization.).

25. Justice Marshall, an activist Justice of the United States Supreme Court, observes: "Because enforcement of the Bill of Rights…frequently requires this Court to rein in the forces of democratic politics, this Court can legitimately lay claim to compliance with its directives only if the public understands the Court to be implementing 'principles founded in the law rather than in the proclivities of individuals.'" Payne v. Tennessee, 501 U.S. 808, 844 (1991) (Marshall, J., dissenting) (quoting Vasquez v. Hillary, 474 U.S. 254, 265 (1986)).

Activism: Taking a Step Further

The court in Tanzania has shown a willingness to move toward bridging the "yawning gap between the letter of the law and reality in the field…"[26] In 2000, Parliament amended the Constitution to explicitly include a prohibition on gender discrimination.[27] Although this represents a significant advancement for women in Tanzania, the court must also articulate a test to determine what types of differentiation on the basis of sex amounts to unconstitutional discrimination. This part offers some thoughts on possible interpretative avenues that may take the law, specifically constitutional law, a step further in favor of women's rights.

Equal protection of laws prohibits sexual discrimination but does not prohibit all differentiation on the basis of sex. In other words, distinctions based on sex as a class would be justified if the differences between the sexes are highly relevant for the legitimate purposes of a given law or act. This kind of searching judicial inquiry, the norm in applying equal protection clauses to discrimination claims,[28] is necessary to differentiate between distinctions based on actual differences and those that are motivated by notions of female inferiority and a desire to subjugate women.

Courts in other countries have developed standards for determining whether or not laws discriminate on the basis of sex.[29] One must be cautious

---

26. Kabudi, *supra* note 1, at 275.

27. Article 13 provides for equal protection before the law and a right to non-discrimination. As amended in 2000, Article 13(5) reads:

For purposes of this Article 'discrimination' means to satisfy the needs, rights or other requirements of different persons on the basis of their nationality, tribe, place of origin, political opinion, color, religion, *gender*, or station in life such that certain categories of people are regarded as weak or inferior and are subjected to restrictions or conditions whereas persons of other categories are treated differently or are accorded opportunities or advantages outside the specified conditions or the prescribed necessary qualifications. [Emphasis added.]

TANZ. CONST., art. 13, §5.

28. For instance, the position of the Human Rights Committee is that "[t]he enjoyment of rights and freedoms on equal footing…does not mean identical treatment in every instance.…For example, article 6, paragraph 5 [of the International Covenant on Civil and Political Rights], prohibits the death sentence from being imposed…on pregnant women." *Compilation of General Comments and General Recommendations Adopted by Human Rights Treaty Bodies, General Comment 18*, U.N. Human Rights Committee, 37th Sess., at 26, U.N. Doc. HRI/GEN/1/Rev.1 (1994).

29. *See, e.g.,* Craig v. Boren, 429 US 190, 197 (1976) (In this case, the United States Supreme Court articulated the standard used to assess claims of sex discrimination. To pass

in adopting an appropriate standard. Courts should protect both non-discriminatory laws and government actions made for legitimate remedial purposes, such as affirmative action, and move beyond the realm of formal equality. Courts should adopt a test that considers the wording and substantive effect of the challenged law.[30] A substantive equality standard would enable the courts to consider broad-based legal, social, and economic consequences of laws when deciding a case and would allow them to do so in a consistent and predictable manner that will not invite complaints of partiality or judicial law making. The standard would embrace "living customary law"[31] designed to take women's needs into consideration. There would be no fear of loosing the positive aspects of customary laws, because discriminatory laws would have to pass not only the test of present usage, but also proof of acceptable objectives.[32] This type of standard will help to achieve substantive justice for all.

The Need for Expansive Interpretation

Some laws may pass the constitutional test but work injustice to women in application. An expansive interpretation of such laws is necessary for society to achieve justice for women. Take the example of the Law of Marriage Act (LMA).[33] The Court of Appeal in *Bi Hawa Mohamed v. Ally Seif*[34] took an ex-

---

muster, such a law must (a), serve an important governmental objective, and (b), must be substantially related to achievement of that objective.).

30. One possible test may be "whether the rule or practice that is being challenged contributes to the actual inequality of women, and whether changing the [law] will actually produce an improvement in the specific material conditions of the specific woman or Women...." Gwen Brodsky and Shelagh Day, Canadian Charter Equality Rights for Women: One Step Forward or Two Steps Back? 191–92 (Canadian Advisory Council on the Status of Women 1989).

31. *See* Wanitzek, *supra* note 22, at 4.

32. This method has to make use of both historical and socioeconomical studies and data. This data must demonstrate to the court that it is meaningless and unjust today to deny a woman rights to property using customary laws, when reciprocal systems of care by the community no longer exist. They must also make apparent to the court the need for new rules, rules that will enable application of a fundamental principle of customary law, namely that property is owned in a manner which takes care of the economic needs of both men and women, as was the case when these rules evolved.

33. For a full discussion of the Law of Marriage Act *see* Salma Maoulidi, Rethinking Property: Women and Matrimonial Property Rights in Tanzania (unpublished manuscript, on file with editor).

pansive approach to the LMA and recognized that societal expectations of women often disadvantaged them under the law. The court recognized that "women, most of whom being not salaried workers, used to invest their entire youthful and active years in the marriage only to be told at divorce that they have no share in the family assets because they were mere wives who performed wifely duties for free."[35] The court understood that a narrow approach to the law denied women's economic rights. In *Bi Hawa,* the court reviewed the reasoning underlying competing schools of thought and decided that domestic work constitutes a contribution towards the acquisition of property:

> On examination of the Law of Marriage Act, 1971 and the law as it existed before its enactment, one cannot fail to notice that the mischief which the law...sought to cure or rectify was what may be described as the traditional oppression of married women by their husbands. It is apparent that the Act seeks to liberate married women from such exploitation and oppression by reducing the traditional inequality between them....[36]

The same approach might be used to expand the reach of matrimonial property. The courts must evaluate how much the housewife's work should be worth in light of the socioeconomic realities of Tanzania and the needs of spouses. Most women are housewives who perform work that is difficult to quantify or value in modern monetary terms. In the absence of a state social security system, the wife's domestic work contributes to both present and future economic security. Couples in urban areas where only one spouse is engaged in paid employment usually have few physical assets to divide, except future earnings. This makes provision of maintenance for the non-employed spouse an important part of the matrimonial property.[37]

Possible Methodologies for Change

Successful judicial activism depends on the availability of relevant socioeconomic data to inform the decision making process. Judicial access to such

---

34. Court of Appeal Civil Appeal No.9\1983 decided, 29/11/1983 (Unreported).

35. *Id.*

36. *Id.*

37. *See* Maoulidi, *supra* note 33, at 72–77, for further discussion on possible expansion of the definition of matrimonial property.

information presupposes the existence of supporting legal structures, such as provisions in the law permitting the courts to receive and consider socioeconomic factors not traditionally considered in ordinary pleadings between parties. In order to produce law that is just for women, judicial officers must understand the particular ways that law affects women. Women's rights activists, both lawyers and plaintiffs, must be willing to bring well-conceived and developed cases before the court. The last part of this essay offers some ways these goals can be achieved.

Use of Amicus Curie Briefs

When a court is faced with a dispute between parties that involves a divisive and controversial issue, "its decision has a dimension that the resolution of the normal case doesn't carry...."[38] The decision may threaten the very legitimacy of the court and must be of such a quality as "to counter inevitable efforts to overturn it and thwart its implementations."[39] To make such a decision, the court must be aware of broad-based legal, social, and economic consequences flowing from its decision. *Amicus curiae*—or friend of the court—briefs may play that critical role.

Typically, amicus briefs are filed by non-parties, either individuals or groups with an interest in the outcome of the case beyond the individual interest of the parties involved. These individuals or groups most often concern themselves with the overall development of the law in a particular area. The briefs often take a broad approach, exploring the larger context of the particular issue before the court and assessing the impact of various outcomes on particular groups or society at large.[40] The briefs are not *evidence* but help the court to assess the case in its totality.

---

38. Planned Parenthood of Southeastern Pennsylvania v. Casey, 505 U.S. 833, 867 (1992). (O'Connor, J.) (in a case involving a controversial issue—the women's right to abortion).

39. *Id.*

40. *See* Robert L. Stern et al., Supreme Court Practice: For Practice in the Supreme Court of the United States 559–66 (7th ed. 1993). (In U.S. Supreme Court practice, such amici are required to: 1. Obtain consent of the parties to the suit (or permission of the Court), 2. Identify the amicus and the interest of the amicus in the case, and 3. Describe in what way the amicus will assist the Court. An effective brief brings something new and interesting to the case. This might be better research, more cogent analysis or more convincing demonstration of the impact of the decision to the public.)

Instead of relying on the court's own, possibly limited, understanding of the ramifications of a case,[41] *amicus curiae* briefs provide the court with significant input from groups or individuals of particular expertise. In a sense, the court hears an extra voice from the people. A decision in a constitutional case affects the lives of many citizens, not only those immediately involved in a suit, such that democratic principles are well-served when the court reaches a decision with the benefit of a variety of perspectives.[42] An activist decision grounded in such expertise and support is likely to be more informed and is better able to withstand challenge.

Training for Judicial Officers

Judicial activism in the area of women's rights depends on a judiciary that understands and appreciates the need for gender equality, especially for equal rights in property ownership. Although there appears to be a formal acceptance of women's rights, belief in the inferiority of women is still prevalent, and members of the judiciary are often influenced by the value system of the society in which they live. Toward this end, it is important to have some gender equality training programs.[43] Given the current economic situation in developing countries like Tanzania, a recommendation involving substantial financial costs will not likely be well-received. Judicial training, however, need not be expensive. Trainers may distribute relevant scholarly papers to judges and magistrates or convene regular seminars. The distribution of literature and training could be expanded to include feedback on judicial decisions from the general public and legal professionals. Facilitating open discussion of their judgments, in conjunction with scholarly papers, is necessary and beneficial.

---

41. Indeed, the need for amici briefs is more because the courts in Tanzania do not have the benefits of modern information technology like computerized research.

42. BRODSKY, *supra* note 30 at 134. (This argument was raised by the Canadian Civil Liberties Association in regard to litigation involving the Canadian Charter of Rights and Freedoms.).

43. Kathleen Mahoney notes that "[t]o the extent that the justice system suffers from gender bias, the system fails in its primary societal responsibility to deliver justice impartially." It should be in the court's interest to avoid using "societally induced assumptions and untested beliefs…that judge individuals on their group membership rather than individual characteristics…" Kathleen Mahoney, *Canadian Approach to Equality Rights and Gender Equity in the Courts, in* HUMAN RIGHTS OF WOMEN, *supra* note 23, at 452–53.

Active Women's Rights NGOs

The success of all the strategies described above depends on the availability of willing and able women's rights activists. Litigation for women's rights is fragmented; groups need to coordinate their efforts. These organizations suffer from resource constraints, operating on a part-time or voluntary basis, often with inadequate financial and communication resources. Women's rights organizations must, however, coordinate their efforts and face these challenges together.

Conclusion

Laws can and do act as instruments of social change by signaling acceptable norms and standards. Because of the complexities of representative politics, the legislature often fails to act when those actions would threaten the interests of powerful groups in society. The women's rights agenda often falls victim to such inaction. In these circumstances, the courts, as final arbiters of justice, are justified in intervening. In so far as women are still powerless in the political processes, judicial activism is their immediate weapon. The courts have shown a willingness to take on an activist stance in this area. Women rights activists should now take on the task of supporting and informing that activism to improve the legal status of women in Tanzania.

CHAPTER TWO

VIOLENCE AGAINST WOMEN

Chapter Introduction, *Johanna Bond*

Violence against women, whether it is at the hands of family members, community members, or representatives of the State, touches the lives of countless women worldwide. The violence takes a variety of forms, including physical, sexual, and psychological harms. It includes, but is not limited to, domestic violence, sexual abuse, rape, sexual harassment, trafficking in women, dowry-related violence, honor crimes, and female genital mutilation (FGM) and other forms of harmful traditional practices.

Perhaps more than any other substantive issue, violence against women has galvanized women's human rights activists around the world. Largely as a result of antiviolence campaigns around the world, the United Nations General Assembly unanimously adopted the Declaration on the Elimination of Violence Against Women (DEVAW) in December 1993.[1] Although not a legally binding document, DEVAW reflects the global consensus that systemic violence against women is a serious human rights violation. The Declaration defines violence against women broadly[2] and sets forth the responsibilities of

---

1. *Declaration on the Elimination of Violence Against Women*, G.A. Res. 48/104, U.N. GAOR, 48th Sess., Supp. No. 49, at 217, U.N. Doc. A/48/49 (1994) [hereinafter DEVAW].

2. The Declaration states: "Violence against women shall be understood to encompass, but not be limited to, the following:

(a)   Physical, sexual and psychological violence occurring in the family, including battering, sexual abuse of female children in the household, dowry-related violence, marital rape, female genital mutilation, and other traditional practices harmful to women, non-spousal violence and violence related to exploitation;

(b)   Physical, sexual and psychological violence occurring within the general community, including rape, sexual abuse, sexual harassment and intimidation at work, in educational institutions and elsewhere, trafficking in women and forced prostitution;

governments, international organizations, and nongovernmental organizations in combating gender-based violence.

Major Factors Contributing to Violence Against Women

Although the factors that contribute to violence against women around the world are too numerous to mention, several of the primary influences deserve special mention. The specific manifestations of the violence and the community responses to violence often differ depending on social, legal, and geographic contexts. There are, however, many similarities in the patterns of violence against women around the globe, making some cautious generalizations possible.

Throughout the world, women's subordination to men contributes to violence against women. In its preamble, DEVAW states, "violence against women is a manifestation of historically unequal power relations between men and women....."[3] Because social constructions of gender often dictate that men enjoy more power and privilege than women in their families and communities, men sometimes use violence as a tool to ensure women's adherence to this construct.

Cultural and traditional norms may exacerbate women's subordination and result in violence against women. In Uganda, for example, men who wish to marry must often pay a "brideprice" or "bridewealth" to the family of the intended bride. As a result of colonial efforts to regulate and standardize bridewealth, the contemporary understanding of brideprice leads some men to conclude that they have "purchased" a wife and that they may, therefore, treat her however they see fit, including using violence against her.[4] As Fitnat Adjetey points out in this chapter, societal efforts to control women's sexuality in Ghana include FGM. In the case of both brideprice and FGM, women's subordination leaves them vulnerable to violence—either perpetrated by their husbands in the form of domestic violence or by the community in the form of FGM.

(b)   Physical, sexual and psychological violence perpetuated or condoned by the State, wherever it occurs.
Id.

3. *Id.*

4. Sylvia Tamale, When Hens Begin to Crow: Gender and Parliamentary Politics in Uganda 35 n.18 (1995).

In many cases, women's lack of economic independence contributes to violence against women. Women who lack economic self-sufficiency may be unable to escape a violent situation, such as violence in the family or sexual harassment in the work place. Although women from all economic backgrounds, including wealthy women, may experience violence, women with economic means tend to have more options for escaping the violence or for accessing the legal system to seek redress. Similarly, race and ethnicity often affect women's ability to rely on the State for protection against violence.

The Responsibility of the State

Human rights violations have traditionally been understood as abuses committed by the state, such as the torture of a political prisoner by a representative of the government. Although women do experience torture and other forms of custodial abuse, they more commonly suffer abuse at the hands of private individuals such as spouses. Since the early 1990s, women's rights activists fought for an expanded understanding of the role of the state in combating violence committed by private, non-state actors.[5]

Significantly, this expanded concept of state responsibility—the notion that a state is responsible for the violations of private individuals if it systematically fails to act with "due diligence" to prevent, investigate, and punish those acts—has gained acceptance within the international human rights community. DEVAW reflects this progress by declaring that it is necessary for states to "exercise due diligence to prevent, investigate and, in accordance with national legislation, punish acts of violence against women, *whether those acts are perpetrated by the State or by private persons*."[6] Other international documents also reflect this trend of assigning to the state greater responsibility for human rights violations perpetrated by private actors.[7] This expanded understanding of state responsibility has been critical for women's human rights activists working to combat domestic violence, rape, and other forms of "private" abuse.

---

5. *See, e.g.*, Dorothy Q. Thomas & Michele Beasley, *Domestic Violence as a Human Rights Issue*, 58 ALB. L. REV. 1119, 1132 (1995).

6. DEVAW, *supra* note 1, at 218.

7. *See, e.g.*, *Report of the Convention on the Elimination of All Forms of Discrimination Against Women* [CEDAW], *General Recommendation 19 (11th Sess.): Violence Against Women*, U.N. GAOR, 47th Sess., Supp. No. 38, at 1, U.N. Doc. A/47/38 (1993).

Progress at the United Nations and Relevant International Law

Several international instruments delineate the specific rights that may be violated in incidents involving violence against women. They include the right to life; the right to equality; the right to liberty and security of person; the right to equal protection under the law; the right to be free from discrimination; the right to the highest standard attainable of physical and mental health; the right to just and favorable conditions of work; the right not to be subjected to torture, or other cruel, inhuman, or degrading treatment or punishment; the right to equal protection during armed conflict; and the right to equality in the family.[8]

The Convention on the Elimination of All Forms of Discrimination Against Women (CEDAW) is a legally binding treaty that prohibits discrimination against women. CEDAW, which was drafted in the mid-1970s, does not specifically mention violence against women. However, the United Nations committee that oversees implementation of the treaty, the CEDAW Committee, issued a general recommendation on violence against women in 1992. The general recommendation, which is intended to guide states parties to CEDAW in their efforts to implement its provisions, describes gender-based violence as a form of discrimination, bringing violence against women within the purview of the treaty. The CEDAW's Committee's General Recommendation No. 19 defines gender-based violence as "violence that is directed against a woman because she is a woman or that affects women disproportionately." It states that gender-based violence "seriously inhibits women's ability to enjoy rights and freedoms on a basis of equality with men."[9]

In 1999, the United Nations General Assembly adopted an Optional Protocol to CEDAW that provides an enforcement remedy to individuals under the jurisdiction of states that have ratified both the Convention and the Optional Protocol.[10] The Optional Protocol allows individuals or groups to sub-

---

8. This list reflects the rights included in DEVAW and CEDAW's Committee's General Recommendation No. 19.

9. *CEDAW*, G.A. Res. 34/180, U.N. GAOR, 34th Sess., Supp. No. 46, at 193, U.N. Doc. A/34/46 (1979).

10. *See generally, Optional Protocol to the Convention on the Elimination of All Forms of Discrimination Against Women*, G.A. Res. 54/4, Annex, 54 U.N. GAOR Supp. No. 49 at 5, UN Doc. A/54/49 (Vol. I) (2000).

mit to the CEDAW Committee allegations of violations of any of the rights enshrined in the Convention. As such, the Optional Protocol may prove to be a significant vehicle for women seeking redress for human rights violations involving violence against women.

In 1994, the United Nations appointed Radhika Coomaraswamy to be the Special Rapporteur on Violence Against Women: Its Causes and Consequences. Since that time, the Special Rapporteur has conducted an intensive study concerning all forms of violence against women around the world. Through her extensive research and adroit advocacy, the Special Rapporteur has raised public awareness about violence against women as a human rights violation and has moved the antiviolence agenda forward at the international level.

In addition to the growing international recognition of violence against women as a human rights abuse, there has been significant progress at the regional level. Although the African Charter does not address violence against women per se, it does prohibit gender discrimination. If violence against women is seen as a form of discrimination, as it is in the CEDAW Committee's General Recommendation No. 19, the nondiscrimination provisions of the African Charter may be useful to antiviolence activists in Africa.

Moreover, on July 11, 2003, the African Union adopted the Protocol on the Rights of Women in Africa, a comprehensive supplement to the African Charter on Human and Peoples' Rights. The Protocol will enter into force when fifteen African states have ratified it. The Protocol includes a number of protections designed to combat violence against women, including a denunciation and call for criminalization of harmful practices such as FGM and forced sex, whether they occur in public or private. The Protocol also requires states parties to "enact and enforce laws to prohibit all forms of violence against women...[and] adopt such other legislative, administrative, social and economic measures as may be necessary to ensure the prevention, punishment and eradication of all forms of violence against women..." [11]

---

11. *Protocol to the African Charter on Human and Peoples' Rights on the Rights of Women in Africa, adopted* July 11, 2003, African Union, art. 4(2)(a), (b), *available at* http://www.africa-union.org/Official_documents/Treaties_%20Conventions_%20Protocols/Protocol%20on%20the%20Rights%20of%20Women.pdf (last visited Nov. 7, 2003).

The Right to Be Free from Violence in Ghana, Uganda, and Tanzania

In this chapter, the authors address several forms of violence against women, describing how each manifests itself in their communities and how the law is or is not meeting the needs of victims of gender-based violence. Hilary Gbedemah, for example, describes the practice of Trokosi, a form of female religious bondage that occurs in the Volta region of Ghana. In accordance with the Trokosi system, a family sends a young girl to live at the shrine of a fetish priest, where she performs physical labor and often becomes a sexual slave, in an effort to redeem the family for a crime committed by one of its members. The young girls become victims of rape and sexual servitude, often bearing a number of children while living at the shrine. Gbedemah explores the myriad ways in which the practice violates the human rights of these young girls and proposes strategies for reform that focus on enforcement of existing laws, public education, government intervention, negotiation with the priests, and the enlistment of traditional leaders in the eradication effort.

Like the victims of Trokosi, refugee women are particularly vulnerable to sexual abuse. Hadija Ally examines the plight of refugee women in Tanzania, detailing how the United Nations High Commissioner for Refugees has dealt with the unique protection problems raised by refugee women. Ally describes the particular vulnerability of young girls, who are assumed to be free of HIV infection. Perpetrators also target girls and women while they travel great distances to collect firewood or when they walk to the latrine, which is often a considerable distance from their living quarters. Other women are raped by their husbands; by men living outside of the camps, including Tanzanian soldiers; or by members of local communities, many of whom resent the presence of large numbers of refugees. According to Ally, many refugee women who are victims of sexual assault resort to informal reconciliation within the community rather than take their cases to court. Ally proposes a number of strategies to better protect refugee women, including increasing prosecution for sex crimes, thereby strengthening the deterrent effect on perpetrators; bringing Tanzanian domestic law into conformity with that nation's international human rights obligations; and increasing economic opportunities within refugee populations.

Scholastica Jullu tackles the more general problem of sexual violence in Tanzania. Jullu focuses her analysis on Tanzania's 1998 Sexual Offenses (Special Provision) Act No. 4. Jullu concedes that the Sexual Offenses Act incor-

porates important changes in Tanzanian rape law, including making most offenses gender neutral; broadening the understanding of rape to include perpetrators not commonly associated with rape, such as traditional healers who
rape for "healing purposes"; relaxing the requirement of penetration; eliminating the requirement that a victim physically resist the assault; and expanding the definition of statutory rape. One of the law's most significant
shortcomings, however, is that it fails to criminalize marital rape. Jullu criti-
cizes Tanzanian authorities for a lack of enforcement of the Act and highlights
the ways in which enforcement could be improved to the benefit of all sexual
assault victims in Tanzania.

Kulsum Wakabi explores the legal, social, cultural, and economic facets of
domestic violence in Uganda. Statistics on the prevalence of domestic violence
in Uganda are limited; initial research, however, suggests levels of domestic
violence as high as 80 percent in some parts of the country. Wakabi examines
the causes of domestic violence in Uganda, analyzes the efficacy of the legal
response to the problem, and proposes strategies for eradicating it. Her proposals include the creation of civil as well as criminal remedies to better address the concerns many victims have with the retributive aspects of the criminal justice system.

Beatrice Duncan offers a more detailed look at a particular type of domestic violence in Ghana, namely marital rape. Ghana's criminal law does not recognize marital rape; the criminal code includes marital immunity under the
heading "Justifiable Use of Force and Harm." Duncan explores the social and
cultural reasons for this tolerance of marital rape and refutes potential arguments against eliminating the marital rape exception. Among the powerful
myths that Duncan debunks is the notion that marital rape is more benign
than rape by a stranger. In assessing strategies for reform, Duncan maintains
that any imposition of criminal penalties for marital rape must be carefully
tailored to the victim's specific circumstances to allow, for example, work release when the victim's family would otherwise suffer unduly from the loss of
the perpetrator's income.

Sheila Gyimah's essay elaborates on the social stigma surrounding rape victims in Ghana. Gyimah asserts that the current Ghanaian rape law embodies
sexist stereotypes, many of which were inherited through the adoption of
British law during the colonial period. She analyzes the body of Ghanaian
common law requiring that a victim demonstrate nonconsent by showing
forceful resistance to the rape—an element allowing a defendant to delve into
the victim's prior sexual history and requiring corroboration of the victim's
testimony in rape trials. In addition to reforming the law to eliminate these

anachronistic and gender-biased rules, Gyimah advocates specialized training for police, medical personnel, prosecutors, and judges.

Finally, Adjetey addresses the difficult problem of FGM in Ghana. Adjetey provides a detailed account of the severe physical and psychological harm caused by FGM, including some fatal repercussions such as tetanus and HIV infection. Adjetey systematically refutes many of the justifications that have been offered in support of the practice. She also analyzes the effectiveness of the Ghanaian government's efforts to combat the practice, including criminally prohibiting FGM since1994. Noting that there were only seven arrests for FGM during the first six years of the law's existence, Adjetey advocates a comprehensive approach to eradication that combines increased prosecution with far-reaching public education campaigns.

Conclusion

With the collection of essays in this chapter, the authors join an intense global campaign to combat violence against women in all of its forms. Because of the strength of local, national, and international advocacy efforts, the human rights community now views violence against women as a pernicious violation of human rights. Although the particular manifestations of violence against women vary from region to region, many of the underlying assumptions about women's position in the social hierarchy persist across borders. As a result, many of the strategies to eradicate gender-based violence share the common goal of improving women's legal and social status within their communities.

Trokosi: Twentieth Century Female Bondage— A Ghanaian Case Study

Hilary Amesika Gbedemah

Introduction

These children are among the thousands of female Trokosi or "fetish slaves" who are serving life sentences at the shrines of traditional West African war gods. They are paying for crimes, sometimes as trivial as the theft of a few heads of maize or a goat, committed by distant and even long-dead relatives. Most of the Trokosi women are condemned to a lifetime of hard labour, sexual servitude and perpetual childbearing at the service of the village priest.[1]

The "Trokosi" institution, a form of female religious bondage, involves sending young virgin girls to the shrine of a fetish priest as reparation for crimes committed by other members of their families.[2] The priests hold the girls in deplorable conditions, deprive them of education, and make them perform domestic and farm labor.[3] Their "sentences" may last from three years to a lifetime.[4] There are no precise figures, but it is estimated that about 2,000

---

1. Emma Brooker, *Slaves of the Fetish*, The Independent (London), June 16, 1996, at 12.
2. Sarah C. Aird, Article, *Ghana's Slaves to the Gods*, 7 Hum. Rts. Brief 6, 6 (1999).
3. *Id.*
4. *Compare* Dep't of State, *Ghana*, in Country Reports on Human Rights Practices for 2001, at 303, §5 at 324 (2001) ("Trokosi...is a religious practice involving a period of servitude lasting up to 3 years.") *with* Aird, *supra* note 2, at 7 ("Under most circumstances, a priest will keep a *trokosi* slave for more than ten years, but he may hold her for her entire life, depending in part upon the severity of the crime her relative committed.").

girls are slave to the Trokosi system in the Volta Region.[5] This paper analyzes the conditions under which the girls are held, and offers both legal and non-legal strategies for bringing the practice to an end.

The Trokosi System

Incidents in the Life of a Slave-Girl, Written by Herself[6]

For Christiana, one of the "'slave-girls,'" the day begins with pondering—about how she got to the shrine and the reason for her presence there. Her family left her there at the age of seven, and she is still perplexed about which member of her family committed the crime for which she was "arrested."[7] She still does not know what the crime was.[8]

Patience, whose family took her to the shrine at ten years old, learned why her family left her at the shrine. [9] The family had offended the fetish, and unless she served at the shrine, the whole family would die.[10] It was her duty to "close the gates of death."[11] Her family assured her that her parents would provide for her upkeep, which they did in the beginning, but after a point they just stopped.[12]

---

5. Dep't of State, *supra* note 4, at 325. ("[A]ccording to some reports there were more than 2,000 women or girls in Trokosi shrines, but according to other international observers there are no more than 100 girls serving at Trokosi shrines throughout the Volta Region.").

6. Harriet Jacobs, INCIDENTS IN THE LIFE OF A SLAVE GIRL, WRITTEN BY HERSELF, (Jean Fagan Yellin ed., Harvard University Press 1987) (1861) (Chapter heading adopted from this autobiography, wherein Ms. Jacobs tells her life story as a slave in the United States. This chapter is a summary of the accounts of four of the girls, given by the girls themselves, and recorded verbatim in a report submitted by Sharon Titian, Director of Missions International, a non-governmental organization working with the girls. The girls range in age from fourteen to twenty-three.).

7. Interview by Sharon Titian, Director, Missions International, Ada-Foah, Ghana, with Christiana Lomornuor [hereinafter Christiana Interview].

8. *Id.*

9. Interview by Sharon Titian, Director, Missions International, Ada-Foah, Ghana, with Patience Akpe [hereinafter Patience Interview].

10. *Id.*

11. *Id.*

12. *Id.*

With each daybreak, these girls confronted the problem of what to eat.[13] The fetish priest provided no food.[14] In addition to domestic chores, the priest required the girls to work on his farm as unpaid farm hands for twelve hours every day.[15] To survive, they cut trees and burned charcoal in order to purchase food;[16] they also begged for alms.[17] Not surprisingly, their diet was appalling[18] and they lacked basic necessities and health care.[19] Whenever the girls complained about poor health to the fetish priest, he gave them a mixture of alcohol and herbs to drink as a palliative, or cut their bodies and put black powder into the wounds.[20] The priest never took them to the hospital for treatment.[21]

One day the girls were told that they would become wives to a new priest and bear his children.[22] When a new priest is installed, the girls are forced to engage in sexual relations with him.[23] The girls worried about this arrangement, since they had almost no food to eat and could not provide for children.[24] The priest warned them that refusal would bring another death to their families.[25] In addition, refusing a priest, who has the right of sexual access to all girls at his shrine, results in instant fines.[26] Payment of these fines required the girls to perform additional work.[27]

The priest started having sex with Patience when she was twelve years old.[28] This was in keeping with the priests' practice of having sex with the virgins

---

13. *Id.*

14. *Id.*

15. *Id.*

16. *Id.*

17. Interview by Sharon Titian, Director, Missions International, Ada-Foah, Ghana, with Juliana Dorgbadzi [hereinafter Juliana Interview].

18. *See* Christiana Interview, *supra* note 7 (indicating that they subsisted on a diet without protein mainly made up of carbohydrates, about half cup of garri—a preparation made from cassava similar to tapioca, with a quarter cup of sugar); Patience Interview, *supra* note 9 (describing a diet which at times consisted of pepper—ground up as a sauce—without fish).

19. Interview by Sharon Titian, Director, Missions International, Ada-Foah, Ghana, with Elizabeth Agbemadi [hereinafter Elizabeth Interview].

20. Patience Interview, *supra* note 9.

21. *Id.*

22. *Id.*

23. *Id.*

24. *Id.*

25. *Id.*

26. *Id.*

27. *Id.*

28. *Id.*

after their third menstrual period.[29] She became pregnant soon afterwards, but he contributed nothing to feed and clothe the child.[30] He offered three justifications for his lack of support: the child was hers as well as his, and she too would benefit from whatever the child became in the future; he already had many children; support of the child of a Trokosi girl was contrary to custom.[31] Thus, the responsibility for post-natal care and maintenance of the child became hers alone.

She summarized their daily lives as follows:

> We were living slavery lives, suffering hunger, no soap for bath, [sic] farming under pressure; in fact it was terrible for human beings to live in such a condition. Our parents too were not sending us anything. We were also afraid that if we should run away we would die and, therefore, remained in this predicament....[32]

The Role of the Fetish Priest

In African religion, the priest is the custodian of the religious and moral beliefs of a local community.[33] Priests "embody the presence of God among people...[and] serve as the link between their fellow human beings on the one hand, and God, spirits and invisible things on the other."[34] Aside from their symbolic purpose, priests have a duty "to look after temples and religious places,...to receive presents on behalf of God or other spirit beings, and in some cases to act as seers and mediums."[35] Priests also serve a chronicling function, being "well versed in religious knowledge, in matters of myths, beliefs, traditions, legends, proverbs, and in the religious practices of their people."[36]

The commission of a crime—murder, adultery, or theft, for example— triggers the enslavement of a Trokosi girl.[37] The offended party approaches the

---

29. *See* Brian S. Woods, *The Slave Girls of Ghana*, 17 N.Y.L. SCH. J. HUM. RTS. 875, 876 (2001).

30. Patience Interview, *supra* note 9.

31. *Id.*

32. *Id.*

33. John S. Mbiti, INTRODUCTION TO AFRICAN RELIGION 153 (2d ed. 1991).

34. *Id.*

35. *Id.* at 161.

36. *Id.*

37. Aird, *supra* note 2, at 6.

priest, requesting that the priest petition the gods to invoke punishment on the offender.[38] Once this is done, the family of the offender experiences grave calamities and large death tolls. The procedure for lifting the hex involves bringing items for reparation to the priest—including a young virgin.[39] The priest sets the period of her bondage and the young girl begins her life of servitude.[40] Should she die before she completes her sentence, her family must replace her.[41]

Even today, the communities in which Trokosi is practiced do not doubt its efficacy.[42] They believe in the fetish's power to cause death and calamities.[43] The threat of supernatural sanction, physical coercion, the notion of family abandonment, and assimilation through forced sexual liaisons with the fetish priest all serve to keep the girls incarcerated.

Legal Challenges to the Trokosi System

Legal Challenges to Specific Aspects of Trokosi

Sexual Offenses[44]

Ghana's Criminal Code categorizes rape as a first degree felony.[45] Marital rape however, is not a crime. A woman is deemed to have consented to any sexual act when she marries.[46] Consent cannot be imputed, however, where

---

38. E.K. Quashigah, *Religious Freedom and Vestal Virgins: The* Trokosi *Practice in Ghana*, 10 Afr. J. Int'l & Comp. L. 193, 199 (1998).

39. Amy Small Bilyeu, Comment, *Trokosi—the Practice of Sexual Slavery in Ghana: Religious and Cultural Freedom vs. Human Rights*, 9 Ind. Int'l & Comp. L. Rev. 457, 472 (1999).

40. *Id.*

41. Brooker, *supra* note 1.

42. *See* Aird, *supra* note 2, at 6.

43. *Id.*

44. [Ghana] Criminal Code, 1960 (Act 29) § 98 ("Rape is the carnal knowledge of a female of any age without her consent.").

45. [Ghana] Criminal Code, 1960 (Act 29) § 97 ("Whoever commits rape shall be guilty of first degree felony.").

46. *See* [Ghana] Criminal Code, 1960 (Act 29) § 42 (A person may revoke any consent which he has given to the use of force against him, and his consent when so revoked shall have no effect for justifying force; save that the consent given by a husband or wife at marriage, for the purposes of marriage, cannot be revoked until the parties are divorced

the female has been compelled under duress to contract the marriage.[47] The Criminal Code thus offers some protection to the girls; when the priests have sex with them they are committing rape, because of the absence of consent due to the forced nature of the marriage.

Right to Health

Female religious bondage violates the right to health. The system violates provisions of the 1992 Constitution of the Republic of Ghana (constitution), which recognizes a child's right to be protected from engaging in work that constitutes a threat to her health, education, or development,[48] and protects her from deprivation of medical treatment denied for religious or other beliefs.[49] The United Nations Convention on the Elimination of all Forms of Discrimination Against Women (CEDAW)[50] and the African Charter on Human and Peoples' Rights (African Charter)[51] require States parties to guarantee access of their citizens to health care services. CEDAW also provides for repro-

---

or separated by a judgment or decree of a competent Court.).

47. [Ghana] Criminal Code, 1960 (Act 29) § 100. *See* [Ghana] Criminal Code, 1960 (Act 29) § 14(b) ("[A] consent is void if it is obtained by means of deceit or duress.").

48. THE CONST. OF THE REPUBLIC OF GHANA 1992 ch. V, art. 28, § 2 ("Every child has the right to be protected from engaging in work that constitutes a threat to his health, education or development.").

49. *Id.* at ch. V, art. 28, § 4 ("No child shall be deprived by any other person of medical treatment, education or any other social or economic benefit by reason only of religious or other beliefs.").

50. Convention on the Elimination of all Forms of Discrimination Against Women, *opened for signature* Mar. 1, 1980, art. 12, 1249 U.N.T.S. 13, 19, 19 I.L.M. 33, 40 [hereinafter CEDAW].

   1. States Parties shall take all appropriate measures to eliminate discrimination against women in the field of health care in order to ensure, on a basis of equality of men and women, access to health care services, including those related to family planning.
   2. Notwithstanding the provisions in paragraph 1 of this article, States Parties shall ensure to women appropriate services in connexion [sic] with pregnancy, confinement and the post-natal period, granting free services where necessary, as well as adequate nutrition during pregnancy and lactation.

Id.

51. African Charter on Human and Peoples' Rights, June 27, 1981, art. 16, 1520 U.N.T.S. 217, 248–49 [hereinafter African Charter] ("1. Every individual shall have the right to enjoy the best attainable state of physical and mental health. 2. States parties to the present Charter shall take the necessary measures to protect the health of their people and to ensure that they receive medical attention when they are sick.").

ductive rights by recognizing a woman's right to decide on the number and spacing of their children. [52]

The daily lifestyle of the Trokosi girl, characterized by a strenuous work regime, poor diet, and unprotected sexual activity, is clearly detrimental to her health. In the face of the AIDS epidemic, the girls are particularly at risk, because they have an abbreviated period of sexual abstinence.[53] Early pregnancy and childbearing create unique risks for the Trokosi, particularly because they are under the age of sixteen and lack basic medical and prenatal care.[54] The health dangers affect both the mother ("pre-eclamptic toxemia, anemia, malnutrition, cephalopelvic disproportion, vesicovaginal and rectovaginal fistulas, [and] difficulty delivery") and the infant ("retardation of fetal growth, premature birth, low birth weight, and perinatal mortality").[55] These health risks underscore the violation of the girls' constitutional right to health caused by the Trokosi system.

Educational Rights

The confinement of the girls at the shrine deprives them (and the children born to them) of their right to education. Ghana's constitution mandates that "basic education shall be free, compulsory and available to all."[56] These provisions should be enforced to allow Trokosi girls to attend school. Girls young enough to enter the mainstream educational system should be integrated under the compulsory education provisions.[57] Older girls who were denied education as a result of their slavery should be provided with education consistent with their life goals, including affirmative action programs in education of the kind Parliament may create under the constitution.[58] Ensuring the girls' attendance at school can be done legally by invoking the provisions of the constitution and CEDAW that prohibit children from engaging in work that constitutes a threat to, *inter alia*, their education or development.[59]

---

52. CEDAW, *supra* note 50, art. 16, § 1(e), 1249 U.N.T.S. at 20, 19 I.L.M. at 41.

53. *See* JUDITH SENDEROWITZ, ADOLESCENT HEALTH: REASSESSING THE PASSAGE TO ADULTHOOD 52 (The World Bank 1995) (reporting that higher incidents of HIV in women in Uganda and Zaire resulted from "girls' earlier sexual debut").

54. *See id.* at 1.

55. *Id.*

56. THE CONST. OF THE REPUBLIC OF GHANA ch. V, art. 25, § 1(a).

57. THE CONST. OF THE REPUBLIC OF GHANA ch. V, art. 25, § 1(a).

58. THE CONST. OF THE REPUBLIC OF GHANA ch. V, art. 17, § 4(a) (reserves to Parliament the power to enact laws "for the implementation of policies and programmes aimed at redressing social, economic or educational imbalance in the Ghanaian society").

59. *See supra* notes 48–50 and accompanying text.

Right to Family Life, Consent to Marriage

The Trokosi system violates the right to family life in two ways. First, it deprives girls of their right to remain within their own families. Under the constitution, Parliament has the obligation to pass laws such that "the protection and advancement of the family as the unit of society are safeguarded in the interest of children."[60] Second, the Trokosi system violates the right to family life by coercing the girls into a new family unit in which they perform the functions of a spouse. Because the unions are not officially legalized,[61] the girls have the duties of wives with none of the privileges or legal protections.

Compulsion of marriage is a misdemeanor under Ghana's Criminal Code.[62] As far as the girls are concerned, they are made "wives" of the fetish priest under duress.[63] Their consent to the consummation of the union is irrelevant. The provisions relating to compulsion of marriage should therefore be dispositive in a prosecution under the Criminal Code. Similarly, CEDAW provides for the right to choose a spouse and freely enter into marriage[64] and makes the betrothal of a child invalid.[65] Difficulties lie in the enforcement of the minimum age for marriage, which requires documentation. With customary marriages, however, such documentation is absent, because unions take place in areas far removed from officials.

Right of Maintenance

Under the Maintenance of Children Decree, a child's legal custodian is under a duty to supply the child with the necessities of life.[66] Accounts given by the girls at the shrine indicate that they are abandoned by their parents,

---

60. THE CONST. OF THE REPUBLIC OF GHANA ch. V, art. 28, § 1(e).

61. *See* Amy Small Bilyeu, *supra* note 39 at 473 ("Unlike other wives in Ghana, the Trokosi have no rights, no assets, and cannot leave when they choose.").

62. [Ghana] Criminal Code, 1960 (Act 29) § 109 ("Whoever by duress causes any person to marry against his or her will, shall be guilty of a misdemeanor.").

63. *See* Patience Interview, *supra* note 9 ("The Priest was installed and he told us we were his wives so he had to be sleeping with us…We were told if we could not agree for the Priest to be sleeping with us then another death would enter our families.").

64. CEDAW, *supra* note 50, at art. 16 §§ 1(a)-1(b), 1249 U.N.T.S. at 20, 19 I.L.M. at 41.

65. *Id.* at art. 16 § 2, 1249 U.N.T.S. at 20, 19 I.L.M. at 41.

66. Maintenance of Children Decree, 1977, S.M.C.D. 133 § 4(l) [Ghana] ("A parent or any other person who is legally liable to maintain a child or contribute toward the maintenance of a child is under a duty to supply the necessities of health, life and reasonable education to that child.").

and the fetish priests expect them to fend for themselves.[67] The failure of the parents and priests to provide for these girls subjects them to numerous risks.

Legal Challenges to the System Itself

Criminalization of Trokosi

Throughout the 1990s, Ghanaian women advocated for the criminalization of Trokosi in Ghanaian law.[68] Their efforts resulted in the Criminal Code Amendment Act of 1998, which provides that:

> (1) Whoever – (a) sends to or receives at any place any person; or (b) participates in or is concerned in any ritual or customary activity in respect of any person with the purpose of subjecting that person to any form of ritual or customary servitude or any form of forced labour related to a customary ritual commits an offence and shall be liable on conviction to imprisonment for a term not less than three years.[69]

Despite this amendment, enforcement against Trokosi is virtually non-existent, largely because fear of reprisal from the fetish priest continues unabated.[70] Because of this disappointing lack of action on the part of local law enforcement, it is important to consider other legal tools with which to fight this practice.

Rights of the (Girl) Child

Under the 1992 Constitution of the Republic of Ghana, every child has the right to special care, assistance, and maintenance from her natural parents except where the parents have surrendered those rights in accordance with the law.[71] The girl-child's rights are even more crucial. Since discrimination on the basis of sex starts at an early age, "greater equality for the girl child is a

---

67. *See* Juliana Interview, *supra* note 17 ("Anytime I was in need or hungry and sent [my parents] message to send me something they would only reply me with abusive words…We only had to rely on the Chief Priest's peasant farming which could not properly cater for us because we were more than the food supplied.").

68. *See* Juliette Ayisi Agyei, *African Women: Championing Their Own Development and Empowerment – Case Study, Ghana*, 21 Women's Rts. L. Rep. 117, 124 (2000).

69. [Ghana] Criminal Code (Amendment) Act of 1998 (Act 554) cl. 17 (amends [Ghana] Criminal Code, 1960 (Act 29) by inserting cl. 17 as §314A).

70. *See* Woods, *supra* note 29, at 880.

71. The Const. of the Republic of Ghana ch. V, art. 28, §1(a).

necessary step in ensuring that women realize their full potential."[72] Women's
rights advocates must take steps to change cultural practices and norms that
subordinate women. It is these attitudes that make the girl-child a natural
choice for reparation on behalf of male members of the family.

Equal Protection

Female religious bondage violates the equal protection and non-discrimination provisions of Ghana's 1992 Constitution.[73] To the extent that the
Trokosi practice victimizes only girls in the process of family reparation, it is
discrimination. Justifications for this practice based on tradition—such as a
historic premium on women slaves, women's perceived obedience, or slave
concubinage as protection from the unwanted advances of men—are at best
paternalistic and at worst wholly untenable. Traditional institutions have no
legal basis to engage in practices that discriminate against girls.

Inhuman or Degrading Treatment or Punishment

The Constitution[74] and the African Charter[75] prohibit torture or other
cruel, inhuman, or degrading treatment. The conditions under which most
of the girls are held constitute such treatment. They are required to perform
jobs dictated by the fetish priests without complaint and without remuneration.[76] If the girls do not satisfy the priest, they are often beaten as punishment.[77] The girls become the sexual slaves of the priests;[78] if the girls refuse
they are fined.[79] The treatment the girls receive is cruel, inhuman, and degrading, especially in light of their tender ages of the girls. In addition, it is a
fundamental tenet of human rights that punishment should be personal and

---

72. Report of the Int'l Conference on Population and Dev., Cairo, 5–13 Sept.
1994 para. 4.15, U.N. Doc. A/CONF.171/13/Rev.1, U.N. Sales No. E.95.XIII.18 (1994).

73. The Const. of the Republic of Ghana ch. V, art. 17.

74. Id. at art. 28, §3 ("A child shall not be subjected to torture or other cruel, inhuman or degrading treatment or punishment.").

75. African Charter, supra note 51, at art. 5, 1520 U.N.T.S. at 247 ("Every individual
shall have the right to the respect of the dignity inherent in a human being and to the recognition of his legal status. All forms of exploitation and degradation of man particularly
slavery, slave trade, torture, cruel inhuman or degrading punishment and treatment shall
be prohibited.").

76. A.E. Amoah, Trokosi in Retrospect, Daily Graphic (Ghana), June 6, 1995, at 5.

77. Id.

78. Id.

79. See Patience Interview, supra note 9.

imposed only on the offender.[80] Contrary to this, not only does the Trokosi girl receive punishment for another's crime, but should she die before the end of the "sentence," she must be replaced with another virgin from the family.[81]

Slavery/Forced Labor

The most far-reaching consequence of the practice of female religious bondage is the fact that it represents a form of modern-day slavery. The Trokosi girls have physical labor and sexual obligations to priests while other young men and women are living privileged lives, acquiring modern skills, and equipping themselves for contemporary challenges. Unlike other forms of slavery, escape for the Trokosi girl is not a viable choice; escape among the Trokosi often leads to social ostracism[82] and, without education or training, few economic opportunities outside of prostitution.[83] In fact, Trokosi girls do not consider escape an option, because fear of reprisal of the fetish operates as a strong disincentive to escape.[84] Protection from slavery, servitude, and forced labor is provided for in the Constitution[85] and Ghanaian criminal law.[86]

Religion, Tradition, Cultural Rights, and the Law

Even with legal advancements, such as the criminalization of Trokosi, customs growing out of religious beliefs are difficult to erase. Trokosi's persistence as religious authority is not only attributable to "a complex web of economic, social, and political factors, that reflect the existing power relations within the community,"[87] but also to the complicity of government officials who should be leading the charge for eradication of the practice.[88] The theo-

---

80. *E.g.*, African Charter, *supra* note 51, at art. 7, §2, 1520 U.N.T.S. at 247 ("Punishment is personal and can be imposed only on the offender.").

81. Amoah, *supra* note 765.

82. *See* Brooker, *supra* note 1.

83. *See* Aird, *supra* note 2, at 6.

84. *See* Brooker, *supra* note 1.

85. The Const. of the Republic of Ghana ch. V, art. 16, §1-2 ("(1) No person shall be held in slavery or servitude. (2) No person shall be required to perform forced labour.").

86. [Ghana] Criminal Code, 1960 (Act 29) §§314-314A. *See supra* note 69.

87. Abdullahl Ahmed An-Na'im, *State Responsibility Under International Human Rights Law to Change Religions and Customary Laws*, in Human Rights of Women, 167, 176 (Rebecca Cook ed., 1992).

88. *See* Brooker, *supra* note 1. ("Senior members of Ghana's armed forces, police service and a handful of government ministers are said to visit the shrines seeking promotion, protection and success in their operations.").

cratic nature of the Ewe state makes it is difficult for the body politic to draw the line between divine and secular authority; the fetish priest is obeyed because he embodies both.[89] The dilemma is where and how the government should draw the line to avoid charges of circumscribing freedom of religion and cultural imperialism.

In spite of assurances to the contrary,[90] the fetish priests believe that opposition to Trokosi is the work of Christian elements whose wish to disband African religion.[91] The priests suggest that opponents of the Trokosi system view Christianity and Western modernity as politically correct, and traditional practices as primitive.[92] The priests argue that Western influences have only had a retrogressive effect on the nation, and the only remedy is to preserve traditional institutions.[93] It is important to avoid frame the challenge to Trokosi as Christian/civilized/progressive in contrast to a traditional/primitive/retrogressive mould. Reformers should emphasize that it is in the interest of the community to the practice, since the African concept of human rights is perceived from a communitarian rather than individualistic perspective.[94] Without this approach, even the individual whom one seeks to assist may resist change.[95]

---

89. *See* Brooker, *supra* note 1 ("[P]olitical and religious power went hand in hand, and the priest acted as law-maker, adjudicator and enforcer...they remain the most revered, feared and powerful figures in many rural communities.").

90. *See* Ann M. Simmons, *'Wife of the Gods' Stirs up Ghana; to Ward off Evil, Animists Send Girls to Shrines, Where Human Rights Activists Say They Are Enslaved by Priests. Those Who Defend the Practice Declare They Are Upholding Tradition—And Resisting Western Ways*, Los ANGELES TIMES, June 24, 1999, at A1 ("We've always maintained that we're not against the shrines themselves, not against traditional worship like the invocation of the gods," said Emile Short, who heads Ghana's Commission on Human Rights and Administrative Justice, which investigated the shrines and deemed them discriminatory.").

91. Vincent Azumah, *Trokosi Priest Attacks Christians*, THE MIRROR (Ghana), June 3, 1995 at 1.

92. *See* Ann M. Simmons, *supra* note 90.

93. Ellior Kudivo, *Letters to the Editor*, WEEKLY SPECTATOR, August 12, 1995.

94. African Charter, *supra* note 51, at art. 29, §7, 1520 U.N.T.S. at 251 ("The individual shall also have the duty...(7) To preserve and strengthen positive African cultural values in his relations with other members of the society, in the spirit of tolerance, dialogue and consultation, and, in general, to contribute to the promotion of the moral well being of society.").

95. *See* Azumah, *supra* note 91 (One Trokosi woman is reported as saying that the Christian organizations were disgracing the system: "Why should they say we are slaves, sleep on the bare "floor, eat poor food and serve as baby producing machines?").

Reform Strategies

Activists should focus reform efforts on three fronts. First, the government must begin to enforce existing legislation, and if necessary, create legislative instruments to implement the law. Formal, non-formal, and basic legal literacy education of women, their families, and the fetish priests should address the myths and fears surrounding the system. Lobbying and public education that utilizes both national and international pressure to increase public awareness about the Trokosi system will lead to greater recognition of this form of modern slavery and increase support for its eradication. These strategies are not mutually exclusive, and may be used simultaneously, or in combination with one another.

Second, the government must actively negotiate to end this practice. The government may have to financially compensate the chiefs for the release of Trokosi girls or explore non-monetary compensation to redress losses from the cheap labor the girls produced. This should not be viewed as a purchase or a ransom, but as liberation for the girls.

Third, the use of customary law and institutions should not be underestimated. Queenmothers, who approximate the priests in political power and serve as role models within the community, have the potential to bring about change by spearheading informal education in the community. They can also play the role of negotiators in the transition process, since they are close enough to the principal actors to gain support and avoid charges of imperialism. Queenmothers should also encourage programs to rehabilitate and reintegrate girls who have been subject to female religious bondage.

Conclusion

The Ghanaian government must take concerted action to eradicate the Trokosi system as practiced today. The government should respect freedom of religion, but not at the cost of the human rights of others. According to its own Constitution and international human rights law, the Ghanaian government must act to end this discriminatory and violent practice. If a free woman chooses to make an informed choice to practice her religion by being a martyr for another's crimes, that is a choice worthy of respect, as long as it is consistent with the law. A child, however, should be entitled to all the protections the law affords.

The Plight of Refugee Women: Protection from Sexual Violence in Refugee Camps— A Case Study of Tanzania

Hadija Ally

Introduction

"Refugees as a group are doubly disadvantaged and thus particularly vulnerable to actions that threaten their protection."[1] Apart from being "victims... of human rights abuses, conflicts and other acts of aggression," they are unwillingly outside their own countries; outside their own familiar and traditional social structures; divorced from the protection of their own governments; and without roots in the local host community.[2] As a group, refugee women share all of the protection problems experienced by male refugees, such as a need for "protection against forced return to their countries of origin; security against armed attacks and other forms of violence; a legal status that accords adequate social and economic rights; and access to such basic items as food, shelter, clothing and medical care."[3] On top of these problems, however, women suffer from specific gender-related protection problems such

---

1. Office of the United Nations High Commissioner for Refugees, Guidelines on the Protection of Refugee Women para. 1 (1991) [hereinafter 1991 Guidelines].

2. *Id.*

3. *Id.* at para. 2. Refugee camps in Zaire and Tanzania are insecure and dangerous. *Update on Rwanda Emergency*, U.N. GAOR Executive Committee of the High Commissioner's Programme, 45th Sess., para. 5, at 2, U.N. Doc A/AC 96/825/Add.1 (1994) (UNHCR describes the situation as follows: "A high level of violence characterizes the situation in refugee camps, particularly Zaire. Murders, assault and harassment of refugees are daily occurrences. Even relief workers have been physically threatened with machetes and axes.").

as sexual and physical abuse and exploitation as well as discrimination in the distribution of food, goods, and services.[4]

Tanzania has a history of being one of the leading countries in the world for hosting refugees from various countries such as Rwanda, Burundi, Democratic Republic of Congo, Uganda, Mozambique, Angola, and South Africa.[5] As of May 1, 2002, approximately 500,000 Burundian, Congolese, and Rwandan refugees were living in camps in Tanzania, mostly in the Kagera Region (on the western part of Lake Victoria).[6] As of September 2002, approximately 350,000 Burundian refugees were living in camps, and nearly half a million more were living on their own in settlements, outside refugee camps in Tanzania.[7] The numbers have been steadily increasing, and despite pressure from the Tanzanian government and public to repatriate, return rates are below entrance rates.[8]

This essay will examine Tanzanian refugee law as it relates to protection of refugee women against sexual violence in refugee camps. The first part describes the problem of sexual violence, particularly rape, against refugee women in the Tanzanian camps. The second part of the paper briefly examines the relevant international human rights standards in relation to the protection of refugees, particularly protection of refugee women against rape. The third part describes the present Refugee Act, with an analysis of the law in relation to the country's international obligations regarding refugees. Finally, the essay outlines current strategies employed by the United Nations High Commissioner on Refugees and makes recommendations for additional steps to be taken to meet the legal standard for the protection of refugee women.

---

4. 1991 Guidelines, *supra* note 1, at para. 3.

5. *See Tanzania: The Largest Refugee Settlements in Africa*, UNHCR, Spring 1979, at 4. Tanzania's refugee population has remained high, despite the voluntary repatriation of refugees from Mozambique and Angola following the independence of their countries in the mid-seventies. The number of refugees from Zaire following the Amnesty Declaration by Mobutu in the late seventies has steadily increased. *Id.* (In late 1979 there were about 160,000 refugees mainly from Burundi, Uganda, and South Africa). In early 1986, that number shot up to about 200,000 refugees, BUREAU FOR REFUGEE PROGRAMS, DEP'T OF STATE, WORLD REFUGEE REPORT 16 (1986), making Tanzania rank the eleventh worldwide and fourth in Africa, *see id.* at 87–99; and by May 1987 the records showed a total of 233,900 refugees, BUREAU FOR REFUGEE PROGRAMS, DEP'T OF STATE, WORLD REFUGEE REPORT 61 (1987).

6. U.S. COMM. FOR REFUGEES, WORLD REFUGEE SURVEY 2002 101–2 (2002).

7. *Id.* at 101.

8. *Id.* at 101–2.

Sexual Violence against Women
in Refugee Camps

Sexual violence against refugee women in refugee camps includes rape,[9] abduction, sexual exploitation, forced prostitution, forced marriage, and family violence.[10] Refugee women and girls often experience sexual violence in three distinct scenarios. First, rape may be the cause of a woman refugee's flight to the host country: "The occurrence, or realistic fear, of rape by members of military forces, in violation of international humanitarian law, is one of the factors contributing to the flight of women and their families from many situations of armed conflict."[11] Second, refugee women face sexual violence during their flight itself.[12] The third scenario, which is the concern of this paper, is sexual violence in the country of asylum. Women and girls "have been subjected to widespread sexual violence in the country of asylum at the hands of bandits, security forces and other refugees."[13]

---

9. Rape is defined under the Tanzanian law as a male having sexual intercourse with a female "not being his wife…without her consenting to it at the time of the sexual intercourse." The Sexual Offences Special Provisions Act, 1998 (Act No. 4 of 1998) [Tanzania] § 130(2)(a). Additionally, it is rape to have sexual intercourse "with her consent where the consent has been obtained by the use of force, threats or intimidation or by putting her in fear of death or of hurt or while she is in unlawful detention," *Id.* § 130(2)(b), or "with or without her consent when she is under eighteen years of age," *Id.* § 130(2)(e). Other provisions prohibit consensual sexual intercourse if the female is of "unsound mind," *Id.* § 130(2)(c), or if she has been misled into believing that the male is her husband when he, in fact, is not, *Id.* § 130(2)(d).

10. *See e.g., Note on Certain Aspects of Sexual Violence Against Refugee Women*, U.N. GAOR Executive Committee of the High Commissioner's Programme, 44th Sess., para. 12, at 7, U.N. Doc. A/AC.96/822 (1993) [hereinafter Note].

11. *Id.*

12. *Id.* at para. 13 ("The perpetrators of sexual violence against refugee women in the course of their flight include bandits, smugglers, border guards, police, members of military and irregular forces on either side of the border, and even element of local populations."). *See also* Claude Lewis, *Women Are Uniting to Battle Rape and Murder in War Zones*, PHILA. INQUIRER, Mar. 31, 1993, at A11.

13. Note, *supra* note 10 at para. 15.

Rape in the Camps

In May 1995,the Women's Commission for Refugee Women and Children (Commission) sent a delegation to Tanzania to investigate the situation of Rwandan and Burundian refugees, specifically to see whether the United Nations High Commissioner for Refugees (UNHCR) [14] Guidelines on the protection of women against sexual violence were being followed,[15] both in the smaller refugee camps in Kigoma District[16] as well as the massive sites in Ngara District. An American health worker told delegates that "[rapes while collecting wood] have become common, even expected."[17] Conducting research in 1998 and 1999 on Burundian refugees, Human Rights Watch found that "a significant proportion of women had experienced repeated physical assaults by their husbands or intimate partners" including sexual assault.[18] UNHCR research recorded a total of 209 reported rapes in and around the camps and an additional 64 attempted rapes between April and December 2000. Because many rapes are never reported, no reliable statistics about rape cases exist, but UNHCR social and protection workers consistently report that rape is prevalent in the Tanzanian refugee camps.[19]

---

14. United Nations Convention Relating to the Status of Refugees, July 28, 1951, pmbl., para. 6, 189 U.N.T.S. 137, 152 as amended by United Nations Protocol Relating to the Status of Refugees, Jan. 31, 1967, 19 U.S.T. 6223, 606 U.N.T.S. 267 [hereinafter UN Convention] ("Noting that the United Nations High Commissioner on Refugees is charged with the task of supervising international conventions providing for the protection of refugees.").

15. WOMEN'S COMMISSION FOR REFUGEE WOMEN AND CHILDREN, REFUGEE WOMEN IN TANZANIA: ASSESSING THE IMPLEMENTATION OF THE UNHCR GUIDELINES ON THE PROTECTION OF REFUGEE WOMEN 1 (1995) [hereinafter Women's Commission].

16. *Id.* Camps in the Kigoma Region bordering Lake Tanganyika (Kanembwa, Karago, Mtabira-1, Mtabira-2, Mtendeli, Myovosi, and Nduta) host approximately 239,000 refugees from Burundi. OFFICE OF THE UNITED NATIONS HIGH COMMISSIONER FOR REFUGEES, STATISTICAL YEARBOOK 2001 45 (2002). The camps in Kigoma were established in 1994 after thousands of Burundians fled political violence in their homeland. *See* U.S. COMMITTEE FOR REFUGEES, WORLD REFUGEE SURVEY 1994 71 (1994).

17. Women's Commission, *supra* note 15, at 1.

18. HUMAN RIGHTS WATCH, SEEKING PROTECTION: ADDRESSING SEXUAL AND DOMESTIC VIOLENCE IN TANZANIA'S REFUGEE CAMPS 23 (2000) [hereinafter SEEKING PROTECTION].

19. Interviews with UNHCR Protection Staff, Karagwe, Tanzania (Dec. 1995). Other common protection problems facing refugee women and girls involve prostitution and sexual exploitation. There is an increase of adolescent sex in the camps, mostly young girls partnering with older men—often as second wives—in order to obtain better food or more

The Victims

Young girls are most vulnerable to rape in the camps,[20] as demonstrated by the increasing number of refugee girls who seek treatment for rape and other forms of sexual abuse.[21] Refugee men are well aware of the prevalence and dangers of AIDS,[22] and they target young girls in the hope that they are still virgins and thus free from HIV.[23] The susceptibility of young girls is further aggravated by the fact that they form the main group responsible for wood collection, an activity where the risk of rape and other sexual attacks is very high.[24] Women and girls walk long distances in search of firewood.[25] A woman can spend up to eight hours searching for wood and, over time, she has to go further from the camp as the immediate surroundings are stripped.[26] Consequently, girls as young as twelve have been raped.[27]

Perpetrators target refugee women for assault at latrines, because these facilities are typically located far from the living quarters, and at night because of poor lighting in the camps.[28] As explained by one UNHCR protection officer in Kigoma Region, "'Early in the life of the camps women were being as-

---

clothes or as physical protection. *Id.* The economic insecurity has also led many women into prostitution. *Id.* The categories of women involved in prostitution are mostly single women and girls who are unaccompanied, as well as female heads of households because of absence of adequate income. *Id.* Unless alternative income-generating opportunities are made available prostitution might remain as the only option for many women. Another category of women suffering sexual exploitation is single women who are housed with other families and are expected to take on conjugal roles in the new households. *Id.*

20. *Id.*

21. Women's Commission, *supra* note 15, at 10.

22. Women's Commission, *supra* note 15, at 10. There is no data on HIV in the refugee camps; however, before the civil war broke out in Rwanda, 1994, the infection rate in Rwanda's major cities was approximately 30%. *Id.* at 2.

23. *Id.*

24. *See* SEEKING PROTECTION, *supra* note 18, at 42. Also, during my visit to the camps in Karagwe in December 1995, I witnessed long lines of young girls and boys descending steep mountains back to the camp. On their heads they carried big bundles of firewood.

25. *See* SEEKING PROTECTION, *supra* note 18, at 45.

26. *Id.*

27. Women's Commission, *supra* note 15, at 5 ("While the Women's Commission delegation was visiting, a UNHCR officer reported the rape of a 12-year-old girl while she and four teenage friends were in the forest collecting wood.").

28. *See* Marc Sommers, *The Haunted Lives of Rwandan Refugees*, ST. PETERSBURG TIMES (Florida), Nov. 6, 1994 at 1D (noting the danger of rape presented by the latrines in Benaco camp for Rwandan refugees in Tanzania).

saulted as they walked to and from the latrines and from collecting water. One woman was killed by her assailant.'" [29] Subsequently, UNHCR gave women torches, encouraged them to walk in groups and assisted communities in setting up neighborhood watches.[30]

The Perpetrators

Perpetrators of rape and related abuses include male refugees, military personnel of the host country, resistance forces, bandits, and local people.[31] "Tanzanian soldiers have been accused of attacking groups of refugees, and raping women and girls."[32] For example, in early May 1995, "a group of refugees from Burundi crossed the border, and was stopped by the Tanzanian military."[33] The group arrived in Ngara and "reported that three of the women with them had been raped."[34] "In another incident in late May, a woman crossing the border from Rwanda was allegedly caught by Tanzanian soldiers who raped and beat her."[35]

Male refugees commit a high percentage of rapes that occur in the camps.[36] "The dislocation and violence experienced by displaced and refugee populations often destroy family and social structures, and with them, the norms and taboos that normally would have proscribed sexual violence against women."[37] "Moreover, the anger, uncertainty, and helplessness of male refugees unable to assume their traditionally dominant roles are often translated into violent behavior towards women."[38]

Alcohol consumption in the camps also contributes to the high incidence of rape. "[M]any of the men in the camps have nothing to do and spend their days drinking in the bars that have sprung up around the camps."[39] Drinking

---

29. Women's Commission, *supra* note 15, at 15 (quoting an interview by the Women's Commission for Refugee Women & Children with Clementine Nkweta-Mura, UNHCR Protection Officer).

30. *Id.; see also* SEEKING PROTECTION, *supra* note 18, at 17.

31. *See supra* notes 10–11 and 13 and accompanying text.

32. Women's Commission, *supra* note 15, at 9.

33. *Id.*

34. *Id.*

35. *Id.*

36. *See supra* notes 10–11 and 13 and accompanying text.

37. HUMAN RIGHTS WATCH, THE HUMAN RIGHTS WATCH GLOBAL REPORT ON WOMEN'S HUMAN RIGHTS 102 (1995) [hereinafter GLOBAL REPORT].

38. *Id.*

39. *See* Women's Commission, *supra* note 15, at 10.

is regarded as the dominant mode of socializing.[40] As such, it often starts early in the morning and continues through the night. "When men leave the bars they take out their frustrations on other family members."[41] UNHCR officers have attempted to address this problem by liming the hours that bars are open in the camps.[42]

Finally, local people also rape refugees.[43] Refugee women and girls, who walk to nearby villages in search of work, report being raped by locals.[44] In one case, a local man raped a young girl and then locked her up in his house.[45] Her whereabouts were discovered after a few days, but she refused to go back to her parents.[46] Her father's efforts to hold the perpetrator responsible and bring his daughter home were defeated when the girl accepted a marriage offer by the man who had raped her.[47] She contended that even if she agreed to go back to the camp she had no future to look forward to.[48] She had lost her childhood and there was no means for her to continue with her education that had been terminated by the war in her home country.[49]

Under-Reporting of Rape

Despite the prevalence of rape in the camps, only a few cases have been reported either to police or to UNHCR officials.[50] Cultural indifference to rape

---

40. *See id.*

41. *Id.*

42. *See* Royce Bernstein Murray, Note, *Sex for Food in a Refugee Economy: Human Rights Implications and Accountability,* 14 GEO. IMMIGR. L.J. 985, 996 n.78 ("To limit sexual abuses by drunken Burundian men in Tanzanian refugee camps, UNHCR moved to limit the drinking hours of camp bars to 2:00 to 6:00 p.m. daily.").

43. Interviews with UNHCR Protection Staff, Karagwe, Tanzania (Dec. 1995), *supra* note 19.

44. *Id.*

45. *Id.* (This incident happened to a refugee girl who was living at Chabalisa camp in Karagwe. Victim's name withheld for confidentiality.)

46. *Id.*

47. *Id.*

48. *Id.*

49. *Id.*

50. Interview with Sharon Berndard, Head of UNHCR Sub-Office Karagwe, (Dec. 28, 1995) (For example, in the four Karagwe camps which hosts about 250,000 refugees only few incidents of rape were reported—about 15—despite evidence of many more incidents.).

among the refugee communities in Tanzania results in a lack of community support for victims, discouraging them from reporting rape.[51] The situation is even worse where the victim is a young girl, whose decision-making power is still dependent upon her parents or guardians taking the initiative.[52] Such attitudes indicate the extent to which both male and female refugees, including the victims themselves, are ignorant of the impact of rape on the victim.[53] People believe a victim suffers nothing from rape, a point demonstrated by the fact that even when a rapist pays fine, it is not always given to the victim, but to her family instead.[54]

The refugee community is convinced that reconciliation between the rapist's family and the victim's family is a better method for handling rape cases than seeking recourse in courts of law.[55] A court case involves complicated, time-consuming procedures. The law as applied is too burdensome for the victim (as a witness), and the result is rarely a conviction.[56] Reconciliation, however, is simple and fast. In court, a rape case could take a year or more to be completed.[57] In contrast, the parties typically spend only a few hours in reconciliation, often resulting in a fine for the rapist that is paid to the victim's family.[58] The perpetrator is almost always willing to cooperate,

---

51. Interview with Cecilia Ryberg, Senior Social Services Officer, UNHCR Branch Office, Dar es Salaam, Tanzania, (Jan. 10, 1995).

52. *Cf.* MARTIN S. GREENBERG & R. BARRY RUBACK, AFTER THE CRIME: VICTIM DECISION MAKING 8–11 (1992) (study of the factors, including age, that affect an individual's decision to report crime, especially sexual violence).

53. Victims of rape suffer both physically and psychologically. A victim can suffer from post-traumatic disorder or rape traumatic syndrome, with symptoms including "persistent fear, a loss of self confidence and self esteem, difficulty in concentration, an attitude of self-blame, a pervasive feeling of loss of control and memory loss or distortion." Nancy Kelly, *Guidelines for Women's Asylum Claims*, 6 INT'L J. REFUGEE L. 517, 534 (1994). In certain incidents rape results in unwanted pregnancies and maternal mortality particularly in young girls. *See* JUDITH SENDEROWITZ, ADOLESCENT HEALTH: REASSESSING THE PASSAGE TO ADULTHOOD 1 (The World Bank 1995). Also by being forced to carry unwanted pregnancy a victim's right to liberty is impaired. Furthermore, when rape results in infection of the HIV virus (causing AIDS) the ultimate result is death, hence violation of the victim's right to life. Sometimes where there is a strong cultural stigma attached to rape the victim stands to face ostracism. *See, e.g.*, GLOBAL REPORT, *supra* note 37, at 102–3.

54. GLOBAL REPORT, *supra* note 37, at 135.

55. SEEKING PROTECTION, *supra* note 18, at 78.

56. *See supra* note 19.

57. *Cf.* GLOBAL REPORT, *supra* note 37, at 136.

58. *Cf. id.* at 135.

usually by admitting to have committed the offence.[59] The reconciliation procedures, however, not only fail to sufficiently redress the problems of the victim, but they also fail to prevent future rapes. The procedure lacks a deterrent effect, because in most cases, the fines imposed are negotiable and usually limited to the perpetrator's ability to pay.[60] It is therefore possible for the same man to repeat the offence because the punishment is affordable.

International Human Rights Standards for Protection of Refugee Women

Tanzania ratified both the United Nations Convention Relating to the Status of Refugees (UN Convention)[61] and the Organization of African Unity Convention Governing the Specific Aspects of Refugee Problems in Africa (OAU Convention),[62] the regional instrument relating to the status of refugees. Although both documents advance universal standards concerning the protection of refugees,[63] there are no provisions in either convention that specifically confer to refugees the right to protection against physical and sexual violence.[64] Furthermore, the UN Convention as written does not have a sex

---

59. The reason behind this willingness is rather obvious that the perpetrator is saved from facing a much harsher procedure, which might send him to jail.

60. *See supra* notes 54, 57–58, and accompanying text. Given the apparent poor economic position of refugees, the amount agreed upon is minimal or even if it is high, what is affordable is almost negligible. *Id.*

61. UN Convention, *supra* note 14, 187 U.N.T.S. at 137 (Tanzania ratified the convention in 1964 and the protocol in 1968).

62. OAU Convention Governing the Specific Aspects of Refugee Problems in Africa, 1969, 1001 U.N.T.S. 45 [hereinafter OAU Convention] (Tanzania ratified on Jan. 27, 1975).

63. In essence the UN Convention and the OAU Convention are elaborating on the content of the right to seek asylum, *see* UN Convention, *supra* note 14, at pmbl., para. 4, 189 U.N.T.S. at 152 ("Considering that the grant of asylum may place unduly heavy burdens on certain countries, and that a satisfactory solution...cannot therefore be achieved without international co-operation."); OAU Convention, *supra* note 62, at art. II, paras. 1–6, 1001 U.N.T.S. at 48, which right is included in both the Universal Declaration of Human Rights, G.A. Res. 217, U.N. GAOR, 3d Sess., at art. 14, para. 1, U.N. Doc. A/810 (1948) [hereinafter UDHR], and the African Charter on Human and Peoples' Rights, June 27, 1981, art. 12, para. 3, 1520 U.N.T.S. 217 [hereinafter African Charter].

64. In general the UN Convention provides for the right to: asylum, UN Convention, *supra* note 14, at art. 1–11, 189 U.N.T.S. at 152–60, property, *id.* at art. 13–14, 189 U.N.T.S. at 162, association, *id.* at art. 15, 189 U.N.T.S. at 162, freedom of movement, *id.* at art. 26, 189 U.N.T.S. at 172, access to court of law, *id.* at art. 16, 189 U.N.T.S. at 164,

category in its non-discrimination provision.[65] Fortunately, "most internationally guaranteed human rights standards attach to individuals as human beings, not as citizens. Thus refugees do not lose their entitlement to these rights by fleeing their own countries and becoming refugees."[66] "In law, refugees enjoy two overlapping sets of rights: those accorded to them as individuals and guaranteed under international human rights standards (as well as national law), and specific rights relating to their status as refugees."[67]

Although the UN Convention focuses on the generally applicable standards of protection of refugees, these standards are deeply rooted in the wider context of human rights to which all states are bound.[68] The UN Convention is founded on the wider principles set forth in the Universal Declaration of Human Rights that "human beings shall enjoy fundamental rights and freedom without discrimination."[69] The UN Convention aims "to assure refugees the widest possible exercise of these fundamental rights and freedoms."[70] Invoking other instruments not only supplements the UN Convention's substantive inadequacies on protection, but also provides valuable mechanisms for addressing these rights. The UN Convention lacks an enforcement mech-

---

employment (both wage-earning and self-employment), *id.* at art. 17–18, 189 U.N.T.S. at 164–65, welfare (mainly rationing, housing, elementary education, public relief and labor legislation), *id.* at art. 20–24, 189 U.N.T.S. at 166–70, identity papers, *id.* at art. 27, 189 U.N.T.S. at 172, travel documents, *id.* at art. 28, 189 U.N.T.S. at 172, naturalization, *id.* at art. 34, 189 U.N.T.S. at 176, and voluntary repatriation, *id.* at art. 32–33, 189 U.N.T.S. at 174–76. In general the OAU Convention provides for the right to: asylum, OAU Convention, *supra* note 64, at art. I–IV, 1001 U.N.T.S. at 47–49, voluntary repatriation, *id.* at art. V, 1001 U.N.T.S. at 49, and travel documents, *id.* at art. VI, 1001 U.N.T.S. at 49.

65. UN Convention, *supra* note 14, art. 3, 189 U.N.T.S. at 156 (providing only that: "The Contracting States shall apply the provisions of this Convention to refugees without discrimination as to race, religion or country of origin.").

66. Lawyers Committee for Human Rights, African Exodus 91 (1995) [hereinafter Lawyers Committee].

67. *Id.* Refugees remain a privileged class of non-nationals under the refugee convention and international law generally, guaranteed certain civil and political rights as well as national treatment regarding most social benefits. *See supra* notes 64–65 and accompanying text.

68. *See* Lawyers Committee, *supra* note 66, at 34–36.

69. UN Convention, *supra* note 14, pmbl., para. 1, 189 U.N.T.S. at 150.

70. *Id.* at pmbl., para. 2, 189 U.N.T.S. at 150. Likewise, in adopting the OAU Convention of 1969 in Addis Ababa, the heads of state of African countries were "desirous of finding ways and means of alleviating [refugees'] misery and suffering as well as providing them with a better life and future." OAU Convention, *supra* note 62, at pmbl., para. 1, 1001 U.N.T.S. at 46.

anism, and UNHCR, entrusted with protecting refugees from physical harm, plays largely an advisory role vis-à-vis member states. [71] International law generally, and especially the Declaration on the Elimination of Violence Against Women[72] and the Convention on the Elimination of all Forms of Discrimination Against Women (CEDAW),[73] prohibit sexual violence and urge states to ensure that laws against rape, sexual assault, and all other gender-based violence give adequate protection to all women and respect their integrity and dignity.[74]

Rights and Protection of Refugees under Tanzanian Law

The new Refugee Act (The Act),[75] promulgated in 1998 with support of the United Nations High Commissioner for Refugees, represents significant

---

71. UN Convention, *supra* note 14, pmbl., para. 6, 189 U.N.T.S. at 150.

72. Declaration on the Elimination of Violence Against Women, G.A. Res. 104, U.N. GAOR, 48th Sess., pmbl., para. 7, U.N. Doc. A/RES/48/104 (1993) [hereinafter Women's Declaration] (noting that refugee women are especially vulnerable to violence).

73. Convention on the Elimination of all Forms of Discrimination Against Women, *opened for signature* Mar. 1, 1980, art. 12, 1249 U.N.T.S. 13, 19, 19 I.L.M. 33, 40 [hereinafter CEDAW]. CEDAW "is taken to provide evidence of human rights standards that are specifically applicable to women on a general basis" because of its comprehensive obligation to states. Chaloka Beyani, *Toward a More Effective Guarantee of Women's Rights in the African Human Rights System*, in Human Rights of Women, 285, 286 (Rebecca Cook ed., 1992). "It may be viewed as direct amplification of the UN Charter's obligation to promote universal protection of human rights for all without discrimination as to sex and in relation to women." *Id.* at 290.

74. *See, e.g.,* Women's Declaration, *supra* note 72, at art. 4 ("States should pursue by all appropriate means and without delay a policy of eliminating violence against women."). States are required to submit reports on a periodic basis to various international human rights committees. *Id.* at art. 4, cl. (m). Specifically in 1989 the Committee on the Elimination of Discrimination Against Women requested that states include in their reports information about violence against women and the measures taken to eliminate such violence. *Report of the Committee on the Elimination of Discrimination Against Women*, U.N. GAOR, 44th Sess., at para. 392, General Recommendation No. 12, U.N. Doc. A/44/38 (1989). For a full discussion of the contravention of international and regional human rights norms by state's failure to adequately address sexual violence against women please see the preceding article on international law and violence against women.

75. The Refugees Act, 1998 (Act No. 9 of 1998) [Tanzania] [hereinafter The Act]. "[T]he Refugee Control Act adopted by Tanzania in 1966, and subsequently mirrored by

progress in national refugee law, including a definition of refugee,[76] the creation of a National Eligibility Committee,[77] and a provision for the education of refugee children.[78] Despite Tanzania's humanitarian attitude toward refugees,[79] the Tanzanian refugee law remains inadequate in the protection of refugee women from rape and other types of gender-motivated violence.

The Act's primary weakness is that its scope includes only the control and administration of refugees; there is no provision for refugee protection.[80] Specifically, there is no section dealing explicitly with refugee women or with sexual violence.[81] As explained above, international human rights law demands the protection of refugee women from sexual violence.[82] Thus, in fulfilling its international obligations, Tanzania must ensure protection of all people within its territory by guaranteeing them adequate legal protection to enable their enjoyment of rights and freedoms on an equal basis. In an effort to fulfill this obligation, some countries have enacted progressive and comprehensive refugee legislation by not only adopting the UN Convention but also by guaranteeing rights and protections beyond those expressly provided therein. For example, in Sudan, "the 1974 Regulation of Asylum Act...contains an express requirement to give due consideration to international instruments concerning refugees" and states that "these instruments take priority over its own pro-

---

Zambia in 1970 and Botswana in 1976...[are] substantively uniform in character and [have] the essential purpose of controlling the entry, movement, settlement and activities of refugees." Lawyers Committee, *supra* note 66, at 36.

76. The Act, *Id.* note at pt. I, §4.

77. *Id.* at pt. II, §6. Under the old law, Tanzania's entire asylum system was based on wide discretionary powers granted to individual officials, leading into both uncertainty and non-uniformity in the law and its implementation. *See* Lawyers Committee, *supra* note 66, at 36–37.

78. The Act, *supra* note 75, at pt. V, §31.

79. *See supra* notes 5–8 and accompanying text.

80. Indeed, over 75% of the space covered by the Act deals with the administration and control of refugees touching upon points of entry, The Act, *supra* note 78, at pt. III, §10, departure or routes for refugees, *Id.*, surrender of weapons, *Id.* at pt. III, §11, detention of their vehicles, *Id.* at pt. III §14, slaughter of their animals, *Id.* at pt. III, §13, the deportation of refugees, *Id.* at pt. V, §28, of refugees who prejudice peace and foreign relations, *Id.* at pt. V, §27, refugee work permits, *Id.* at pt. V, §32, control of their residence in specified areas and control and administration of such areas set aside for refugees and the restrictions placed upon entry into such settlements, *Id.* at pt. IV, §§16-20.

81. *See supra* note 75 (containing a breakdown of the sections of The Act and highlighting its emphasis on administration and control).

82. *See supra* notes 72–74 and accompanying text.

visions."[83] "Zimbabwe's 1983 Refugee Act is the most comprehensive and impressive model of legislation for protection of refugees in Africa."[84] In addition to adopting the UN and OAU Conventions, "[i]t gives direct effect in domestic law to the application of international standards for the protection of refugees and the relevant instruments are provided for in an annex."[85] Canada has gone even further by including a gender category as one of the grounds for granting asylum.[86] Tanzania should follow these examples.

Tanzania could argue that as a matter of governmental policy the country observes humanitarian norms and that refugees, like all aliens, are entitled to protection under national law, particularly the Constitution, which incorporated the Bill of Rights.[87] This is a plausible argument as far as a theoretical guarantee of these rights is concerned. The argument loses credence, however, when it comes to the practical implementation of these rights by the government and, in cases of a violation, their enforcement by refugees. Refugees lack power to participate in the political process and therefore are without representation to ensure actual realization of such rights.

The situation is worse when it comes to rights of refugee women and their legal protection. Like all other aliens, the rights of refugee women cannot be isolated from the general standard of legal protection accorded to national women by domestic legislation.[88] In short, refugee women are entitled to enjoy no more protection than that accorded to national women unless the national protection standard is below the international standard.[89] Refugee women who

---

83. Lawyers Committee, *supra* note 66, at 37.

84. *Id.* at 38 ("The act amends the Immigration Act no. 18 of 1979, the Interpretation Act, Cap. 1 of the Laws of Zimbabwe, and the Prison Act, Cap. 21 of the Laws of Zimbabwe, where these are inconsistent with Zimbabwe's international obligations toward refugees.).

85. *Id.*

86. IMMIGRATION AND REFUGEE BOARD [CANADA], GUIDELINES ISSUED BY THE CHAIRPERSON PURSUANT TO SECTION 65(3) OF THE *IMMIGRATION ACT*: GUIDELINE 4: WOMEN REFUGEE CLAIMANTS FEARING GENDER-RELATED PERSECUTION: UPDATE (1996).

87. CONST. OF THE UNITED REPUBLIC OF TANZANIA, 1977, ch. 1, pt. III. In 1985 the bill of rights was incorporated in the constitution to become part of the law; before that it was in the preamble to the constitution. *See* HUMAN RIGHTS LAW IN AFRICA 1996, 355–61 (Christof Heyns ed., 1996).

88. *See infra* pp. xx–xx Scholastica Jullu, *Sexual Violence Against Women in Tanzania: Sexual Offences (Special Provision) Act No. 4 of 1998 as a Case Study* (extensive discussion of the Tanzanian law pertaining to sexual violence and exploitation). Specifically, the law falls short of adequately protecting all women in Tanzania, including those in refuge camps, because of issues of evidence, definitions of consent, and under-enforcement. *Id.*

are victims of rape are not different from any other national women who face the same problem. Thus, even if the government claims that the Tanzania rape law adequately addresses the problem of rape of refugee women, this is only true as far as redressing past rapes.[90] The frequency of rape in refugee camps, however, calls for aggressive preventive measures. Tanzanian rape law cannot achieve this, because, unlike many other penal sanctions, it lacks deterring force or effect.[91] Moreover, special requirements for proving rape operate to the disadvantage of the victims, allowing most accused rapists to go free.[92] This is why many refugee women have decided to avoid seeking recourse in courts of law, and have instead opted for reconciliation.[93]

Recommendations

The Role of the United Nations High Commissioner for Refugees

Recognizing the prevalence and detrimental effects of sexual and gender-based violence in the refugee camps in Tanzania, the UNHCR bases its approach to sexual and gender-based violence on the UNHCR Sexual Violence

---

89. J.L. BRIERLY, THE LAW OF NATIONS, 278–79 (6th ed. 1963).

90. *Cf.* Committee on the Elimination of Discrimination Against Women, *Consideration of Reports Submitted by States Parties Under Article 18 of the Convention on the Elimination of All Forms of Discrimination Against Women, Second and Third Periodic Reports of States Parties, Tanzania,* para. 30–34, U.N. Doc CEDAW/C/TZA/2–3 (1996). "To start with, an amendment to the law on defilement of girls under 14 years of age was effected in 1992 making defilement a scheduled offence whereby a convicted accused is punished with a minimum of 35 years imprisonment. However, stringent punishment has not deterred the practice." *Id.* at para. 34.

91. *See* Dep't of State, *Tanzania* in COUNTRY REPORTS ON HUMAN RIGHTS PRACTICES FOR 2001 at 668, §2d at 682 (2001) ("The Government does not adequately investigate, prosecute, or punish perpetrators of abuses in refugee camps.").

92. Law Reform Commission of Tanzania, Discussion Paper: Criminal Law as a Vehicle for the Protection of the Right to Personal Integrity, Dignity and Liberty of Women, Agenda No. 48.8, Presented to the 48th Commission Meeting, ch.5, §6, *available at* http://www.lcrt-tz.org/criminal_law.pdf (Last accessed June 27, 2003) ("One factor that is most known to impede effective application of our criminal law as a means for the protection of the dignity, integrity and liberty of women, is the strict, and we may add, conventional requirement of corroboration in all sexual offences.").

93. *See supra* notes 57–60 and accompanying text.

Guidelines.[94] UNHCR, in collaboration with its implementing partners and the refugee community, has been working to implement adequate prevention and response mechanisms. Eleven refugee camps in four districts offer UNHCR sexual and gender-based violence (SGBV) services. Most camps had some sort of system in place for support and monitoring of SGBV, but UNHCR has examined these disparate strategies, coordinated the efforts into a unified program, created protocols to clarify responsibilities of individual actors, evaluated program outcomes, and strengthened reporting lines.[95]

Facilitating Reporting and Education

Reliable maintenance of sexual and gender-based violence statistics remains a problem at the camps, as it is the world over. It has, however, improved since April 2000, when UNHCR implemented a new set of procedures. Reporting procedures are only effective if women are willing to step forward with their stories and if officials receiving the information are sensitive. Education is therefore an important part of increasing reporting. The UNHCR provides regular training on SGBV and the governing Tanzanian laws and procedures for UNHCR staff, government officials, police, the judiciary, and non-governmental organizations (NGOs). UNHCR also conducts education for the refugee community, raising awareness of human rights, promoting self-esteem, and building capacity for mobilization for change. Community Services agencies in all the camps conduct awareness-raising specifically concerning vi-

---

94. United Nations High Commissioner for Refugees, Sexual Violence Against Refugees: Guidelines on Prevention and Response (1995). The guidelines have recently been replaced by new guidelines entitled: Sexual and Gender-Based Violence Against Refugees, Returnees and Internally Displaced Persons (May 2003) [hereinafter 2003 Guidelines]. The Guidelines were developed in consultation with UNHCR's partners and have been tested in 32 countries around the world with the participation of more than 60 partners. The Guidelines reflect progress made over the past years and underscore the importance of an inter-agency, multi-sectoral approach to addressing SGBV against not only refugees, but also returnees and IDPs.

95. This work was made possible by funds provided by businessman and philanthropist Ted Turner, who donated U.S. $1 billion to the United Nations in 1997, establishing the U.N. Foundation. "In February 1999, the U.N. Foundation gave UNHCR the first installment of a US$1.65 million award to strengthen UNHCR's efforts to prevent sexual violence against women and adolescent girls in refugee situations in five countries in Sub-Saharan Africa," including Tanzania. Seeking Protection, *supra* note 18, at 63 n.172.

olence against women, reaching not only the refugee community as a whole, but also refugee leaders, local councils, "sungu-sungus," and women and peer educators. Furthermore, actors in various relevant sectors meet every week to examine SGBV issues and develop new strategies for protection and response.

Meeting the Needs of Victims

Following the food shortage that began in May 2000, the UNHCR has struggled to prevent the misappropriation of food shares by batterers. To that end, UNHCR has placed women on the food distribution committees and has begun to split ration cards, making it easier for women to access rations. New Drop-In Centres offer temporary shelter and other emergency assistance, and Women's Forums offer women support in an informal setting.[96] When solutions at a camp are inadequate for an individual woman, she may be considered for resettlement under the "women-at-risk" criteria. To eliminate sexual assaults that occur when women and girls trek to find firewood, the UNHCR provides, to the best of its ability, fuel to those most vulnerable to attack. The UNHCR and its implementing partners acquired vehicles, generators, computers, and improved facilities including the Drop-In Centres. Despite the current funding, the UNHCR continues to seek support from various agencies to fund these efforts.

Encouraging Legal Recourse

One of the UNHCR's biggest challenges is discouraging refugee councils from resolving SGBV cases informally. Because the councils are important to the refugee communities both culturally and practically, UNHCR focuses on awareness-raising and training within the councils. UNHCR also believes that getting women on the councils will help to address some women's rights concerns, including violence against women in the camps. Slowly, the councils are beginning to report SGBV incidents to the UNHCR. Women must be informed of their options to turn to the state justice system as opposed to relying on the council's reconciliation efforts, and then supported in the decision to bring suit. The legal system in Tanzania, however, is an over-burdened, understaffed, expensive, and insensitive alternative. To ameliorate this situation, the UNHCR developed a strong relationship with the Tanzanian judiciary, training magistrates and judges on refugee issues, including SGBV, and pro-

---

96. *Id.* at 17.

viding copies of relevant legislation. Transportation is a huge obstacle, and UNHCR furnishes vehicles for travel to the courts by witnesses, victims, and suspects. The UNHCR has hired two Tanzanian lawyers specifically to work on the legal aspects of the SGBV program. Combined, these efforts have increased the number of perpetrators convicted.

Further Recommendations for the UNHCR

There is room for improvement, however. UNHCR should maintain and increase its physical presence in refugee settlements and provide a stable, well-trained staff at all UNHCR locations. A 1992 study by the Lawyers Committee for Human Rights concluded that the lack of UNHCR's physical presence in refugee camps resulted in a failure to ensure protection against sexual and other forms of violence.[97] Given the number of refugees and the persistent problem of rape incidents in the Tanzanian camps, [98] UNHCR should assign a reasonable number of Protection staff to work in the field offices to ensure their regular presence and follow-up of such cases in the camps.

Training for police/investigators, prosecutors, and the courts improves enforcement. These courses should address the peculiar nature and impact of rape and other forms of sexual violence on the victim. Training should include instruction about the technicalities of the procedures and how best to assist victims in preparing their cases for prosecution. All of these efforts, together, can alleviate the unnecessary burden on victims and may eventually lead to higher conviction rates. Convictions will not only punish the offenders, but they have a deterrent effect on others.

Training the refugee community about their rights and potential liability under the Tanzanian rape law and the human rights implications of rape is important. Training should demonstrate that reconciliation, the method to which most refugees have resorted, lacks deterrent force,[99] an essential element in prevention of the problem. Refugees should thus be encouraged to take their cases to the courts. The UNHCR should continue its efforts to combat the use of reconciliation in gender-based violence situations by providing awareness raising and training for refugees and the refugee councils specifically.

---

97. *See* Lawyers Committee, *supra* note 66, at 171–72.
98. *See* SEEKING PROTECTION, *supra* note 18, at 45.
99. *See supra* notes 89–94 and accompanying text.

Voluntary repatriation is the last but most effective long-term measure, as it restores refugees into their country of origin.[100] Refugees and the relevant authorities, however, should resort to repatriation only where there is no danger of refugees facing persecution. Most importantly, it must be voluntary and unforced.[101]

The Role of Non-Governmental Organizations

As in many countries in Africa, human rights non-governmental organizations (NGOs) in Tanzania have not been fully involved in the protection of refugee women against sexual violence.[102] This lack of involvement may be due to a fear of being involved with a group (the refugees) whose presence in the country has been met with hostility from the local population.[103] That the Tanzanian refugee law mainly provides for refugees' obligations and sanctions and not their rights reflects such hostility.[104] The law sends a message that refugees are bad people. NGOs can play an important role in changing the public's attitude toward refugees.

Educating the Population

NGOs should educate the Tanzanian population about the rights of refugees and refugee women in particular. NGOs can do this through media, seminars, and simple brochures written in the national language. Education about refugees will result in less hostility directed at refugees and will, in turn, reduce violence against refugee women by the local population. This will be a difficult task due to the economic sacrifices made by villages bordering refugee camps.[105] It is not surprising that many Tanzanians applauded Tanzania's 1995 closure of its borders.[106] NGOs must make efforts, however, to transform this hostility toward refugees into increased sensitivity and a stronger commitment to eradicating suffering within the refugee population.

---

100. *See, e.g.,* OAU Convention, *supra* note 62 at art. V, 1001 U.N.T.S. at 49.

101. *E.g., id.* at art. V, para. 1, 1001 U.N.T.S. at 49.

102. *See* Lawyers Committee, *supra* note 66, at 175.

103. *Id.* at 177.

104. *See* notes 76–81 and accompanying text.

105. *See, e.g.,* Chris McGreal, *Locked out to Ease Tension Within,* THE GUARDIAN (London), Apr. 3, 1995, at 11.

106. *See id.*

Defending Refugee Rights

NGOs can defend refugee rights and advocate for the protection of refugee women against sexual violence by providing legal advice and representation,[107] researching and documenting sexual abuses against refugee women (women refugee victims of rape may be willing to talk to NGO representatives even when unwilling to tell police or other officials),[108] invoking international human rights mechanisms, including submission of shadow reports,[109] and using the African Charter by filing complaints to the African Commission on Human and Peoples' Rights about Tanzania's violation of its duty under Art. 18(3) of the African Charter.[110] NGOs can complain to the Commission about the failure of Tanzania's refugee law to comport with international standards.

Advocating for Law Reform

Tanzania should amend its refugee law to incorporate all international human rights provisions on the protection of refugees from physical violence, particularly the protection of refugee women from sexual violence. Specifi-

---

107. Lawyers Committee, *supra* note 66, at 178–79.

108. *Id.* at 179–80.

109. *Id.* at 180–81. Although Tanzania is a party to the International Covenant on Civil and Political Rights, *opened for signature* Dec. 19, 1966, S. TREATY DOC. No. 95-2, 999 U.N.T.S. 171 [hereinafter ICCPR], it has not ratified the Optional Protocol to the Convention in which case neither NGOs nor individuals can file communications under the protocol. *Id.* at 999 U.N.T.S. 302. However, because Tanzania is a member to CEDAW, *see supra* note 74, NGOs can compel the Tanzanian government to comply with its obligation under Article 2 of CEDAW, CEDAW, *supra* note 74, at art. 2, 1249 U.N.T.S. at 16, by invoking the provisions of Article 18 which requires state members to submit to the Secretary-General of the UN for consideration by a committee measures taken by the state to meet its obligation. *Id.* at art. 18, 1249 U.N.T.S. at 22. Article 2 specifically requires member states to abolish all discriminatory laws and to take effective measures to ensure protection of rights of women. *Id.* at art. 2, 1249 U.N.T.S. at 16. Such reports of non-compliance could force Tanzania, for example, to pay attention to discriminatory laws and possibly result in their reform.

110. African Charter, *supra* note 63, at art. 18, para. 3, 1520 U.N.T.S. at 249. ("The State shall ensure the elimination of every discrimination against women and also ensure the protection of the rights of the woman as stipulated in international declarations and conventions."). Because regional or international complaints may expose the fact that although Tanzania purports to abide by humanitarian laws, it still has discriminatory provisions in its laws. *See* Lawyers Committee, *supra* note 66, at 51–54. Such exposure, particularly at this time of multi-party democracy, can be a very useful tool for reform.

cally, the law should incorporate the non-discrimination provision required by CEDAW[111] and apply the definition of sexual violence provided by the Committee on the Elimination of Discrimination Against Women.[112] Alternatively, Tanzania can follow the Zimbabwe Refugee Act approach[113] by simply adopting the UN and OAU Conventions and annexing all relevant international instruments to make them part of the law.

The express acknowledgement of the rights and protection of refugees in the refugee legislation is vital for two reasons. First, by bringing the relevant domestic law into conformity with the internationally recognized standards of human rights and refugees, a state achieves uniformity and consistency in the way it treats to refugees. Second, it helps raise public awareness that refugees have rights both as individuals and refugees.[114] Most Tanzanians do not know that refugees have rights, including an entitlement to protection from both physical as well as sexual violence.[115] A law that imposes obligations on refugees without describing any of their rights reinforces this lack of awareness and sends the message that refugees are bad people. Because the host country typically incurs significant costs in housing and caring for refugees, this message compounds the usual bitterness and hatred local people feel toward refugees.[116] The consequences of such hostility range from indifference to violation of refugee rights, including, for example, the rape of refugee women by local people and local military personnel.[117]

The law should comprehensively provide for the rights of refugees, particularly economic rights. This will trigger economic measures from intergovernmental and non-governmental organizations that offer financing for small enterprise businesses. Problems like prostitution and sexual exploitation will be reduced because of the availability of alternative income-generating opportunities.[118] Likewise, rape cases will be reduced because the refugee popu-

---

111. CEDAW, *supra* note 74, at art. 2, 1249 U.N.T.S. at 16.

112. *Report of the Committee on the Elimination of Discrimination Against Women, Eleventh Session*, U.N. GAOR, 47th Sess., Supp. No. 38, para. 6, U.N. Doc. A/47/38 (1992).

113. *See supra* notes 84–85 and accompanying text.

114. Throughout Africa, "many key officials dealing with refugees had very little knowledge of the rights of refugees." Lawyers Committee, *supra* note 66, at 27.

115. *See* SEEKING PROTECTION, *supra* note 18, at 55.

116. *See* Chris McGreal, *supra* note 105. The big influx of refugees have led to food shortages in areas neighboring the refugee camps due to high demand from refugees who buy food in order to supplement their diet. *See id.*

117. *See* SEEKING PROTECTION, *supra* note 18, at 39.

118. *See supra* note 19 and accompanying text.

lation will start thinking of a possible future, instead of dwelling in hopelessness which, coupled with the usual idleness of camp life, particularly for male refugees, leads to violence against women.[119]

Conclusion

Refugees living in Tanzania deserve adequate protection under the law. They are a minority group with no right to vote in the host country and thus have no representation in Parliament. As such, refugees in Tanzania depend on the government's benevolence and willingness to reduce strife in the camps. The government should demonstrate its commitment to refugees by incorporating relevant international human rights standards into national refugee law. Such a law would provide legal support for various measures taken to implement the rights of refugees and ensure their protection. The law will enable human rights NGOs, UNHCR, and other interested groups to implement financial assistance programs. Male refugees will have a future to look forward to if development programs are available to them. This will reduce the idleness and frustrations that contributed to violence against refugee women. Together with education and implementation of UNHCR guidelines, these measures will help to shield refugee women from sexual violence.

Long-term solutions for refugee women, children, and men will never be found in camps where food, water, and firewood are scarce and opportunities for employment are severely limited. The ultimate solution to these problems lies in the refugees' country of origin. The international community must therefore support justice by holding accountable those who allegedly committed atrocities and making the country peaceful to enable voluntary repatriation.

---

119. *See supra* notes 36–42 and accompanying text.

Sexual Violence Against Women in Tanzania: A Case Study on the 1998 Sexual Offences (Special Provision) Act No. 4

Scolastica Jullu

Introduction

In an effort to fulfill its obligation under international law and to provide the protection guaranteed under the Constitution of the United Republic of Tanzania,[1] the Parliament enacted the Sexual Offences (Special Provisions) Act[2] in 1998 to protect women from sexual violence.[3] Despite the new law, sexual violence[4] directed towards women has drastically increased.[5]

Law enforcement's failure to recognize sexual violence as a violation of women's human rights hinders implementation of the Act and international

---

1. TANZ. CONST. art. XXII §1 (1977) provides that "all people are born free, and are all equal," and art. XXII §2 provides that "every person is entitled to recognition and respect of his dignity."

2. The Sexual Offences (Special Provisions) Act (Act No. 4 of 1998) (Tanzania).

3. *Id.* at pmbl.

4. The term "sexual violence" is broad and may be used to describe rape by acquaintances or strangers, by authority figures (including husbands), incest, child sexual abuse, pornography, stalking, sexual harassment, and homicide. Most fundamentally, sexual violence describes the deliberate use of sex as a weapon to demonstrate power over and to inflict pain and humiliation upon another human being.

5. The extent of abuse increased from 40% in 1995 to 80% in May 2000. DAR ES SALAAM CITY COMMISSION, REPORT ON SAFE CITIES AND WOMEN SAFETY (2000).

human rights law. Discriminatory attitudes towards women and a shortage of personnel with expertise on sexual violence contributes to the poor administration of the Act.[6] Unless Tanzania improves implementation of the Act, its laudable goals of protecting women and children against sexual abuse will not be realized.

History of Legal Response to Sexual Violence in Tanzania

The traditional system of legal administration in pre-colonial Tanzania, as in most parts of Africa, was characterized by the absence of specialized institutions and personnel and a lack of a clear distinction between civil and criminal wrongs.[7] The primary goal of dispute settlement mechanisms was to restore the parties in conflict to a mutually agreeable position. These mechanisms were generally informal and involved direct or indirect participation of community members. Dispute settlement was accomplished through various forms of mediation, arbitration, and adjudication.[8]

When the British took over control from the Germans,[9] Tanganyika (now Tanzania) found itself a recipient of British law. The criminal law, codified in the Penal Code,[10] contained various statutes describing offences or providing special punishments for both common and customary laws. Chapter XV of the Code provided for offences against morality that are now called sexual offences, including rape, attempted rape, defilement, and statutory rape.[11] The offences were punishable for sentences ranging from thirty years to life imprisonment.

---

6. Although the focus of this essay is sexual violence as a women's rights issue and law reform occurred in the substantive law of sexual offences, it must be emphasized that legal change is only worthwhile when accompanied by changes in attitudes and practice. As a method of social control, criminal law has inherent limitations and should not be looked upon as the only means by which society can respond to social problems.

7. Twaib Fauz, Legal Profession in Tanzania: The Law and Practice 17 (1997).

8. While there is some literature that describes mediating and supportive functions assigned to certain persons in traditional settlement of disputes, there are yet no in-depth studies on the types of the settled disputes.

9. Tanganyika passed through four stages of legal status: it fell under de facto British administration in 1916 and become a protectorate and a mandatory territory under the League of Nations in 1920. It became a trust territory under the United Nations in 1946 and its dominion in 1961 and attained republic status in 1962.

10. Penal Code, Cap 16 (Tanz.).

Customary law existed in Tanganyika before colonialism and persists today. The British-imposed Courts Ordinance[12] of 1920 gave the native courts jurisdiction over criminal matters involving Africans.[13] Each court was to administer and enforce customary law so far as it was applicable, not repugnant to natural justice and morality,[14] and not in conflict with the provision of any law in force in the territory. Under these native courts, traditional tribunals were created to deal with rape and defilement cases. This system was a form of patriarchal natural justice where the concerns of female victims could not be thoroughly addressed because women had no right to speak in traditional courts. [15] Traditional courts punished those guilty of sexual assault by ordering perpetrators to pay cows or goats to the victim or her family as compensation.[16] Customary law allowing victims to settle their disputes out of court hindered laws governing sexual offences. Many people considered customary law to be effective, faster, and easier to access than court procedures that were seen as corrupt and staffed with inexperienced police officers who were unable to deal with sexual violence cases.[17]

---

11. *Id.* §§130, 132 and 136.

12. Courts Ordinance, (Act No. 6 of 1920) (Tanganyika).

13. As part of British indirect rule, the applicable laws in its colonies (Tanganyika being no exception) were divided into two systems. The indigenous population was governed by African customary law, which was administered in native courts. The native courts operated outside the profession of the judiciary. At the lowest level, African chiefs under the control of lay administrative officers within the colonial administration presided over these courts. The other system was established mainly for Europeans and their courts were presided over by qualified magistrates and judges.

14. §9 of JALO stated that "in all cases, civil and criminal to which person subjected to native and customs, every court shall be guided by native law and customs so far as it is applicable…and shall decide all such cases according to substantial justice without undue regard to technicalities of procedure and undue delay."

15. J.S.R. COLE & W. N. DENISON, TANGANYIKA: THE DEVELOPMENT OF ITS LAWS AND CONSTITUTION, 130 (1964).

16. In many cases, the offender was asked to marry the girl after compensating the victim's family. In some tribes like the Chagga of Northern Tanzania and the Sukuma of the Lake region, rape was the recognizable form of marriage respected at that time.

17. People resort to customary dispute settlement due to the bureaucratic nature of the legal system in dealing with sexual violence cases. Customary method is believed to be quicker in solving various disputes than courts of law. Lack of police posts in various wards associated with lack of medical facilities and transport are the main factors that contribute in resorting for customary disputes resolution. In many cases women look to non-litigation community based mediation and counseling to settle sexual disputes. Mediation and counseling is working well in some areas, in other areas such alternatives leave women vul-

After independence, Tanzania developed its own Constitution.[18] Although the Constitution does not specifically enumerate the rights of women, the founding provisions discuss the values of human dignity, freedom, equality,[19] privacy, and personal security.[20] The Constitution promotes equality in the country's value system and protects the dignity, life, and personal liberty of all individuals. Advocates have successfully used the Constitution to address violence against women and redress inequalities.[21]

Tanzania amended inherited colonial criminal laws to suit local circumstances and to reflect its own legal system. The Penal Code contains Tanzania's criminal law as it did under the colonial regime, and most of the provisions dealing with offences against morality remain the same.[22] In declaring certain types of behavior to be criminal, legislation plays a crucial role in the development and maintenance of community attitudes and expectations and represents a moral denunciation of unacceptable conduct.

Sexual Offences Act as a Human Rights Document

As a signatory to various regional and international human rights instruments, Tanzania has a responsibility to combat sexual violence and violence against women in general.[23] Sexual violence contravenes the right to personal

---

nerable to other serious forms of sexual violence as local leaders do not have power to enforce their judgments. *See* Dr. Mtengeti Migiro, Customary Law as a Hindrance to Criminal Prosecution, Discussion Paper with Tanzania Media Women Association and Sexual Offences Draft Bill Conducted on May 2, 1998.

18. In April 1964, Tanganyika and Zanzibar united and became one country called Tanzania, and in 1977 the political parties also united and the Union constitution was made in the same year but Zanzibar has its own Constitution.

19. The Constitution provides that "All human beings are born free, and all are equal." Tanz. Const. art. XXII (1977).

20. *Id.* at art. XVI.

21. For an example, *see* Bi Hawa Mohamed v. Ally Seif, Civil Appeal No. 9 of 1983 (Unreported).

22. *See* Penal Code, Cap. 16 (Tanzania).

23. For a brief discussion of how sexual violence violates international human rights law, *see* Introduction to Violence Against Women and International Human Rights at pages xx–xxx, *infra.*; *see generally* Human Rights of Women: National and International Perspective 143 (Rebecca Cook ed., 1994).

integrity, right to life,[24] right not to be subjected to torture or cruel inhuman degrading treatment,[25] right to freedom and security of persons,[26] the right to choose and form a family,[27] and the right to enjoy the best attainable state of physical and mental health.[28] The Tanzanian Constitution also provides for those rights, giving further protection for women against sexual violence.[29]

In March 1998, the Sexual Offences (Special Provision) Act replaced the existing rape law in Tanzania.[30] The ultimate goal of the Act was to enhance government efforts to protect women and children from sexual violence, and to promote the integrity, dignity, liberty, and security of women.[31] The enactment of the Sexual Offences Act is a step toward ensuring that women have

---

24. UDHR Art. 3, ICCPR Art. 6 (1), African Charter Art. 5. Sexual violence enforces a restricted lifestyle on all women. The threat of an attack causes females to limit their behavior and activities throughout their lives. Many women feel obliged to conceal their own sexual abuse, and some women continue to live in violent relations out of fear of being cut off from family or community support. A woman may also feel that her inability to avoid sexual abuse makes her inadequate, deserving of abuse or powerless to escape to it. *See* TANZANIA MEDIA WOMEN ASSOCIATION, WOMEN AND SEXUAL VIOLENCE (Seminar paper presented to a Media Workshop on June 22, 1999).

25. UDHR art. 5, ICCPR art. 7, African Charter art. 5. Rape, like torture, is a purposeful behavior intentionally perpetrated to keep women in a subordinated position and deny them the right to participate in society. Just as with torture, rape is committed for specific purposes including punishment, intimidation, and diminution of women's personalities.

26. ICCPR art. 9, UDHR art. 3, African Charter art. 6.

27. ICCPR art. 23, CEDAW art. 16, African Charter.

28. African Charter Art. 16(1). Victims of rape suffer depression, stress, anxiety, trauma, schizophrenia, and other mental illnesses. The physical health effects range from cuts and bruises inflicted in the violence, to transmission of STDs including HIV/AIDS. Sometimes a woman's whole reproductive system will be complete destroyed, especially after gang rape.

29. The international human rights of women discussed in this section derived from international human rights instruments that have been signed and ratified by the government of Tanzania. Tanzania is not, however, party to Convention against Torture and Other Cruel, Inhuman or Degrading Treatment or Punishment (1987).

30. Sexual Offences (Special Provisions) Act (Act No. 4 of 1998) (Tanzania). The emergence of female non-governmental organizations that championed the rights of women and children contributed to the enactment of Sexual Offences Act. These organizations prepared the sexual offences bill and submitted it to the Minister for Community Development and Children affairs.

31. *Id.* at pmbl. The Act does much to protect the interests of children, who are particularly vulnerable to abuse. A full examination of its real implications for children ought to be undertaken but that is beyond the scope of this paper.

access to legal justice once their rights have been violated. The major imped-iment to realizing this goal is only in small part the law itself and more im-portantly, the implementation of the law by the police and the judiciary. Tan-zania must have a clear mechanism and coordinated effort to ensure proper enforcement of the Act.

Defining Sexual Offenses

Under the new legislation either a male or female can be classified as a vic-tim or an offender, except in rape cases where the offender is always a man. With this change, legislative drafters intended to remove the stigmatization of female victims and create equitable provisions covering both sexes. The sig-nificance of this change is questionable however; it has more theoretical than practical meaning. It provides some consistency of labeling and may serve to protect the Act from constitutional challenge. Although the majority of sex-ual assault cases involve male perpetrators and female victims, there may be some educational value in the message that men can be victimized in a simi-lar way.

Section 130 of the Penal Code defines rape as a male person having sex with a girl or a woman without her consent, or when her consent is obtained by use of force, threat, or intimidation, including putting a woman in fear of death;[32] when a woman is of unsound mind or in a state of intoxication in-duced by drugs administered by the man;[33] or when the man knows that he is not her husband but the woman has been made to believe him to be her law-ful husband.[34] Unlike in the past, the new Act mentions groups of people who can commit rape. The Act includes persons in position of authority who take advantage of their positions to commit rape: staffs of remand homes and places of custody established by law,[35] doctors and hospital staff,[36] traditional healers who rape girls and women for healing purposes,[37] and religious lead-ers who rape women and girls under the pretense of blessing them.[38]

---

32. Penal Code, Cap. 16 (Tanzania) § 130(2) (b) (as amended by the Sexual Offences (Special Provisions) Act (Act No. 4 of 1998)).

33. Section 130(2)(c) of the Penal Code as amended by Act No. 4 of 1998.

34. *Id.* §130 (2) (d).

35. *Id.* §130 (3) (b).

36. *Id.* §130 (3) (c).

37. *Id.* §130 (3) (d).

38. *Id.* §130 (3) (e).

Penetration as Proof to Rape Cases

Under the 1998 law, the state needs to prove only slight penetration of the vagina by the penis.[39] The requirement of slight penetration, however, excludes other forms of sexual assault, such as insertion of objects (for example bottles, sticks, or hands), anal rape, fellatio, and cunnilingus that result in similar and sometimes greater trauma and injury to women.[40] The Act classifies such sexual assaults as secondary indecent assaults rather than principal assaults. Including all acts of sexual violence in the definition of rape could prevent indecent assaults from receiving lighter sentences.[41]

Consent of Victim to Intercourse

The new law removed the requirement that the victim prove she physically resisted sexual intercourse. Section 130(4)(b) of the Penal Code provides that "evidence of resistance such as physical injuries to the body is not necessary to prove that sexual intercourse took place without consent." Although this provision removed the requirement of proof of injury, most courts still require such proof in the form of scars, bruises, and injury to the victim or offender. Rape is the only offence in which the complicity of the victim becomes a relevant consideration in the trial and punishment of the offender.

Marital Rape

The new law exempts husbands from rape prosecution.[42] The Act does not recognize marital rape, and some people argue that husbands, by virtue of

---

39. Section 130 (4)(a) provides that "For the purposes of proving the offence of rape penetration however slight is sufficient to constitute the sexual intercourse necessary to the offence." *Id.* § 130 (4)(a).

40. Kathryn Ross, *An Examination of South African Rape Law*, in WOMEN, RAPE AND VIOLENCE IN SOUTH AFRICA 8 (Cape Town Community Law Center, 1993).

41. ASIA AND PACIFIC WOMEN'S RESOURCE AND ACTION SERIES: LAW 30.

42. While the Sexual Offences bill was before Parliament, the provision prohibiting marital rape was included, but the following discussion resulted in removal of the provision: "Now the law won't interfere with our relationship with our wives by detecting the manner of having sexual intercourse, Honorable Speaker! It must be noted that our customs allow rape for purposes of getting a wife. If marital rape provision becomes a law, this Parliament will be acting contrary to our ancestors. We shouldn't forget that we members of Parliament are the leading rapists." "No we don't rape, we simply undertake the process of reproduction." Due to the controversy, Parliament eliminated the provision prohibiting marital rape.

paying bride-price, have a legal right to have unlimited sexual access to their wives. At the time of marriage, brides are told that if the husband enters the bedroom the wife must obey him. It is believed that the husband has the right to have sexual intercourse at any time, making marital rape a non-issue.[43]

Statutory Rape

The new law amended the statutory rape law by including a provision that a girl under eighteen is not capable of consenting to sexual intercourse unless she is married to the man and they have not separated.[44] For an offender under the age of eighteen, the maximum penalty for having unlawful sexual intercourse with a girl below eighteen is ten years imprisonment with corporal punishment and payment of compensation.[45] For those over eighteen who commit statutory rape, the sentence is thirty years to life.[46]

Problems with Enforcement of the Act

Limited Jurisdiction

Primary courts in Tanzania are the lowest courts. They are accessible to the people and have jurisdiction over matters related to customary law and minor criminal offences. Given their accessibility, primary courts could be effective in dealing with sexual offences if given the power to adjudicate rape cases. The legislation uses language that hinders the application of the Act by magistrates who are not conversant with the English language. In order for the Act to be effectively applied, it must be translated to Swahili, and these local courts must be given permission to apply the Act. The primary courts need guidelines to explain how the Act should be applied. Otherwise, the spirit of the Act will be undermined by primary courts that continue to adjudicate rape cases according to customary law.[47]

43. *See generally* OEF INTERNATIONAL, EMPOWERMENT AND THE LAW 104 (Margaret Schuler ed., 1986).
44. Penal Code, Cap. 16 (Tanzania) §130(2) (e) (as amended by the Sexual Offences (Special Provisions) Act (Act No. 4 of 1998)).
45. *Id.* §138 (a).
46. *Id.* §130 (3).
47. It must be noted that primary courts have power of solving rape and defilement cases customarily by applying customs applicable to its jurisdiction. The government requires abolishing the application of customary laws in rape and defilement cases by extending the application of the Sexual Offences Act to primary courts. It is time now for the primary courts to improve its performance by employing graduates to serve as magistrates

Victims' Access to Courts

Some areas of Tanzania lack police forces and courts to deal with cases of rape and sexual violence.[48] Lack of transportation and medical services leave victims with little support and no legal recourse. Given the time sensitive nature of much medical evidence in sexual assault cases and the trauma that accompanies such abuse, delays can be devastating to the victim and the prosecution. For the victim of sexual abuse, obtaining justice often means hours of travel, hours of waiting for attention, and unsympathetic treatment from police and medical personnel. Even when women travel to the appropriate court, they may be unable to obtain relief. Clerks in some courts are not even aware of the passage of new sexual offences law.[49] Lack of medical services, legal aid services, and police posts often make victims resort to customary dispute resolution, which is quicker but more discriminatory toward women.

Police Performance

The greatest obstacle to the effective implementation of the legislation is the police, many of whom do not know the law despite efforts to educate them. The police force must take steps to ensure that all police officers at all stations and posts are systematically informed of the new Sexual Offences Act and of the police duty to enforce its provisions. The police response to rape and sexual violence cases needs to be improved and standardized to ensure that cases reported to police are prosecuted and the assailants punished accordingly.[50]

The basic police training in Tanzania resembles military training in that it instructs the police how to use firearms and how to work in specialized units. NGOs recently introduced trainings related to human rights protection. Police, however, still receive no specialized training regarding the handling of rape cases. There is no special police unit that deals with rape and defilement cases, making it difficult for victims to receive sympathetic treatment.[51]

---

rather than continuing with its tendency of employing unqualified magistrates who are not conversant with human rights issues.

48. Geographically the country has twenty regions within the mainland, and five regions in the Island of Zanzibar. Sexual Offences Act is not applicable to Zanzibar as the Island has its own legal system.

49. *See* HUMAN RIGHTS WATCH, GLOBAL REPORT ON WOMEN'S HUMAN RIGHTS 403 (1995).

50. *Id.* at 397.

51. *See* CONFRONTING SEXUAL ASSAULT: A DECADE OF LEGAL AND SOCIAL CHANGE 129

Unfortunately, the problems with the police are more complex than simple lack of human rights training and lack of familiarity with the Sexual Offences Act. Police officers frequently fail to act on rape complaints because they hold discriminatory views about women that undermine the proper functioning of the law. The police, who are the first official point of contact for victims of rape and sexual violence, decide if a case will be presented to the prosecutor. Whether a case makes it to court depends on how the police record a victim's charges,[52] and many rape cases are recorded inaccurately. If the police inaccurately record the particulars of a case, the case will be dismissed. Most cases reported to police stations are dismissed because the police designate the charges as unfounded,[53] the victim did not make a formal complaint, [54] the police dropped the charges, or the police failed to apprehend a suspect.[55]

Rape and Forensic Evidence

A major obstacle to successful rape investigation in Tanzania is the mandatory requirement that survivors submit to a medical examination at a government hospital. This requirement is unduly burdensome because medical staff frequently collect the medical evidence incorrectly, and lose valuable ev-

---

(Robert V. Julian & Renate M. Mohr eds.,1994).

52. Charges are formal complaints, usually in writing, made before the court of law alleging that a particular person has committed an offence.

53. The police may designate a case "unfounded" for either subjective or practical reasons. Sometimes the police do not believe that rape or attempted rape occurred. In other cases, police foresee that the prosecutor will have difficulty proceeding with the charges and designate the charges as unfounded.

54. In some instances, the victim refuses to make a formal complaint after relating the offence to the police. In other cases the victim decides to drop the charges at the police level before it goes to the prosecutor's office. A victim might change her mind and decide that she did not want to participate in the lengthy process required by a criminal prosecution. The probability of reliving the rape while testifying in the courtroom is a deterrent to many victims in the initial stages of police action.

55. Police failure to apprehend the suspect is a normal occurrence in Tanzania. There are some reports made by the police where the victim wanted to proceed with rape charges, but a failure to apprehend the offender renders further police action impossible. Sometimes the victim does not get a good enough look at the offender to give the police an adequate description, and in other instances, the offender will be apprehended, released on bail, and disappear. The absence of witnesses during the offence further complicates police attempts to apprehend the suspect.

idence. This is particularly troubling because medical evidence may be the only corroboration for a rape victim's testimony.

Forensic doctors, who lack training in the treatment of sexual assault victims, are often biased against women. This bias affects their investigatory procedures. Forensic doctors often fail to focus on critical evidence and appear to privilege virginity as evidence of rape. Despite the crucial role of medical evidence, women have enormous difficulty accessing official medical centers and obtaining sufficient admissible evidence of sexual assault.[56] Investigators often compound the problem by failing to inform women of the importance of being examined as soon as possible after being raped.

Prosecutorial Behavior

Prosecutors have wide discretion in deciding whether to prosecute a rape case. Prosecutors note that unless the woman agrees to the prosecution, it is unlikely that they will bring charges. A case may take five to ten years to reach its final determination, often leaving victims tired and disappointed. In addition, prosecutors and magistrates are often poorly remunerated, which makes them vulnerable to bribes by wealthy suspects. Courts often dismiss cases for want of prosecution or lack of evidence.

Corroboration Requirement

The law eliminated the requirement of corroborative evidence of sexual assault, such as cuts, torn clothing, or witnesses to an offence. Legally, prosecutors can now obtain a conviction without additional proof that a complainant's testimony is truthful. In practice, corroboration is still an important factor in obtaining a conviction. Evidence like vaginal bruising is still expected in any rape or defilement case. Despite the elimination of the corroboration requirement, the traditional view that sexual assault complaints may be motivated by personal factors such as vengeance or guilt still undermine women's credibility. False accusations, however, are no more likely in cases of rape than in any other case.

---

56. With widespread corruption, it is normal to find two contradictory medical reports in the victim's court file, which makes it difficult for magistrates to assess their authenticity. Police often fail to issue Police Form Number 3, which enables the victim to receive medical examination at a government owned hospital. In some cases, investigators (especially if they know the accused person) refused to issue a PF3 and told the women to come two days later or even a week—at which time critical evidence like blood and semen were lost.

Recommendations

Organize Special Training Programs

The Ministry of Justice and Constitutional Affairs should establish a special training unit to deal with rape cases. As is already the trend, each resident/district magistrate court should identify and train prosecutors who will specialize in cases of rape and sexual abuse. Likewise, primary courts should have trained public prosecutors.[57] Rape cases require courts to use exceptional care in assessing the credibility of a rape survivor, and these standards must be included in new legislation.

The Ministry should also educate judges and magistrates on women's human rights and human rights in general. Public prosecutors and police also need to receive training in human rights and women's rights in particular.[58] Trainings should encourage prosecutors to be sensitive in dealing with rape and other sexual violence cases. Police colleges must also extend curricula beyond arms training to include human rights courses. Police investigators handling sexual assault cases should specialize in such investigations and should be trained in the issues surrounding violence against women and the use of medical and forensic evidence. In addition, the police should handle rape cases as soon as possible to ensure that forensic evidence is not lost.

Medical schools and other medical training institutions should develop and make compulsory specialized curricula in clinical forensic medicine. A specialty in clinical forensic medicine, similar to that for forensic pathologists, should be developed and made available to those doctors who wish to concentrate in this area.

Include Prohibition of Marital Rape in the Act

To promote equality in marriage, new legislation or amendments to current legislation must include a prohibition on marital rape. Protecting a

---

57. The Chief justice should issue directives that will help in translating the new legislation and make it applicable to Primary Courts. Application of the legislation to the primary court will reduce the problem of transport and access to justice that are facing rural women.

58. For example, in South Africa, the development of specialized sexual offence courts staffed by trained professionals produced conviction rates almost 20% higher than other courts.

woman's right to sexual determination must start at the family level. Making husbands immune to rape prosecution violates international standards of equality in the family. Tanzania must enact an anti-marital rape provision to implement international human rights standards promoting equality in the family and protecting the family from violence.

Rehabilitate Offenders

Tanzania must reform its prison system to rehabilitate sexual assault offenders and ensure that they do not leave prison with similar attitudes towards women as when they entered. Under the current system, prison may even contribute to recidivism among perpetrators of rape crimes. Political actors need to make prison reform a priority on the national political agenda.

Assist Victims

Tanzania should make therapeutic and legal aid services available to rape victims. The availability of these services would encourage victims to report rape. The treatment of post-traumatic stress disorder demands specialization, and in Tanzania, there are no counseling services or legal aid services available to rape victims.[59] Social support, both within and outside of the family, aids in the process of recovery. Appropriate social support requires sensitivity, commitment, and a non-judgmental attitude regarding the victim's conduct.

Raise Awareness

Raising awareness and disseminating information to the general public will play a great role in engendering respect for women's human rights. Government, the private sector, and non-governmental organizations should coordinate their activities and help to collect and disseminate information about sexual assault and women's human rights generally.[60] The Ministry of Educa-

59. Legal aid service is available in civil matters that do not involve the police force.

60. A national directory of non-governmental, governmental, and private sector services available to women and children victims of rape should be developed and information be distributed to medical officers, hospitals, health care facilities, police stations, and magistrates.

tion, in connection with non-governmental organizations[61] and religious leaders, must organize training programs to educate people regarding the effects of rape and other forms of sexual violence. Seminars, workshops, informal and formal talks, debates, public rallies, and school curricula focusing on human rights will promote awareness of the right to equality and freedom from sexual violence within Tanzanian society.

Abolish Customary Law Dispute Settlements

Because it privileges the position of men in society, customary law is a hindrance to women's human rights in Tanzania. The repeal of the Customary Law (Declaration) Order will help women to realize their freedom from all forms of violence. The government's silence regarding customary law settlement of sexual assault cases encourages underreporting of sexual offences. Redress through the formal court system must be readily available to victims who would otherwise pursue settlement of sexual assault outside of the court system. Unless Tanzania eliminates customary law as an avenue to resolve sexual assault cases, the Sexual Offenses Act will not succeed in its objectives, hindering the creation of a nation that respects women's human rights.

Conclusion

Eradicating myths about rape and defilement is an arduous task in a male-dominated society. New legislation alone cannot remedy the situation. The law is only as innovative as the individuals who use, interpret, and apply it. If victims do not report sexual assault, the pervasiveness of the offence remains cloaked in secrecy; victims are left without redress, and the perpetrators of the crime are not held accountable. The legal system must accept responsibility for improving victims' remedies and access to the legal system.

Communities must initiate public education campaigns to raise awareness about sexual violence. Public education that recognizes discriminatory laws, myths, and stereotypes helps to dispel them over time. Efforts of women's

---

61. NGOs have a critical role to play in terms of monitoring and reporting sexual violence as abuses of human rights, in vigorously promoting the rights of victims and prosecution of offenders, and in reminding the government and international agencies of their responsibilities within the context of UN policies and charters, and the plan of action of the relevant international conferences.

non-governmental organizations in raising the collective consciousness of the society have promoted women's human rights and led to important revisions in rape laws. Although these innovations have resulted in increased public awareness and legal and social advancements for women, they must be accompanied by strong advocacy to bring about further changes. Advocates must challenge discriminatory stereotypes that rely on women's inferiority and legitimate male authority. The progression from authority to violence is only a matter of degree.

Domestic Violence: Strategies for Combating Wife Battery in Uganda

Kulsum Wakabi

Introduction

Despite the lack of adequate documentation, a few surveys and numerous articles in the local media indicate that domestic violence is a serious problem in Uganda.[1] Domestic violence in general, and wife battery in particular, are especially prevalent in Ugandan society because they are seen as part of a marital relationship.[2] For instance, in Acholi, in northern Uganda, the estimated occurrence of violence is at 80 percent.[3] In a study of violence against women

---

1. There is still insufficient information and data on domestic violence because of problems such as unreported cases. Even where cases are reported they are not specifically broken down in terms of gender, frequency of occurrence, or even the manner in which these cases are handled. The problem of domestic violence is not unique to Uganda. Women all over the world are forced to endure years of violence perpetrated by their families, their communities and even by their states. Domestic violence is a universal problem that cuts across all cultures and is found in all nations of the world. For instance, in the United States, rape is committed every six minutes, in Peru, 70% of crimes reported to the police are of women beaten by their partners; in Thailand 50% of married women are beaten; in Ecuador, over 80% of the women interviewed have been beaten; in Brazil, 18,000 cases of battery were reported regularly; in Austria, 54% of all murders are committed in the family and 90% of the victims are women and children. Further, in the United States a woman is battered every 15 seconds, a level of violence that constitutes the largest cause of serious injury to women there. Lori Heise, *Crimes of Gender*, WORLD WATCH 14 (March–April 1989).

2. For instance, among the Bakiga tribe in Western Uganda, wife battery is estimated to occur in between 75–80% of the population. Letitia L.E.M. Mukasa-Kikonyogo, Case Study on Violence Against Women in the Family in Uganda 5 (1987). In Southern Uganda, as well as in Iteso, Busoga, and Lango (parts of eastern and northeastern Uganda), wife battery is estimated to occur in 75% of the community. *Id.* at 5; *see* MINISTRY OF FINANCE AND ECONOMIC PLANNING, UGANDA'S POPULATION AND HOUSING CENSUS STATISTICS (1991).

3. Mukasa-Kikonyogo, *supra* note at 2.

in Kampala District, 81 percent of the 80 women interviewed had suffered violence at the hands of their husbands or male friends.[4]

In this essay, I examine the causes of domestic violence in Uganda and the legal response and mechanisms presently available to address this problem. I argue that domestic violence is a significant problem in Uganda that is not being addressed by the existing legal system. I also argue that the Ugandan government has a duty to act affirmatively both under its national laws and international obligations to eliminate domestic violence. Finally, I will set out proposals for law reform within the existing legal structure that could help to combat domestic violence.[5]

The Causes of and Factors Contributing to Domestic Violence in Uganda

Before proposing legal strategies to address domestic violence, it is useful to examine the factors that cause or contribute to the occurrence of domestic violence in Uganda. These factors have negatively affected the legal system that, in turn, has served to perpetuate domestic violence by forcing victims to remain in abusive relationships.

Political Strife

Violence caused by political strife has a direct effect on the incidence of violence against women in general and domestic violence in particular.[6] The United Nations Special Rapporteur on Violence Against Women has observed

---

4. *Id.*

5. However, it is important to keep in mind that the problem of domestic violence is a complex one and legal remedies alone without other supportive measures and policies will not combat domestic violence. Strategies to eliminate domestic violence should not only be legal, but should be multi-dimensional because domestic violence does not arise out of a single cause but is a phenomena so deeply ingrained in all sectors and institutions within society that legal remedies alone may not suffice. *U.N. Center for Social Development and humanitarian Affairs, Report on Violence Against Women in the Family, 1989*, at 74, U.N. Doc. ST/CSDHA/2, U.N. Sales No. E.89.IV.5 (1989) [hereinafter *U.N. Report 1989*].

6. Preliminary Report submitted by the Special Rapporteur on Violence Against Women, its Causes and Consequences, U.N. ESCOR, 15th Sess., Agenda Item 11(a) at 17, U.N. Doc. E/CN. 4/1995/42 (1994) [hereinafter U.N. Preliminary Report 1994].

that patterns of social conflict within the larger society often affect the incidence of violence against women.[7] Militarization and extreme levels of repression have been found to increase violence against women.[8] Uganda has endured a troubled and volatile political history. Since independence, Uganda has had seven different governments within a twenty-five year period, four of which took power through the force of arms.[9] Throughout this period Uganda has used violence and terror as a means of conflict resolution.[10] Such a history of political violence and chaos has undeniably taken its toll on Ugandan society, breeding a culture of violence, accepting the use of force to resolve disputes even within the family, and contributing to the incidence of domestic violence.

Culture

Cultural socialization and traditional practices have been significant factors in relegating women to an inferior position as compared to men, leaving them vulnerable to abuse.[11] According to many cultural beliefs and stereotypes, women are not considered to be male equals, but subordinates who must obey their husbands. An attempt by women to assert themselves may be seen as a threat to the existing power relations and may be suppressed through physical violence or psychological means.[12]

In many societies in Uganda, wife battery is permissible and is considered to be an inherent part of a marital relationship. Major tribes in Uganda such as the Bakiga, Iteso, Soga, Langi, Acholi, Baganda, and Karamajong deem wife

7. *Id.*

8. *Id.*

9. These occurred in 1962 at Independence, in 1967 under Milton Obote, in 1971 under Idi Amin, 1979 under the Uganda National Liberation Front, 1980 under Yusuf Lule, in 1980 under Milton Obote, and in 1986 under Yoweri Museveni. *See* E.A. Brett, The Military and Democratic Transition in Uganda, in *From Chaos to Order: The Politics of Constitution-Making in Uganda* 78 (Holger Bernt Hansen & Michael Twaddle eds., 1995).

10. *Id.* at 78.

11. *See generally* U.N. Report 1989, *supra* note at 5 .

12. *Id.* at 31. In order to preserve the male dominant power relation within the family, Ugandan women are taught to behave as a "good wife:" "A good wife endures many years of drudgery, hardships, but never complains, otherwise she is bad. She must have the ability and stamina to endure physical and emotional pain…When her husband disciplines her occasionally, she must be grateful; a good beating is a symbol of love, it shows that a man cares." Hope Bagyendera Chigudu, *Characteristics of a Good Wife*, ARISE, Oct.–Dec. 1991, *quoted in* Victoria Mwaka et al, Women in Uganda: A Profile, 12 (1994).

battery acceptable so long as it does not cause serious harm, injury, or death.[13] Wife battery is not only a form of chastisement or punishment, but a way of reminding the woman who is "boss" so that she is not tempted to disobey the man in the future (preventive beating).[14] In one case, a husband who decapitated his wife with an axe was reported to have made the statement, "What do you do if your cow becomes unruly?"[15] Such cultural attitudes, instilled through socialization, increase the incidence of domestic violence by condoning the behavior of violent husbands.

The practice of bridewealth also perpetuates the inferior status of women. Although bridewealth gifts are supposed to be tokens of appreciation given by the man's family to the woman's parents, they have often been regarded as a price or payment for the woman.[16] Bridewealth encourages male domination and control and reinforces the concept of women as property, possession, or chattel of men. As such, it perpetuates violence against women.[17]

Similarly, the cultural practice of polygamy increases the incidence of domestic violence because of jealousies, rivalries, constant suspicion, and feelings of insecurity among multiple wives.[18] Any attempt to sever the relation-

---

13. For example, among the Karamojong in northeastern Uganda, it is customary for women to physically resist the advances of their partners before sexual intercourse on the wedding night such that the man has to physically subjugate the woman and overpower her before he can have intercourse as a demonstration of his manhood. Mukasa-Kikonyogo, *supra* note 2, at 5.

14. Some women describe reasons for wife beating: He didn't want me to argue with him or correct him when he did something wrong. He was drunk and wants to fight whenever he is drunk. He wanted sex whenever he was drunk and I did not. He suspected I was unfaithful. I asked for money for sugar. He loved another girl and no longer wanted me. I went for a meeting without his consent. He and his relatives kept claiming I was barren. *Id.*

15. Othin, Husband Kills Bride, The New Vision (Kampala, Uganda), Jan. 14, 1993, at 12.

16. Most cultures in Uganda demand that bridewealth be paid to male relatives of the women where women are exchanged for cattle, money, meat, sugar, and salt. Mwaka, *supra* note 12, at 109.

17. For instance, during an interview, one woman stated that she had been married for five years, during which time she had constantly been battered by her husband. When she went back to her family, she was rebuked by her father because her husband threatened to claim the bridewealth he had paid for her. Under severe duress she was forced to go back to her husband. She has been hospitalized several times since and her body is visibly mutilated. It's interesting to note that the husband always pays all the hospital bills and takes her back home only to continue the cycle of violence. *Id.*

18. *See generally* Hope Mwesigye & Yeri Wakabi, Violence Against Women in Uganda:

ship with their polygamous husbands is usually met by violence.[19] In other cases, men resort to beating up their older wives to intimidate them and force them out of their home to make room for a new wife.[20]

Poverty

Although domestic violence exists in all classes of society, whether rich or poor, it is particularly prevalent among poor women living in rural areas and urban slums.[21] Despite statutory laws that give women the right to own property, customary practices keep women economically and financially dependent on men, making them vulnerable to acts of violence.[22] Most women in Uganda are therefore forced to depend on men as breadwinners. Women who are financially dependent on men often have nowhere to go and have no means of supporting themselves or their children and are thus forced to endure domestic violence. Batterers also exert control over their partners through financial coercion. It is not uncommon for a man to refuse to let his wife work, because this would mean giving up power and control to the woman. [23]

Religion

Certain religious beliefs also contribute to the prevalence of domestic violence. Most religions preach or emphasize the sanctity of marriage. For instance, the Catholic Church does not allow divorce.[24] Christianity seems to

---

A Comparative Study on Rural and Urban Settings 17–21 (Uganda Gender Resource Center 1993).

19. Mukasa-Kikonyogo, *supra* note 2 , at 6.

20. *Id.*

21. *Id.* at 5.

22. Irene Bazalaki, Wife Battery, ARISE, June 1993 [hereinafter Bazalaki Wife Battery]. In this article, a woman who had been constantly beaten by her husband said, "There is no more love between me and my husband. Probably that is why he beats me. I cannot go anywhere else because I am old now. He is the sole breadwinner; and what would happen to my young children if I went away?"

23. *See generally* Mwesigye & Wakabi, *supra* note 18, at 12–14.

24. *Id.* Reported a story where Imat Okot, a devoted Catholic woman, who believes that divorce is a greater sin than her husband's harshness is willing to preserve her marriage. She stated that her children were entitled to a father at whatever cost, and that she had no right to deny them that.

foster the notion that women are subordinate to men because of the "rib" theory, i.e., that God made woman of a man's rib and that women are therefore inferior to men.[25]

The Islamic religion encourages women to obey men; any act of disobedience is punishable by the husband. In Islam, men act as guardians of women. Women are dependent on their husbands or the nearest male kin.[26] This dependence leaves women vulnerable to domestic abuse because they are often not able to fend for themselves financially should they opt to divorce their husbands. Further, although the concept of divorce is acceptable in Islam, Islamic teachings discourage it.[27]

Just as religion frowns upon divorce, Ugandan culture too regards divorce as something undesirable. There is a stigma attached to divorced or unmarried women.[28] Women and society, in general, tend to regard divorced or unmarried women as failures.[29] As a result, women tend to endure beatings, harassment, and torture at the hands of their husbands for the sake of staying married.

Alcoholism

A debate exists as to the relationship between alcoholism and domestic violence.[30] Research has shown that excessive consumption of alcohol and drugs can contribute to increased incidents of domestic violence.[31] Arguing alco-

---

25. For a historical perspective on the subordination of women, *see* Augustine Rössler, Inferiority of Body and Soul, in Gender Identities in American Catholicism 56 (Paula Kane et al eds., 2001). Since the 1960s, however, this attitude has yielded ground to a view of gender equality publicly espoused by the church. Some authors feel that the stance is ineffective at discouraging domestic violence and other gender-weighted issues. *See* Christine E. Gudorf, *Encountering the Other: The Modern Papacy on Women, in* CHANGE IN OFFICIAL CATHOLIC MORAL TEACHINGS 269 (Charles E. Curran ed., 2003).

26. Asma Mohammed Abdel Halim, *Challenges to Women's International Human Rights in Sudan*, in HUMAN RIGHTS OF WOMEN 405 (Rebecca Cook ed., 1994).

27. *See generally* YUSUF QARADAWI, THE LAWFUL AND THE PROHIBITED IN ISLAM 202–7 (1994).

28. Mukasa-Kikonyogo, *supra* note 2 , at 14.

29. *Id.*

30. Compare Jerry P. Flanzer, *Alcohol and Other Drugs Are Key Causal Agents of Violence*, in CURRENT CONTROVERSIES IN FAMILY VIOLENCE 171 (Richard J. Gelles & Donileen R. Loseke eds., 1993) with Richard J. Gelles, Alcohol and Other Drugs Are Associated with Violence—They Are Not Its Cause, in Current Controversies, *supra*, at 182.

31. In a U.N. study of 60 battered women, 93% of the violent incidents were reported to have occurred after consumption of alcohol. U.N. Report, 1994, *supra* note 6 , at 28. In

holism is the cause of domestic violence, some people believe that curing alcoholism will stop domestic violence. Solving substance abuse without addressing other factors, however, is not enough to stop domestic violence. With poverty and high rates of unemployment contributing to a high rate of alcoholism, men drink for a variety of reasons. Then, with alcohol-lowered inhibitions and alcohol inflamed tempers, they beat their wives to exert their power, as described above.

Inadequacies of the Present Legal Remedies

Currently, both the laws and the legal structures lack sufficient safeguards to protect women from domestic violence. By failing to adequately address domestic violence, the Ugandan legal system has contributed to the problem. Present laws are flawed, rendering them inadequate as a means of redress. This, coupled with attitudes held by judicial and law enforcement officials, discourages battered women from seeking protection.[32] The following section will examine the attitudes of judicial and law enforcement officers who are responsible for implementing the law and assess how the law itself falls short in addressing domestic violence cases.

Attitudes of Judicial and Law Enforcement Officers

Judicial and law enforcement officers have been unresponsive and unsympathetic towards victims of domestic violence. For instance, one Ugandan High Court Judge said, "It is better for one person to suffer than risk a complete breakdown of family life."[33] One male member of parliament in Uganda remarked on the subject of wife beating, "Wife beating my foot! Please stop wasting our time as we intend to discuss development issues of our country. We should have something better to discuss."[34] Such remarks made by people

---

Uganda too, studies on the causes of domestic violence have revealed that drunkenness and alcohol consumption is a contributing factor in the increase in domestic violence. MWESIGYE & WAKABI, *supra* note 18, at 8. *See also* MUKASA-KIKONYOGO, *supra* note 2, at 8.

32. Judicial officials here includes Resistance committee court members, magistrates and judges; police officials includes police, prosecutors and, for the purpose of this paper, even people who intervene to preserve the peace for instance clan elders, church leaders, and legislators. *See* Mwesigye & Wakabi, *supra* note 18, at 8.

33. Mukasa-Kikonyogo, *supra* note 2 , at 22.

34. Yeri Wakabi, Domestic Violence in Uganda: Does It Make a Difference Where One

occupying some of the highest government offices demonstrate that these attitudes are pervasive in Ugandan society and that many people do not take domestic violence seriously.

The police, too, have been known to encourage battered wives to drop charges and opt for reconciliation.[35] This preference for reconciliation is not peculiar to the police. Resistance Committees, clan elders, and church leaders favor reconciliation and preservation of the family.[36] Cultural and religious beliefs, traditional notions of sanctity and privacy of the home, and notions of male superiority have resulted in this preference for reconciliation.

These traditional gender biases are so embedded in the social structure that domestic violence is not regarded as a violation of women's rights or as a crime deserving serious attention. Because domestic violence is not seen as a crime, there is a pervasive permissive attitude, a tolerance of wife abusers both at a conscious and subconscious level throughout the legal system. Thus, domestic violence is commonly regarded as a private matter with which the state or other outsiders should not interfere. As a result, judicial and law enforcement officers are reluctant to investigate, prosecute, and punish domestic violence.[37] Judges have a lot of discretion in sentencing and imposing fines. Judges often impose very lenient sentences, such as a small fine or warning, on perpetrators of domestic violence. Courts typically do not impose prison sentences unless the assault was very serious or resulted in death. The police and judiciary do not like to intervene in such cases and favor mediation over prosecution or imprisonment. The police and the judiciary send out a message to the battered woman that such acts are acceptable, forcing her to remain in the abusive relationship.

Institution of Criminal Prosecutions

At present, Uganda has no specific legislation addressing domestic violence. There are, however, general criminal laws against threatening violence,

Lives? 16 (1993) (unpublished paper delivered at a conference on Urban and Community Development in Africa).

35. Interview with FIDA client in Uganda Association of Women Lawyers Legal Aid Clinic in Kampala (Jan. 1995); *see also* U.N. Report 1989, *supra* note 5, at 56.

36. *See generally* Action for Development (ACFODE) Survey, Highlights of Findings from Focus Group Discussion, Key Informant interviews with Mukono Town Council Community Members Women's and Men's Exclusive Interviews (1993).

37. *See also* U.N. Report 1989 *supra* note 5 , at 56–57, 71–72.

common assault, assault occasioning bodily harm, grievous harm, affray, murder, and manslaughter.[38] In Uganda, however, it is not a crime to rape or sexually assault a woman to whom one is married and from whom one is not legally separated.[39] A woman is presumed to have consented to all sex with her husband at the time of marriage. The present scope of criminal law does not cover this form of domestic violence and is thus too narrow. Although the general provisions appear to offer sufficient protection for battered women, in practice, these laws do not provide an effective remedy to battered women. The implementation of these criminal provisions is severely crippled.[40]

Criminal laws, although gender neutral, can have a different impact on men and women. As described above, attitudes towards the role of women must change, because legal remedies have proved to be ineffective when there is a gap between the law and the commitment of judicial and law enforcement officers to utilize the law. A law on the books is meaningless unless it is enforced.

Prosecution and investigation of domestic violence cases is problematic. The battered woman is usually living or at least having contact with her abuser until the time of trial. It is not, therefore, uncommon for the victim to be threatened or sweet talked into withdrawing the charges against her abuser.[41] Many victims want the violence to end but do not want the abuser to be jailed or to suffer greatly. Imprisonment and fines affect not only the abuser, who usually is the breadwinner, but also the family as a whole. A battered woman's evidence forms the basis of the prosecution's case, and yet because the woman is dependent on the abuser financially and emotionally, she may not be willing to testify against her abuser. Wives are competent but not compellable witnesses. When the wife refuses to testify against her abuser, the police cannot

---

38. The Penal Code Act, Cap 106 §§ 74, 76, 182–83, 212, 227–28 (Uganda) (1978 reprint).

39. Uganda adopted the British Common Law System at the time of independence, which did not recognize marital rape. Though the British have changed their laws today, Uganda has not yet done so.

40. In addition to criminal proceedings, a battered woman has the right to institute proceedings under tort law and may claim damages for assault. However, where two people are married or living together and have had children together, compensation in form of damages may affect the family's financial resources to the detriment of the family as a whole. Further, the abuser may not have the money to pay. In addition, the battered woman most times cannot afford to pay for a civil suit which may be lengthy and time consuming, as well as costly.

41. Mukasa-Kikonyogo, *supra* note 2 , at 16–17.

force her to do so. This is another reason why, in dealing with domestic violence cases, the police tend to be reluctant to intervene.

Institution of Divorce or Separation Proceedings

Although divorce or separation proceedings appear to be a way for a battered woman to escape an abusive marital relationship, this is very rare in practice. The statutory divorce law governs only marriages solemnized in churches[42] and those contracted at the District Executive Secretary's office.[43] Under this statute, no person may be granted divorce merely on the grounds of cruelty. [44] Cruelty must be coupled with some other ground such as adultery, bigamy, or desertion. These other grounds are often difficult to establish, creating another hurdle for abused women seeking a divorce. [45]

The Customary Marriage (Registration) Decree governs marriages contracted under customary law, but it addresses neither the grounds for divorce nor the meaning of cruelty. [46] Customary marriages and their dissolution are governed by the customs and traditions under which they were performed. As discussed earlier, most customs and traditions in Uganda condone wife battery unless it becomes very serious. Therefore, here too, divorce is rarely a viable remedy and battered women remain bound in marriages that are oppressive and harmful to their health.

The Marriage and Divorce of Mohamadans Act governs marriages contracted under Islamic law. As it does in customary marriages, the Act neither lays down specific grounds for divorce nor mentions cruelty or wife battery anywhere in its provisions. Islamic norms pertaining to the dissolution of marriage are interpreted from the Koran. As discussed earlier, though Islam does not permit wife beating, it demands obedience from the wife and treats the woman as a ward under the control of man who has the right of chastisement.[47] As in other religions, divorce is generally disfavored in Islam and is supposed to be a last resort if the marriage has failed.[48] This law also fails to

---

42. Here, church means a licensed place of public worship under the Marriage Act.

43. The District Executive Secretary's office is an office designated by government to perform and license marriages.

44. The Divorce Act, Cap 215 (Uganda) (1906).

45. *Id.* §2(v).

46. *See* The Customary Marriage (Registration) Decree, Cap 213 §3(1) (Uganda) (1906).

47. *See* Yusuf Qaradawi, The Lawful and the Prohibited in Islam 205 (1994).

48. *Id.* at 207. Quotes the prophet Mohammed (SAW) as having said "Among lawful

offer a battered woman an adequate remedy, especially if she is a devout believer.[49]

Specific Domestic Violence Legislation

Parliament must enact specific domestic violence legislation to prevent and protect women from domestic violence. Advocates for specific criminal prohibitions of domestic violence argue that arrest, prosecution, and conviction with punishment sends out a clear message that society condemns the abuser's conduct and holds him personally responsible for the act.[50] Although criminalization is desirable, it does not take into account the tremendous influence of cultural, economic, and emotional factors that affect the victim, the abuser, and the actors in the legal system. In Uganda, where society is heavily influenced by tradition and the majority of women have not acquired sufficient political, economic, social, and cultural independence, bolstering enforcement of current criminal law and creating new civil legislation to provide specific remedies to victims will prove most effective.

Criminal Law

The primary problem with the criminal justice system is not the law itself, but the practice of trivializing domestic violence and treating it as an offense within the private sphere that does not warrant public intervention. Although there are criminal laws that seemingly offer protection to battered women, there is a gap between the law in theory and the law in practice. The government must direct its efforts toward closing this gap such that battered women who wish to prosecute their abusers face no attitudinal or structural obstacles in their pursuit of justice.

Since the police and law enforcement officers, such as resistance councils, in Uganda play a significant role in crime prevention and the maintenance of law and order in the community, training the government must ensure that programs discussing domestic violence constitute part of the curriculum in

---

things, divorce is most hated by Allah." *Id.*

49. A similar situation is faced by battered women who are devout Catholics.

50. *See* U.N. Preliminary Report 1994, *supra* note 6, at 30.

law enforcement or judicial training. Non-governmental organizations should also sponsor refresher training programs at regular intervals.[51]

The government, in consultation with NGOs, should also establish clear guidelines governing how domestic violence cases should be handled, investigated, and prosecuted. There should also be a requirement that these cases are recorded accurately, complete with all of the details that may assist in the prosecution. Such provisions ensure that police, prosecutors, and judges give domestic violence cases the attention that they deserve and allow the government and NGOs to keep track of the incidence of and actions taken in such cases. The police should also provide victims of domestic violence with information that will assist them in getting medical treatment, counseling, and other services.

Enactment of New Civil Legislation

A new form of legislation based on protection rather than retribution may be more familiar and attractive and result in less drastic consequences for the victim.[52] An ideal approach would be the enactment of flexible legislation that prevents and reduces recidivism while still accommodating the needs of the victim. In other words, the legislation should provide for, where necessary, the arrest and detention of the abuser in criminal cases and civil remedies, such as an injunction requiring the offender to stop battering.

Scope of Relationship to be Covered

Although this essay focuses on domestic violence as violence occurring between a husband and wife, that is not the only kind of violence that a woman

---

51. A good example of such training programs is the Musasa Project in Zimbabwe, which aims at raising awareness about violence against women within the legal system in Zimbabwe. This project has enjoyed considerable success. This Zimbabwean aims to raise the consciousness of the police through a series of workshops on the plight of battered women in an effort to change negative attitudes held by the police. Sheelagh Stewart, *Working the System: Sensitizing the Police to the Plight of Women in Zimbabwe, in* FREEDOM FROM VIOLENCE: WOMEN STRATEGIES FROM AROUND THE WORLD 160–67 (Margaret Shuler ed., 1992). Organizations such as such as FIDA (The Uganda Association of Women Lawyers), ACFODE (Action for Development) other Human Rights Organizations as well as the Ministry of Women should work on these programs.

52. Traditionally, any marital problems between the parties were reported to elders with a view to protecting or preventing further violence.

in a family suffers. Studies show that women are not only beaten by their husbands or male friends, but are also beaten by other relatives, *e.g.*, brothers-in-law, sisters-in-law, their husband's girlfriends, or their co-wives, and even by their step-children, usually with the approval of the husband.[53] Most families in Uganda consist of extended families and potentially polygamous relationships, and therefore any domestic violence legislation must cover a variety of familial relationships to afford women the greatest protection against violence.

Definition of Domestic Violence

The statute's definition of domestic violence should cover a broad range of acts by the offender, including physical and psychological harm, *e.g.*, common assault, assault occasioning physical bodily harm, grievous harm, wrongful confinement, threats, intimidation, coercion, stalking, destruction of property, forcible or unlawful entry, sexual violence, marital rape, bridewealth related violence, arson, and humiliating verbal abuse or acts intended to demean the woman or intended to cause psychological abuse.[54]

Persons Who May Make Complaints or Institute Proceedings

Battered women may not be in a position to make complaints or to institute proceedings against their abusers.[55] The law should allow other categories of people to initiate complaints on behalf of women who have been battered. These may be friends, relatives, resistance council members, health care providers, witnesses, or the police.

Remedies Available

Remedies available should include an *ex parte* temporary protection order when the offender immediately endangers the safety or welfare of the victim or any person assisting the victim. Such a remedy would protect the battered

---

53. *See generally* Mwesigye & Wakabi, *supra* note 18, and Mukasa-Kikonyogo, *supra* note 2.

54. *See, e.g.*, Women in Law and Development International, State Responses to Domestic Violence: Current Status and Needed Improvements 79 (1996).

55. In most civil cases, it is the person who has suffered harm who may institute proceedings except in cases of disability or death. However, in criminal cases, any person in the community can make complaints and the complaint can then be investigated by the police.

woman or any person assisting the battered woman. Long-term orders for protection should also be available to prohibit further attacks, threats, or undesirable conduct and to specifically order the abuser to stay away from the victim or persons assisting the victim. Remedies such as fines and orders for payment of medical and/or legal expenses incurred would deter the abuser from abusive acts and hold the abuser personally responsible for the consequences of his acts. Remedies such as temporary orders for child custody, visitation, child and other maintenance issues, counseling, or costs of temporary resettlement or accommodation of the victim and her children would prove invaluable. An order for the offender to vacate the dwelling premises and an order for arrest without warrant should be available when the offender disregards the protection order. These remedies should be available either alone or in combination with others depending on the circumstances of each case. Moreover, these remedies must be available in addition to and not exclusive of criminal action, such as prosecution of assault charges.

Other Recommendations

In addition to the enactment of new domestic violence legislation and the improvement and strengthening of the existing laws, the following are recommended:

1. Establishing a family court that will be able to deal exclusively with family issues, including domestic violence. The court should deal with these cases expeditiously.

2. Establishing coordinated social services such as shelters, counseling and support groups, and free legal services.

3. Introducing economic development programs for women such as microfinance programs to enable them to acquire economic independence.

4. Encouraging peaceful means of conflict resolution at all levels within society.

5. Encouraging and promoting policies that will promote higher education of women.

Conclusion

Domestic violence is a pervasive problem in Uganda. It is rooted in a culture characterized by violence as a means of conflict resolution, cultural socialization, and traditional practices that treat women as subordinates of men, lack of economic independence for women, and religious beliefs that preach obedience to men and foster notions of male superiority. In spite of this, however, there is no specific law dealing with this problem in Uganda. The present laws that could be used to deal with this problem are inadequate and do not address the special circumstances and problems that a battered wife faces. Uganda has a duty both under its new constitution and under its international commitments to rectify this situation by enacting a new law that will adequately address the problem of domestic violence, strengthen and improve the justice system, and make the necessary amendments to civil remedies such as divorce laws. Uganda must also modify criminal and civil procedures by making them more accessible, cheap, easier to use, and less cumbersome to enable battered women to access the legal system to protect themselves from domestic violence.

Marital Rape as a Form of Domestic Violence and the Need for Law Reform in Ghana

Beatrice Akua Abrekna Duncan

Introduction

"A woman's place is in the kitchen.
A man's place is in the bedroom."

In Ghana, no legal remedy exists for women who are victims of marital rape, by virtue of an exemption that serves as a bar to the prosecution of men who rape their wives. This lack of protection stems partly from the nature of marital rape itself, as well as from the general attitude of society toward sexual offenses. This tolerance of marital rape creates an unfair situation for married women because it underestimates the severity of marital rape. This essay addresses marital rape as a form of domestic violence and underscores the need to provide adequate protection to women who are raped in the context of marriage.

The "Culture of Silence" of Marital Rape

It seems this subject is still very much a taboo around here where Machismo is so deep and so strong; women are certainly not ready to share their experiences about rape in marriage with anybody, maybe they don't even acknowledge it themselves.[1]

Frank and open discussions about sex are quite alien to Ghanaian society, even though society recognizes that sex is an important component of life. In

---

1. Diana E. H. Russell, Rape in Marriage 349 (rev. ed., Indiana Press 1990) (1982).

a country like Ghana, where having children is desirable, sex is regarded as one of the most essential activities of men and women. In spite of this reverence for sexual activity, oral communication about it is taboo. This lack of communication on the subject of sex makes it impossible to talk about marital rape.

Most people use euphemisms to describe sex, and Ghanaian society perpetuates a "culture of silence" in matters related to sex. When a young woman is about to get married, her mother commonly instructs her about "the facts of life." Instead of using words that explicitly describe the sexual experience, her mother will refer to a "meeting" or "conference" with her husband. More importantly, mothers often instruct that a daughter must never say "no" to her husband's sexual advances, even if she has good reason to do so. Men receive similar instruction from their fathers and are made to understand that it is their absolute privilege to have sex. At this stage, men begin to embrace the notion that a woman's refusal to have intercourse is meaningless. This kind of "sex education" among men and women accounts for widespread societal acceptance of marital rape.

In most jurisdictions where the offense exists, rape is defined as intercourse without the consent of the victim.[2] The law often limits its definition of victim to a female who is not the wife of the perpetrator.[3] Thus, marital rape does not qualify as rape, even though the wife is a female whose consent is clearly absent. The exemption for marital rape demonstrates the extent of the ignorance about marital rape, not just among the general populace but also among the politicians who shape the law.

In Ghana, there is a dearth of information on the subject of marital rape. This lack of information stems from a reluctance on the part of the state to interfere in the domestic affairs of its citizens. Marital rape, being domestic in nature, has enjoyed shelter from public scrutiny or state intervention. Wives who are victims of marital rape face significant obstacles and social stigmas in even talking about their experience to family members or friends. For most Ghanaian women, especially for those who are married, revelations of this kind in an open court require tremendous courage.

---

2. *See, e.g.*, Criminal Code (Amendment) Act, 1998 § 98 (Ghana).

3. RUSSELL, *supra* note 1, at 17.

The Legal Genesis of the Marital Exemption

In Ghana, the marital exemption is embodied in section 42(g) of the Criminal Code, Act 29 of 1960.[4] A careful reading of the law reveals that the code condones marital violence. Although the law groups rape and incest under the heading of "Sexual Offenses," marital immunity is subsumed under the general heading "Justifiable Use Of Force And Harm."[5] The implication of this law—that marital rape is not considered a sexual offense—raises the need for law reform in Ghana.

Potential Arguments against the Need to Abolish Marital Immunity

The process of law reform is bound to be met with opposition. In Ghana, the task will be difficult because of the male-dominated Parliament. At the moment, women account for only 9.5 percent of Parliament.[6] Bearing in mind the myths associated with marital rape, discussions about this subject in Parliament will be contentious. Also, many of the male parliamentarians are husbands themselves and they may be embarrassed by the subject.

Reformers can anticipate potential arguments against reform of marital rape law based upon the experiences of other countries and the writings of opponents who have displayed a total lack of understanding of the subject. One common argument against reform is a contention that marital rape is different from rape by a stranger.[7] The stranger rape/marital rape dichotomy holds that marital rape does not carry with it the devastating consequences

---

4. Criminal Code, 1960 (Act 29) §42(g) (Ghana) (The code provides that "the use of force against any person may be justified on the grounds of his consent, but a person may revoke consent which he has given to the use of force against him, and his consent when revoked shall have no effect for justifying force; save that the consent given by a husband or wife at marriage for the purpose of marriage, cannot be revoked until parties are divorced or separated by a judgment or decree of a competent court.").

5. *Compare* Criminal Code, 1960 (Act 29) §98 *and* §108 *with* Criminal Code, 1960 (Act 29) §42(g) (Ghana).

6. Lisa Aubrey, *Gender Development and Democratization in Africa*, 36 J. ASIAN & AFRI. STUD. 87, 92 (2001).

7. *See* Michael Gary Hilf, *Marital Privacy and Spousal Rape*, 16 NEW ENG. L. REV. 31, 40–41 (1980).

and gruesome circumstances of rape by a stranger, and therefore cannot be as serious as stranger rape.[8] This argument, however, suffers from the weaknesses described below and reflects the widespread acceptance of marital rape as normal marital behavior.

The limited notion of rape as solely an ambush experience is untenable. Rape does not depend on the type of relationship in question; rape is rape whether committed by a stranger or by a husband.[9] Similarly, both a husband and a stranger can be prosecuted for the murder of a woman, whether or not she happened to be in a spousal relationship with her murderer.[10] Viewed in this light, the distinction between stranger rape and marital rape is—at best—arbitrary and—at worst—a reflection of state-sanctioned violence against women.

Marital rape has extremely serious consequences for victims. In every marital relationship, there is a reasonable expectation of love and mutual trust from both sides. Rape in a marital relationship is antithetical to these ingredients. Also, although rape by a stranger is humiliating and often devastating, it may occur just once; rape by a husband, however, may occur every day.[11] In order to understand the impact of marital rape, it is essential to consider the opinion of women who have been victims of marital rape.

Marital rape can lead to suicidal thoughts.[12] More importantly, marital rape is often accompanied by life-threatening violence, including verbal threats; the use of weapons such as guns, knives, belts, and cigarettes;[13] slaps or severe beatings;[14] and other harmful sexual practices.[15] Of fundamental importance here are the negative long-term effects of marital rape on women. These include negative feelings towards men in general; lack of confidence in oneself; severe depression; anger; desire to hurt; and a general hatred of sex.[16] Findings suggest that women who are victims of marital rape suffer additional risks of other bodily injury and even murder.[17]

---

8. *See* RUSSELL, *supra* note 1, at 190.
9. *Id.* at 359.
10. *See id.*
11. *See id.* at 111 (noting the frequency of rape in marriage).
12. *Id.* at 194.
13. *Id.* at 112.
14. *Id.* at 178–79.
15. *Id.* at xii.
16. *Id.* at 190–205.
17. *Id.* at 113.

Another argument offered in favor of maintaining the immunity is that prosecution for marital rape would destroy every opportunity for reconciliation between the parties.[18] This contention overlooks the aforementioned dangers associated with marital rape and reflects the notion that reconciliation is a natural societal response to marital rape. Successful reconciliation in cases of marital rape is only a remote possibility; the law must provide adequate protection for victims in the majority of cases that will not benefit from reconciliation. In addition, the criminal justice system operates to condemn behavior that society deems harmful. Imposition of criminal penalties does not depend on the potential for reconciliation in certain types of cases. It is very important to treat marital rape strictly as a crime and not to make the availability of protection dependent on the remote possibility of reconciliation.

Others maintain that prosecution will involve a disclosure of intimate details of the matrimonial relationship,[19] and that this might prove to be a tedious and stressful process for the parties involved. This argument is meritless because the same argument is never offered in relation to other cases requiring revelations of an intimate character. Some maintain that prosecution for marital rape is unnecessary in light of other existing remedies, such as assault and battery laws under criminal law and divorce proceedings under civil law.[20] This view does not take into account the seriousness of marital rape; indeed, in many jurisdictions, assault and battery carry lesser sanctions than rape. Making use of divorce laws would also leave the crime of marital rape unpunished because divorce laws do not impose sanctions, and therefore would not have a deterrent effect. Rape is a crime of violence accompanied by physical and psychological damage that is often permanent,[21] and warrants corresponding punishment.

Some argue that wives could use the criminal justice system to seek vengeance and to ensure punishment of their spouses.[22] This proposition ignores the checks and balances inherent in the evidentiary process of the judicial system. In all criminal cases, the prosecution must prove the guilt of the accused beyond a reasonable doubt. It would be up to the police to consider whether a case can be made from a complaint of spousal rape. An alleged vic-

---

18. *See* GR. BRIT., LAW COMMISSION REPORTS: CRIMINAL LAW RAPE WITHIN MARRIAGE, LAW. COM. NO. 205, at 11 (1992).
19. *See* Hilf, *supra* note 7, at 41.
20. GR. BRIT., *supra* note 18, at 10.
21. Warren v. State, 336 S.E.2d 221, 222 (Ga. 1985) (describing martial rape).
22. GR. BRIT., *supra* note 18, at 14.

tim offering testimony in court would also be subjected to cross examination. In addition, the possibility of perjury charges for a fabricated complaint would deter false reports.

The Treatment of Marital Rape under International Law

My husband was a very violent man and used sex as another means of hurting and degrading me. He would order me to do things and if I refused or gave any sign of being unwilling, he would hit me until I obeyed, and then hit me for getting it wrong or being too slow. Subsequently, he would just walk in, order me to strip and then rape me....He said he'd cut me up if I tried to leave. He would go at me until I bled, and humiliate me verbally at the same time. He would finish by ejaculating or even urinating over me, preferably in my face if I could not avoid it. When he thought I'd told my doctor what was happening, he punished me with sodomy. That damaged me, and the fear of that overrode my fear of leaving him, and I ran off with the children. I am still running, and he's still trying to find me.[23]

The treatment of marital rape under international law is important because marital rape is not a problem peculiar to just one country, but is universal in character. Under international human rights law, violence against women is understood to encompass physical, sexual, and psychological violence occurring in the general community, including rape, sexual abuse, sexual harassment, and martial rape.[24] In its Declaration on the Elimination of Violence Against Women, the United Nation called upon the international community to eliminate violence against women, calling such violence "a violation of the rights and fundamental freedoms of women."[25] Under its "Directive Principles of State Policy," Ghana has expressed its intent to abide by obligations arising under international law.[26] Because marital rape exemptions violate the

---

23. RUSSELL, *supra* note 1, at 351 (narration of Mrs. Christie from Wales, United Kingdom, of her experience of domestic abuse by her husband).

24. *Declaration on the Elimination of Violence Against Women*, G.A. Res. 104, U.N. GAOR, 48th Sess., Supp. No. 49, at 217, U.N. Doc. A/48/49 (1993).

25. *Id.*

26. GHANA CONST. ch. VI, art. 40.

principles set forth in various human rights instruments, the case for ending this practice is even stronger.

Recommendations for the Application of Penalties in Ghana

The application of penalties to would-be offenders deserves serious attention. Because of the level of dependency of Ghanaian women on their husbands, the imposition of an unqualified jail term on spousal rapists could be extremely detrimental to many women. It is essential to devise a system of penalties that would best suit the circumstances of Ghanaian women. One solution is to impose a jail term that would permit men to go to their regular places of employment during the day and return to prison after work. This arrangement would ensure the continued monetary support of the rapist's wife and children. Additionally, legal reformers should seek mandatory counseling for offenders, to enable spousal rapists to receive education on sexual limitations in marriage and respect for women's human rights.

The extended family system in Ghana is of tremendous importance. In traditional society, as long as the husband is providing the essentials for his family, his bad behavior, no matter how serious, is treated as merely incidental to the marriage. A woman under those circumstances would be regarded as ungrateful by her extended family if she ever placed her husband at risk of prosecution or imprisonment, and she would be torn between protecting her rights and losing the support and confidence of her in-laws.[27] The extended family system, however, should not be viewed as static; instead, it should be a dynamic institution that is capable of reflecting changes that have taken place in society. As such, the extended family will have to adjust its expectations to comport with a new marital rape statute and will ultimately have to recognize that it will benefit female members of the family.

Ghana must also work to change the attitude of police. All police stations in Ghana are male dominated. The police believe that they are not supposed to meddle in the internal affairs of married couples. Unfortunately, the police

---

27. *See* Rosemary Ofeibea Ofei-Aboagye King, *Domestic Violence in Ghana: An Initial Step, in* GLOBAL CRITICAL RACE FEMINISM 317, 320 (Adrien Katherine Wing ed., 2000) (noting that most women hesitate to report domestic violence cases for fear that they would be blamed for the breakdown in the relationship by their partners and both families).

in Ghana are also susceptible to bribery and may refuse to prosecute cases where the perpetrator has given them money. In this context, the police are more likely to deny women justice because of their economically disadvantaged position. In order to change the attitude of the police towards cases of domestic violence, Ghana must address domestic violence as a serious issue during police training.[28] Training more female police would also help to meet the special needs of women victims. Ghana should also establish an affirmative action program to create at least one female-only police station in each region. This would likely increase the participation of women police in domestic violence cases, facilitate reporting of marital rape cases, and increase the likelihood of the prosecution of marital rape cases that are reported to police stations.

The final point reformers should consider is how to prevent marital rape. First, marriage counseling should be encouraged prior to and during marriage. Counseling normally consists of educating each party on their roles in marriage; sex is discussed within the context of procreation. Instead, sex should also be discussed as a source of mutual enjoyment for both parties; then, sex could be seen not as a weapon of violence but as an act of love.

Conclusion

The road to law reform is not an easy task and there will undoubtedly be tremendous opposition, especially from men who form the majority of the current Parliament. Nevertheless, it is hoped that Ghana will soon be in a position to declare to its women that when they say "I do," it does not take away their right to say "I won't."[29]

---

28. *See id.* at 327.

29. Moira K. Griffin, *In 44 States, It's Legal to Rape Your Wife*, 9 STUDENT LAW. 20, 20–22 (1980).

Attitudes Toward Victims of Rape that Affect the Reporting, Prosecutions, and Convictions for Rape: The Need for Law Reform in Ghana

Sheila N.Y. Gyimah

Introduction

There are very few reported cases on rape in Ghana's law reports,[1] but the issue of underreporting of rape is not peculiar to Ghana. Underreporting has been an issue in many countries that derive their criminal laws from the English common law, including the United States of America.[2] Under common law, a man commits the offense of rape if he has carnal knowledge of a woman

---

1. The only law reporter in Ghana is the Ghana Law Reports (G.L.R.). The cases that are reported in this report are some cases from the superior courts in Ghana, which consists of the High Court, the Court of Appeal, and the Supreme Court. Rape cases can be tried in the High Court with a jury or in the Circuit Court with the aid of assessors, that is two lay people. Thus rape cases that are tried in the Circuit Court and which do not go on appeal, will never get reported. *See* Criminal Code, 1960 (Act 29) § 97 (Ghana) *and* Criminal Procedure Code, 1960 (Act 30) §§ 2(2), 2(4) (Ghana).

2. *See, e.g.,* Susan Brown miller, Against Our Will: Men, Women and Rape 175 (1975) (noting that only one out of every five rapes, or possibly, one in twenty, may actually be reported in the United States); U.S. Dep't of Just., FBI Uniform Crime Reports 14 (1977) (reporting that rape has been recognized by law enforcement as one of the most underreported of all index crimes).

not his wife; by force or threat of force; against her will; and without her consent.[3] Apart from the formal definition of rape, certain procedural rules that developed at common law were based on highly sexist and stereotypical attitudes about rape and rape victims, making the conviction of rapists difficult. These factors not only contribute to underreporting, sparse prosecution, and few convictions for rape, but also heighten the trauma that victims endure during a rape trial.

Definition of the Crime

Labeling of the Crime: Rape or Sexual Assault

In the common law tradition, rape was defined in gender-specific terms. This led to the development of sexist stereotypes about the offense, leading feminists to advocate for a sex-neutral definition. Others argue for retaining gender-specific categorization to maintain the uniqueness of a crime directed primarily at women.[4] Section 98 of Ghana's Amended Criminal Code defines rape as "carnal knowledge of a female of age 16 or higher without her consent."

Laudable though it is to maintain the uniqueness of the crime, it is important to challenge the attitudes and stereotypes associated with rape. Making the offense sex neutral may result in a new approach toward victims by law enforcement and juries alike, helping to remove some of the negative attitudes toward victims.[5] This, in turn, may encourage adult women to report rapes and pursue prosecution.

Making rape a gender-neutral offense will equalize the position of both sexes when they are victims of sexual assault and will help to promote gender equality in Ghana, in addition to removing some of the myths around the offense. In addition, the indecent assault provision of the Criminal Code, which makes sexual abuse that does not involve penile penetration a misdemeanor, should be subsumed under a general, gender-neutral sexual assault law along with rape.[6]

---

3. Susan Estrich, Real Rape 8 (1987).

4. See id. at 81.

5. See Camille E. Legrand, Comment, *Rape and Rape Laws: Sexism in Society and Law*, 16 Cal. L. Rev. 919, 941 (1973).

6. See Criminal Code (Amendment) Act, 1998 (Act 554) ch. 6, §103 (Ghana).

Standard of Consent

Consent is an important element in the definition of rape in Ghana.[7] For sexual intercourse to amount to rape, it must occur without the woman's consent. However, it is not certain how the Ghanaian courts will interpret non-consent.[8]

Section 14 of Ghana's Criminal Code sets out circumstances in which consent will be negated, including consent given for the commission of a criminal act.[9] This section holds that consent is void if it is given by a minor,[10] an incompetent person,[11] or given as a result of deceit, duress,[12] the undue exercise of parental authority,[13] or by a fundamental mistake of fact.[14]

Further guidance on the standard of consent can be gleaned from *Agbemenya v. The State*,[15] a rape case that was appealed to the Ghanaian Supreme Court on a procedural issue.[16] The case involved a seventeen year old girl who had been raped by her mother's relative. In the Supreme Court's opinion, all that the perpetrator had to prove was a reasonable probability that the victim consented to sexual intercourse.[17] The court considered two factors in establishing the existence of this reasonable probability: first, the victim's acquaintance with the alleged rapist; and second, the undamaged condition of

---

7. *See* Criminal Code, 1960 (Act 29) §98 (Ghana); *see also* P. K. TWUMASI, CRIMINAL LAW IN GHANA 283 (1985).

8. A recent publication which is an annotation to Ghana's criminal code cites only English cases on the issue of consent. This indicates that the Ghanaian courts probably have not clearly articulated any standard. *See* HENRIETTA J.A.N. MENSAH-BONSU, THE ANNOTATED CRIMINAL CODE OF GHANA 73 (1994).

9. *See* Criminal Code, 1960 (Act 29) §14 (Ghana).

10. A minor for the purposes of the section is a person aged ten years and below, but for the purposes of a crime involving indecency, a minor should be a person under fourteen years. *See id.* §14(a).

11. *Id.*

12. *Id.* §14(b).

13. *Id.* §14(c)-(d).

14. *Id.* §14(e).

15. Agbemenya v. State, [1964] G.L.R. 663 (Ghana).

16. The appellant in the case had been convicted of rape by a High Court judge sitting with the aid of assessors. He had appealed on the ground that the judge misdirected the assessors on crucial factual matters and therefore prevented them and himself from forming a true opinion. It was held that the judge misdirected the assessors and prevented them and himself from considering all the important issues in the case, including the issue of consent, therefore the conviction was quashed and appellant was acquitted. *Id.* at 664.

17. *Id.*

the underwear the victim was wearing on the day of the rape, which the court concluded to signify willingness remove it and allow the appellant to penetrate her.[18] Relying on a combination of these two factors, the court concluded that the alleged rapist was wrongly convicted and reversed his conviction.[19] The opinion of the Supreme Court, which emphasized the struggle between the parties, indicates that the standard of non-consent was that of forceful resistance.

Ghanaian courts should disregard this interpretation of consent and avoid adopting the resistance standard. A woman should not be required to put her life at risk before the court will accept that she did not consent. This denies her right to sexual autonomy and her right to justice and equal treatment under the law. Rather, the courts should adopt the ordinary meaning of lack of consent, thereby ensuring that the courts do not adopt a standard that reflects discriminatory stereotypes. With such an interpretation, once a woman in a trial claims to have rejected sexual intercourse, the burden will shift to the assailant to prove otherwise. Such an interpretation will also make it easier to prosecute rape cases and less of an ordeal for victims.

Requirement of Penetration

Under Ghana's current law, the only acceptable evidence of rape is proof of penetration of the vagina by the penis.[20] Any sexual penetration, however slight, by the penis in the vagina is sufficient to complete the crime.[21] This requirement is unfair to women because there are equally harmful instances of sexual molestation that fall short of penile penetration. A woman could, for instance, be forced to engage in oral or anal sex, which would not amount to rape due to the penetration requirement. However, she may feel as violated by such an act, or she may even feel worse. In addition, where the assault consisted of both penal-vaginal penetration and anal penetration, it would be inefficient to prosecute the assailant under rape provisions for the former offense and indecent assault laws for the latter.

---

18. *Id.* at 668.

19. *Id.* at 671.

20. *See* Criminal Code, 1960, (Act 29) §99 (Ghana) ("Whenever, upon trial of any person for an offense punishable under this Code, it is necessary to prove carnal knowledge, the carnal knowledge shall be deemed complete upon proof of any least degree of penetration only.").

21. Nat'l Inst. of L. Enforcement & Crim. Just. Assistance Admin., U.S. Dep't of Just., Forcible Rape 5 (1975).

The acts constituting sexual violation (or carnal knowledge) in Ghana's Criminal Code need to be broadened. Limiting the harms associated with rape to penal-vaginal penetration does not ensure adequate protect of victims from many other harms. Prohibited acts should be labeled "prohibited sexual conduct or acts" and not "sexual penetration," which is a definition in male genital terms.[22]

This change in the law will send a message to would-be rapists that they will be held accountable for any unwelcome physical act against a woman's body. Additionally, the trial of rape cases will focus on the perpetrator's actions instead of the actions of the victim, thereby making prosecutions easier and convictions surer.

Evidentiary Rules

In addition to the formal definition of rape, courts under the common law tradition also developed many subsidiary rules of evidence unique to the crime of rape. Most of these rules evolved from myths and sexist stereotypes associated with rape.

Sexual History of Victim and Rape Shield Laws

One evidentiary rule that evolved under traditional common law was the rule that a defendant could offer evidence of the complainant's prior sexual history.[23] This rule conjures up two myths: that women lie about sexual matters, and that an unchaste woman[24] would consent to intercourse with any man.[25]

There is no formal provision in Ghanaian criminal law requiring evidence of a victim's prior sexual history at a rape trial. However, dicta of some

---

22. *See* Catharine A. Mackinnon, *Feminism, Marxism, Method, and the State: Toward Feminist Jurisprudence*, 8 SIGNS: J. WOMEN IN CULTURE & SOC'Y 635, 647 (1983).

23. *See* Leon Letwin, *"Unchaste Character," Ideology, and the California Rape Evidence Law*, 54 S. CAL. L. REV. 35, 38 (1980).

24. Unchaste women are women that have had sex outside marriage; *See* People v. Benson, 6 Cal. 221, 223 (1856) ("It must be obvious to all that there would be less probability of resistance upon the part of one already debauched in mind and body, than there would be in the case of a pure and chaste female").

25. *See* People v. Abbot, 19 Wend. 192,195 (N.Y. Sup. Ct. 1838)(where the court colorfully put it as "And will you not more readily infer assent in the practiced Messalina, in loose attire than in the reserved and virtuous Lucretia?").

Ghanaian courts in cases involving sexual offenses reveals that the rule is operative and is therefore likely to be invoked in a rape trial.[26]

This evidentiary practice is unjust to victims of rape because there is no logical connection between promiscuity and consent in rape cases. Since the probative value of evidence of a victim's prior sexual history is outweighed by its prejudicial impact, such evidence should not be admitted in a rape trial.[27] It is equally illogical to use this type of evidence to determine the victim's credibility. There is no correlation between a person's sexual laxity and her credibility. Instead, this practice is simply based on sexist stereotypes about women who are not virtuous. It should have no relevance whatsoever in a rape trial.[28] Consent given once to intercourse cannot be transformed into consent for all intercourse, nor should a victim's sexual history be a barometer for her honesty.

Ghana should enact rape shield laws to protect victims of rape from unnecessary inquiry into their private lives. A possible constitutional challenge, however, could be raised against the exclusion of such evidence under Article 19 of the Ghanaian Constitution, which guarantees a defendant's right to a fair trial.[29] In balancing this right against the right to privacy, courts are likely to uphold the right to a fair trial. Even if any constitutional argument in favor of the right of privacy fails, a further argument could be made that evidence of the victim's past sexual history is not required by Ghana's Criminal Code[30] and therefore should not be used in rape trials.

Rape shield laws are very useful because they help to defuse some of the institutionalized bias against rape victims. These laws protect the privacy of women and remove the prejudicial effect of introduction of evidence of their past sexual conduct in court.[31] Such protection would promote fairness in rape trials.

Requirement of Corroboration

Traditional common law also requires corroboration.[32] Rape corroboration rules were founded on Lord Hale's assertion that rape is "an accusation easily

---

26. *See* TSUMASI, *supra* note 7, at 287.

27. *See* NAT'L INST. OF L. ENFORCEMENT & CRIM. JUST. ASSISTANCE ADMIN., *supra* note 21, at 23.

28. *See* Letwin, *supra* note 23, at 40.

29. *See* GHANA CONST. ch. V, art. 19.

30. *See* Criminal Code, 1960 (Act 29) §4(b) (Ghana).

31. *See generally* ESTRICH, *supra* note 3, at 80.

32. *See generally* Note, *The Rape Corroboration Requirement: Repeal Not Reform*, 81 YALE L. J. 1365, 1365–91 (1972) [hereinafter, *The Rape Corroboration Requirement*].

to be made, and hard to be proved, and harder to be defended by the party accused, though ever so innocent."[33] In Ghana, there is no statutory requirement for corroboration in rape cases.[34] In practice, however, the courts do require it for all sexual offense trials, including rape.[35] This special corroboration requirement has been criticized as imposing a sexually discriminatory rule that severely inhibits convictions for the offense of rape.[36]

Available evidence suggests that the basis for Lord Hale's assertion is unfounded.[37] Considering the stigma associated with rape and the negative attitudes of law enforcement agents toward victims, it is unlikely that many women will make unfounded rape accusations. The screening process by the police and the prosecution is likely to eliminate unfounded claims. Also, research has indicated that jury attitudes favor the defendant, not the victim, and that few rape cases lead to convictions.[38]

The special rape corroboration requirement should be done away with because it leads to the underreporting of rape by requiring rapes to fit into a certain stereotype, leading to difficulty in prosecuting rape cases, and hampering convictions.

The Cautionary Instruction

In the absence of corroborative evidence of rape, some common law courts issued cautionary instructions to the jury. These instructions proposed that rape is a charge easily made but difficult to prove, and therefore information about the victim should be examined with caution.[39] There is no direct indication that Ghanaian courts use the cautionary instruction in rape trials. However, because of frequent reliance on English criminal practice in Ghanaian

---

33. SIR MATTHEW HALE, THE HISTORY OF THE PLEAS OF THE CROWN 635 (1736).

34. *See* TWUMASI, *supra* note 7 , at 285–87.

35. *See, e.g.*, Agbemanya, [1964] G.L.R. at 666; Commissioner of Police v. Sem, [1962] 2 G.L.R. 77 (Ghana) (allowing the dismissal of a rape conviction due to lack of corroboration of evidence besides the victim's own story); State v. Ohene-Kesson and Mensah, [1961] 2 G.L.R. 708, 714 (Ghana) (holding that medical evidence of the victim's condition consistent with his or her story afford adequate corroboration as required by the law).

36. *See The Rape Corroboration Requirement, supra* note 32, at 1370.

37. *See generally* Thomas A. Morris, *The Empirical, Historical And Legal Case Against The Cautionary Instruction: A Call For Legislative Reform,* 1988 DUKE L.J. 154 (1988).

38. *See* NAT'L INST. OF L. ENFORCEMENT & CRIM. JUST. ASSISTANCE ADMIN., *supra* note 21, at 29; HARRY KALVEN & HANS ZEISEL, THE AMERICAN JURY 249 (1966).

39. Morris, *supra* note 37, at 154–55.

courts, there is a strong likelihood that it is used. Since there is no justifiable basis for such instructions, which prejudice victims of rape, they have no place in the courtroom. The Ghanaian legislature should be urged to pass a law to abolish this practice if it is in use.

Victim Services

The perception of law enforcement agents plays a role in determining whether a victim will report crime to the relevant authorities. Existing evidence concerning societal beliefs about rape victims suggests that rape myths are accepted not only by laypeople, but by professionals responsible for providing services to sexual assault victims.[40] Interactions with victims that are characterized by these negative beliefs cause victims to experience what has been termed a second rape.[41] In Ghana, there is a need to sensitize law enforcement agents so that they will approach rape victims without prejudice.

The Police

The police department is usually the first place that a victim turns after a rape. Police initially determine whether the crime is worth investigating.[42] Consequently, police officers must be knowledgeable about rape and rape victims so they can effectively handle complaints. In the absence of sensitization, police may allow their cultural attitudes to work to the detriment of rape victims.

In Ghana, there are no special police units to handle sexual offenses, and police personnel are not given any special training in dealing with rape victims. Ghana can learn from the United States' example and include training on rape victimology in the curriculum for police training.[43] Furthermore, special units should be set up at police stations to handle rape cases and should be staffed by officers of both sexes. This will enable female victims who cannot talk about intimate sexual matters with men to open up to female officers.

---

40. Connie L. Best et al., *Medical Students' Attitudes About Female Rape Victims*, 7(2) J. INTERPERSONAL VIOLENCE 175–76 (1992).

41. LEE MADIGAN & NANCY C. GAMBLE, THE SECOND RAPE 5–6 (1991) (The second rape is defined as the act of violation, alienation and disparagement a survivor receives when she turns to others for help and support.).

42. *See id.* at 73–74.

43. *See* NAT'L INST. OF L. ENFORCEMENT & CRIM. JUST. ASSISTANCE ADMIN., *supra* note 21, at 42.

Moreover, special guidelines can be set up to help determine whether or not to prosecute a rape case. These changes may result in better handling of rape complaints and encourage adult women in Ghana to report rapes.

Medical Personnel

Hospitals have an important role to play because collection of forensic evidence is essential to the prosecution of rape cases. Hospitals are a critical force in either aiding the victim or causing greater distress immediately following the crime. Hospital personnel, like police, are products of society and subject to its myths and stereotypes.[44] Moralizing by hospital staff can further traumatize the victim, increasing her sense of guilt.[45] Also, the victim's medical examination may be intrusive and amount to a second rape if it is not done with sensitivity and if it involves unwanted procedures.[46] If the hospital handles a victim in an unsympathetic manner, she may feel that her body is being subjected to another form of abuse.

The attitude of medical personnel about rape and rape victims is related to both societal conditioning and deficits in educational preparation.[47] In Ghana, no special training is given to medical personnel on how to deal with victims of sexual assault, and there are no special hospital units to deal with such cases. To resolve this problem, Ghanaian medical schools and nursing colleges should include training on rape trauma syndrome in their curricula. This may help to de-legitimize rape myths and improve the care of rape victims by medical personnel. Better treatment of victims may encourage adult women in Ghana to seek medical care when they are raped, and thereby encourage overall reporting as well.

Prosecutors

Prosecutors may also play a role in discouraging victims from reporting rapes.[48] They can decide not to prosecute if the victim's story does not fit an

---

44. *See* Cindy Cook Williams & Reg Arthur Williams, *Rape: A Plea for Help in the Hospital Emergency Room, in* THE RAPE VICTIM 92, 93 (Deanna R. Nass ed., 1977).

45. *Id.*

46. *See, e.g.,* MADIGAN & GAMBLE, *supra* note 41, at 85–87 (noting that a rape victim may have to undergo AIDS tests, or blood tests for alcohol content, which is sometimes even used by the defense against her).

47. *See* William & Williams, *supra* note 44, at 97.

48. *See generally* NAT'L INST. OF L. ENFORCEMENT & CRIM. JUST. ASSISTANCE ADMIN.,

accepted stereotype. Furthermore, the failure of prosecutors to take into account the trauma of the victim may lead to disbelief of her story for reasons of inconsistency; this can lead to a second traumatization of the victim.[49] Prosecutors do not always tell the victim the real reasons for their refusal to prosecute, culminating in the victim's further distrust of the legal system.

There is a need to sensitize prosecutors in Ghana to the trauma of victims to avoid causing further distress. This can be done by organizing seminars or other in-house training programs for prosecutors. Specialization in rape cases should also be considered. Additionally, plea bargaining in rape cases should be avoided as much as possible. It should be used only with the knowledge and consent of victims, so that victims do not feel that they have been denied justice.

Rape Trials

In a society like Ghana, where people avoid talking openly about sexual matters, having to give evidence about rape in open court will be a very embarrassing and traumatic experience for the victim. This is one of the main reasons why adult women in Ghana refrain from reporting rapes.

The best solution to this problem is to hold rape hearings for adult victims in camera, which is a private judicial forum rather than a public one. The Ghanaian Constitution gives the court power to hold criminal cases in camera to protect the private lives of persons concerned in the proceedings.[50] Sensitizing judges to the problems of rape victims should make them respond positively to appeals to hear rape cases in camera.

Rape Crisis Centers and Victim Advocacy Services

Rape represents a crisis and an interruption in a victim's life[51] and causes unsettling reactions.[52] Crisis intervention helps victims develop and maintain

U.S. DEP'T OF JUST., FORCIBLE RAPE: A NATIONAL SURVEY OF THE RESPONSE BY PROSECUTORS (1977).

49. MADIGAN & GAMBLE, *supra* note 41, at 92.

50. *See* GHANA CONST. ch. V, art. 19(15)(a)-(b).

51. LYNDA LYTLE HOLMSTROM & ANN WOLBERT BURGESS, THE VICTIM OF RAPE 127 (1978).

52. Ann Wolbert Burgess & Lytle Holmstrom, *Rape Trauma Syndrome, in* THE RAPE VICTIM 119, 121 (Deanna R. Nass ed., 1977) (the rape trauma syndrome, is the acute phase and the long term reorganization process that occurs as a result of forcible rape or at-

realistic perceptions of the event, manage affective responses, and develop coping strategies appropriate for the client's post-victimization state.[53] Thus, there is a need for rape crisis centers in Ghana. Crisis counselors should provide advocacy and counseling services for victims of rape,[54] and professional advocates should work with the institutions that serve victims.[55] In a country with limited resources, it is unlikely that the government will take the initiative to start a crisis center. Therefore, private rape crisis centers should be established to assist victims of rape. These centers will go a long way toward encouraging women to report rape in Ghana and ensuring that victims are treated fairly by the criminal justice system.

Conclusion

Women in Ghana should come together to form a legal action group that will work to reform the law on rape. If these suggestions are realized, women will be spared the embarrassing and humiliating re-victimization that accompanies many rape trials. This may encourage adult victims of rape in Ghana, who are currently hiding, to report the crime. By increasing the reporting of rape, the chances of catching and prosecuting rapists will be higher, and Ghanaian women, in turn, will be safer.

---

tempted forcible rape. This syndrome of behavioral, somatic, and psychological reactions is an acute stress reaction to a life-threatening situation.).

53. *See* KATHRYN QUINA & NANCY L. CARLSON, RAPE, INCEST, AND SEXUAL HARASSMENT 42–43 (1989).

54. *Id.* at 42.

55. *Id.* at 43.

FEMALE GENITAL MUTILATION: TRADITION OR TORTURE?

Fitnat N-A. Adjetey

Introduction

Female Genital Mutilation (FGM) refers to several operations that entail the removal of part or all of the female external genitalia.[1] FGM affects some seventy-five million women and children globally.[2] It exists in Indonesia, Malaysia, Yemen, and at least twenty-five African countries: Somalia, Djibouti, Sudan, Ethiopia, Egypt, Mali, Gambia, Ghana, Nigeria, Liberia, Senegal, Sierra Leone, Guinea, Guinea Bissau, Burkina Faso, Benin, Cote d'Ivoire, Tanzania, Togo, Uganda, Kenya, Chad, Central African Republic, Cameroon, and Mauritania.[3] FGM is also practiced in immigrant communities in some European countries and Australia.[4]

Short-term effects of FGM include acute pain, post-operative shock, cuts in the vaginal walls, hemorrhage, and infection that could lead to death.[5] Long-term effects include infertility as a result of infection, chronic infections of the uterus and vagina, painful sexual intercourse, painful menstrual peri-

---

1. *See* LILIAN PASSMORE SANDERSON, AGAINST THE MUTILATION OF WOMEN 14 (1981).

2. United Nations Dep't of Pub. Info., *Traditional Practices Affecting the Health of Women and Children*, [1991] 23 OBJECTIVE: JUSTICE (No. 2) at 35, 35, U.N. Doc ST/DPI/1182 [hereinafter OBJECTIVE: JUSTICE].

3. Commission on Human Rights, Sub-Commission on Prevention of Discrimination and Protection of Minorities, *Review of Further Developments in Fields with Which the Sub-Commission Has Been Concerned, Study on Traditional Practices Affecting the Health of Women and Children, Final Report by the Special Rapporteur, Mrs. Halima Embarek Warzazi*, U.N. ESCOR, 43d Sess., at 3, para. 11, U.N. Doc. E/CN.4/Sub.2/1991/6 (1991) [hereinafter Warzazi].

4. *Id.* at 3, para. 12.

5. EFUA DORKENOO & SCILLA ELWORTHY, FEMALE GENITAL MUTILATION: PROPOSALS FOR CHANGE 8 (3d ed. 1992).

ods, and obstructed child birth.[6] The United Nations Commissioner on Human Rights has stated that FGM "is not only dangerous to health, but injurious to women's dignity."[7] The World Health Organization has condemned FGM as a serious health risk.[8]

FGM is an age-old practice that has been maintained by traditional and religious leaders. Entrenched and supported by other traditional institutions such as polygyny and the dowry and bride price systems, FGM amplifies the notion that women are chattel. FGM is practiced for reasons ranging from religion and custom to hygiene and aesthetics.[9] Many women have chosen to speak out against the practice as cruel, inhuman, and degrading treatment because of the long-lasting and harmful health implications, and because it is practiced using crude surgical methods and without anesthesia.[10]

In this essay, I appraise the different types of FGM and their short and long-term effects on girls and women. Then I analyze and critique the arguments for and against FGM. I then examine the actions that have been taken to address FGM under the national laws of Ghana. Lastly, I suggest further action that might be taken to address FGM in Ghana.

Female Genital Mutilation: The Facts

"Female genital mutilation [(FGM)] is the collective name given to several traditional practices that involve the cutting of female genitals."[11] FGM is per-

---

6. *Id.* at 8–9.

7. OBJECTIVE: JUSTICE, *supra* note 2, at 37.

8. *Id.*

9. *See* DORKENOO & ELWORTHY, *supra* note 5, at 13–15.

10. *See id.* at 5.

11. NAHID TOUBIA, FEMALE GENITAL MUTILATION: A CALL FOR GLOBAL ACTION 9 (1993). Female Genital Mutilation is also commonly known as Female Circumcision (FC), but this is a misnomer. Circumcision "implies an analogy to nonmutilating male circumcision, which is not the case. Male circumcision is the cutting off of the foreskin from the tip of the penis without damaging the organ itself." *Id.* Most of the penis would be amputated if the equivalent of clitoridectomy were to be performed on men. *Id.* "[R]emoval of all the penis, its roots of soft tissue, and part of the scrotal skin" would be equivalent to infibulation. *Id.* Likening female circumcision to male circumcision therefore understates the extent of physical and other damage caused by FGM. For this reason I shall use the term Female Genital Mutilation (FGM) to collectively describe the three genital operations.

Female Genital Mutilation is also sometimes called Female Genital Cutting (FGC). *Note*

formed on a female from the age of only a few days to the age of sixteen.[12] There are three different types of FGM namely, clitoridectomy, excision, and infibulation or "pharaonic circumcision." Clitoridectomy is the "removal of the clitoral prepuce or tip of the clitoris."[13] Excision is the removal of the clitoris and the labia minora (small, inner lips of the vagina).[14] Infibulation or "pharaonic" circumcision is the most extreme of these operations and involves the removal of the clitoris, labia minora, and parts of the labia majora (large, outer lips of the vagina).[15] The remaining skin of the labia majora is then scraped to form raw surfaces and stitched together with thorns.[16] The wound is further kept together by binding the woman, with pieces of cloth made into a rope, from thigh to ankle for several weeks to enable scar tissue to form, covering the urethra and most of the vagina.[17] A small aperture, the size of "the head of a match stick or the tip of the little finger," is left open for the flow of urine and menstrual blood.[18] "Approximately 85 percent of all women who undergo FGM have clitoridectomies," or the excision procedure, and fifteen percent have undergone infibulation.[19]

FGM is usually performed by unskilled "traditional surgeons," such as an old woman of the village.[20] The "surgeons" use non-sterilized "razor blades, iron knives, and pieces of cut glass, or similarly constructed home-made tools."[21] "The degree of hygiene under which the operation is performed, the expertise of the practitioner, the general health of the girl or woman being circumcised, and the amount of struggling she does will all influence" the degree of severity of the effects of the operation.[22] Generally, FGM is performed with-

on Terminology, FEMALE GENITAL MUTILATION: A GUIDE TO LAWS AND POLICIES WORLD-WIDE x (Anika Rahman & Nahid Toubia, eds. 2000).

12. See DORKENOO & ELWORTHY, supra note 5, at 7.

13. Note, What's Culture Got to Do With It? Excising the Harmful Tradition of Female Circumcision, 106 HARV. L. REV. 1944, 1946 (1993) [hereinafter Culture].

14. Id.

15. SANDERSON, supra note 1, at 2.

16. Culture, supra note 13, at 1947.

17. Id.

18. TOUBIA, supra note 11, at 10.

19. Id.

20. DORKENOO & ELWORTHY, supra note 5, at 7. For a detailed description of an FGM operation, see HANNY LIGHTFOOT-KLEIN, PRISONERS OF RITUAL: AN ODYSSEY INTO FEMALE GENITAL CIRCUMCISION IN AFRICA 53 (1989).

21. Culture, supra note 13, at 1947.

22. Id. at 1947–48.

out anesthesia or the use of antiseptic.[23] After the procedure, the girl's mother and relatives provide follow-up care, and the girl lies in bed until her wounds have healed enough to allow her to move about with the help of a stick but with both legs still bound together.[24] The girl's legs stay bound together for at least forty days to ensure that the two sides of her vulva have coalesced and healed.[25]

FGM has severe physical and psychological consequences for the woman.[26] Women undergoing FGM may feel "anxiety prior to the operation, terror at the moment of being seized by an aunt or village matron, unbearable pain; the subsequent sense of humiliation and of being betrayed by parents, especially the mother."[27] Beginning with the operation, "[p]rotracted bleeding commonly leads to anemia,…[and] [i]f bleeding is very severe and uncontrolled, it can result in death."[28] Bad eyesight of the operator or struggling by the child or woman during the operation can cause cuts to the urethra, bladder, anal sphincter, vaginal walls, and Bartholin's glands.[29] Using unsterilized equipment also exposes females to tetanus infection, which can be fatal.[30] It is common for "traditional operators" to work on a group of girls at the same sitting with the same instrument, thereby increasing the risk of transmission of infection particularly for HIV.[31]

Infibulated women must be re-opened for sexual intercourse.[32] According to a description of a wedding night in Somalia, a husband uses a dagger to open up his wife and has prolonged and repeated intercourse with her for eight days to prevent the scar from closing again.[33] Needless to say, infibulated women suffer severe pain during sexual intercourse (dyspareunia).[34] Women will feel anxiety, trauma, and pain prior to and during sexual intercourse.[35]

---

23. DORKENOO & ELWORTHY, *supra* note 5, at 7.

24. *See* LIGHTFOOT-KLEIN, *supra* note 20, at 54.

25. DORKENOO & ELWORTHY, *supra* note 5, at 7.

26. The following discussion of effects of FGM is extremely limited. For a more complete discussion, *see generally* NAHID TOUBIA & SUSAN IZETT, WORLD HEALTH ORGANIZATION, FEMALE GENITAL MUTILATION: AN OVERVIEW (1998).

27. DORKENOO & ELWORTHY, *supra* note 5, at 10.

28. TOUBIA, *supra* note 11, at 13.

29. DORKENOO & ELWORTHY, *supra* note 5, at 8.

30. *Id.*

31. *Id.* at 9.

32. *Id.*

33. *Id.* at 8.

34. SANDERSON, *supra* note 1, at 39.

35. *Id.*

FGM destroys a woman's ability to achieve sexual satisfaction or gratification. Removal of the clitoris takes away the primary specialized sexual organ of a female, while her reproductive organs are left intact.[36] FGM does not affect the hormonal stimulants for sexual desire and arousal.[37] While a woman may feel sexually aroused and may be stimulated by other sexually sensitive parts of her body, a woman who has undergone FGM is unable to have an orgasm.[38] This leaves her with a physical and psychological sense of dissatisfaction and frustration.[39]

The Reasons for FGM: A Critique

Several reasons have been given for the practice of FGM, including "maintenance of tradition, the promotion of social and political cohesion, the enhancement of fertility, the fulfillment of religious requirements, the prevention of promiscuity, the preservation of virginity, the maintenance of feminine hygiene, and the pursuit of aesthetics."[40] Mutilation by FGM is "not merely cultural: it was psychosexual, sociological, and pseudo-hygienic and a part of the phenomena of discrimination against women, which has existed in every age and in most societies."[41]

For some African tribes, such as the people of Northern Sudan, the Kikuyu of Kenya, the Tagouana of Cote d'Ivoire, and the Bambara of Mali, FGM is a part of the initiation rites for development into adulthood.[42] Elaborate ceremonies accompany the event, and special songs are sung with dancing and chanting intended to teach a young girl her duties and desirable behavior as a wife and mother.[43] These initiation ceremonies affect other social relationships.[44] Robin Cerny Smith notes that several theories argue that this system

---

36. *See* DORKENOO & ELWORTHY, *supra* note 5, at 9.

37. *See id.* at 13.

38. *See id.* at 10.

39. *See* TOUBIA, *supra* note 11, at 17–18.

40. Culture, *supra* note 13, at 1949.

41. Commission on Human Rights, Sub-Commission on Prevention of Discrimination and Protection of Minorities, *Summary Record of the 910th Meeting*, UN ESCOR, 34th Sess., at 2, para. 3, U.N. Doc E/CN.4/Sub.2/SR.910 (1991).

42. DORKENOO & ELWORTHY, *supra* note 5, at 14.

43. *Id.*

44. Robyn Cerny Smith, Note, *Female Circumcision: Bringing Women's Perspectives into the International Debate*, 65 S. CAL. L. REV. 2449, 2459–60 (1992).

says a lot for group cohesion,[45] but the question to be asked is whether, bearing in mind the health risks, FGM is so crucial to group identity that performing the initiation rites without FGM would destroy group identity.[46] Studies of the practical value of FGM today indicate that conducting initiation rites without FGM would not destroy the group identity.[47]

In Mali, for example, ceremonies that once accompanied FGM have in most cases disappeared.[48] Where FGM is still practiced, 98 percent of the operations are carried out before puberty, with 53 percent occurring before the age of one.[49] This indicates the purpose of FGM, to teach a young girl her duties and desirable behavior as a wife, is no longer achieved by the performance of the operation. In the cities, FGM is performed in hospitals and clinics with the use of anesthesia.[50] Many educated women in these societies have escaped undergoing FGM and continue to be a part of these societies without harming group identity.[51]

"In some communities, [FGM] is the traditional ritual that confers full social acceptability and integration into the community upon the females."[52] In Akwa Ibom State and in villages in the Calabar area of Cross River State of Nigeria, women who have not undergone FGM face derision from other women who have undergone FGM.[53] FGM is a prerequisite for acceptance as a member of an ethnic group and a woman's right to belong, contribute to, and participate in her community as a full member.[54] The late Jomo Kenyatta commented that "[n]o proper Gikuyu would dream of marrying a girl who has not been circumcised"[55] and that "clitoridectomy...is regarded as the *conditio sine qua non* of the whole teaching of tribal law, religion, and morality."[56]

In cultures where the bride price system operates, a bride's family cannot obtain a bride price if the bride is not "pure."[57] In Nigeria, for example, a po-

---

45. *Id.* at 2470.
46. *See id.* at 2473–81.
47. *See* DORKENOO & ELWORTHY, *supra* note 5, at 14.
48. *Id.*
49. *Id.*
50. *Id.* at 7.
51. *See* Robyn Cerny Smith, *supra* note 44, at 2459, 2481–90.
52. Culture, *supra* note 13, at 1949.
53. *Id.* at 1950.
54. *Id.* at 1949.
55. JOMO KENYATTA, FACING MOUNT KENYA 132 (AMS Press 1978) (1938).
56. *Id.* at 133.
57. DORKENOO & ELWORTHY, *supra* note 5, at 14. Bride price, also referred to as dowry or "bridewealth," is a practice in which the prospective husband gives his future wife's fam-

tential mother-in-law uses FGM to discover whether or not the bride to be is a virgin.[58] If the woman is found not to be a virgin, her husband-to-be has the right to reject her and to demand a return of the bride price.[59] When a woman is rejected in this manner, her family is disgraced and stigmatized, leaving the woman with little choice but to leave home and marry outside of her community.[60] Preservation of virginity as an excuse for the practice of FGM is odd from a strictly practical level "since refibulation is easily done to look like the original one, whereas a ruptured hymen is more difficult to repair."[61] Although this argument is flawed, if society continues to base its rewards on the presence of FGM, then women have little choice but to succumb to the practice.

Assumptions about differences in male and female sexuality promote FGM. "The belief that [women who have not undergone FGM] cannot help but exhibit an unbridled and voracious appetite for promiscuous sex is prevalent in all societies that practice [FGM]."[62] The belief is that FGM not only protects a woman from her own sexuality, "saving her from temptation, suspicion and disgrace," but preserves her chastity as well.[63] Within polygynous relationships, a man cannot possibly satisfy all his wives regularly if they are sexually active.[64] It is not surprising that such men believe that the clitoris provokes women to make uncontrollable sexual demands on their husbands.[65] Thus FGM is not used to protect a woman from her sexuality as the argument for FGM purports; on the contrary, it is used to facilitate the ability of males in a polygynous society to satisfy their wives. FGM is also believed to protect a female from sexually aggressive males.[66] After a female has been infibulated, only a small opening, the size of the tip of a finger is left in the vagina.[67] Thus, sexual intercourse is supposed to be impossible, preventing her from having sex

---

ily a payment, typically in the form of livestock, in exchange for the privilege of marrying her. T.W. BENNETT, A SOURCEBOOK OF AFRICAN CUSTOMARY LAW FOR SOUTHERN AFRICA 195 (1991).

58. DORKENOO & ELWORTHY, *supra* note 5, at 14.
59. *Id.*
60. *Id.*
61. *Id.* at 13.
62. LIGHTFOOT-KLEIN, *supra* note 20, at 39.
63. DORKENOO & ELWORTHY, *supra* note 5, at 13.
64. *Id.*
65. *Id.*
66. LIGHTFOOT-KLEIN, *supra* note 20, at 39.
67. *See supra* note 18 and accompanying text.

before marriage. This argument does not hold up in the light of reports of young girls who have undergone FGM getting pregnant.[68] Furthermore, if aggressiveness stems from the men, then the best way to cure that would be to control the sexuality of males and not females.

Another myth that supports the practice of FGM is that FGM heightens male sexual pleasure.[69] The belief is that the smaller the vaginal opening of a female, the greater the sexual pleasure a man gets from having sex with her.[70] Surveys show that men report that they enjoy sex more with uninfibulated women.[71] The belief that FGM heightens male sexual pleasure is therefore just an illusion.

FGM is also incorrectly believed to enhance fertility, to make child birth easier, and to have healing powers.[72] The Egyptians and the people of Katiola in Mali believe that the clitoris is ugly and must be removed to make a woman clean.[73] In some parts of Somalia and Sudan, the aim of infibulation is to produce a smooth skin surface that it is believed makes a woman cleaner.[74] Although these superstitious beliefs about female sexuality are biologically and factually incorrect,[75] cultures that practice FGM hold onto their beliefs with tenacity, remaining ignorant of or overlooking factual inaccuracy.

Lastly, religion is another major reason given for the practice of FGM.[76] FGM, however, is a cultural, not religious, practice.[77] FGM preceded Islam in Africa.[78] "Not only is there no specific call for FGM in the Quran," but also there is a virtual absence of FGM in most Islamic countries.[79] Furthermore,

---

68. Mary Ann French, *The Open Wound; at Last, the World Comes Face to Face with What is Being Done to All Little Girls, in the Name of God and in the Service of an Ancient Ideal of Chastity*, WASH. POST, Nov. 22, 1992, at Fl.

69. RODNEY HEDLEY & EFUA DORKENOO, CHILD PROTECTION AND FEMALE GENITAL MUTILATION 7 (1992).

70. *Id.* at 6.

71. *Id.* at 7.

72. LIGHTFOOT-KLEIN, *supra* note 20, at 38–39. FGM is "claimed to have cured women suffering from melancholia, nymphomania, hysteria, insanity, and epilepsy, as well as kleptomania and proneness to truancy." *Id.* at 39. "[I]f a girl is ill and not gaining weight she is assumed to have the 'worm disease.' [FGM] is believed to cure this malady by releasing the worm." *Id.*

73. DORKENOO & ELWORTHY, *supra* note 5, at 14.

74. *Id.*

75. *See* LIGHTFOOT-KLEIN, *supra* note 20, at 38.

76. TOUBIA, *supra* note 11, at 31.

77. *Id.*

78. DORKENOO & ELWORTHY, *supra* note 5, at 13.

79. TOUBIA, *supra* note 11, at 32.

FGM is not practiced in Saudi Arabia.[80] Additionally, Islamic theologians have refuted the argument that FGM is based on religious doctrine.[81] The people who tend to practice FGM are not religious scholars and do not know that FGM is not required by Islam.[82] Thus, "it is most likely that newly converted leaders, seeking to continue the practice of FGM, linked it with Islam."[83]

It is not difficult to understand why FGM continues unabated if one puts oneself in the shoes of a Sudanese woman who has no education and who believes, or has been brought up to believe, that her only goal in life is to marry, to satisfy her husband sexually and otherwise, and to bear him many children.[84] For such a woman, tradition plays a very important part in her life, and her tradition, she is told, demands that she undergo FGM. Dahabo Elmi Muse, in her prizewinning poem on FGM, speaks about the "three feminine sorrows" her grandmother told her about "the day of circumcision, the wedding night and the birth / of a baby."[85] A rural woman is brought up to expect these three feminine sorrows and to see them as natural. It would be difficult for her to believe otherwise.

FGM under the Law in Ghana

FGM is practiced in Northern Ghana.[86] The prevalence of FGM in Northern Ghana is 30 percent.[87] The Government issued a formal declaration in

---

80. LIGHTFOOT-KLEIN, *supra* note 20, at 41.

81. DORKENOO & ELWORTHY, *supra* note 5, at 13.

82. *See* ELLEN GRUENBAUM, THE FEMALE CIRCUMCISION CONTROVERSY 60–66 (2001).

83. TOUBIA, *supra* note 11, at 31.

84. *See* LIGHTFOOT-KLEIN, *supra* note 20, at 68–70.

85. Dahabo Elmi Muse, "Poem on Female Genital Mutilation," *reprinted in* LULA J. HUSSEIN AND MARIAN A.A. SHERMARKE, DEP'T OF JUSTICE CANADA, WORKING DOCUMENT, FEMALE GENITAL MUTILATION: REPORT ON CONSULTATIONS HELD IN OTTAWA AND MONTREAL, app. C (1995), *available at* http://canada.justice.gc.ca/en/ps/rs/rep/wd95-8a-e.pdf (Last visited July 8, 2003). "This poem won the First Prize in the Poetry Competition for Female Poets of Benadir and was recited during the closing ceremony of the International Seminar on the Eradication of Female Circumcision held in Mogadishu, Somalia in 1988." LULA J. HUSSEIN AND MARIAN A.A. SHERMARKE, DEP'T OF JUSTICE CANADA, WORKING DOCUMENT, FEMALE GENITAL MUTILATION: REPORT ON CONSULTATIONS HELD IN OTTAWA AND MONTREAL, app. C (1995), *available at* http://canada.justice.gc.ca/en/ps/rs/rep/wd95-8a-e.pdf (Last visited July 8, 2003).

86. TOUBIA, *supra* note 11, at 25.

87. *Id.*

1989 against FGM.[88] In 1994, the Government formally criminalized the practice; the new law reads as follows:

> (1) Whoever excises, infibulates or otherwise mutilates the whole or any part of the labia minora, labia majora and the clitoris of another person commits an offense and shall be guilty of a second degree felony and liable on conviction to imprisonment of not less than three years.
>
> (2) For the purposes of this section 'excise' means to remove the prepuce, the clitoris and all or part of the labia minora; 'infibulate' includes excisions and the additional removal of the labia majora.[89]

Although this constitutes positive legal reform, it is unclear whether this legislation has had any effect on the ground. Seven years after enactment of the criminal prohibition the prevalence rate remains 30 percent.[90] There were only seven arrests pursuant to the law between 1994 and 2000.[91] As of 2000, only two of the arrested "operators" had been prosecuted and convicted,[92] including one "operator" who was sentenced to three years after "operating" on 3 girls, ages 12 to 15, who had consented but without the knowledge of their parents.[93] In addition to under-enforcement, the law often fails to hold parents liable and typically does not reach people who travel out of the country for the procedure.[94]

---

88. OFFICE OF THE SENIOR COORDINATOR FOR INT'L WOMEN'S ISSUES, DEP'T OF STATE, GHANA: REPORT ON FEMALE GENITAL MUTILATION (FGM) OR FEMALE GENITAL CUTTING (FGC) (2001) *available at* http://www.state.gov/g/wi/rls/rep/crfgm/10100.htm (Last visited July 8, 2003).

89. [Ghana] Criminal Code (Amendment) Act, 1994 (Act 484). The Act inserted §69A into the [Ghana] Criminal Code, 1960 (Act 29).

90. THE CENTER FOR REPRODUCTIVE LAW AND POLICY, WOMEN OF THE WORLD: LAWS AND POLICIES AFFECTING THEIR REPRODUCTIVE LIVES, ANGLOPHONE AFRICA, PROGRESS REPORT 2001 40 (2001).

91. Dep't of State, *Ghana*, in COUNTRY REPORTS ON HUMAN RIGHTS PRACTICES FOR 2001, at 303, §5 at 322 (2001). The police arrested one practitioner and a set of parents in March of 1995 after the press revealed that an eight-day-old girl was brought to the hospital to seek care for severe bleeding following FGM. FEMALE GENITAL MUTILATION: A GUIDE TO LAWS AND POLICIES WORLDWIDE 166 (Anika Rahman & Nahid Toubia, eds. 2000) [hereinafter Guide].

92. Dep't of State, *supra* note 91, §5 at 322.

93. Guide, *supra* note 91, at 166.

94. Dep't of State, *supra* note 91, §5 at 323. At least one set of parents, however, have been arrested under the law. *See supra* note 91.

The 1992 Ghanaian Constitution (the Constitution) is replete with clauses protecting women from practices such as FGM.[95] To begin with, FGM is not only contrary to the fundamental rights and freedoms declared in the Constitution, but also antithetical to the commitments that form the basis of the Constitution and are affirmed in the preamble of the constitution.[96] The preamble to the Constitution affirms a commitment to "the protection and preservation of Fundamental Human Rights and Freedoms."[97] The Constitution talks about the protection of right to life and protection of personal liberty.[98] Article 15(2) proclaims that no person shall be subject to torture or cruel, inhuman, or degrading treatment or punishment, or any other condition that detracts from the dignity and worth of a human being.[99] FGM is torture, cruel, inhuman, and degrading treatment and is injurious to the health and well-being of women and children, as defined by the Torture Convention,[100] the United Nation Commission on Human Rights,[101] and the World Health Organization.[102] Children are explicitly protected; the Constitution prohibits subjecting a child to torture or other cruel, inhuman, or degrading treatment.[103] The Constitution also prohibits discrimination on the grounds of gender,[104] and it gives Parliament the power to enact laws that are reasonably necessary for "implementation of policies and programs aimed at redressing social, economic or educational imbalances in the Ghanaian society."[105] FGM is discrimination against women on the basis of their gender, and

---

95. *See* The Const. of the Republic of Ghana 1992 ch. V. (entitled "Fundamental Human Rights and Freedoms").

96. *See id.* at pmbl.

97. *Id.*

98. *Id.* at ch. V, art. 13–14.

99. *Id.* at ch. V, art. 15(2).

100. *Declaration on the Protection of All Persons from Being Subjected to Torture and Other Cruel, Inhuman or Degrading Treatment or Punishment*, G.A. Res. 3452, U.N. GAOR, 30th Sess., Supp. No. 34, at 91, U.N. Doc. A/100034 (1975).

101. *See* Commission on Human Rights, Sub-Commission on Prevention of Discrimination and Protection of Minorities, *Updating of the Report on Slavery Submitted to the Sub-Commission in 1966, Report by Mr. Benjamin Whitaker, Special Rapporteur*, U.N. ESCOR, 35th Sess., at 19, para. 46–47, U.N. Doc E/CN.4/Sub.2/1982/20 (1982). The report condemns FGM as "slavery-like practices of which women are the particular victims." *Id.*

102. World Health Organization, Female Genital Mutilation: A Joint WHO/UNICEF/UNFPA Statement 7–9 (1997).

103. The Const. of the Republic of Ghana 1992 ch. V, art. 28(3).

104. *Id.* at ch. V, art. 17(2).

the Ghanaian parliament has a duty to pass legislation banning FGM to re-dress the social imbalance created by it. Article 26(l) of the Constitution en-titles every person "to enjoy, practice, profess, maintain and promote any cul-ture, language, tradition or religion subject to the provisions of the Constitution."[106] Article 26(2), however, states that "all customary practices which dehumanize or are injurious to the physical and mental well being of a person are prohibited."[107] Even prior to passage of the criminal prohibition on FGM, this article alone is sufficient to constitute a ban on FGM in Ghana.

Plan of Action for Eradication of FGM in Ghana

The Criminal Code of Ghana[108] and the Ghanaian Constitution[109] provide avenues to protect women from FGM in Ghana. Under the Criminal Code, practitioners of FGM can be prosecuted as felons.[110] Before such cases can be prosecuted, however, victims of FGM must realize that FGM is detrimental to their health and that legal remedies are available to them. Massive legal lit-eracy campaigns will have to be mounted all over the country to educate peo-ple on their rights and obligations under the Constitution. The Constitution provides for the establishment of a National Commission for Civic Education (NCCE)[111] that shall "educate and encourage the public to defend this Con-stitution at all times, against all forms of abuse and violation"[112] and "to for-mulate for the consideration of Government, from time to time, programmes aimed at realising the objectives of this Constitution."[113]

Women's rights groups must lobby the Commissioner for Civic Education to make the public aware that FGM is criminal and unconstitutional. In light of all the above contraventions of the law by the practice of FGM, the NCCE should formulate programs at the national, regional, and district levels aimed at making the citizens of Ghana aware that FGM is illegal. This education should take the form of symposia, documentary films on television, radio pro-

---

105. *Id.* at ch. V, art. 17(4)(a).
106. *Id.* at ch. V, art. 26(1).
107. *Id.* at ch. V, art. 26(2).
108. *See supra* notes 89–94 and accompanying text.
109. *See supra* notes 95–99, 103–7 and accompanying text.
110. [Ghana] Criminal Code (Amendment) Act, 1994 (Act 484) pt. 1.
111. The Const. of the Republic of Ghana 1992 ch. XIX.
112. *Id.* at ch. XIX, art. 233(b).
113. *Id.* at ch. XIX, art. 233(c).

grams and articles in the newspapers, both in English and the major Ghanaian languages, in order to get the information to as many people as possible.

Women's rights groups should also approach the Commission on Human Rights and Administrative Justice (CHRAJ),[114] the body charged with the duty "to investigate complaints of violations of fundamental rights and freedoms;"[115] "to investigate complaints concerning practices and actions by persons...where those complaints allege violations of fundamental rights and freedoms under this Constitution,"[116] and to take appropriate action to remedy constitutional violations, including "bringing proceedings in a competent Court for a remedy to secure the termination of the offending action or conduct."[117] The Constitution does not specify who may bring a complaint, but non-governmental organizations may present such complaints and/or reports in an advisory capacity to governmental organizations. In the past, this has led to reform in other areas of law relating to women.[118]

Advocates for women should present the CHRAJ with a complaint stating that the practice of FGM violates the fundamental rights and freedoms enshrined in the Constitution. This complaint would call for an investigation and for an action to be brought in court for a declaration that FGM is unconstitutional. Advocates could then present the CHRAJ with a request that after the investigation, the CHRAJ should bring an action under the Constitution to secure the termination of the practice of FGM.[119] Advocates should present evidence on FGM, elucidating its health consequences for women and children, and attach copies of recommendations made by the Special Rapporteur appointed by the U.N. Sub-Commission on Prevention of Discrimination and Protection of Minorities, to study traditional practices affecting the health of women and children.[120] In such a case, advocates could also put in evidence expert testimony on the health risks involved in the practice of FGM and also present a film clip of an FGM "operation." In light of the fact that FGM contravenes the provisions of the Constitution and the directive principles of state policy, the Supreme Court should declare FGM unconstitutional and abolish it in Ghana.[121]

---

114. *See id.* at ch. XVIII.
115. *Id.* at ch. XVIII, art. 218(a).
116. *Id.* at ch. XVIII, art. 218(c).
117. *Id.* at ch. XVIII, art. 218(d)(iii).
118. *See* THE CENTER FOR REPRODUCTIVE LAW AND POLICY, *supra* note 90, at 43.
119. *See supra* notes 111–17 and accompanying text.
120. *See* Warzazi, *supra* note 3, at 36, para. 154.
121. *See* THE CONST. OF THE REPUBLIC OF GHANA 1992 ch. V, art. 33.

The CHRAJ also has a duty under the Constitution "to educate the public as to human rights and freedoms"[122] and "to report annually to Parliament on the performance of its functions."[123] Accordingly, in its annual report, the CHRAJ should educate the public on FGM and make recommendations to Parliament for expanding and enforcing the law criminalizing FGM.

Women's rights advocates should also present the Attorney General and Director of Public Prosecutions with a statement showing that FGM is a crime and should be prosecuted. Although FGM is a crime under §69A of the Criminal Code of Ghana, "operators" are rarely prosecuted for the practice of FGM.[124] The advocate's statement would list "operators" whom the advocates have identified through interviews with women in areas where FGM is practiced. The statement would recommend that parents and guardians of minors be charged with abetment of assault. A court may be reluctant to imprison a parent for this offense, but since the court has discretion to levy a fine or impose imprisonment or both,[125] the court could merely fine the parents to serve as a deterrent to committing these crimes. Prosecutors should vigorously pursue cases of FGM.

Finally, advocates must promote education on the problem of FGM. Symposia should be held and documentary films run by the mass media to sensitize the populace to the problems caused by FGM. Publicity must be given to the criminal proceedings taken against FGM "operators." In particular, the public must recognize that victims of FGM can bring several kinds of actions for redress. Victims may press criminal charges against "operators." They may also be able to bring a civil action in tort for battery. Because Ghanaians can bring a claim to the High Court when constitutional rights have been, are being, or are likely to be infringed upon, a would-be victim of FGM can obtain a court order prohibiting anyone from performing the operation on her. A victim of FGM can also obtain a declaration from the courts, stating that the FGM operation is an infringement of the rights of women enshrined in the Constitution. Victims may also contact the State prosecutors, who shall asses their complaints and bring the appropriate charges against the "operators" for "assault" and "causing harm."

For any country to ban and effectively eradicate FGM, any legislative action must be backed by the elimination of polygyny and the dowry and bride

---

122. *Id.* at ch. XVIII, art 218(f).
123. *Id.* at ch. XVIII, art. 218(g).
124. *See supra* notes 91–94 and accompanying text.
125. *See* [Ghana] Criminal Code, 1960 (Act 29) §20.

price systems and supported by affirmative action for women in the areas of health and education. These actions will serve to combat the notion that a woman is a piece of property that can be passed from one man to another. This cannot be done, however, without the help of the traditional rulers and religious leaders who have helped maintain the practice of FGM. If traditional leaders have helped to perpetuate the practice of FGM, they can also be the agents of change.

Customary practices die hard, but history has shown that they can be eradicated through education and exposure to other cultures and ways of life. Any plan to eradicate FGM must be supported by education and health programs and eradication of other customary practices that reinforce the practice of FGM like dowry, bride price, and polygyny. FGM is deeply ingrained in traditional society, but, with continuous pressure on the governments of countries where it is practiced and education of women on the impact of the practice, FGM can and must be eradicated.

CHAPTER THREE

WOMEN'S RIGHTS WITHIN THE FAMILY

Chapter Introduction, *Johanna Bond*

Because women have been largely relegated to the private sphere, as discussed in chapter one, women's rights within the family are critically important to their quality of life. The level of autonomy, or lack thereof, that women enjoy within the family is both derivative of and a reflection of the freedom they enjoy within the larger society. Stereotypes that limit women's participation in public life often reinforce women's expected, stereotypical role within the family—as a caregiver who contributes neither to the financial well-being of her family nor to the leadership of her community.

The first two essays in chapter three describe traditional marriage practices in Ghana, including polygamy. The essays describe the gender-based inequalities that stem from polygamy and the social and legal forces that contribute to the perpetuation of the practice. The essays also suggest courses of action that combine legal, social, and economic strategies to combat it. The following two essays address marriage and divorce in Ghana and Uganda, respectively. The first of the two essays focuses on the ways in which marriage and divorce under Ghanaian customary law discriminates against women, while the second explores divorce in Uganda under customary, statutory, and religious laws and examines its implications for women's rights in Uganda. The next essay examines the treatment of matrimonial property within the Tanzanian legal system and describes the ways in which the legal system disadvantages women. Similarly, the subsequent essay addresses the treatment of marital property within the Ugandan legal system. The final essay in the chapter takes on the critical issue of women's inheritance rights in Tanzania and proposes specific legal reforms that would increase women's legal rights to inheritance and contribute to women's economic empowerment.

Women's Rights within the Family and Multiple Systems of Law

As former British colonies, Ghana, Uganda, and Tanzania each have a pluralistic legal system—one in which multiple systems of law operate simultaneously. As a result, the extent to which a woman is able to realize her right to equality within the family may depend, in part, on whether a court is applying statutory law, customary law, or religious law to her case. During the colonial period, British authorities initiated a dual legal system in which trial courts applied the "received" law, or the law in force in Great Britain, in cases involving non-Africans and local courts applied customary law in cases involving African parties.[1]

Today, family law in each of these countries reflects this colonial legacy. In Ghana, for example, a couple may choose to marry according to statutory law pursuant to the Marriage Ordinance, according to customary law, or according to Islamic law pursuant to the Marriage of Mohammedans Ordinance. The rights that a woman may legally enjoy during her marriage and at its dissolution depend upon the type of marriage into which she has entered. Statutory law often, but by no means always, provides more protection for women's human rights than other systems of law, creating disparities among women who have married pursuant to different legal systems within the same country. Uganda employs a similar pluralistic system, in which an individual may marry according to statutory law, customary law, Islamic law, or Hindu law.[2]

In some countries, such as Tanzania, independence from colonial rule inspired efforts to dismantle the pluralistic legal system.[3] As a result, Tanzania

---

1. Marsha A. Freeman, *Measuring Equality: A Comparative Perspective on Women's Legal Capacity and Constitutional Rights in Five Commonwealth Countries*, 5 BERKELEY WOMEN'S L.J. 110, 118 (1989–90).

2. Because the Hindu law of marriage is rarely invoked by Ugandan women, it will not be discussed in detail. *See,* Sylvia Tamale, *Law Reform and Women's Rights in Uganda*, 1 E. AFRICAN J. OF PEACE AND HUM. RTS. 164, 170 (1993).

3. As Bart Rwezaura observes, "Plural legal systems…are a product of colonial occupation." Bart Rwezaura, *Tanzania: Building a New Family Law Out of a Plural Legal System*, 33 U. Louisville J. Fam. L. 523, 523–24 (1994–95). Rwezaura also notes that the unified

has unified the marriage laws in one statute—the Law of Marriage Act (LMA)—that governs all marriages in Tanzania, regardless of the customary or religious beliefs of the parties. Tanzania's LMA does not, however, govern legal matters involving inheritance, leaving women susceptible to discrimination in inheritance depending on whether statutory, customary, or Islamic inheritance law applies.

Women's Rights During Marriage: Polygyny, Brideprice, and Other Discriminatory Aspects of Marriage

Polygyny

In Ghana and Uganda, customary and Islamic marriages are potentially polygamous. Even in Tanzania, the LMA does not prohibit polygamy, but does allow women in customary or Islamic marriages to register an official "objection" to a husband's decision to take a new wife.[4] Bernice Sam and others argue that polygamy creates an inherently unequal relationship between a husband and his wives. Sam also notes that the practice allows men to abandon older wives, who may be beyond their childbearing years.[5]

As the authors in this chapter point out, polygamy substantially increases women's risk of contracting HIV/AIDS, may exacerbate domestic violence by creating a home environment in which multiple wives compete for the affection and resources of one man, and leads to smaller shares of inheritance particularly if the husband in a polygamous marriage dies intestate. However, despite the social, legal, and economic problems created by polygamy, several of the authors in this chapter caution against a rigid prohibition of the practice. Angela Dwamena-Aboagye, for example, recommends a prospective ban on polygamous unions with two narrow exceptions involving circumstances in which sexual intercourse is impossible or the female partner is infertile.

---

marriage law was intended to simplify complex choice of law questions and to elevate the status of women in Tanzania. *Id.* at 526.

4. Tanzania Law of Marriage Act, §§ 20–21 (1971).

5. *See infra* p. 211.

Brideprice

According to customary law in Ghana, Uganda, and Tanzania, the family of a prospective groom must pay a brideprice, or compensation to the family of the prospective bride. In Tanzania, the LMA does not prohibit the payment of brideprice. Sam points out that bridewealth traditionally functioned to "compensate the bride's family for the loss of a daughter" and to "serve as a means of distinguishing marriage from concubinage."[6] Sam also notes, however, that bridewealth has changed from a traditional symbol to a means of "purchasing" a wife, and clearly this notion of women as chattel reinforces men's domination over women.

Women's Rights in the Dissolution of Marriage: Divorce or the Death of a Spouse

Divorce

In Ghana and Uganda, women's rights to property at divorce largely depend upon whether statutory, customary, or Islamic marriage law controls. In Ghana, the Matrimonial Causes Act governs the dissolution of marriages contracted according to statutory law under the Marriage Ordinance and certain other marriages meeting narrow requirements.[7] Customary and Islamic law governs divorces for marriages contracted within those legal systems. When a statutory marriage is dissolved, a Ghanaian court may order maintenance or the transfer of moveable or immovable property in an effort to reach a settlement that is "just and equitable."[8] Despite additional constitutional guarantees requiring that assets jointly acquired during marriage be "equitably" distributed upon divorce,[9] women continue to be at the mercy of

---

6. *See infra* p. 212.

7. The Matrimonial Causes Act may govern non-monogamous marriages (i.e., customary and Islamic) upon application by the parties. Under such circumstances, the court must apply the provisions of the Act subject to the "peculiar incidents of that marriage," referring to the customary law of the parties involved. Matrimonial Causes Act, 1971 (367) (1971) (Ghana), art. 41(2)(a).

8. CENTER FOR REPRODUCTIVE LAW AND POLICY, WOMEN OF THE WORLD: LAWS AND POLICIES AFFECTING THEIR REPRODUCTIVE LIVES, ANGLOPHONE AFRICA (Center for Reproductive Law and Policy 1997), at 43.

9. Ghana Constitution, art. 22 (3)(b).

judges' discretion in a legal and social environment in which women's financial and nonmonetary contributions to the marriage are minimized or ignored.

Women generally fare no better under customary or Islamic divorce law. Customary law varies according to the ethnic group of the parties, and the details of the marriage dissolution must often be negotiated between the families of the parties.[10] Customary divorce often involves the return of bridewealth to the husband's family, particularly if the wife is deemed to be at fault in causing the divorce.[11] Because families are often financially unable to return the bridewealth, many women remain in unhappy or violent relationships.[12] Customary law generally provides no support for an ex-wife other than a token "send-off" amount.[13] Islamic law gives a husband the right to unilaterally divorce his wife by simply pronouncing *talaq* three times; no similar right exists for Muslim women.[14] Islamic law does not expressly address the distribution of marital assets at divorce, which as Regina Mutyaba points out, "often works to the advantage of men."[15] According to Mutyaba, however, a divorcing Muslim husband must often pay maintenance during *iddat*, the period of approximately three months following a divorce.[16] The situation for divorcing women is similar in Uganda, with variable relief available to women depending upon the type of marriage they have contracted.

Unlike the laws in Ghana and Uganda, Tanzania's LMA reflects a unified marriage law—applicable to all marriages in Tanzania—that delineates women's rights upon marriage and at divorce. Under the LMA, women have the same rights as men to acquire, hold, and dispose of property. Section 114 of the LMA, however, gives courts considerable discretion in dividing property between divorcing spouses. Among other things, the court may consider "the custom of the community to which the parties belong" and "the extent of the contributions made by each party in money, property, or work towards the acquiring of the assets."[17] In the landmark case of *Bi Hawa Mohammed vs.*

10. Center for Reproductive Law and Policy, *see supra* note 8, at 43.
11. Sylvia Tamale, Law Reform and Women's Rights in Uganda, E. African J. of Peace & Hum. Rts. 1, 173 (1993).
12. *Id.*
13. Center for Reproductive Law and Policy, *supra* note 11, at 43.
14. Shaheen Sardar Ali, Gender and Human Rights in Islam and International Law 60 (2000).
15. Regina Mutyaba, this chapter, 222.
16. *Id.*
17. LMA, section 114.

Ally Sefu, the Court of Appeals of Tanzania determined that a woman's domestic work constituted a "contribution" within the meaning of section 114
of the LMA, recognizing her right to matrimonial assets upon divorce.[18] In
practice, however, courts often still give preference to husbands, who are generally higher wage earners, in the division of matrimonial assets.[19]

Inheritance

In Uganda and Tanzania, statutory, customary, and Islamic law also governs inheritance when a spouse dies intestate. Because women often perform
domestic labor or labor in the informal labor market, they have few avenues
for amassing wealth. Therefore, when her husband dies, a woman's very survival may be at stake. The laws in Uganda and Tanzania, however, fail to reflect this reality and afford women incomplete and inequitable remedies in
cases involving intestate succession.

In Tanzania, for example, courts must first determine whether to apply
statutory, customary, or Islamic law in intestate succession cases.[20] There is a
presumption in favor of customary law unless the court is satisfied that it is
"apparent from the nature of any relevant act or transaction, manner of life
or business, that the matter is...to be regulated other than by customary
law."[21] In other words, customary law is presumed to apply unless an examination of the deceased's life, under the "mode of life" test, reveals that statutory or Islamic law should apply. Under customary law, which the courts most
commonly apply, a spouse—regardless of gender—will not inherit property
if there are surviving male children or other male family members of the deceased's lineage.[22] In practice, when a man dies intestate, his side of the family will sometimes raid his home, "grabbing" property with no regard for the
surviving widow or her children. In other cases, the deceased man's family expects to "inherit" the widow along with the man's property, forcing her to wed

---

18. Bart Rwezaura, *supra* note 3, at 523, 532 (*citing* Court of Appeal (Dar es Salaam)
Civ. App. No. 9 or 1983).

19. Jennifer L. Rakstad, et al., *The Progress of Tanzanian Women in the Law: Women in
Legal Education, Legal Employment, and Legal Reform*, 10 S. CAL. REV. OF L. & WOMEN'S
STUD. 35, 98 (2000).

20. Hindu law may also apply in rare intestate succession cases involving Hindu parties.

21. Judicature and Application of Laws Ordinance, Cap. 453, ord. 1961, No. 57, Section 9(1).

22. Rakstad et al, *supra* note 19, at 95 (describing degrees of inheritance for possible heirs).

a surviving brother or other male relative of the deceased. In other instances, widows serve as "custodians of their sons' inheritance" and are entitled to use the family home until they die.[23]

Under Islamic law, a widow is entitled to receive one-eighth of her husband's estate if there are surviving children and one-quarter if there are no children.[24] A widower, by contrast, is entitled to one-quarter of his wife's estate if there are children and one-half if there are not.[25] This inheritance scheme discriminates against women on its face. A Tanzanian statutory law, the Indian Succession Act of 1865, grants widows and widowers the same rights to the estate, but the law is rarely applied. As a result of this fragmented system of laws, Tanzanian women face varying degrees of discrimination in the administration of a deceased husband's estate.

Ghana, however, has taken steps to integrate its statutory and customary laws by passing the 1985 Intestate Succession Law, [26] a law that was designed, in part, to improve the plight of widows.[27] As the memorandum accompanying the law stipulates, the law applies "irrespective of the class of the intestate and the type of marriage contracted by him or her."[28] The law, which applies to self-acquired property rather than lineage or clan property, grants surviving spouses and children absolute rights to the household chattels and one house of the estate. The law includes a formula to determine division of the residue of the estate, including a one-eighth share to be distributed according to customary law.[29] Although the Intestate Succession Law represents a significant step forward for women in Ghana, customary rules of inheritance remain a resilient force because many people are unaware of the law or lack the means to enforce it in court.[30]

---

23. *Id.*

24. ULLAH, AL-HAJ MAHOMED, MUSLIM LAW OF INHERITANCE 69 (Law Publishing Company 1940).

25. *Id.*

26. Intestate Succession Law, P.N.D.C.L. 111 (1985)(Ghana).

27. Jeanmarie Fenrich & Tracey Higgins, *Promise Unfulfilled: Law, Culture, and Women's Inheritance Rights in Ghana*, 25 FORDHAM INT'L L. J. 259, 268 (2001).

28. Republic of Ghana, *Provisional National Defence Council Laws on Intestate Succession, in* LAWS OF THE PROVISIONAL NATIONAL DEFENCE COUNCIL TOME 1, at ii (1982).

29. Jeanmarie Fenrich and Tracey Higgins, *Promise Unfulfilled: Law, Culture, and Women's Inheritance Rights in Ghana*, 25 FORDHAM INT'L L. J. 259, 289 (2001) (noting that where there is no surviving parent, the share to be distributed according to customary law increases to one fourth).

30. *Id.*

International Human Rights Law Relevant to Equality within the Family

Article 16 of the Convention on the Elimination of All Forms of Discrimination Against Women (CEDAW) protects women's rights to equality in "marriage and family relations."[31] Article 16 specifically requires states parties to ensure that men and women enjoy "the same rights and responsibilities during marriage and at its dissolution" and the same rights in the "ownership, acquisition, management, administration, enjoyment, and disposition of property."[32] Like CEDAW, article 23 of the International Covenant on Civil and Political Rights requires states parties to ensure equality in marriage and at its dissolution.[33]

In 1994, the CEDAW Committee issued General Recommendation No. 21 to guide states parties in the implementation of articles 9, 15, and 16 of the Convention. General Recommendation No. 21 condemns polygyny, noting "with concern that some States parties, whose constitutions guarantee equal rights, permit polygamous marriage in accordance with personal or customary law."[34] With respect to women's property rights, General Recommendation No. 21 unequivocally states, "any law or custom that grants men a right to a greater share of property at the end of a marriage or de facto relationship, or on the death of a relative, is discriminatory and will have a serious impact on a woman's practical ability to divorce her husband, to support herself or her family and to live in dignity as an independent person."[35] The Recommendation also specifically addresses the consideration of nonmonetary contributions to the household in the division of marital assets[36] and the need for inheritance law to provide equal shares to men and women who are "in the same degree of relationship to a deceased."[37]

---

31. *Convention on the Elimination of all forms of Discrimination Against Women*, GA res. 34/180, 34 UN GAOR Supp. (No. 46) at 193, UN Doc. A/34/46.

32. *Id.*

33. International Covenant on Civil and Political Rights, GA res. 2200A (XXI), 21 UN GAOR Supp. (No. 16) at 52, UN Doc. A/6316 (1966); 999 UNTS 171.

34. Committee on the Elimination of Discrimination against Women, General Recommendation 21, Equality in marriage and family relations (Thirteenth session, 1992), at para. 14, Compilation of General Comments and General Recommendations Adopted by Human Rights Treaty Bodies, U.N. Doc. HRI\GEN\1\Rev.1 at 90 (1994).

35. *Id.*, para. 28.

36. *Id.*, para. 32.

37. *Id.*, para. 34.

The African Charter also protects women's rights within the family. Article 18 requires states parties to eliminate "every discrimination against women." The Protocol to the African Charter on Human and Peoples' Rights on the Rights of Women in Africa takes a more conservative position on polygyny than does the CEDAW Committee, encouraging monogamy "as the preferred form of marriage."[38] The Protocol also requires states parties to ensure that women and men "enjoy the same rights in case of separation, divorce, or annulment of marriage."[39]

---

38. Protocol to the African Charter on Human and Peoples' Rights on the Rights of Women in Africa, Art. 6(c).

39. Protocol to the African Charter on Human and Peoples' Rights on the Rights of Women in Africa, Art. 7.

Polygamy, Equality, and the Gender Debate: A Comparative Study of Ghana and the United States

Angela Dwamena-Aboagye

Introduction

In Ghana, polygamy is a legally recognized form of marriage. In the United States, polygamy exists as a religious practice despite longstanding criminalization. This essay compares the practice of polygamy in Ghana and the United States by analyzing the condition of gender equality in these two countries.

United States — Background

Monogamy, the union of a single man and a single woman, is the only legally recognized form of marriage in the United States.[1] Polygamy has been illegal since the early 1800s.[2] Fundamentalist Mormons and members of the

---

1. 1 U.S.C. §7 (2003); *see* Richard A. Posner and Katharine B. Silbaugh, A Guide to Americas Sex Laws 141–54 (1996); *but see, e.g.,* Kobogum v. Jackson Iron Co., 43 N.W. 602, 605 (Mich. 1889) (an exception has been made for Indian Tribes in the United States because the practice is part of their tribal law).

2. *See, eg.,* Reynolds v. United States, 98 U.S. 145 (1878) (The Court upheld a statute which outlawed polygamy in a areas where the United States had exclusive jurisdiction); *see also* Howard Roberts Lamar, The Far Southwest 1846–1912 A Territorial History 402 (1966) (Utah was required to give up polygamy before Congress would consider granting it statehood).

Church of Jesus Christ of Latter-Day Saints,[3] who are almost all concentrated in the western states, practice polygamy.[4] The Mormon Church abandoned polygamy as an officially sanctioned practice in 1890,[5] but break-away fundamentalists continue to support the practice.[6]

As of 1985, approximately 10,000 to 20,000 polygamists lived in Utah alone.[7] In 1991, estimates from the Rocky Mountain states revealed 50,000 polygamists living in communes.[8] Despite official opposition, these numbers are growing.[9]

The Law

In 1882, Congress passed the Edmunds Act, making polygamy illegal in the United States.[10] Before the Edmunds Act, *Reynolds v. United States,*[11] in which the plaintiff was prosecuted and convicted for concurrent marriages to two women, settled the question of the illegality of the practice in the United States. The court rejected Reynolds' contention that the free exercise clause of the First Amendment should protect an individual from conviction if his act was based on a good faith religious belief. The court declared that "[l]aws are made for the government of actions, and while they cannot interfere with mere religious belief and opinions, they may with practices."[12]

---

3. Founded by their leader Joseph Smith, around the early 1830s. JOAN SMYTH IVERSEN, THE ANTIPOLYGAMY CONTROVERSY IN U.S. WOMENS MOVEMENTS, 1880–1925, 3 (1997).

4. RICHARD N. OSTLING AND JOAN K. OSTLING, MORMON AMERICA THE POWER AND THE PROMISE 56–57 (1999) (polygamy practitioners are mainly found in parts of Utah, Arizona, and Colorado with a few scattered in other western states).

5. *See generally* Jeremy M. Miller, *A Critique of Reynolds Decision,* 11 W. ST. U. L. REV. 165, 182 (1984).

6. OSTLING, *supra* note 4, at 57.

7. *See, e.g.,* Janice Perry, *Polygamy and the State: Despite Laws Against it, the Practice Seems to be Gaining,* L. A. DAILY J., Apr. 24, 1985, at 4.

8. *See* Dirk Johnson, *Polygamists Emerge from Secrecy,* N.Y. TIMES, Apr. 9, 1991, at A22.

9. For example, Short Creek, a polygamist community in the West, was raided by Arizona state officials in 1953. The strategy failed woefully. MARTHA SONNTAG, KIDNAPPED FROM THAT LAND 112, 182–83 (1993).

10. IVERSEN, *supra* note 3, at 113.

11. 98 U.S. 145.

12. *Id.* at 166.

The U.S. Supreme Court has yet to overturn the *Reynolds'* decision in subsequent cases,[13] despite changes in free exercise jurisprudence that raise questions about the validity of the *Reynolds* belief/action dichotomy.[14]

Ghana — Background

British colonization left Ghana with a legacy of English law[15] co-existing with traditional law. Couples may choose to marry according to statutory law or traditional African customary law. Apart from English statutory and customary law, Islamic law[16] governs marriages between Muslims.[17] The existence of three systems of law operating simultaneously creates some confusion for courts attempting to apply different rules to different communities.[18]

Laws on Marriage

Both customary[19] and Islamic marriages[20] are potentially polygamous.[21] Statutory marriage under the Marriage Ordinance,[22] on the other hand, is

---

13. *See, e.g.,* Davis v. Beason, 133 U.S. 333 (1890); Mormon Church v. United States, 136 U.S. 1 (1889); In re Snow, 120 U.S. 274 (1887).

14. *See* MILLER, *supra* note 5, at 190–91.

15. *See* KWAME OPOKU, THE LAW OF MARRIAGE IN GHANA: A STUDY IN LEGAL PLURALISM, 1–2 (1976) (English law was formally introduced into Ghana through the enactment of the Gold Coast Supreme Court Ordinance, 1876, by the colonial legislature. Although Ghana gained independence from Britain in 1957, the Common Law System is still very much with us.).

16. Ghana has a substantial number of practicing Muslims especially in the northern part of the country which came under Islamic teaching influence introduced from Northern Africa. *See,* U.S. Department of State, *International Religious Freedom Report 2002: Ghana,* § 1 (2002), *at* http://www.state.gov/g/drl/rls/irf/2002/13835.htm.

17. Marriage of Mohammedans Ordinance, cap. 129 (1907) (Ghana).

18. *See* OPOKU, *supra* note 15, at 9.

19. The Ghanaian Constitution formally incorporates customary law into the legal regime. Ghana Const. art 11 §2: "The common law of Ghana shall comprise the rules of law generally known as the common law, the rules generally known as the doctrines of equity and the rules of *customary law* including those determined by the Superior Court of Judicature." Article 11 §3: "For the purposes of this article, '*customary law*' means the rules of law which by custom are applicable to particular communities in Ghana." [emphasis added].

20. The Marriage of Mohammedans Ordinance, cap. 129 (1907) (Ghana) governs marriages contracted under Islamic Law.

strictly monogamous. The statutory law disallows polygamy and provides sanctions against bigamy.

Statistical research on the number of practicing polygamists is not readily available in Ghana.[23] Monogamous marriages are more common than polygamous unions, and although customary law permits polygamy, most couples married under customary law are in monogamous unions. Absent a statutory marriage, however, the choice between monogamy and polygamy depends almost entirely on the wishes of the male partner, who may decide at any time to exercise his right to take another wife.[24]

Constitutional Debate in the United States

Free Exercise

In the United States, the polygamy question hinges almost entirely on *Reynolds v. United States*,[25] which recognized the petitioner's right to freely exercise his religious beliefs but held that this right did not cover his conduct, still considered criminal under the law.[26]The Court's rationale was that because

---

21. *See* OPOKU, *supra* note 15, at 33.

22. Marriage Ordinance cap. 127 §42 (1884) (Ghana); *see generally,* W. C. Ekow Daniels, *Towards the Integration of the Laws Relating to Husband and Wife in Ghana, in* INTEGRATION OF CUSTOMARY AND MODERN LEGAL SYSTEMS IN AFRICA 351, 353–58 (1971).

23. The Ghana Demographic and Health Survey 1988, 11 (1988) (32.6% of married women were in polygamous unions); George Panyin Hagan, *Marriage, Divorce and Polygyny, in* FEMALE AND MALE IN WEST AFRICA 192, 198 (Christine Oppong ed., 1983) (a survey of 328 married men among the Guans of Winneba found that 27% of them were in polygamous marriages); ESTHER N. GOODY, CONTEXTS OF KINSHIP 82 (1973) (a 1968 survey among the Gonja tribes of Ghana found that 18% of married men were in polygamous unions); G. K. NUKUNYA, KINSHIP AND MARRIAGE AMONG THE ANLO EWE 157 (London School of Economics Monographs on Social Anthropology No. 37, 1969) (in a 1962–63 census 42.4% of Woe and Alakple men were in polygamous marriages).

24. *See* cap. 127 §44 (Ghana).

25. 98 U.S. 145.

26 The Court upheld Section 5352 of the Revised Statutes which stated:

"Every person having a husband or wife living, who marries another, whether married or single, in a territory or other place over which the United States has exclusive jurisdiction, is guilty of bigamy and shall be punished by a fine of not more than $500 and by imprisonment of not more than 5 years."

harmful consequences flowed from plural marriages and because prohibition affected actions not beliefs, the state was right in prohibiting the practice.[27]

The test that has emerged from modern Supreme Court analysis of the free exercise clause requires the government to prove the existence of some compelling state interest in order to justify a limitation on an individual's free exercise right.[28] The second prong of the Court's balancing test is that the legislation must be the least restrictive means of accomplishing the state interest. Thus, where the state's objective can be served by granting an exemption to people whose religious beliefs are burdened, the court would demand that the exemption be granted.[29]

This development in free exercise jurisprudence has resulted in calls for overruling *Reynolds*[30] because some contend that the state's reasons for the continued criminalization of polygamy are not "compelling" enough to override an individual's free exercise right, or that an exemption should be granted to people who practice this religious tradition.[31] It is becoming increasingly

---

27. Though the court was not very clear on the exact nature of the "evil consequences" apart from the general interest in the preservation of monogamy and references to history and tradition, Justice Waite quoted Professor Leiber as saying that "polygamy leads to the patriarchal principle—and fetters people in stationary despotism." 98 U.S. 145, 166. Also mentioned was the fact that "there has never been a time…when polygamy has not been an offense against society.…" *Id.* at 165. A third "evil" was the mention of third parties affected by the practice "[P]ure minded women and innocent children.…" The nature of the harm to them, however, was not explained. *Id.* at 168.

28. *See, e.g.,* Wisconsin v. Yoder, 406 U.S. 205, 219–20 (1975); Sherbert v. Verner, 374 U.S. 398, 403 (1963).

29. *See eg.,* Sherbert 374 U.S. 398 (where a Seventh Day Adventist was fired for being unwilling to work on Saturdays and the state refused to give her unemployment benefits based on this reason, the Court held that exemptions could be made here without undermining the unemployment compensation system); Yoder 406 U.S. 205 (invalidating Wisconsin's refusal to exempt 15 year old Amish students from the requirement of attending school until age 16); *But see* Employment Div., Dep't. of Human Res. v. Smith, 494 U.S. 872 (1990) (where defendants make a free exercise claim to the use of the drug peyote as a central part of their religious rites. Held: The applicable criminal law on the use of prohibited drugs is enforceable, regardless of the degree of burden it causes on an individual's religious beliefs.). Note that concurring and dissenting Justices in *Smith* observed that the applicable test should be compelling state interest necessary to justify an infringement on an individual's free exercise right as set forth in Sherbert. Congress has enacted legislation confirming this test. *See* the Religious Freedom Restoration Act of 1993 107 Stat. 1488.

30. *See, e.g.,* LAURENCE H. TRIBE, AMERICAN CONSTITUTIONAL LAW 826–28 (1978); Harrop A. Freeman, *A Remonstrance for Conscience,* 106 U. PA. L. REV. 806, 822–26 (1958).

31. Even one Justice of the Supreme Court expressed the sentiment that "in time,

apparent that the government must either come up with a compelling interest for banning polygamy, or the *Reynolds* rationale may crumble.[32]

The Privacy Right Argument

The second major attack on anti-polygamy statutes utilizes the substantive
due process clause of the U.S. Constitution.[33] This clause confers a constitutional right to marry[34] and some contend that this right should be extended
to cover polygamous marriages.[35]

Although the state's compelling interest in preventing polygamous unions
is not currently grounded in case law, the Court may not require the state to
prove this interest if it does not see polygamy as within the realm of protected
privacy rights.

Equal Protection and the New Debate

The potential for reconsideration of the polygamy question in the light of
modern Supreme Court free exercise jurisprudence indicates that the government must redefine its defense against polygamy or risk the overruling of

---

Reynolds will be overruled." Justice Douglas J. (dissenting in part) in Wisconsin v. Yoder,
406 U.S. 205, 247, observed, "the court rightly rejects the notion that actions, even though
religiously grounded, are always outside the protection of the free exercise clause....In so
ruling, the court departs from the teaching of Reynolds v. United States...."

32. It does seem that third party "victims" of polygamy asserted by the state as women
and children, may be a compelling reason sufficient to uphold the state's objective, depending on how the argument is constructed, because in the eyes of certain pro-polygamy
commentators and the defendants in these polygamy cases, the women in the polygamous
communes are happy with their choice, and the children are in absolutely no danger of becoming wards of the sate because of neglect or poverty. In fact, it is asserted that the children are better off than those in monogamous marriage, and are more secure. Is there another way in which the state could show just how women and children may be "victimized"
or harmed by the practice? This remains to be seen. *See also* PERRY, *supra* note 7.

33. Substantive due process privacy rights have been found inherent in the 14th Amendment and include rights to contraception, abortion, marriage, family relations, upbringing, and education of one's children. Homosexual sodomy, however, has not been included.
See Bowers v. Hardwick, 478 U.S. 186, 190 (1986).

34. *See* Zablocki v. Redhail, 434 U.S. 374, 385–86 (1978); Loving v. Virginia, 388 U.S.
1, 11–12 (1967).

35. *See, eg.,* G Keith Nedrow, *Polygamy and the Right to Marry: New Life for an Old
Lifestyle*, 11 MEMPHIS ST. U. L. REV. 303, 327–29 (1981).

Reynolds. The most persuasive argument is that polygamy violates the Equal Protection Clause of the Fourteenth Amendment[36] because it grants the male partner in marriage a right to marry more than one spouse, while denying the female spouse a corresponding right. Therefore, giving legal recognition to the practice, whether pursuant to good faith religious belief or not, means that the state itself is in danger of violating the Constitution. Polygamy discriminates against women and reinforces stereotypical notions of the inferiority of females in conjugal relations. As such, prohibiting polygamy is necessary for Constitutional compliance.

The harms of polygamy fall upon only the female partner in the union. Polygamy does not restrict the male in the number of wives he can acquire or in his sexual pursuits. Therefore, the man is not subject to the mental insecurity and stigma that his wives, who compete for family resources and his attention, suffer. The women involved are short-changed in the satisfaction of their sexual desires and needs because although the man may demand his sexual satisfaction from them at any time, his wives have no such right to demand the same from him.[37] Even if the men and women willfully consent to these arrangements, the government should not recognize a system of marriage that clearly flouts the principle of equality between the sexes and the guarantee of the equal protection under the law.

The equal protection argument against polygamy offers stronger support for a prohibition than prior cases that relied on unsubstantiated claims of the evils of polygamy and the duty to protect monogamy. Nevertheless, any argument based on a compelling interest in equality for women requires political will.

Constitutional Debate in Ghana

Legislation alone cannot eradicate polygamy in Ghana because a prohibition of the practice is likely to generate strong opposition. Proponents of polygamy are likely to offer two primary arguments, which will be discussed below.

---

36. *See generally* Craig v. Boren, 429 U.S. 190, 197–98 (1976) (the Court held that "statutory classifications that distinguish between males and females are subject to scrutiny under the Equal Protection Clause." Gender based classifications will only withstand a Constitutional challenge if they serve important government objectives and are substantially related to achieving those objectives.).

37. *See, eg.*, Carmen Thompson and Celeste Fremon, *Memories of a Plural Wife*, GOOD HOUSEKEEPING, Mar. 7, 1999, at 118.

The Culture-Religion Argument

The Ghanaian Constitution contains certain provisions that are similar to the free exercise[38] and substantive due process[39] clauses of the U.S. Constitution. These rights arise under the Fundamental Human Rights and Freedoms Chapter of the Ghanaian Constitution.[40] The combined effect of these provisions guarantees protection against infringement on religious beliefs, thoughts, conscience, culture, tradition, and practices. There is no dichotomy between protection of beliefs and practices.

Some of the justifications for polygamy in African societies focus not only on social and economic factors or cultural norms but also on African traditional religion. The traditional marriage, which is celebrated as an integral part of African culture, has important religious significance.[41] Marriage in West African societies, including Ghana, is the concern of the entire community and is seen not as the union of the individuals involved but rather as a union of the families.[42]

Culture and religion function to normalize polygamy. For example, the notion that a woman in her menstrual period is unclean and therefore should not come into the company of men[43] suggests that it is alright for the husband to have a second wife when the other is "incapacitated." Although there is no scientific basis for this uncleanliness belief, for Africans, the emission of blood from a woman's body assumes an aura that clashes with a man's

---

38. U.S.Const. amend. I.

39. U.S.Const. amend. XIV §1 (the Substantive Due Process clause).

40. Art. 21 §1 states in part as follows: "All persons shall have a right to:
    (b) freedom of thought, conscience and belief, which shall include academic freedom;
    (c) freedom to practice any religion and to manifest such practice."
Article 26 §1 also states: "Every person is entitled to enjoy, practice, profess, maintain any culture, language, tradition or religion, subject to the provisions of this Constitution." This section is labeled "cultural rights and practices" and is directly relevant to this discussion. Ghana Const. Chpt. 5. These rights are enforceable by the courts. Ghana Const. art. 33.

41. One writer describes it this way:
"For the African peoples, marriage is a focus of existence. It is the point where all members of a given community meet: the departed, the living and those yet to be born. All dimensions of time meet here, and the whole drama of history is repeated, reviewed and revitalized.… [M]arriage is a duty, a requirement from the corporate society, and a rhythm of life in which everyone must participate.…" JOHN S. MBITI, AFRICAN RELIGIONS AND PHILOSOPHY 130 (2d ed. 1990).

42. DANIELS, *supra* note 22, at 354.

43. *See* PETER SARPONG, GHANA IN RETROSPECT 78 (1974).

spirit, or spirituality, and against which the man must be protected. Sociological concepts of culture and religion form the basis of a constitutional and
legal defense of polygamy under the religious and cultural rights clauses of
Ghana's Constitution.

The Privacy Argument

Another constitutional argument, similar to the privacy right argument
under the U.S. Constitution, stems from Ghana's constitutional guarantee of
non-interference with the privacy of the home.[44] This provision shields those
who see marriage as the individual's private choice; whether a polygamous or
a monogamous union, this is a matter within the home with which the state
should not interfere.

Nevertheless, the rights to freedom of religion, culture, and practices, and the
right of non-interference with the privacy of one's home are not absolute. Article 26, section 2 of the Constitution of Ghana limits the enjoyment of cultural
rights and practices by providing that "all customary practices which dehumanize or are injurious to the physical or mental well-being of a person are prohibited." As a result, the challenge is to demonstrate how the practice of polygamy
dehumanizes or injures women in order to bring it outside of the private realm.

Ghana: Polygamy and the Equality Provisions of the Constitution

Article 17[45] of the Constitution of Ghana[46] contains provisions dealing with
equality and freedom from discrimination.[47] The Ghanaian non-discrimina-

---

44. Ghana Const. art. 18 §2.

For the purposes of this study, "privacy of his home" is the operative phrase. "Privacy
of his home" may be taken to mean any number of things including a right against illegal
searches and seizures, non-interference with the physical structure of an individual's place
of abode, or the way in which he/she chooses to order his/her family life and relations
within that abode, or simply the way in which the individual orders his own private or personal life, as distinct from his public life.

45. Found under the Fundamental Human Rights and Freedoms Chapter (Chpt. 5).

46. Fourth Republican Constitution (1992).

47. Of special relevance is section 1 which states as follows: "All persons shall be equal
before the law."

Section 2 of the same article provides: "A person shall not be discriminated against on
the grounds of gender, race, color, ethnic origin, religion, creed or social or economic status."

tion provision prohibits different treatment of people who are similarly situated and explicitly includes gender discrimination. To date, Ghana has not tested these constitutional equality provisions on gender grounds. In Ghana, written laws rarely discriminate against women, and generally, written law and legislative enactments, as distinct from customary law, give both sexes equal opportunity. Deeply embedded attitudes stemming from our cultural and traditional norms, however, have generally relegated women in Ghanaian society to an inferior status.[48]

Nevertheless, women's rights advocates may use the Constitution to correct imbalances in the society that disadvantage women as a class. As mentioned above, Article 26, Section 2 of the Constitution prohibits harmful customary practices. This provision clearly states that the enjoyment of cultural rights and customary practices is not absolute. It is likely that once activist prove that a customary norm is injurious or dehumanizing, the legislature or the courts will prohibit it.[49] In fact, Article 26, Section 2 is the strongest weapon women's rights activists have in the struggle against polygamy.

Judicial Challenge

Women's rights activists interested in bringing a test case must first find a qualified plaintiff. Under Article 33 of the Ghanaian Constitution, such a plaintiff must not only have a significant stake in the controversy, she must also show that a provision of the Constitution has been or is likely to be con-

---

Section 3 defines "discrimination" for the purposes of the Article and states that "discriminate" means to give different treatment to different persons attributable only as mainly to their respective descriptions by race, place of origin, political opinions, color, gender, occupation, religion or creed, whereby persons of one description are subjected to disabilities or restrictions to which persons of another description are not made subject or are granted privileges or advantages which are not granted to persons of another description."

This definition in the Constitution has been quoted in full to give one the sense of how close the definition of discrimination or different treatment comes to the U.S. Supreme Court's analysis of discriminatory legislation, facially, by impact, or as applied when it is put under the scrutiny of equal protection.

48. *See* JOHANNA O. SVANIKIER, WOMEN'S RIGHTS AND THE LAW IN GHANA 75–77 (1997). This attitude is gradually changing with societal education on the value of formal education for girls. Even though in matrilineal societies girls belonged to their family even after marriage, fathers felt they were of no use to them once they got married, and so saw educating girls as a non-investment venture.

49. Ghana follows the Common Law system and decisions of the Superior Court of Judicature if not overturned become part of the law. Ghana Const. art. 11 §2.

travened in relation to *her*. In this instance, the ideal plaintiff is a woman who married under customary law in Ghana and now finds herself facing a polygamous situation either because her husband has just married a second wife or is about to do so.

District Court

In District Court, the plaintiff should claim that, as a practice, polygamy violates the Constitution because it discriminates against women contrary to Article 17, Sections 1 and 2 and injures their mental well-being. The District Court is unlikely to grant the plaintiff either an injunction against her husband or a divorce because the wife has no such right under customary law. Because of the constitutional nature of the suit, however, Article 130(2)[50] of the Constitution requires the District Court to stay proceedings and refer the matter to the Supreme Court for determination.

Supreme Court

If the constitutionality of polygamy is brought before the Court, the plaintiff/petitioner should urge that the state has no reasonable or objective justification for maintaining a practice that disadvantages married women compared to their spouses. The enjoyment of the religious, cultural, and customary rights is not absolute; any customary practice that dehumanizes or injures the physical or mental well-being of a person is prohibited. The evidence of psychological harm and indignities caused by sharing one husband among multiple wives and the fact that these harms affect only the women indicate that the practice of polygamy contravenes the Constitution.

Although it is unclear how the Court may respond, a judicial challenge by women's rights activists in Ghana is worth trying because the publicity may propel women's issues into the forefront of the national debate and generate a series of other cases in the courts challenging other discriminatory practices.

---

50. Article 130 §2 states: Where an issue relates to a matter or question referred to in Art. 33 (the enforcement of the Fundamental Human Rights and Freedoms) arises in any proceedings in a court other than the Supreme Court, that court shall stay proceedings and refer the question of law involved to the Supreme Court for determination, and the court in which the question arose shall dispose of the case in accordance with the decision of the Supreme Court.

Legislative Reform

The discrimination inherent in the marriage law is borne out by the differences found under each of the three systems of marriage—customary law marriage, Islamic marriage under the Mohammedan's Ordinance, Cap. 129,[51] and statutory marriage under the Ordinance, Cap. 127. In order to achieve fairness and equality, formalities governing marriage should uniformly apply to everyone. Although each woman is legally married under any of the systems, the law discriminates between them, preferencing the Ordinance wife over the customary law wife by giving more security to the former and leaving the latter to the whims of her male partner. Since the Constitution's nondiscrimination guarantee is being contravened, a new law should provide an integrated and uniform set of rules applicable to all Ghanaians, irrespective of status, religion, ethnic group, or creed.

Ghanaian marriage laws, taken as a whole, violate the equality principle and the prohibition against discrimination in the Ghanaian Constitution. The three marriage systems offer women vastly different protection against discrimination. Monogamy cannot exist side by side with polygamy or potentially polygamous marriages without perpetuating inequalities and injustice among the very citizens whom the law is supposed to benefit and unify.

A proposed legislative ban on polygamy is unlikely to succeed because many influential Ghanaian men, including some of the honorable Parliamentarians, are currently in polygamous marriages, or in unions similar to polygamy.[52] A proposal for total reform of the marriage laws to provide uniformity within the three marriage systems, however, might be more successful.

Recommendations for Change

Legislative Reform

Legislation can restrict polygamy if effectively combined with enforcement and education.

---

51. For purposes of this study, I shall limit myself mainly to the differences between customary law marriage and the ordinance marriage. Marriage under the Mohammedan's Ordinance is also polygamous and has very similar incidents and effects as customary law marriage on women.

52. I personally knew a number of them in such relationships.

The proposed act should include:

(a) Abolition of the three systems of marriage,[53] and the establishment of a uniform marriage law for all citizens, which shall require registration of the marriage.

(b) Inclusion of customary traditions and symbols, if the couple would like to celebrate their marriage in a customary fashion. However, the law should make clear that the performance of the customary rites does not confer legal marital status to the couple unless the statutory registration requirement is met.

(c) A prohibition of polygamy with narrow exceptions.[54] The prohibition should not have retrospective effect because of the social upheaval it would cause.[55] The Act should preserve the validity of polygamous unions existing prior to the date the Act comes into force. The Act should, however, allow women in pre-Act polygamous marriages to sue for divorce.[56]

(d) Violators of the law, both the man and woman involved in the violation, should be sanctioned, unless it is shown that one partner obtained the consent of the other by fraud, deceit, or coercion.

(e) A comprehensive system of statutory registration of marriage should be established and accessible to all.

(f) Local district courts should have legal jurisdiction over all matrimonial claims including divorce, which can only be legal if granted by a district judge.

-----

53. For example, the Intestate Succession Law of Ghana applies to every intestate death, irrespective of the personal law, religion, status, or ethnic group of the deceased person. P.N.D.C.L. 111 § 1 (1985) (Ghana).

54. The only two exceptions I would suggest with respect to polygamy are: (i) where it is established that the female partner is unable to have children as a result of infertility or disease; and (ii) where it is shown that the female partner is unable to have sexual intercourse with her spouse because of a serious illness or a disability. *See also* Esther Mayambala, *Changing the Terms of the Debate: Polygamy and the Rights of Women in Kenya and Uganda*, 3 E. Afr. J. Peace & Hum. Rts. 200, 232–38 (1997) (she makes the same arguments as to why a total ban on polygamy may operate to the disadvantage of women in special cases).

55. *See, e.g.*, Daniels, *supra* note 22, at 392.

56. For example, Egypt is one country that gives women the right to ask for divorce on that ground. However, the women must prove a material or moral injury suffered as a result of her husband's act. *See* Jamal J. Nasir, The Status of Women Under Islamic Law 25–26 (1990). It should be noted that the right should be given to women in pre-Act marriages, because the proposed Act would place a ban on polygamy in Ghana, unlike the Egyptian provision which actually recognizes polygamy as a legal form of marriage. I would also suggest that no proof of injury should be required by the law, since this would place an onerous burden on the woman.

(g) The legislature should amend all other statutory provisions concerning marriage to bring them in conformity with the new law. These other statutes include: the Intestate Succession Law,[57] the Customary Marriage and Divorce Registration Law,[58] the Administration of Estates Decree,[59] and the Matrimonial Causes Act.[60]

Judicial Challenge

Because of delays in the adjudicatory system in Ghana, advocates should use a judicial challenge only as an alternative to a proposal for Parliamentary reform. If the court refuses to interpret the Constitution as prohibiting polygamy, it will be difficult to have the case reopened. This would only reinforce the validity of the practice; therefore, advocates should only use this method of reform with caution.

Education

Legislative reform without vigorous education will not work. Governmental agencies, commissions, international bodies, and non-governmental organizations all need to educate citizens on women's rights, including the right to equality within marriage.

Raising Women's Consciousness

Women themselves will impede implementation of a law prohibiting polygamy if they do not understand what equality of treatment under the law means. Programs focused on educating women about their rights, especially rural women, should be developed.

International Law

Ghana is party to a number of human rights conventions, such as the Convention on the Elimination of All Forms of Discrimination Against Women,[61]

---

57. P.N.D.C.L. 111 (1985) (Ghana).
58. P.N.D.C.L. 112 (1985) (Ghana).
59. Act 63 (1961) (Ghana).
60. Act 367 (1971) (Ghana).
61. G.A. Res. 34/180, U.N. GAOR, 34th Sess., Supp. No. 46, at 193, U.N.Doc.A/34/46 (1979).

the International Covenant on Civil and Political Rights,[62] the International Covenant on Economic and Social Rights,[63] Convention on the Political Rights of Women,[64] and the African Charter on Human and People's Rights.[65] Application of these treaties in Ghana through incorporation into national law or use as interpretive aides by the Courts will discourage polygamy because of its discriminatory character.

Conclusion

In spite of the vast differences in the economic, cultural, and social developments in the United States and Ghana, the underlying concern for the principle of equality ties the women of the two nations together. While the legal and cultural history of women's equality renders women in the United States more secure than in Ghana, both countries have a compelling interest to ensure that this principle is not violated to satisfy any religious or cultural system of rules or laws. Polygamy is an institution designed only to control women through oppression and domination. Now is the time for change and for equality.

---

62. G.A.Res. 2200A(XXI), U.N.GAOR, 21st Sess., Supp. No. 16 at 52, U.N.Doc.A/6316 (1966).

63. G.A.Res. 2200A(XXI), U.N.GAOR, 21st Sess., Supp. No. 16 at 49, U.N.Doc.A/6316 (1966).

64. G.A.Res 640(VII), 193 U.N.T.S. 135 (1952).

65. OAU Doc. CAB/LEG/67/3 rev. 5.

DISCRIMINATION IN THE TRADITIONAL MARRIAGE AND DIVORCE SYSTEM IN GHANA: LOOKING AT THE PROBLEM FROM A HUMAN RIGHTS PERSPECTIVE

Bernice Sam

Introduction

Traditional marriage and divorce systems in Ghana have placed women in an unequal and disadvantaged position for decades. Polygamy, bride price, sororate, leviratic, child marriages, and fault-based divorce all hamper a woman's ability to achieve equality with men. The subordinate role of women leads to their widespread poverty and prevents full participation in sustainable development efforts in Ghana. Women's lack of reproductive rights results in unchecked population expansion and increased health risks for women and children alike. In addition, traditional marriage and divorce rules violate several human rights norms. Ghana must redress this inequality in the law.

Traditional Law Marriage

As of 1991, approximately 86 percent of couples in Ghana contracted marriages under traditional or customary law.[1] In pre-colonial times, marriage

---

1. Ulrike Wanitzek, *Integration of Personal Laws and the Situation of Women in Ghana: The Matrimonial Causes Act of 1971 and its Application by the Courts, in* THIRD WORLD LEGAL STUDIES 75, 78 (1991).

was a family matter rather than an individual concern. Although the situation is somewhat different today, due in part to increased mobility and diversity in society, marriage remains a union of two families.

Requirements

Requirements for customary law marriage vary by region, but certain commonalities have been judicially recognized.[2] These are: (1) agreement by the parties to live together as man and wife: (2) consent of the husband's family; (3) consent of the wife's family, indicated by acceptance of dowry, and (4) consummation of the marriage.[3]

Consent

Consent of the parties is a requirement for any marriage. The principle of consent is negated in child marriage[4] because girls are too young and lack the capability to give informed consent. Although customary law traditionally had no minimum age for marriage, it is a criminal offense to marry any person against his or her consent.[5] The Children's Act of 1998 fixed the minimum age of marriage at eighteen years with the exception of children between sixteen and eighteen years who obtain parental consent.[6] Despite the law, in some parts of northern Ghana it is still customary to marry off girls at an early age. This is but one illustration of the dichotomy between customary and statutory laws.

Consent of the families of both parties is also necessary for a valid customary marriage. A spouse becomes an addition to the family and must accept certain familial obligations.[7] Parents or family members of the man initiate arrangements that culminate in the marriage; it is unusual and improper for a young man to make a formal marriage proposal to the family of the bride. Despite the traditional importance of familial consent, the increase in migration from rural areas has diluted this concept, leading one commentator to observe that today "parental consent amounts to passive ratification of

---

2. *See* Quartey v. Martey & Anor., [1959] G.L.R. 377 (Ghana).

3. *Id.*

4. *See infra* notes 50–52 and accompanying text.

5. Criminal Code, 1960 (Act 29) § 109 (Ghana).

6. The Children's Act, 1998 (Act 560) § 14 (Ghana).

7. Each spouse has to attend significant activities in either family, which include marriages, naming of newborns, funerals, and traditional festivals.

a relationship—marriage—that is a fait accompli for all intents and purposes."[8]

Dowry

Dowry, or bride price, has both symbolic and practical importance in traditional marriage. Dowry is a *quid pro quo* arrangement that compensates the bride's family for the loss of a daughter and grants the husband legally enforceable rights over the wife and her children.[9] The terms and conditions of the dowry are settled between the two families and ratified by the prospective husband through the transfer of money or gifts to the bride's family.[10] If the wife is found to be at fault in divorce her family must return the dowry to the husband. On the other hand, the dowry serves as a guarantee to the wife's parents that she will be properly treated; the wife's family may refuse to return the dowry if the husband's mistreatment leads to divorce.[11] In a society with little or no state intervention in the formation of a traditional marriage, the dowry is proof that the couple has married and serves as a means of distinguishing marriage from concubinage.[12]

Consummation

At common law, non-consummation of a marriage due to impotence is grounds for nullification.[13] Although it is unclear whether non-consummation of a traditional marriage would have the same consequence, the high value Ghanaian society places on children suggests that impotence would preclude customary marriage.[14] Some scholars argue that non-consummation

---

8. Kofi Oti Adinkrah, *The Essentials of a Customary Marriage: A New Approach*, 12 Rev. Ghana L. 40, 41 (1980).

9. He has a right to claim *damages* from the third party in the event of the wife's infidelity. He also has an exclusive right to her body and a right to profit by the fruits of her labor and that of her children. Kwame Opoku, The Law of Marriage in Ghana 34–35, 60, 70 (1976).

10. The dowry may include kola, cowries (a type of river shell), drinks, cows, sheep, or other gifts agreed on between the families. *Id.* at 34.

11. *Id.* at 35.

12. *Id.*

13. *See* Harthan v. Harthan [1949] P. 115; *cf.* Pettit v. Pettit [1962] 3 W.L.R. 919 (Eng.) (applying *Harthan*, but refusing to grant the husband's prayer for nullity on the grounds of impotence under the circumstances).

14. *See* Matrimonial Causes Act, 1971 (Act 367) §41(3) (Ghana).

should not invalidate a customary marriage because marriage is not only for procreation.[15]

Types of Traditional Marriages

Child Marriage

Child marriage, in which an older man indicates to the parents of a pre-pubescent girl that he or his son desires to marry her, still occurs in Ghana today. The man may assume financial responsibility for the girl's welfare, including her education.[16] In some instances, the girl's family may send her to her prospective in-laws for rearing until she is ready for married life and child bearing.[17] In other cases, a girl's family may withdraw her from school to start married life; this is a way of ensuring that she does not become so-phisticated or fall in love with someone else.[18] In some communities in northern Ghana, a girl may be freed from this difficult situation if her chosen or desired boyfriend can refund all money expended on her behalf to the rejected man.[19]

Leviratic Marriage or Widow Inheritance

Leviratic marriage or widow inheritance is a practice in which a man is obliged to marry his brother's widow.[20] Although the man is usually the successor to the decedent, in some communities, the widow has a right to choose a husband among the decedent's brothers.[21] Although the widow has a right to refuse to marry a brother, her family may have to return the dowry. Some widows consent to this type of marriage because it is the only way to guarantee their continued care, since in many instances the successor inherits the decedent's property.[22]

---

15. Adinkrah, *supra* note 8, at 48.

16. Florence Abena Dolphyne, The Emancipation of Women, An African Perspective 11 (1991).

17. *Id.*

18. *Id.* at 12.

19. *Id.*

20. The Oxford English Dictionary 870 (2d ed. 1989).

21. A customary successor may be older or younger than the decedent.

22. Inheritance by the successor of a decedent has been formally abolished by the Intestate Succession Law, 1985, (P.N.D.C.L. Law 111) §3 (Ghana) (which gives the surviving spouse and children an absolute right to the estate).

Sororate Marriage

In a sororate marriage, a sister of the wife replaces a wife who flees her marriage or dies before giving birth. The replacing sister steps into the shoes of the "ex-wife" and performs all the duties and customs her husband requires of her.

Traditional Law Divorce

In ancient times, customary marriage was almost indissoluble, as societies considered it a permanent social and spiritual bond between families and between the man and women themselves.[23] Today, however, divorce is common and fairly easy to obtain. Divorce under customary or traditional law may be done extra-judicially or judicially.

Before Family Elders

Customary law does not provide specific grounds for divorce, but communities generally accept certain justifications. Due to the dynamic nature of custom, acceptable reasons have expanded with time, giving men more freedom to divorce their wives than vice versa. Still, both men and women have the right to request divorce. Grounds for divorce include adultery, impotence or sterility, neglect of the family, desertion, witchcraft, cruelty, discord between spouse and inlaws, and extreme favoritism by the husband to a co-wife.[24]

Formalities for divorce differ among the various tribes in the country.[25] A panel comprised of elders from the two families or the community typically undertakes dissolution of a traditional law marriage. Usually, the party seeking divorce makes a complaint before family members; if reconciliation fails, the panel convenes to make a determination of fault, followed by decisions on return of gifts and dowry, property distribution, and child custody.[26] If the

---

23. OPOKU, *supra* note 9, at 91.

24. *Id.* at 91–93.

25. In some parts of Ashanti, a woman is "chalked" (smeared with white powder) by the husband which she must show to the public to signify the completed process of dissolution of the marriage. Among the Gonja tribe, the husband smashes the water pot kept at the back of her room or breaks down her fireplace. *Id.* at 94.

26. *Id.* at 93.

families or panel find the woman to be at fault, her family must return the dowry and end the marriage without any property. Usually she receives a "send off," an amount of money enabling her to resettle.[27] The families or panel may distribute property between the couple if the wife was hardworking and supportive during the marriage. When the man is at fault, he loses only a refund of the dowry.[28]

Judicial Dissolution

The Matrimonial Causes Act,[29] which regulates statutory marriages, also applies to customary and Islamic marriages, which are potentially polygamous. The 1993 Courts Act[30] decentralized the court system.[31] As a result, community tribunals closer to the people and spouses in both rural and urban centers have the option of applying to courts in matrimonial disputes. Although it is obligatory to dissolve a statutory marriage in court, it is optional for customary marriages.[32] The Matrimonial Causes Act provides better protection for women in divorce and does not automatically apply to divorces within traditional marriages, resulting in disparities in the treatment of divorcing women.

"Free Note" Dissolution

A growing phenomenon peculiar to the central and western regions of Ghana is the use of free notes to dissolve customary law marriages. An aggrieved spouse, usually the husband, writes a letter stating the reasons for the grievance. This note, addressed to the head of the extended family or his spouse's biological father, rarely contains any provision relating to property distribution.

This "free note" method is a way to bypass formal dissolution and to avoid a property settlement. Interestingly, the "free note" is accepted in the aforementioned regions as conclusive. In at least one case in the western region, however, the High Court pronounced the "free note" non-binding.

---

27. *Id.* at 95.

28. *Id.*

29. Matrimonial Causes Act, 1971 (Act 367) (Ghana).

30. Courts Act, 1993 (Act 459) (Ghana).

31. Ghana's court system is divided hierarchically into the Supreme Court, the Court of Appeal, the Circuit court, the District court, and the Community Tribunal system.

32. *See* Wanitzek, *supra* note 1, at 84.

Factors that Impede Equality

From inception to conclusion, traditional marriages are characterized by discrimination against women. The following section will explore some of the discriminating attributes of traditional or customary law marriages in Ghana.

Polygamy

Polygamy allows men to have as many wives as they desire. It has becomes a status symbol for a man to have many wives. The non-discrimination principles enshrined in Ghana's Constitution require either abolishing this male right or permitting women to have more than one husband. This view enjoys little support in any social or political forum in Ghana. Nevertheless, the need to treat women as equals remains, whether or not polygamy survives.

Polygamy lowers the status of women. A wife must share her husband with other women, yet she dares not breach fidelity to her husband lest she be shamed before family elders or be made to appease the husband. Although the husband enjoys a right to compensation by a man with whom his wife has sex, the mere allegation of adultery, even if unsubstantiated, by a husband means serious trouble for a wife.[33] Additionally, polygamy gives men greater opportunity for sexual gratification than women.

Women in polygamous marriages have little control over their reproductive lives. Wives may compete among themselves by having children to please their husband, which has serious consequences for women's physical and mental health as well that of their children. Although having many children is a status symbol for men, studies show that primarily women perform the work of child-rearing.[34] Men use polygamy to abandon older women who are past child-bearing age, whereas a statutory marriage protects such women. Also, women are at greater risk of contracting HIV/AIDS in polygamous marriages, as they have no right to insist on the husband's fidelity.[35]

Proponents of polygamy have advanced religious and cultural justifications for the practice.[36] These are not compelling reasons for granting women fewer

---

33. *See* Opoku, *supra* note 9, at 60.

34. *See* Aminata Traore, *Evolving Relations Between Mothers and Children in Rural Africa*, 31 Int'l Soc. Sci. J. 486 (1979).

35. *See* Irene Martyniuk, Institute for Research on Women, Women in Ghana Face Dilemmas (1992).

36. *See* Dolphyne, *supra* note 16, at 17.

rights than men in marriage. The idea of partnership and mutual gratification is completely lost in polygamy, as are principles of gender equity and justice.

Dowry

The dowry, originally a mere symbol, is now seen as the purchase of a wife. Families of prospective brides demand huge sums of money in addition to other gifts. A woman's education, family history, and personal wealth are all factors that determine the dowry price.[37] Some traditional councils[38] have by-laws that set fixed amounts of money for a woman depending on whether she has been previously married or widowed.

The dowry system is problematic for many reasons. When women's parents are unable to return the dowry money, women cannot escape bad or abusive marriages. The dowry system and other discriminatory practices like widow inheritance and sororate marriages reinforce the notion that men possess women. In addition, young men often delay marriage, because they do not have the financial means to provide the dowry. This results in increased cohabitation and concubinage, in which women have no rights.

Property Rights of Spouses

Women have few property rights under traditional law. Customary law treats the husband as the manager and owner of all property acquired during a marriage. In many cases, traditional law treats property received prior to marriage different from property acquired individually during the marriage.[39] Many women, however, are not economically positioned to acquire property either before or during marriage. Thus, at divorce, a woman is usually at the mercy of the traditional and statutory legal systems.

Property Distribution Before Family Elders

Customary law requires a woman to assist her husband in his undertakings but mandates that all property acquired belongs exclusively to him.[40] At dis-

---

37. *See* DOLPHYNE, *supra* note 16, at 7.

38. A traditional council is composed of chiefs of towns and villages within a designated traditional area within the Chieftaincy Institution.

39. Akua Kuenvehia, PROPERTY RIGHTS OF SPOUSES, 5, paper presented for consultation of Ghana Const. Art. 22(2) in Accra, 1998 (hereinafter Property Rights of Spouses).

40. Quartey v. Martey & Anor., [1959] G.L.R. 377, 380 (Ghana).

solution of a traditional marriage before family elders, men's exclusive property rights often leave women with nothing, particularly when family elders
determine that a woman is at fault in a divorce. In some instances, the wife
actually leaves the marriage worse off than when she entered it. Unlike the Intestate Succession Law, which was changed in 1985 to give a woman a share
in a deceased husband's property,[41] the traditional distribution of property at
divorce remains plagued by inequality.[42]

Although the Matrimonial Causes Act of 1971[43] ostensibly offers improved
protections for women, judges continue to rely on customary norms that discriminate against women when applying the statutory law. Sections 20 and 21
require judges to ensure that property distribution is just and equitable, regardless of who holds title to any property.[44] Many judges, however, have used
this discretion to continue to divide property according to who has financially
contributed to the acquisition of property.[45] This places women in a double
bind. Because society demands women eschew their education and career
goals in favor of housework and child care at home, they are rarely in the position to contribute money to family property acquisition. Simultaneously, the
system fails to acknowledge that their domestic work is indispensible to building family wealth.[46]

Necessaries

Under traditional law, a man has an obligation to financially maintain his
wife, even if the wife can maintain herself.[47] This reinforces the stereotypical
notion that women are children who must be provided for by men. A majority of married women in Ghana are capable of providing necessaries for
themselves and assisting in maintenance of the family. Therefore, this provision should be limited to extreme situations such as medical and surgical

---

41. *See* Intestate Succession Law, 1985 (P.N.D.C.L. Law 111) (Ghana).

42. *See* Wanitzek, *supra* note 1, at 93.

43. This Act governs all monogamous marriages, and couples in polygamous marriages
may request the application of the Act when seeking divorce. Matrimonial Causes Act, 1971
(Act 367) (Ghana)

44. *See id.* §§ 20–21.

45. *See* Clerk v. Clerk, [1981] G.L.R. 583 (Ghana) (holding that when a husband pur-
chases property with his earnings, that property is solely his upon divorce).

46. *See id.* at 597 (standing for the proposition that a wife's domestic work, including
her "moral and material support to the husband," did not entitle her to a share in the matrimonial home upon divorce).

47. *See* OPOKU, *supra* note 9, at 62–63.

treatment or in clear cases in which the wife is unemployed and dependent on the husband.

Send Off

Traditional law does not provide for maintenance after divorce. Community elders may grant a woman "send off" money at divorce if she is not at fault. There is no corresponding rule requiring a woman to give a man "send off" money.

Judicial Intervention in Property Settlement

Despite the important role courts have played in addressing inequalities between men and women, the decisions of most judges still reflect stereotypical and traditional notions of the inferiority of women. Judges have wide discretion in applying the provisions of the Matrimonial Causes Act. Caselaw reveals that if judges determine that a wife has made a "substantial contribution" to matrimonial property she may receive a fair portion of property at dissolution.[48] Although the Act does not explicitly mention "substantial contribution" as a condition for equitable distribution of property,[49] this court-developed standard has left many women without property at divorce. Courts ignore homemaking as a contribution. Many women do not pursue their cases in court for fear of being unable to prove "substantial contribution." Many women assist husbands in marriage and forgo property acquisition for fear of creating disagreement in the home. The law should explicitly recognize and value women's contributions during marriage and should ensure women's right to property and economic empowerment even after a marriage has ended.

Child, Leviratic, and Sororate Marriages

The practice of marrying off female children to husbands at an early age deprives girls of crucial opportunities available to their male counterparts. Child marriage hinders their education, restricts their economic autonomy, and often adversely affects their reproductive health.[50] Those who support the

---

48. *See* Wanitzek, *supra* note 1, at 89–95.
49. *See* Matrimonial Causes Act, 1971 (Act 367) (Ghana).
50. *See generally* Susanna Louis B. Mikhail, *Child Marriage and Child Prostitution, in* GENDER, TRAFFICKING, AND SLAVERY 43 (Rachel Masika ed., 2002).

practice maintain that it ensures the moral virtue of society's women and future mothers by preventing them from wayward development.[51] Nevertheless, this practice contributes to the continued subordination of women. In the past, girls unquestionably accepted such arrangements by parents, but in recent times, many young girls refuse to marry elderly men. Some of these young brides run away to other parts of the country, while others end up as prostitutes or porters.[52]

Sororate and leviratic marriages treat women as their husband's possessions. Leviratic marriage, or widow inheritance, restrains a woman from marrying the person of her choice, thrusting her into an often unwanted marriage and putting her in a position of economic dependence on the husband's successor. In rural and farming communities, a woman is deprived of access to land whether it belongs exclusively to the husband or is jointly owned by the couple. This practice, as well as the tradition of forcing women to reproduce in place of their "defective" sisters, perpetuates negative stereotypes of women, affects women personally, and limits the development of their skills and independence.

Recommendations

Legislation

Legislation encompassing and reforming all aspects of traditional marriage and divorce rules will promote certainty, equity, and justice for married women.[53] The law should abolish all harmful customary practices of marriage such as widow inheritance and sororate marriages. Because dowry plays an important role in maintaining Ghanaian cultural tradition, communities will resist legal restrictions of this practice and circumvent regulation by increasing the value and number of gifts. The law, therefore, should not prohibit dowry but should require that both families provide gifts. The law should,

---

51. DOLPHYNE, *supra* note 16, at 13.

52. Betrothal and child marriage is prevalent in the northern parts of the country. Runaways end up as "kaya yoo," i.e., porters who carry wares of market women and shoppers at markets. They are often exposed to diseases and unwanted pregnancies as they live on the streets of the cities. *See* CHRISTIAN CHILDREN'S FUND OF CANADA, CHILD ALERT UPDATE (2003).

53. *See generally* Wanitzek, *supra* note 1, at 105–7.

however, abolish dowry refunds. In order to modify this practice, the government and women's rights advocates should conduct widespread education on the negative effects of exorbitant dowries.

Similarly, the law should not ban polygamy, because such a ban would be difficult, if not impossible, to enforce. A complete ban on polygamy will also encourage men to enter into informal unions, which offer women little or no support under the existing laws. Increasing the perception of women as independent, capable persons whose rights as individuals must be respected and protected is important in order to combat polygamy.[54] Women's rights advocates must also refute the religious justifications of the practice.

Judicial Education

When family elders fail to resolve the dispute, divorcing parties find themselves before the courts. As a result, judges need to receive gender sensitization training to appreciate the male–female power dynamics in society and their adverse impact on women. Judges also need to understand Ghana's obligations under international law in order to avoid making decisions that conflict with the country's commitment to respect human rights.

Population

Widespread education of the population, especially women, would increase awareness of women's rights at divorce. Public education regarding women's human rights is a critical tool in addressing inequality and discrimination against women. As such, the government cannot abdicate responsibility to understaffed and underfunded non-governmental organizations (NGOs). The government must become actively involved.

Gender Training

Until recently, legal institutions offered no courses in gender or the human rights of women at legal institutions. Introduction of these courses at the university level would create awareness of the plight of women among

---

54. Cote D'Ivoire is one of the few countries in Africa that has abolished polygamy.

law students and inspire them to join human rights organizations after school.

Research and Data Collection

Research is crucial to any movement for policy reform. Research and data collection also often elicits constructive comments from the public.[55] Public data collection ensures that information is available to the community as well as to lawmakers and NGOs.

Special Courts

Creating courts to handle matrimonial disputes will provide judges with expertise and accelerate the process of correcting inequalities in the system. Small, local community tribunals enable people in the rural areas to settle disputes before courts without the added disincentive of trekking long distances.

Matrimonial Act

Until Ghana enacts legislation specifically addressing the property rights of spouses under the traditional or customary law system, advocates must use the Matrimonial Causes Act to ensure equality in divorce. The Act provides for settlement of property and financial support on the application of either party.[56] It is up to lawyers to persuade judges to interpret the Act favorably to women.

Conclusion

The dual system of divorce, with statutory and customary law operating side by side, has created a myriad of rules and standards that can no longer be tolerated in light of Ghana's constitutional commitment to equality and non-discrimination. Divorce affects women's development, reproductive autonomy, and ability to contribute meaningfully to the economy of the country. Ghana must reform divorce law to reflect women's rights.

---

55. Wanitzek, *supra* note 1, at 105; *see* Matrimonial Causes Act, 1971 (Act 367) § 20 (Ghana).

56. Wanitzek, *supra* note 1, at 105; *see* Matrimonial Causes Act, 1971 (Act 367) § 20 (Ghana).

Comparative Study of the Status of Women under the Law of Divorce and of their Economic Status in Uganda, Britain, and Bangladesh

Regina Lule Mutyaba

Introduction

Although many societies recognize that women and men are equal, few fully incorporate notions of gender equality into the law. For instance, Ugandan women have made great advances in the areas of higher education, law, and business, and they contribute constructively and monetarily to the home.[1] The laws that govern divorce, however, fail to recognize women's equal contribution and worth. Uganda must eliminate this inconsistency and reform divorce law to reflect equality between husband and wife. This essay offers a

---

1. *See Consideration of Reports, Submitted by State Parties Under Article 18 of the Convention on the Elimination of All Forms of Discrimination Against Women, Initial and Second Periodic Reports of State Parties, Uganda,* U.N. CEDAW, 14th Sess., U.N. Doc. CEDAW/c/UGA/1–2 (1995) [hereinafter Uganda's Initial and Second Periodic Reports to CEDAW]. For example, in 1955, government Ministries employed almost no women; in 1987, of 102,899 employees in the civil service, 21,102 were female. *Id.* at 45–46 tbl.17. However, progress has been slower in getting women into management positions; in 1995, only 6% of public and government management positions were held by women. *See Consideration of Reports, Submitted by State Parties Under Article 18 of the Convention on the Elimination of All Forms of Discrimination Against Women, Initial and Second Periodic Reports of State Parties, Addendum, Uganda,* U.N. CEDAW, 14th Sess., U.N. Doc. CEDAW/c/UGA/1–2/Add.1, at 18 (1995).

brief comparative study of women's status under divorce laws in Uganda, Britain, and Bangladesh and proposes that Uganda reform its divorce laws to reflect the principle of equality.

Grounds for Divorce

Uganda

Depending on the type of marriage she contracted, a Ugandan woman may divorce under the Divorce Act, customary law, or Mohammedan law. Statutory law, customary law, and Islamic law require grounds for divorce in most instances and place at least one party at fault for the breakdown of the marriage. Under all systems, women seldom instigate divorce because of the disproportionate stigma and burden of proof it entails.[2] Under the Divorce Act, a husband may divorce his wife if she has committed even one transgression, but a wife must prove that her husband committed at least two offenses.[3] Local traditions, which are not recorded and vary widely from tribe to tribe, govern both creation and dissolution of customary marriages. For women who marry under customary law, the greatest problem is that divorce, instigated by either party, requires the return of bridewealth. Customary law allows men and women to divorce for reasons that differ according to the custom and traditions of particular ethnic groups or tribes. Under Islamic law, a husband may unilaterally divorce his wife simply by pronouncing the word *talaq* three times.[4] A wife cannot exercise this right, but she may repudiate her marriage under Islamic law through the exercise of *khula*, which is permitted only upon

---

2. *Consideration of Reports, Submitted by State Parties Under Article 18 of the Convention on the Elimination of All Forms of Discrimination Against Women, Third Periodic Reports of State Parties, Uganda*, U.N. CEDAW, Extraordinary Sess., U.N. Doc. CEDAW/c/UGA/3, at 62 (2002) [hereinafter Uganda's Third Periodic Report to CEDAW].

3. The Divorce Act, Cap. 215 §5 [Uganda]; [Dieter Nauman v. Herman Stella Joanila Nauman, Divorce Cause No. 6 of 1973 (Uganda 1973).] *See also* Julie Mertus, *State Discriminatory Family Law and Customary Abuses, in* WOMEN'S RIGHTS HUMAN RIGHTS 159 (Julie Peters & Andrea Wolper eds. 1995) (quoted in Judith Armatta, *Getting Beyond the Law's Complicity in Intimate Violence Against Women*, 33 WILLAMETTE L. REV. 773, 793 n.110 (1997)). *But see* Uganda Const. art. 31(1).

4. ALAMGIR MUHAMMAD SERAJUDDIN, SHARI'A LAW AND SOCIETY: TRADITION AND CHANGE IN SOUTH ASIA 198 (2001). However, some legal precedent (at least in Bangladesh) suggests that invoking *talaq* requires good cause, beyond just the whim of the husband. *Id.* at 202–7.

a showing of a husband's cruelty, failure to provide spousal maintenance, or failure to provide shelter.[5]

Bangladesh

Marriage and divorce in Bangladesh is governed by Shari'a or Islamic law.[6] Divorce under Islamic law takes different forms: it can be achieved by *talaq*, as in Uganda, where a husband unilaterally dissolves the marriage by pronouncing *talaq*;[7] by mutual consent or by judicial decree;[8] or by a right, known as *talaq-i-tafwid*, explicitly included in the marriage contract.[9] If *talaq-i-tafwid* is not included in the Mohammedan marriage deed, the wife must obtain a court-ordered divorce.[10]

Britain

British law gives both parties the same rights in divorce. Both husband and wife may petition for divorce under the Matrimonial Causes Act on grounds of irretrievable breakdown of marriage.[11] Britain has also considered

5. Ashgar Ali Engineer, The Rights of Women in Islam 137–38 (1992).

6. All Muslims in Bangladesh are subject to the Muslim Family Laws Ordinance of 1961. See Muslim Family Laws Ordinance of 1961, 1961 Ord. VIII, §1 [Bangladesh].

7. Id. §7. See Serajuddin, supra note 4, at 198. However, today divorces must be registered, meaning that a pronunciation of *talaq* is no longer immediately effective. See Consideration of Reports, Submitted by State Parties Under Article 18 of the Convention on the Elimination of All Forms of Discrimination Against Women, Third and Fourth Periodic Reports of States Parties, Bangladesh, U.N. CEDAW, 17th Sess., U.N. Doc. CEDAW/c/BGD/3–4, §2.15.3 (1997) [hereinafter Bangladesh's Third and Fourth Periodic Reports to CEDAW].

8. Serajuddin, supra note 4, at 198–99.

9. See Muslim Family Laws Ordinance of 1961, 1961 Ord. VIII, §8 [Bangladesh]; Serajuddin, supra note 4, at 206.

10. Serajuddin, supra note 4, at 207.

11. The Matrimonial Causes Act, 1973, c. 18, §1(1) (Eng.). However, the petitioner has to satisfy the court that one of the following facts has occurred:

"(a) That the respondent has committed adultery and the petitioner finds it intolerable to live with the respondent. (b) That the respondent has behaved in such a way that the petitioner cannot reasonably be expected to live with the respondent. (c) That the respondent has deserted the petitioner for a continuous period of at least two years immediately preceding the presentation of the petition. (d) That the parties to the marriage have lived apart for a continuous period of at least two years immediately preceding the presentation of the petition

steps to move away from a combined fault and no-fault system to pure no-fault divorce.[12]

Consequences of Divorce

Maintenance

Uganda

Divorce Act

Uganda's Divorce Act entitles a wife to alimony until she dies, remarries, or attains a better financial position.[13] The Court may order a husband to pay sums of money as permanent alimony in divorce cases or in cases involving a decree of judicial separation.[14] In making its determination, the Court considers the husband's ability to pay, the conduct of the parties, and the fortune of the wife (if any).[15] The court may order the alimony payments altered or suspended if the husband is later unable to pay due to disability.[16] Although a wife may petition for divorce, she is not obliged to pay alimony to the husband.

Women are not fully protected by this law because they often find it difficult to amass evidence about their husbands' income. In most cases, even husbands with discoverable salaries have peripheral businesses generating income that is difficult to track. Uganda courts must take pains to consider all of the husband's income-generating projects in the calculation of alimony.

Customary Law

Uganda's Customary Marriage (Registration) Decree[17] does not mention alimony. According to custom, however, a woman is not entitled to mainte-

---

and the respondent consents to a decree being granted. (e) That the parties to the marriage have lived apart for a continuous period of at least five years immediately preceding the presentation of the petition." *Id.* § 1(2).

12. However, a pure no-fault system is still not in place. *See* James Copson, *The Attitude of the English Court to Conflict of Jurisdiction in Divorce and Related Financial Proceedings,* 34 FAM. L.Q. 177, 179–80 (2000).

13. The Divorce Act, Cap. 215 §§ 24–25 [Uganda].

14. *Id.* § 25(1).

15. *Id.*

16. *Id.* § 26.

17. The Customary Marriages (Registration) Decree, Decree 16 of 1973 [Uganda].

nance after divorce, especially if she is at fault for the divorce. Society expects her to return to her parents and disassociate herself completely from her former husband and his family.[18]

The Uganda Law Reform Commission, in its comments concerning the proposed Domestic Relations Bill, recommended that former husbands should maintain or compensate their wives even when the divorce is performed under customary law.[19] A similar survey soliciting public comments from women included the following quote from one respondent: "[the husband] has spoilt all your chances, made you old, you have left him riches and children and you have even grown sick and unable."[20] Policymakers must take into account the real-life circumstances of women divorced under customary law when formulating a new divorce law for Uganda.

Mohammedan Law

Islamic law expressly provides for maintenance of a divorced wife. The amount a divorced Muslim woman receives depends on her husband's means at the time of divorce.[21] A wife must be maintained through the period of iddat, the period of approximately three months following divorce.[22] Some males contend that a husband is not required to pay maintenance after the period of iddat.[23] Most interpretations of the Koran's divorce provisions come from male scholars. Women should develop alternative interpretations to the Koran when appropriate and should challenge restrictive interpretations that seek to deny women this vital economic support.

Bangladesh

In Bangladesh, the Dissolution of Muslim Marriage Act governs Muslim women's right to maintenance in divorce.[24] Husbands, however, still have wide discretion in determining the amount of maintenance given to former wives after divorce.[25] Islamic law requires that a groom pay *mahr*, payable either on

---

18. *See* Jacqueline Asiimwe, *Making Women's Land Rights a Reality in Uganda: Advocacy for Co-Ownership by Spouses*, 4 YALE HUM. RTS. & DEV. L.J. 171, 175 n.19 (2001).

19. Uganda's Third Periodic Report to CEDAW, *supra* note 2, at 69.

20. On file with the author.

21. SERAJUDDIN, *supra* note 4, at 278; *see also* ENGINEER, *supra* note 5, at 129–32.

22. SERAJUDDIN, *supra* note 4, at 207–8.

23. *Id.* at 309–11.

24. The Dissolution of Muslim Marriage Act of 1939, 1939 Act 8, §2 [Bangladesh].

25. SERAJUDDIN, *supra* note 4, at 306–26.

demand or upon divorce.[26] However, the amount to be paid depends on the ability of the husband.[27]

Britain

In Britain, unlike in Uganda or Bangladesh, a Court granting a divorce may order either party to pay maintenance to the other.[28] Moreover, the court is given considerable discretion to determine what financial distribution is most equitable, looking at a number of factors and the parties' reasonable needs.[29] Britain has therefore come closest to achieving equality in the application of its laws.

Reform for Uganda

Divorced women in Uganda are economically, socially, and politically disadvantaged. Women often get married at a young age and are not educated like their male counterparts. After divorce, they are unable to make enough money to support themselves. Divorced women carry a social stigma and are ostracized. The laws in Uganda do very little to protect the interests of the divorced woman. The law must recognize these inequalities and provide maintenance for divorced women.

Although only women receive maintenance after divorce, maintenance should not be based solely on the income of the husband. Courts must take into account a wife's contribution in the home and should also consider the duration of the marriage. Moreover, the Court should not consider fault in assessing alimony, as it is very difficult to appraise fault in monetary terms.[30]

---

26. *Id.* at 40–41. *See also* Bangladesh's Third and Fourth Periodic Reports to CEDAW, *supra* note 7, §2.15.2.

27. SERAJUDDIN, *supra* note 4, at 278, *see also* ENGINEER, *supra* note 5, at 129–32.

28. The Matrimonial Causes Act, 1973, c. 18, §23(1) (Eng.). *See generally* STEPHEN M. CRETNEY & JUDITH M. MASSON, PRINCIPLES OF FAMILY LAW 410 (6th ed. 1997).

29. The Matrimonial Causes Act, 1973, c. 18, §25 (Eng.); *see also* Cretney, *supra* note 28, at 408–10, 433–54, 481–82.

30. *See* Cretney, *supra* note 28, at 448–53.

Property Rights

Uganda

Divorce Act

Uganda's Divorce Act is silent as to property distribution to a wife upon divorce. In Britain, the Married Women's Property Act of 1882 codified women's rights to property separate from their husbands.[31] Similarly, Uganda's Law Reform Commission has recommended (in regard to pending reforms of the Domestic Relations Bill) that property jointly acquired during marriage should be treated equitably as the property of both spouses.[32] In practice, however, courts typically deny divorcing wives the right to a share of the property despite their contribution to the family accumulation of wealth. Additionally, where divorce is based on fault, Uganda's Divorce Act penalizes a wife for committing adultery by removing her right to property.[33] In contrast, the statute does not remove the right of a husband to property when the marriage is dissolved because of his adultery.

The only area in which the Divorce Act addresses a wife's share of the property is in the calculation of alimony *pendente lite*, whereby "the court may order one-fifth of the husband's average net income for the three years just preceding the date of the order."[34] Yet, the wife does not receive a substantial amount because the courts do not consider inflation and the absence of financial records make it difficult to determine how much money the husband is making.

Even if courts were willing to safeguard the needs of women, very few divorce cases ever reach the courts. Most women do not go to court to fight for their rights[35] because they are ignorant of the existence of the law, they lack the resources to bring suit, they are too far from courts, or they succumb to societal pressure to reconcile.

---

31. The Married Women's Property Act, 1882, 45 & 46 Vict., c. 75 (Eng.).

32. Uganda's Third Periodic Report to CEDAW, *supra* note 2, at 69.

33. The Divorce Act, Cap. 215 §27 [Uganda].

34. *Id.* §24.

35. This is a fact known by the author of this paper through her experience in assisting women through the Association of Women Lawyers FIDA(U), which provides free legal services to women.

Customary Law

Women own very little under customary law. According to custom, a wife is "purchased" by her husband through the payment of bride wealth.[36] As a result, a wife is considered to be her husband's property. When they divorce, she does not share in the family property and may keep only a few personal items.[37] Because the two families, not the individuals, arrange the marriage and because a wife moves to a husband's home with just the necessaries of life, society does not view women as entitled to a share of the property she uses with her husband.[38] When the matrimonial home stands on communal or inherited clan land, a wife who married into the clan is unlikely to obtain a share of this land upon her departure.

Mohammedan Law

Islamic law is silent as to the distribution of marital property at divorce, which often works to the advantage of men in practice. Theoretically, at least, men and women enjoy equal status and should get equal shares of the marital property.[39] Islam's broad mandate of equality provides a wide area from which to fashion an equitable remedy.

Bangladesh

Women in Bangladesh do not acquire any marital property upon dissolution of the marriage by divorce, apart from dowry and *mahr*. It is undisputed, however, that these women contribute to the family's accumulation of wealth. Lack of access to marital property forces poor divorced women to resort to non-traditional work, such as manufacturing. They receive less pay than men for equal work and are often unable to support themselves.[40]

Britain

Women in Britain have equal property rights in divorce. A court, primarily concerned with providing a home and resources for the children,[41] may order

---

36. Uganda's Initial and Second Periodic Reports to CEDAW, *supra* note 1, at 74–75.
37. *Id.* at 76.
38. *Id.*
39. Engineer, *supra* note 5, at 42, 54–55.
40. *See* Bangladesh's Third and Fourth Periodic Reports to CEDAW, *supra* note 7, §2.10.4.

either party of a marriage to transfer property to the other or to a child.[42] In ordering the transfer of property, the Court is also guided by the "clean break" principle, meaning that financial and property issues should be settled as quickly as would be just and reasonable.[43] Divorcing parties may also draft consent orders for financial and property adjustments.[44]

Reform for Uganda

A wife's share in property upon divorce must be based on principles of equality and fairness. All property acquired during the marriage and to which a spouse has contributed, with the exception of property comprising the burial grounds, should be equally shared by law. Although the customs of the parties should not be considered in property distribution, a wife's direct or indirect contributions as a homemaker should be considered. For example, the Uganda Domestic Relations Bill incorporates the wife's contributions when considering the division of property.[45]

The reform effort should encourage consensual property distributions modeled after British law. An exception should be made for communal clan land, which has historically remained the property of the clan. Any consensual proceedings, however, should take into account Ugandan women's relative lack of bargaining power. Some mechanism should be devised to ensure that a woman's consent is freely given.

Custody

Uganda

Divorce Act

Uganda's Children Statute, in accord with principles of the Uganda Constitution, requires courts granting custody to take into account the best interest of the child.[46] Although the statute does not explicitly delineate the factors to determine the welfare of the child, examples include: the character of

---

41. *Id.* §§24(1)(a), 25.

42. The Matrimonial Causes Act, 1973, c. 18, §24(1)(a) (Eng.).

43. *Id.* §25A. *See generally* Cretney, *supra* note 28, at 454–67.

44. The Matrimonial Causes Act, 1973, c. 18, §33A (Eng.).

45. The Domestic Relations Bill (Uganda).

46. The Children's Statute, Act 6 of 1996, §7 (Uganda); Uganda Const. art. 34; *see* Mayambala v. Mayambala, Divorce Cause No. 3 of 1998, at 17 (Uganda 1998).

the parent; the child's sex, age, and upbringing; and the facts surrounding the custody dispute.[47] The best interest standard is broad and the court has wide discretion in awarding custody upon divorce.[48] While no one factor explicitly outweighs the others, courts place a high value on economic status. Because women generally depend on their husbands for economic security, courts often award custody to the husband. Courts will make an exception for very young children and grant custody to the mother.[49]

Customary Law

Customary practices breed inequality between husband and wife in matters regarding child custody. Although the "welfare of the child principle" applies in customary cases, in patrilineal Uganda, children belong to the husband and courts award custody accordingly.[50] In some cases, the husband decides who will get custody of the children on divorce, and the courts have affirmed this custodial right of the husband.

Mohammedan Law

Under Islamic law, custody of children upon divorce is based on the interpretation of the Koran. The Koran recognizes the father's superior right to custody of the children; not surprisingly, many jurists conclude that children should revert to their father.[51] Another interpretation of the Koran holds that nursing children belong to their mother for a period of two years only.[52] An

---

47. *See* Wambwa v. Okumu (1975) EA 578; Lough v. Ward (1945) 2 All ER 338 (Eng.) (not a divorce case, but upholding a father's control over his sixteen year old daughter as against a religious organization she had joined and that had effectively asserted custody over her).

48. The Uganda Divorce Act provides that: "In suits for dissolution of marriage or for nullity of marriage, or for judicial separation, the court may at any stage of the proceedings, or after a decree absolute has been pronounced, make such order as it thinks fit, and may from time to time vary or discharge the said orders, with respect to the custody, maintenance and education of the minor children of the marriage or for placing them under the protection of the court." The Divorce Act, Cap. 215 §30 [Uganda].

49. Uganda's Initial and Second Periodic Reports to CEDAW, *supra* note 1, at 77.

50. For example, courts have relied on "the father's natural and superior right to the custody of the child as against the mother." Nakagwa v. Kiggundu, 1978 HCB 310, 312 (Uganda 1978); *see also* Lough v. Ward (1945) 2 All ER 338, 348 (Eng.); Uganda's Initial and Second Periodic Reports to CEDAW, *supra* note 1, at 77.

51. Engineer, *supra* note 5, at 149.

52. *Id.* at 150.

alternative interpretation gives women custody of daughters up to puberty and sons up to the age of seven.[53] If a wife's right to custody of the children on divorce is relinquished in the *khula* divorce agreement, the only remedy available to the wife is to sue for invalidation of the agreement.

Bangladesh

Interpretation of Islamic law in Bangladesh gives a woman custody of her children upon divorce. While a woman may assert a custody right in court, it is neither infinite nor absolute. Custody of a daughter lasts only until puberty, and custody of a son lasts until the age of seven. [54] Furthermore, the right to custody is conditioned on the mother's good conduct and care of the child. The woman is not left without a remedy; she may apply to court for variation of the period of custody.[55]

Britain

In Britain, husbands and wives have equal rights to custody of children upon divorce. British courts apply the welfare principle to determine custody of and access to the child. [56] The court has broad powers in making custody orders for children who are under sixteen years old. In cases where the parties demonstrate a willingness to cooperate, the court will award joint custody. Much like other jurisdictions, the courts consider parental fitness and may order supervised custody when the need arises.[57] British custody disputes generally result in more favorable outcomes for women than those in Uganda and Bangladesh.

Reform for Uganda

A comprehensive reform in the law of Uganda must provide that either party can obtain custody of the children. The Domestic Relations Bill (Draft) 2000 of Uganda states that courts should apply the welfare principle, based on

---

53. *Id.* at 149; *see also* SERAJUDDIN, *supra* note 4, at 25.
54. *See* Bangladesh's Third and Fourth Periodic Reports to CEDAW, *supra* note 7, §2.15.5.
55. Convention On The Elimination Of All Forms Of Discrimination Against Women, *opened for signature* Mar. 1, 1980, art. 16 §1(d), 1249 U.N.T.S. 13, 20. Bangladesh acceded to the Convention on Nov. 6, 1984.
56. The Matrimonial Causes Act, 1973, c. 18, §41 (Eng.).
57. *See* Cretney, *supra* note 28, at 814–16.

the best interest of the child, when making orders related to maintenance and custody of children. Also, parental fitness should be included as a factor for consideration. Courts should not consider customary practices in custody matters, and parties should be able to settle.

In addition, there should be an age limit for custody. The women of Uganda recommended to the Uganda Constitutional Commission that eighteen be the age limit for child custody.[58] Finally, the court should be able to vary custody arrangements in the event of changed circumstances.

Child Support Maintenance

Uganda

Divorce Act

The Divorce Act gives wide discretion to the Court to award maintenance of the children and to vary the order as needed.[59] Child support should be awarded to the custodial parent on dissolution of marriage. The Act, however, is silent as to the factors the court should consider in reaching a conclusion.

Customary Law

The husband traditionally maintains his children only when he has custody of them. This arrangement is unfair to the ex-wife because in addition to not receiving a share in the marital property, she must support the child or children alone.

Mohammedan Law

Women may receive child support during the period of iddat (depending on the grounds for the divorce); after that period the child support usually ceases.[60] The maintenance amount depends on the husband's ability to pay.[61]

---

58. Recommendations Made by the Women of Uganda to the Constitutional Commission (Ministry of Women in Development, 1991).

59. The Divorce Act, Cap. 215 § 30 [Uganda]. However, the Children's Statute requires that both parents help to maintain the children after separation or divorce. See Uganda's Third Periodic Report to CEDAW, *supra* note 2, at 38. Moreover, women are entitled upon divorce to a fixed monthly support payment per child (2000 Ugandan shillings), but most never receive it. See Anne Akia Fiedler, *The Laws of Love*, Orbit, vol. 72 (Spring 1999), *available at* http://www.vso.org.uk/publications/orbit/72/love.htm (last visited on July 28, 2003). *But see* Mayambala v. Mayambala, Divorce Cause No. 3 of 1998, at 17–18 (Uganda 1998).

Bangladesh

Fathers have a duty to pay child support. If a husband fails to pay, the wife can enforce her rights in court.[62] Many such cases, however, never reach the court, because women do not have the economic means to pursue their rights in court.

Britain

Courts may order child support either before or after the dissolution of marriage. Either party may make periodic payments for the benefit of the child under the Matrimonial Causes Act.[63] Maintenance is also provided for in the Child Support Act.[64] When making a determination, the court looks at the needs of the child, the income of the parties, the status of the family before breakdown of marriage, and any disability that may affect the child.[65] In doing so, the court tries to place the child in a situation similar to that prior to the divorce.[66]

Reform in Uganda

Uganda must establish clear rules on the computation of child support. In most cases, child support should be paid by the non-custodial parent to the custodial parent until the child has attained eighteen years of age. Guidelines should provide a formula for computing child support for the non-custodial parent that considers the needs of each parent and the costs of raising children.[67] These guidelines will help judges with the difficult task of determining an amount that a non-custodial parent should pay.

---

60. Jamal J. Nasir, The Islamic Law of Personal Status 181–82 (1990).

61. *Id.* at 197.

62. Serajuddin, *supra* note 4, at 285–94, 320. *See also* Hefzur Rahman v. Shamsun Nahar Begum, 47 DLR (1995) 54 [Bangladesh].

63. The Matrimonial Causes Act, 1973, c. 18, §23(1)(d) (Eng.).

64. The Child Support Act, 1991, c. 48, §1 (Eng.). *See generally* Cretney, *supra* note 28, at 512–21.

65. The Matrimonial Causes Act, 1973, c. 18, §25(2) (Eng.). *See generally* Cretney, *supra* note 28, at 546–53.

66. The Matrimonial Causes Act, 1973, c. 18, §25 (Eng.).

67. For example, see the guidelines promulgated by the District of Columbia in the United States. D.C. Code Ann. §16-916.01 (Supp. 2002).

Conclusion

The suggested reforms will go a long way in improving the status of Ugandan women. With a strong women's movement and the cooperation of the government, Uganda will achieve its goal of establishing equal rights for women before, during, and after marriage.

Rethinking Property: Women and Matrimonial Property Rights in Tanzania

Salma Maulidi

Introduction

Property issues affect married women upon termination of the marriage by legal separation, divorce, or death of a spouse. In this essay I will examine matrimonial property in Tanzania[1] under the Law of Marriage Act (LMA),[2] which provides for the interests of legally separated and divorced women.[3]

The Present Law Governing Matrimonial Property

The LMA "regulate[s] the law relating to marriage, personal and property rights between husband and wife, separation, divorce and other matrimonial relief, and other matters connected therewith and incidental thereto."[4] Parliament passed the Act amidst changing political and socioeconomic circumstances in the country.[5] The Act faced much opposition during the parlia-

---

1. My discussion will be limited to Tanzania Mainland.

2. Law of Marriage Act, No.5 (1971) (Tanz.) [hereinafter LMA].

3. The discussion of marital property in relation to inheritance law is beyond the scope of this essay.

4. *See* LMA long title of legislation.

5. In 1967, Tanzania adopted the policy of African socialism, attempting to abandon capitalistic relations inherited from the colonial masters, which were seen as oppressive and exploitative. The Arusha Declaration, passed in 1967, was to guide the implementation of the new political and socioeconomic relations. For a detailed discussion of the colonial pe-

mentary debates because of its pro-women stance, which some members of Parliament viewed as non-traditional.[6] The Act assures women's rights to acquire, hold, and dispose of property, whether movable or immovable. This broad view of women's property rights contradicted elements of customary law, which denies women such authority. Because the Act applies to statutory, customary, and Islamic marriages, women in customary relationships are entitled to enjoy equal rights, liabilities, and status before the law, just like those in statutory unions.[7]

Under the LMA, marriage does not alter the ownership of any property owned by either spouse individually or either spouse's ability to acquire, hold, or dispose of such property.[8] An estate or matrimonial home owned by either spouse in which the other has an interest is not, however, covered by this rule. A spouse can protect her or his interest in matrimonial property by registering the interest in the land, or by petitioning the court to stop a sale or administration of property.[9] A wife or widow can benefit from this provision if the property at issue is land or a home on a surveyed plot of land, which is likely to be located in an urban setting. The majority of Tanzanian women, however, live in the rural setting where land titles are not registered.[10] Where the titles are registered, the Act assumes the spouse's knowledge of the sale.

---

riod in Tanzania and its subsequent influence on post-colonial political and economic thought, *see* Susanne D. Mueller, *The Historical Origins of Tanzania's Ruling Class*, 15 CAN. J. OF AFR. STUD. 459 (1981).

6. See Ministry of Community Development, Culture, Youth & Sports, Situation of Women in Tanzania v (1988). Some of the Act's positive aspects include the recognition of a wife's, including a common law wife's, interest in matrimonial property, women's equal contracting capacity, and the prohibition of domestic violence. LMA, §§ 56–59, 66–67.

7. Id. §§ 25(1)(d), 56.

8. Id. § 58.

9. Id. § 59. The Land Registration Ordinance, Cap 334 (Tanz.), requires all surveyed plots/lands to be registered with the Registrar of Titles. Under section 71, a spouse or widow can register her interest in the house or land. A wife or widow can raise a caveat under section 78 to stop a sale or administration of the property. She is, however, disadvantaged if the buyer is a bona fide buyer and had no knowledge of the other spouse's interest in the property. Land Registration Ordinance, Cap 334, § 78 (Tanz.).

10. Two types of land titles exist in Tanzania, the granted right of occupancy, and the deemed right of occupancy. Both are usufruct in nature; the former recognizes titles issued by the government, mostly on surveyed land, while the latter recognizes customary titles, mainly on unsurveyed land. The government has tried to put in place a system at the village level where by the village chairman allocates and records the distribution of land. This has been primarily implemented in registered and development villages.

This can be detrimental to women since land transactions are exclusively a male domain.[11] Moreover, enforcing a woman's right when she becomes aware of a sale or potential sale by her husband may be cumbersome. Lacking financial resources, a woman's access to legal institutions may be limited. Access to legal institutions entails sacrificing the few financial resources she has, as the woman must often travel great distances to the court, without any certainty as to the outcome of the matter. By pursuing the case, she may fall behind in work needed to sustain herself and her dependents.

The LMA is not without its shortcomings. It creates a rebuttable presumption that property acquired during the marriage belongs exclusively to the party in whose name it is titled.[12] Yet in patriarchal societies, where "business" is a man's affair and women are in charge of the home, it is often the man's name that appears on property as he is more likely to register it. Thus, the wife may be excluded from the title even when she is the sole contributor.

For legally separated and divorced women, the lack of a definition of matrimonial property threatens their access to and share of property that may be rightfully theirs and may be necessary to their survival.[13] It has been difficult for women to argue before the court that property is matrimonial property acquired through joint efforts, particularly when their names do not appear on the deed or they cannot prove a direct contribution. The Act tries to mitigate this problem by empowering the court to divide assets acquired by joint efforts during the marriage.[14] According to the Act, judges should consider the fol-

---

11. I am referring to the gender division of responsibilities in the family where "business" ventures are the realm of the man while domestic affairs are that of the woman. Cases reported in newspapers and coming before the court suggest a common practice of husbands alienating property without their wives' knowledge. These women only discover the alienation upon divorce or death of the husband. Likewise, under customary law, only men were permitted to alienate clan land. In Bernado Ephraim v. Holaria Pastory & Ano [1989] Civ. App. No. 70 (Tanz.), the High Court ruled against the customary law on constitutional equal protection grounds.

12. LMA § 60. Where the names of both spouses appear on the title, there is a rebuttable presumption that their beneficial interests therein are equal.

13. The interpretation section of the LMA, section 2, only defines a matrimonial home. There is another practical problem facing Tanzanian women seeking divorce. Section 114 of the LMA does not specify at what point the court will order division of the property/assets as opposed to division of the proceeds from the sale of the property. Given the repeated devaluation of the shilling, division of the assets through sale may not, in some instances, be the best option for the woman, as it may not adequately reflect the value of the contribution, and of the asset, in terms of the use and actual value from which she might otherwise benefit if the property is not sold.

lowing factors when dividing property: the customs of the community from which the parties belong; the extent of the contributions made by each party in money, property, or work; any debts owing by either party contracted for their joint benefit; and the needs of infant children.[15] Ideally, the court should aim for equal division of the property.[16] The Act, however, leaves considerable discretion to the individual judge to determine what property constitutes matrimonial property. Moreover, since the formula for computing the contributions of each party in acquisition of the property is imprecise,[17] the court has broad discretion to determine the type and extent of each party's contribution.

Customary Law and the LMA

There are two sources of customary law in Tanzania. The first is a codified set of customary rules devised by the colonizers and later adopted on a national scale through the Unification of Customary Law Project.[18] This project eventually produced various Local Customary Law Declaration Orders, "a kind of synthesized restatement of the law for patrilineal peoples...."[19] The Customary Law Declaration Order applies to patrilineal communities that are specified therein, which constitute about 80 percent of the overall population.[20]

The second source is unwritten customary laws and rules of the people that address areas not covered by the written rules. Judges and community leaders ascertain these rules through expert and oral opinions, scholarly works, and other authoritative sources.[21] This source of customary law governs the remaining 20 percent of the population not governed by the Cus-

---

14. LMA §114.

15. LMA §114(2).

16. *Id.*

17. *Id.*

18. SALLY FALK MOORE, SOCIAL FACTS AND FABRICATIONS: "CUSTOMARY" LAW ON KILIMANJARO 1880–1980, 159–60 (1986).

19. *Id.* These declarations included Customary Law Declaration 4 (Tanz.), Rules of Inheritance, Government Notice (GN) 436, 1963, which governs succession, and Local Customary Law Declaration, Law of Persons, (GN) 279, 1963, which governed matrimonial affairs before the enactment of the LMA.

20. *See* Magdalena Rwebangira, Women's Priorities for Legal Reform in Tanzania (1989) (mimeograph, Tanzania Women Lawyer's Association) (copy available in Library of Tanzania).

21. These include anthropological works. Also, an amendment to the Magistrates Court Act of 1963 provides for the use of assessors, or local elders, in determining questions of Islamic and customary law. *Id.* at 158–59.

tomary Law Declaration Order.[22] Regardless of its source, resort to the customary law of the community to guide the division of matrimonial assets in a divorce runs the risk of excluding the wife from receiving any share of the property.

The application of customary law is subjective. In an effort to determine the applicable customary law, courts often employ lay people from the community whose opinions are not binding on the court.[23] The use of these lay people, called assessors, may have negative consequences for women because most of these interpreters of community customs are men. Also, there is no consistent interpretation of customary law.[24] Progressive interpretations of customary law are rare, especially when there is no clear formula to guide the court and too much discretion is left to the individual judge.[25]

Extent of Each Party's Contribution

The LMA does not indicate what types of matrimonial property are jointly owned by the couple. Under the Customary Declaration Order, courts favored financial contribution as "effort" in acquiring matrimonial property. This view has been retained in some post-LMA decisions. In *Bi Zawadi Abdallah v. Ibrahim Iddi*,[26] the court held that the domestic duties of a spouse do not constitute "contribution" within the meaning of section 114, and thus do not entitle a spouse to a share of the matrimonial assets. In this case, the court refused to equate housework and childrearing with the husband's paid work in evaluating each spouse's contribution to the matrimonial property.

This approach risks undervaluing the contribution made by women engaged in the subsistence sector and petty trade, through which they save the

---

22. Unwritten laws and rules apply to matrilineal communities and other patrilineal communities not covered by the order.

23. MOORE, *supra* note 18, at 159.

24. *See* BARTHAZAR ALOYS RWEZAURA, TRADITIONAL FAMILY LAW AND CHANGE IN TANZANIA: A STUDY OF THE KURIA SOCIAL SYSTEM 138–39 (1985).

25. *See id.* at 139–40.

26. Bi. Zawadi Abdallah v. Ibrahim Iddi, Civ. App. No. 10 (Dar-es-Salaam High Court 1981). *See also Tumbo v. Tumbo*, High Court of Tanzania at Dodoma (1982) (acknowledging that property rights arise out of contribution of money, property, or work in the acquisition of an asset, but finding that women's housework alone is insufficient as a contribution; acknowledging also that spouses may contract for automatic joint property ownership of all assets acquired during marriage).

family from expending money on food and other basic needs.[27] Women engage in these activities in addition to other duties such as rearing children, allowing the man to engage in financially profitable ventures, or formal employment.[28] Women in rural areas often bring up families single-handedly, while husbands migrate to urban centers in search of a better future for the family. These sacrifices are in danger of being disregarded absent a broader definition of the kinds of contributions a court should consider and a guideline detailing how these contributions should be evaluated in the distribution of property.

Another case, *Bi Hawa*,[29] has emphasized the need for proof in alleging that particular property is matrimonial property, creating additional problems for women. Courts are requiring a higher standard of proof, making it increasingly difficult for women to meet this burden.[30]

The *Bi Hawa* case indicated that if a husband can show that the wife was adequately compensated during the relationship, she will receive a lesser share of the joint property. In *Bi Hawa*, the husband alleged that he had given his wife money to start a business but she squandered it. He pleaded that if the business were operative, she would have been amply provided for. The court considered this argument, and the wife ended up with very little property because the court found her to be irresponsible for squandering the money given to her.[31]

A second view is more sympathetic to women and recognizes traditional domestic duties of a wife as a contribution entitling the spouse to share in matrimonial property. Nevertheless, feminists are approaching this analysis with caution; recent decisions and professional legal opinion interpret section 114 of the LMA as precluding this broader view of women's contributions.[32]

---

27. *See* Jeffrey Meeker & Dominique Meekers, *The Precarious Socio-Economic Position of Women in Africa: The Case of the Kaguru of Tanzania*, 40 AFR. STUD. REV. 35, 43–44 (1997).

28. *Id.* at 44.

29. Bi-Hawa Mohammed v. Ally Sefu, Dar-se-Salaam, Court of Appeal Civ. App., No. 9 of 1983 (unreported).

30. Interview with Dr. Stephen Z. Gondwe, Professor of Law, University of Dar-es-Salaam (April 22, 1995). Dr. Gondwe indicated that when a woman has good counsel, the courts are more likely to consider *Bi-Hawa's* rationale in identifying matrimonial property. The problem is proof of the contribution is becoming more stringent and absent receipts or title, increasingly hard to meet.

31. Bi-Hawa, Civ. App. No. 9/1983.

32. *See* Rwebangira, *supra* note 20, at 11.

Mixed opinions on women's contributions will continue as long as the definition of key terms such as "joint efforts," "contribution," and "matrimonial property" remain unclear. Thus, even judgments that view a wife's domestic duties as "contribution" can be harsh, since it is still in the discretion of the judge or magistrate to determine to what extent the court will consider it sufficient to amount to an "effort" in acquiring property.[33]

Rethinking Property

Tanzania will not likely succeed in the reform of its property laws by "picking up the pieces which have remained of indigenous property systems, nor... by imposing alien institutions."[34] Instead, meaningful legal reforms should take various issues into account, including social, political, and economic factors.[35] An initial step in the task should be to identify the ways, both legal and extra-legal, that existing property laws discriminate against women.[36] Society, particularly women, must identify problems that perpetuate the discriminatory distribution of property and must develop strategies to best overcome such problems. The legal system must then embrace these aspirations rather than dictate solutions that have very little relevance in people's lives.

Law has a significant role to play in matrimonial relations, and it should be used in a just way to promote women's equality. A just system for the distribution of marital property requires a re-examination of customs and customary law and a rethinking of property relationships in the present socioeconomic situation. Madhu Kishwar notes that:

> [C]ultural traditions have tremendous potential within them to combat reactionary and anti-woman ideas, if we can identify their

---

33. It will be interesting, for instance, to see how the court will rule when a housewife employs a maid to help her in the home. Will the court still rule that she was engaged in "wifely duties," or look at that fact that the duties are performed by someone else. It will also be interesting to see if her share of the property will be affected if the court finds that someone else was performing the duties.

34. H.W.O. Okoth-Ogendo, *Property Systems and Social Organization in Africa: An Essay on the Relative Position of Women UnderIndigenous and Received Law, in* THE INDIVIDUAL UNDER AFRICAN LAW 54 (Peter Nanyenya Takirambudde ed., 1982).

35. I am consciously not including culture in the category because I believe that these other factors greatly influence culture and tradition making it dynamic.

36. ALICE ARMSTRONG, WOMEN AND LAW IN SOUTHERN AFRICA v–ix (1987) (discusses appropriate methodologies).

points of strength and use them creatively. The rejection of the harmful is then made much easier than attempts to overthrow traditions totally or attack them arrogantly from the outside....We must realize that
if we fail to acknowledge and help reinvigorate the deeply humane portions of our heritage, none of our other efforts are likely to succeed.[37]

Customary law is to blame for most of the unfairness to women because it
fails to recognize women's property rights. Using Kishwar's approach, however, some academics have begun to investigate customary law as it applied to
traditional communities pre- and post-colonialism.[38] In this vein, future work
and research should seek to distinguish true tradition from "customary law"
as well as recognize the dynamic nature of custom. Property as we know it
today has an individualistic connotation not present in communal societies.[39]
As a result, traditional rules of land inheritance, though they may have protected women's interests in pre-colonial societies, need to adapt to modern
economic and social relationships in Tanzania.[40]

Not all individuals appreciate the impact of colonialism and post-colonialism on the sexual division of labor in African societies. The introduction of

37. Madhu Kishwar and Ruth Vanita, *In Search of Answers: Indian Women's Voices
from Manushi* 47 (1984). *See also* Radhika Coomaraswammy, *Ethnicity and Patriarchy in
the Third World, in* Empowerment and the Law: strategies of third world women
109 (Margaret Schuler ed., 1986).

38. *See generally* Ifi Amadiume, Male Daughters, Female Husbands—Gender and
Sex in an African Society, (1987).

39. Taking an example of the Kuria tribe, a patrilineal group in the northern part of
Tanzania with very close ties to the Maasai and Luo, a woman was considered head of her
house, although technically the head of household was the man. This was also true in cases
of polygamous unions, where each house headed by a wife was self-sufficient, the individual woman being responsible for the management of her family in terms of feeding it and
protecting cows that were her daughter's bridewealth to be later used for her son(s).
"[A]lthough the husband would exercise some general authority and influence over his
wives on the use of such cattle, he could not overstep his powers," e.g., he could not use
them for his own marriage or that of a stepson. The harsh rules were intended to protect
the property of each house. Thus, a woman enjoyed autonomy in matters of production
and control of bridewealth cattle as well as other cattle and property acquired by her husband, herself and, in some instances, her father. This is an important point as cows were
the basis of wealth in this society yet women had access and control over them. *See*
Rwezaura, *supra* note 24, at 26.

40. Rose Mtengeti-Migiro, *Legal Development on Women's Rights to Inherit Land Under
Customary Law in Tanzania*, 24 law & politics in Africa, asia, & latin America, 362,
370–71 (1991).

cash crops in Africa during this period has led to the exploitation of women's labor. Women have been forced to take on sole responsibility for growing food for household consumption while men engage in cash crop production or other economic pursuits.[41] Some women may also be compelled to help in cash crop production, though their husbands generally control the profits from their work.[42]

Today, women are victims of structural adjustment programs and free-market policies handed down by the World Bank and the International Monetary Fund (IMF). A primary goal of such programs was to devalue Tanzania's currency and to raise agricultural producer prices in order to increase exports.[43] Although an improved balance of trade provides opportunity to import more foreign capital, most women are unable to make capital investments since they do not have the income or property necessary to acquire loans.[44] This situation leaves women vulnerable to impoverished conditions, with the possibility of being dispossessed of land or property. Tanzanian property laws must therefore ensure that women enjoy equal property rights.

Activists can justify legal reform by relying on traditional concepts of property ownership in which women and others had access to land and were able to use the land. Traditionally, land was owned communally and access was more important than ownership.[45] Positive aspects of existing laws can be used to compliment traditional concepts. For example, land law titles that are usufruct in nature can be used to advance the concept of access to women upon divorce thereby defeating the customary practice of denying the widow a share of the estate.

Women's interests in matrimonial property can be protected by creating rules to guide the division in terms of assets, work, monetary contribution, and other non-traditional contributions. For example, in computing the value of housework, there should be a finding of how much it costs to eat at a hotel,

---

41. Meeker, *supra* note 27, at 43–44.

42. *Id.* at 45.

43. Werner Biermann and Jumanno Wagao, *The Quest for Adjustment: Tanzania and the IMF, 1980–1986,* 29 AFR. STUD. REV. 89, 96–97 (1986).

44. Rosebud Kurwijila and Jean M. Due, *Credit for Women's Income Generation: A Tanzanian Case Study,* 25 CAN. J. OF AFR. STUD. 90, 91–92 (1991). For a discussion of the deleterious effects of IMF macroeconomic policy on the urban poor in Tanzania and its resulting economic strain on women, *see* Joe L. P. Lugalla, *Development, Change, and Poverty in the Informal Sector During the Era of Structural Adjustments in Tanzania,* 31 CAN. J. OF AFR. STUD. 424, 435, 443–44 (1997).

45. *See* Mtengeti-Migiro, *supra* note 40, at 363.

to launder clothes professionally, and to have live-in help. The costs for these services can be put together to determine their worth. The value of assets can be evaluated professionally. The court will, following the formula set, compute the value of contribution made by each party in terms of money or services, and apportion the assets accordingly. If the assets cannot be physically apportioned or if a party does not wish to sell an item, then that party should pay the other the difference.

Judicial activism has played a significant role in helping women gain access to property, matrimonial or otherwise.[46] Judges have a pivotal role to play in the just application of the law. Judges can refuse to recognize clan land as capable of alienation and instead allow divorced women a usufruct right to the land. If a woman has children, the land may then be held in trust for them. Similarly, judges can opt to apply the provisions of the Law of Marriage Act if the husband chooses to treat land as individual property, thereby entitling the woman to a share of it, as if it were matrimonial property.

To create a fair system for allocating matrimonial property, separate property should be identified in the marriage contract. Thus, upon dissolution, a court will resort to the marriage certificate to determine which property is subject to division. This will require monitoring and enforcing the LMA's requirement that marriages be registered.[47] Similarly, any private property of the parties that is likely to be jointly used or improved, like a house or a business, can be valued at the time of the marriage contract and revalued upon dissolution to determine the other party's contribution and improvement. The evaluation should take into account inflation and other economic realities. Such a scheme will not necessarily deprive an individual of title to privately owned property, but will recognize the contribution and efforts of the other spouse in its improvement. This will help women as an equal apportionment of the sale proceeds does not consider the increase in the cost of living.

As a result of IMF and World Bank policies, various sectors, including the judiciary, are facing serious cutbacks, inhibiting the role of the judiciary and other legal institutions in applying and enforcing the law. The above scheme attempts to minimize judicial costs as it uses existing structures rather than dramatically increasing the role of public officials. Other institutions and individ-

---

46. Bernado Ephraim v. Holaria Pastory et al, (PC) Civ. App. No. 70 (Mwalusanya J. and Munyera J.) (women can inherit clan land).

47. LMA §§ 42–55.

uals such as elders or religious institutions should be involved in the implementation and application of equitable legal principles in matrimonial issues.

Law schools should require students to enroll in a family law course with a gender-sensitive curriculum. As these students will ultimately influence the administration of justice and policy formulation, schools must expose them to equitable principles of family law. Likewise, social workers, religious leaders, clan elders, village council members, district and regional commissioners, and development officers should undergo short courses dealing with equality in the family and family law.

Legal education should be a significant force in rethinking property issues and instilling respect for women's equality and it should involve all levels of society, particularly grassroots legal education. Given that most women in communal societies and non-industrialized communities depend greatly on communal support, legal education programs aimed at improving women's access to property should focus on community-based institutions. A communal, grassroots approach toward women's property rights will be more effective than one that solely involves the Law Reform Commission or Parliament.

Property in Marriage Relations — Its Legal Implications for Women in Uganda

Margaret C. Oguli Oumo

Introduction

Women in Uganda have almost no opportunities to acquire property, and if they do, their chances of controlling or managing this property are minimal. A woman may receive property upon divorce, but only if she can prove it belonged to her.[1] Most women do not receive a share of the matrimonial property for which they toiled throughout their married lives to acquire or improve, because their contributions, both monetary and in the form of services, are often ignored.[2]

Today, the extended family system, which traditionally ensured that women were protected and provided for, has broken down. Instead, more women are working and financially contributing to the family. In addition, civil strife has left many women as head of the household and has increased the numbers of single mothers.[3] These factors, combined with inflation, have caused many women to want to acquire property, invest, and accumulate matrimonial property. There is no longer any cultural or customary justification for denying women a share in the matrimonial property after a marriage is dissolved.

---

1. Edwin Scott Haydon, Law and Justice in Buganda 104 (1960) (stating that the husband, as head of household, has entire domestic authority).

2. Lule Saloongo v. Mangulata Nandaula Nalongo, HCH. (1982).

3. Evidence from the Household Based Surveys, showed that women head one-fifth of the households in Uganda. UNICEF, Children and Women in Uganda: A Situation Analysis 75 (1989).

The Law

Lack of a clear definition of what constitutes matrimonial property leads to exploitation and discriminatory treatment of women, because women must prove that property belongs to them while men do not. In matters relating to distribution of property, neither customary nor case law explicitly discriminates against women. As will be explained, however, the impact on women is extremely burdensome.

The Divorce Act, which regulates the dissolution of church or civil marriages, does not define matrimonial property, yet presumes that everything in the house belongs to the husband.[4] The wife must, therefore, prove ownership in order to make property claims.[5] Such proof is often difficult to establish because women do not publicly announce their contributions. For example, a woman might give her husband money to purchase various items, but there is no public record of this transfer of funds. Requiring the woman to prove ownership of certain property is also unfair because people often do not keep documentation when they purchase property. Finally, in the home, no distinction is made between the property of the man and the woman, as all is taken as family property; as a result, it would be difficult for witnesses to testify as to what property belongs to whom.

Social customs and economic factors act as informal barriers that prevent women from acquiring property. Although the government does not directly create these social and economic factors, these obstacles are caused by circumstances that are under the control of government. The government has sanctioned the application of custom and religion in the determination of property rights, which has resulted in a detrimental effect on women's ability to acquire property.[6] Likewise, the government has failed to educate the peo-

---

4. The Divorce Act, Cap. 215 (Uganda).

5. Florence Butegwa, *Using the African Charter on Human and People's Rights to Secure Women's Access to Land in Africa, in* HUMAN RIGHTS OF WOMEN 495, 496 (Rebecca J. Cook ed., 1994).

6. In Ugandan courts, it is mandatory to apply Customary law provided it does not conflict with any written law and "is not repugnant to natural justice and equity." The Judicature Act, No. 11, sec. 8(1) (1967) (Uganda). A lot of customs conflict with statutory laws and yet they are operative. This is because customs are strong and the government machinery has not been able to monitor the application of the law, so customs are still applied. The women are also not involved in interpreting the law so their interests and needs are often ignored, and the needs of the men who interpret the law are taken into consideration.

ple about women's contribution to development in order to foster a change in attitude towards women's access, control, and management of property. Such a change would ensure that women have a share in matrimonial property when a marriage is dissolved.

Moreover, the law prevents women from capitalizing on direct and indirect contributions to matrimonial property because of the lack of a clear legal definition of matrimonial property. Direct contributions are difficult to identify when the parties pool their income to acquire joint assets. Indirect contributions also are difficult to quantify; for example, when a woman works while her husband acquires an education or leaves her job to care for the family, she is making an indirect contribution. Many women sacrifice their own education and careers to take care of their families, thereby freeing the man to go to university or to earn a better income. Unfortunately, these contributions by women are routinely ignored in the division of matrimonial property.

Effects of the Law on Women

The effect of these "gender neutral" laws, giving women little or no claim to matrimonial property, is to render wives dependent on their husbands. Many women will not be motivated to acquire property because they know that at the dissolution of the marriage they will receive nothing. Many of them are not able to enforce the rights they have, because they cannot afford a lawyer to represent them in court.[7]

In separation and divorce, women feel pressured to compromise, because they know that courts will not recognize their rights. As a result, women will often accept anything that is offered to them, even if the contested item of property belongs to them. For example, if a husband offered to pay his wife a certain amount of money for support, she is likely to accept it. Also, women are often forced to stay in violent relationships because they know they will not be able to leave with any property.

---

7. Literacy levels of the women are lower (55.5%), as compared to that of men (76.8%). U.N. Development Program, Human Development Report 212 (2001) As a result, women have few chances of getting well paid jobs. Even when they are employed, they are concentrated in the traditionally female jobs, which are characterized by low pay. Even when they are employed, their income goes to meet household needs, leaving them with nothing to save. *See* Sylvia Tamale, *Law Reform and Women's Rights in Uganda*, 1 E. Afri. J. Peace & Hum. Rts. 164, 178 (1993).

This also leads to insecurity in marriage, and women may make secret arrangements to protect themselves, such as registering property in their children's or brother's names. In other instances, women may keep property in their father's home, in the hope that if there is a dissolution of the marriage they will at least have some property to fall back on to sustain themselves in old age.

Finally, women are not motivated to work and acquire property. This leads to loss of self-esteem, because society does not value the work they do in the home. Consequently, the family's standard of living is negatively affected by this loss of women's potential contribution.

Factors that Contribute to Women Being Deprived of Property upon Dissolution of Marriage

Uganda is made up of fifty-six tribes, each with its own customary practices.[8] Because women do not traditionally sit on the clan councils, men have always had the privilege of articulating and shaping the customary laws. In matters of matrimonial property, this translates into ownership by men. Men have broad powers over their wives and their wives' property and they are empowered to enforce these rights in courts.[9]

Early Marriage

Because girls are married off at an early age, often to older men, it is difficult for them to relate to their husbands on an equal basis in matters relating to property. Many girls are married at puberty, and thus do not have the education, skills, and experience necessary to acquire employment. Young brides end up staying at home to look after the family, and those in villages spend most of their time engaged in agricultural work on land that belongs to their husbands.[10] Therefore, they have few chances to acquire and accumulate their own property.

---

8. *See* Const. of Uganda. Third Schedule.

9. World Bank, Uganda, A Country Study 28 (1993).

10. World Bank, Gender, The Evolution of Legal Institutions and Economic Development in Sub-Saharan Africa 27 (1992).

Bride Price

When a man pays a bride price to the wife's family at the time of marriage, the woman is reduced to the status of property. It follows that everything she owns and produces belongs to her husband.[11] Payment of bride price is a feature of customary marriages and is typically paid unless the bride's family chooses not to exercise their right to demand it.[12] Even in a civil or church marriage, payment of bride price is often a prerequisite for the families to give consent for the parties to marry.[13] Although bride price is not required by law, most people feel obliged to pay it because they want to fulfill their customary obligations.

While in theory, the payment of bride price is intended to seal the marriage and symbolize the union of two families, in reality, it means the transfer of the woman's services from her father to her husband and his family.[14] Because of his proprietary "rights" over the wife, even when a husband dies, one of the husband's relatives "inherits" the woman; her refusal means that her family must return the bride price. Because a woman's productive capacity is not her own, but her father's or her husband's, she cannot claim any property.

Polygamy

Under customary law, a man may marry as many women as he desires.[15] Even in church or civil marriages, which are supposed to be monogamous, men take on additional wives.[16] Polygamy is a feature in the African family system and is considered a symbol of wealth. The more money a man has, the more women he will be able to pay bride price for, and the more wives he has, the more people work for him, producing more food.

Polygamy lowers the status of a wife relative to her husband. In a relationship in which there is one man and two women, the status of the man and the women cannot be equal. The husband becomes the master and his wives compete for his

---

11. *Uganda: The Facts About the Tradition of Bride Price*, 26 GENDER NEWS ALERT 56 (2000).

12. Customary Marriages Registration Decree 16 (1973) (Uganda).

13. *See* Tamale, *supra* note 7, at 171.

14. *Id.*

15. Customary Marriage Registration Decree 16 (1973) (Uganda).

16. Lara Santoro, *First Wive's Club in Unites in Africa*, CHRISTIAN SCIENCE MONITOR, Jan. 28, 1998, at 1.

favors.[17] The man takes over the role of allocating resources in the home and the women are reduced to mere laborers. At the same time, because the family assets are pooled together under the man's control, the women lose what they produce individually and cannot claim it at the dissolution of marriage.[18]

Inheritance

In practice, Ugandan law does not recognize the right of women to inherit property and thus forecloses one of the main channels of property acquisition.[19] According to the law of inheritance, when someone dies the division of his property depends on whether he left a will.[20] Although women could inherit property through wills, very few people make wills because of ignorance of the process.[21] If a man dies without a will, however, his property will be divided according to estate law, which holds that all his children, both male and female, are entitled to an equal share.[22]

Although the law provides for equal distribution of property between male and female children when there is no will, these provisions are rarely followed, and the property is divided according to customary law. Customary laws of inheritance do not recognize the rights of female children to inherit their father's property.[23] Many Ugandans believe that female children who marry should not get a share of the family land because their husbands will take over their share, leaving less for the clan. With respect to spousal inheritance, women are denied the right to inherit their husband's property because they do not belong to his clan.[24] Thus, in practice, married women are prevented from inheriting property both from their fathers and their husbands.

Although men are supposed to inherit land so that it will stay within the family, many men sell clan land.[25] Additionally, because of migration, the clan

---

17. *Id.* at 215.

18. *See* Jacqueline Asiimwe, *Making Women's Land Rights a Reality in Uganda: Advocacy for Co-Ownership by Spouses*, 4 YALE HUM. RTS. & DEV. L.J. 173, 174 (2001).

19. *See* Butegwa, *supra* note 5, at 497.

20. Succession Amendment Act, Cap, 139, Uganda)(1964).

21. It is also considered a bad omen for one to make a will. OEF INTERNATIONAL, WOMEN, LAW AND DEVELOPMENT IN AFRICA: ORIGIN AND ISSUES 51 (Margaret Schuler ed., 1990).

22. *Id. See also* The Succession Amendment Decree (1972)(Uganda).

23. *See* Asiimwe, *supra* note 18, at 175–76.

24. Tamale, *supra* note 7, at 175.

25. *See* Butwega, *supra* note 5, at 500.

is in a state of disintegration and more land is held on an individual basis.[26] As a result, the traditional reasons for denying women the right to inherit land no longer exist.

Religion

Religion may have a limiting effect on women's ability to acquire and control property. Christianity, for example, emphasizes the subordination of women to men and maintains that women cannot hold property independently of their husbands.[27] As a result, Christian women are not motivated to acquire their own property. According to the Bible, a woman is subordinate to her husband, the recognized head of the household.[28] As a result of these teachings, many women do not acquire property of their own because they believe either that the husband should have control over property or that the husband's property belongs to them jointly. At the dissolution of the marriage, many women have been disappointed to learn that their husbands sold or squandered their property and that any remaining property was regarded as his.

Social Factors

Women face barriers in acquiring property because the male-dominated society views the control of property as synonymous with power. Ownership of property is seen as a source of power that only men should enjoy. Women are supposed to be under the control of men, and if they acquire property, it is seen as an assertion of independence and a rejection of male authority.[29] Many women do not acquire property for this reason. If they do, they register the property in the names of the husband, sons, or male relatives for fear of breaking their marriages or dissuading prospective husbands. Therefore, at the breakdown of marriage, women have no property of their own, and what once belonged to them becomes subject to the control of a man.

---

26. *Id.*
27. Theodera Ooms, *The Role of the Federal Government in Strengthening Marriage*, 9 VA. J. SOC. POL'Y & L. 163, 164 (2001).
28. *Ephesians* 5:22.
29. *See* CHRISTINE OBBO, AFRICAN WOMEN 44 (1980).

Woman's Role in the Home

Society recognizes a woman's role as family caretaker, and this role allows her no time to work and acquire property. Caring for the family, which includes not only the immediate family but also the extended family, leaves a woman with no time to think about property and its management.[30] Moreover, she knows that her husband handles these concerns, so she does not make an effort to acquire assets of her own. Meanwhile, the man's income goes toward acquisition of valuable assets like a car or a house.

In addition, women have to meet the expenses that relate to their domestic duties. For a woman in a rural area, if the members of the family fall sick, she must take them to the hospital or look for herbs to cure them. For a working urban woman, when a child falls sick she must pay the hospital bills. Upon divorce, women often have no tangible assets of their own to claim because in addition to having no time to acquire anything, they expended their income by meeting the household expenses. Moreover, the law does not consider women's domestic work to be a contribution toward her husband's accumulation of property. Therefore, a wife will not receive a share of the marital property upon distribution unless she can show that she made some monetary contribution towards its purchase.[31]

Economic Factors

Women have limited access to credit and fewer chances of getting well paying jobs that would allow them to earn an income and establish credit. Most of the banks in Uganda are commercial enterprises that operate to maximize profits. As a result, while they often advance credit they always demand collateral in the form of a land title.[32] Because women cannot own land under customary law, they have nothing to give as security.[33] Some institutions de-

---

30. WORLD BANK AND THE MINISTRY OF GENDER AND COMMUNITY DEVELOPMENT, *Report of Study of the Legal Constraints to Women's Economic Empowerment* at 3 (1995).

31. Butegwa, *supra* note 5, at 496.

32. Ewa Qwist, *Women's Access, Control and Tenure of Land, Property and Settlement* (1998), at http://www.sli.unimelb.edu.au/fig7/Brighton98/Comm7Papers/TS26-Qvist.html (last accessed July 23, 2003).

33. *See* ACP-EU TECHNICAL CENTRE FOR AGRICULTURAL AND RURAL COOPERATION, THE ECONOMIC ROLE OF WOMEN IN RURAL AND AGRICULTURAL DEVELOPMENT 16 (2001).

mand the consent of the husband before they undertake any financial transaction with a woman.[34] Many women, who have had few limited educational opportunities, cannot manage credit and ask their husbands to manage it for them; the husband may end up investing the money on his own, or he may misappropriate it. This restricted access to credit often prevents women from acquiring property and making investments.

Employment

Employment opportunities for women are limited in both the formal and informal sector.[35] Women are less educated than men,[36] so very few of them can get well paying jobs. For those who manage to get formal employment, many are concentrated in traditionally female jobs that do not offer high salaries;[37] therefore, women cannot accumulate savings to invest in property acquisition. Some women start small businesses in the informal sector. These jobs are often characterized by low turnover and little pay.[38] The money women earn often goes into maintaining the business and meeting the household needs, leaving women with nothing to invest.

Recommendations

Law Reform

Uganda should revise its matrimonial property laws to eliminate discriminatory rules and ensure equitable sharing of property at the dissolution of the

---

34. *See* Julie Mertus, *State Discriminatory Family Law and Customary Abuses, in* WOMEN'S RIGHTS HUMAN RIGHTS 135, 142 (Julie Peters & Andrea Wolper eds., 1995).

35. Although women make up about 51% of the population, as of 1988, they constituted only 20% of the work force in the formal sector. *Consideration of Reports Submitted by States Parties Under Article 18 of the Convention on the Elimination of All Forms of Discrimination Against Women,* U.N. GAOR, Comm. On The Elimination Of Discrimination Against Women, at 67, U.N. Doc. CEDAW/C/UGA/3 (2000) [hereinafter UGANDA COUNTRY REPORT].

36. The literacy rate for women is 44.9% as compare to 63.5% for men. *Id.* at 39.

37. The majority of Ugandan women are employed in stereotypical female occupations, such as teaching, nursing, stenography, and clerking. Tamale, *supra* note 7, at 178.

38. *Id.*

marriage. Parties who feel compelled to fulfill customary or religious obligations could do so if they wish, but these ceremonies should have no legal implications in legally recognized marriage.

The court structure to deal with divorce should be unified.[39] Since a family court to deal with children's issues has been proposed, the mandate of this court should be expanded to include all family matters. These courts should be located within reasonable walking distances of most villages to make them accessible to all women.[40] The courts, in consultation with lawyers and activists, should write court rules so that women can understand them and file complaints.

In addition, the government should revise laws to incorporate principles of equality and non-discrimination, such as those in the Ugandan Constitution and other regional and international conventions to which Uganda is a party. Uganda should also incorporate some of the measures that have been adopted in other countries, such as defining matrimonial property to include the earning capacity of the partner to which the homemaker contributed.[41]

Customary practices like bride price, polygamy, and the exclusion of women from inheritance should be prohibited. Women themselves should be involved in the process of reforming the law, because they are in the best position to define the problem and suggest workable solutions.

Educational Measures

The government and non-governmental organizations (NGOs) may improve matrimonial property law by educating judicial officers who make decisions on property distribution at the dissolution of the marriage. Trainings should make these officers aware of the barriers women face in acquiring property and the contribution they make in acquiring or improving matrimonial property. Judicial awareness should include knowledge about the hardships women may face when denied a share of the matrimonial prop-

---

39. *See generally* Catherine Harries, *Daughters of the People: International Feminism Meets Ugandan Laws and Customs*, 25 COLUM. HUM. RTS. L. REV. 493, 525–26 (1994).

40. Esther Damalie Naggita, *Why Men Come Out Ahead: the Legal Regime and the Protection and Realization of Women's Rights in Uganda*, 6 E. AFRI. J. PEACE & HUM. RTS. 34, 59 (2000).

41 *See generally* REGINA LULE MUTYABA ET. AL, FIDA RESEARCH ON DIVORCE AND SEPARATION 41–44.

erty, including inability to work, absence of financial savings, and sometimes, inescapable poverty. Giving women a share of the property that they helped earn means they are getting a share of the investment they made; it is a more just resolution.

Lawyers

Changing the curriculum in the law school for undergraduates and organizing trainings, workshops, and seminars for lawyers will go a long way toward improving women's ability to realize their rights to matrimonial property at the dissolution of the marriage. Well-trained lawyers will be able to defend women's rights to matrimonial property, bearing in mind the barriers they face and the contributions they make. Through this training, some may feel obliged to assist the women in order to improve the situation in society.

General Population

Educating the population, especially women, about their rights to property, matrimonial property in particular, will create a culture that encourages respect for rights, knowledge of people's obligations, and resources for women faced with property problems.[42] Communities must understand that while denying women property may be customary, it also violates women's rights that are enshrined in the Ugandan Constitution.

Research and Data Collection

Collection of data and information can facilitate the law reform process and raise awareness because activists will have reliable information concerning the nature of the problem, including its causes and effects.[43] It will also give lawmakers and activists materials on which to rely in arguing for law reform.

Formal Education

The enrollment and retention of girls in school will increase their chances of getting a better education,[44] enhance their skills, and enable them to get

---

42. *See generally* Naggita, *supra* note 40, at 59–60.
43. *See* Tamale, *supra* note 7, at 194.

jobs that pay enough money to allow for property acquisition. Additionally, women's chances of sharing in matrimonial property will increase since such tangible contributions will be more readily recognized by courts in property disputes.

Access to Credit

Providing women more opportunities to acquire credit can improve their chances of acquiring property.[45] Barriers such as requiring collateral in the form of land should be removed and loans should be given based on factors that evidence a person's likelihood to repay in a timely manner. Such factors might include having a stable job, being a resident, and holding a position of authority in the community. The government and the NGO community should train women to run enterprises and to manage credit, including tips on how to start a business and keep accounts.[46] This training will improve women's ability to manage property, to invest, and to earn an income. This will, in turn, allow them to have property of their own to fall back on when they face divorce.

Conclusion

Customs, practices, and policies that prevent Ugandan women from acquiring property must be reformed so that women can contribute tangibly to the development of assets in the home. In addition, the law should define matrimonial property to include the contribution of women, and courts should recognize these contributions during the dissolution of the marriage and ensure equitable distribution of the property. As long as women are denied equal rights to property, justice will not be achieved, and the Ugandan communities will suffer the consequences.

---

44. *Id.,* at 179 (noting that the proportion of girls in schools declined from 46% in primary one to 38% in primary seven).

45. *See generally* Nadia H. Youssef, *Women's Access to Productive Resources: The Need for Legal Instruments to Protect Women's Development Rights, in* WOMEN'S RIGHTS HUMAN RIGHTS 279, 283–84 (Julie Peters & Andrea Wolper eds., 1995).

46. *See, e.g.,* COUNCIL FOR ECONOMIC EMPOWERMENT FOR WOMEN OF AFRICA, UGANDA CHAPTER CASE STUDY (2002).

Impact of Customary Inheritance on the Status of Widows and Daughters in Tanzania: A Challenge to Human Rights Activists

Monica E. Magoke-Mhoja

Introduction

I was very well off before my husband died. I ran a restaurant business. However, after the death of my husband, since I was childless, his children who I had brought up, evicted me from the matrimonial home....I wasn't even allowed to enter the restaurant. This restaurant, which I built together with my husband is no longer in my control. As I no longer have a means of earning an income, I am now begging from relatives.

-Widow[1]

Like the woman quoted above, most widows and daughters suffer under the facially discriminatory customary inheritance law in Tanzania.[2] Customary law completely bars widows from inheriting land from their deceased husbands, even when the land is marital property, and subjects the widows to

---

1. Monica E. Mhoja, Legal Status of Widows, in Exposed to Social Insecurity Vulnerable Women and Girls in Tanzania 27 (Friedreich Ebert Stiftung ed., 1995).

2. In matters of inheritance, three systems operate hand in hand: statutory law, religious laws, and customary law. Native Tanzanian affairs are presumed to be regulated by customary law except where there is an express indication that any other law ought to apply. See Law Reform Comm'n of Tanzania, Report of the Commission on the Law of Succession/Inheritance 34–36 (1995).

being "inherited" by men in her husband's family.[3] It prohibits daughters from inheriting any family or clan land, limits them to inheriting small shares of property, and excludes daughters and widows from administering estates. This discrimination against widows and daughters violates their human rights.[4] The harms inflicted by gender-biased inheritance laws include poverty, harassment, ostracism, ill-health, and psychological damage. The discriminatory effects of these inheritance laws have become magnified as the scourge of HIV/AIDS has greatly increased the number of widows and orphans in Tanzania.[5]

Customary inheritance law came into being during a time when family or clan members supported widows and children upon the death of a husband or a father. These traditions, however, are dissipating in modern society as a result of migration, urbanization, the influx of different cultures, the influence of religious groups, and increased access to education. Customary law regulating inheritance is problematic because widows and children are often left with little or no means of support.

---

3. Widow inheritance connotes a customary practice in which on the death of a husband, the widow is "inherited" by one of the deceased's male relatives. *See, e.g.,* Proceedings of a National Workshop on Women and Law in Eastern Africa 34–35 (M. K. Rwebangira ed., 1993).

4. M.C. Mukoyogo, Theoretical Frame-Work on the Law of Inheritance, in Report on the Law of Inheritance & Research Findings by the Law Reform Commission of Tanzania 19 (Unpublished, Presented to the Minister of Justice in March 1995); *see also* Samuel Sitta, Opening Remarks, in Report on the Law of Inheritance & Research Findings by the Law Reform Commission of Tanzania 13 (Unpublished, Presented to the Minister of Justice in March 1995).

5. It is estimated that between 800,000 and 1,000,000 Tanzanians are infected with AIDS Virus. *See* The United Republic of Tanzania, Bureau of Statistics 130 (1995). More recent estimates indicate that the number of infected Tanzanians is now over 2 million. *See, e.g.,* CIA Factbook (2002).

Customary Inheritance Law and the Harm It Inflicts upon Widows and Daughters

The Scope of the Rules

Regimes of Inheritance: Persons Entitled to Distribution of Different Types of Property

Customary law distinguishes between self-acquired land/property and family or clan land.[6] Certain rights and obligations flow to individuals based on this categorization.

Self-Acquired Land/Property

Historically, self-acquired land referred to the land found by a man through his own efforts. Such efforts included the initial clearing of virgin forest, the planting of permanent crops, and the purchasing of land.[7] Under the inheritance regime, if the deceased has children, male or female, they exclusively inherit all self-acquired property.[8] Customary law, however, discriminates based on gender. Under the Customary Rules, which govern much of customary law, inheritance occurs in three degrees: the deceased's eldest son by his most senior wife inherits in the first degree,[9] a status that assures him a bigger share than any other heirs. All other sons inherit in the second degree. Those in the second degree will each get bigger shares than daughters, who inherit in the third degree.[10]

The Customary Rules establish the mode of distribution of property in the second and third degrees according to the children's ages and gender. Under this regime, males always get more than females and age only comes into play to determine who gets more property as between multiple males or multiple females. In other words, gender always trumps age, with males inheriting more than females, regardless of age.

---

6. *See* R.W. James & G.M. Fimbo, Customary Land Law of Tanzania —a Source Book 295–302 (1973).

7. Z.S. Gondwe, Female Intestate Succession to Land in Rural Tanzania: Whither Equality 30 (1990).

8. Rule 26 of the Customary Rules.

9. Rule 19 of the Customary Rules.

10. Rules 23, 25 of the Customary Rules.

Family and Clan Land

Family land reflects the status of a family as a unit of production and ownership.[11] Rule 20 of the Customary Rules provides that daughters can inherit clan land to use for their lifetime, but have no disposal rights. No such restrictions apply to men. In addition, Rule 27 makes a specific provision for widows regarding their succession to clan land: the widow has no share of the inheritance, and if the deceased left relatives of his clan, her share is to be cared for by her children just as she cared for them.

The unfairness of the Rules is perhaps most clear in the context of marital property. Upon inheritance, courts applying the Rules do not consider whether the property in dispute was matrimonial property obtained by joint efforts as provided for under the 1971 Law of Marriage Act (LMA).[12] The LMA recognizes spouses as partners who toil in a joint undertaking and are entitled to equality of ownership.[13] Logically, this qualification should continue after the death of the husband. The LMA, however, does not apply to inheritance and does not, therefore, supersede customary law in matters of inheritance.

Such mistreatment of widows is counterproductive. In terms of public policy, it seems to encourage divorce. Wives will not devote themselves to their family and community if they are apprehensive about being robbed of the fruits of their labor should their husband(s) die before them. It simply does not make sense for a divorced wife to expect a division of up to 50 percent and a widow to expect nothing.[14]

Wife Inheritance

Customary law provides for widow inheritance. Pursuant to this custom, a widow is required to marry a male relative of her dead husband. Rule 62 of the Customary Rules provides that the deceased's relatives may ask a widow whether she wishes to be inherited. If she agrees to marry one of her deceased

---

11. There is no hard and fast definition of "family land." *See* Gondwe, *supra* note 7, at 31.

12. Law of Marriage Act, Act No. 5 of 1971 (Tanzania), creates a presumption that any property acquired during the marriage belongs either to the husband or wife or it is property of both.

13. *See also* M.K. Rwebangira, The Status of Women and Poverty in Tanzania 15 (Unpublished, Presented at the World Bank Workshop, Socio-Economic Growth and Poverty Alleviation in Tanzania, Dar es salaam, 1995).

14. *Id.* at 34.

husband's male relatives, she can remain there as a wife, but without control over the land.

Women face significant pressure to succumb to widow inheritance. Women are pressured by socioeconomic problems that stem from gender bias. Some widows, for example, agree to be inherited out of fear that their family of origin will be required to refund the bride price paid by a deceased husband's family. This is particularly true in a situation in which the person who received the bride price property has died. The next generation inherits the obligation to refund the bride price.[15]

The practice of widow inheritance is harmful and degrading to women. It treats women as chattel, passing them from man to man through inheritance. After they are passed to a relative as property, their new status as wife subjects them to forced sex in the new marriage.

Other Gender-Biased Aspects of the Customary Rules

Selection of a Guardian

When a wife dies, the clan council does not select a guardian for her spouse and children, but when a husband dies, the clan council does select a guardian to care for the widow and children.[16] The guardian typically is a burden to the widow. He works for free but essentially becomes the head of the household. He is involved in all social and economic family affairs and the widow is required to entertain him with food, yet he does not financially contribute to the house.

Appointment of an Administrator

Rule 5 provides that the administrator of the deceased's property is either the deceased's eldest brother or father; if there is no brother or father, any other male relative may be chosen with the help of the clan council. If there is no male relative, the deceased's sister is the administrator. The Rule excludes widows and daughters in this hierarchy.

---

15. Mugesi Nyitonyi v. Mangazeni Ndege, 1977 L. Rev. Tanzania. No. 27. If the father-in-law received the bride price while he was alive, his main heir is responsible for its return, irrespective of the house to which the wife belongs.

16. The 1st schedule deals with the roles of a guardian for the deceased's estate. If there is an adult son he can be nominated.

The Harm the Rules Inflict on Widows and Daughters

As a result of the Rules, widows and daughters sustain psychological and sometimes physical harms after a man's death. The Rules discriminate against women and deprive them of full participation in society. Although women may file petitions in court for relief from the injustice of the Rules, most judges are conservative and promote sexual inequality in succession. This inequality is harmful to women in many ways.

Daughters

Daughters cannot be the primary heirs unless there are no male offspring. When they do inherit, daughters are placed in the third degree and therefore end up with the most unsuitable land and little property. Also, daughters cannot be selected as administrators of an estate. As a result, daughters feel inferior to sons. Further exacerbating the problem is the false notion that if a person is selected as an administrator, he is also an heir. Administrators tend to squander the entire estate and leave female heirs empty-handed. Thus, daughters are economically and emotionally harmed.

Limited inheritance rights force most orphan daughters to move to town and work as domestic workers. These women face physical harm, such as rape by their employers, and the psychological harm of separation from their mothers. Some daughters stay with their mothers but turn to prostitution to escape poverty. They encounter physically invasive harms of unwanted sex, potential HIV/AIDS infection, sexual abuse, unwanted pregnancy, or sexual harassment.[17] Some impoverished widows fail to provide an education for their children, so daughters miss the opportunity to educate themselves and possibly escape poverty.

Widowhood: Types of Harassment[18]

As widows, women are extremely vulnerable. Under the Rules, they have no inheritance rights of their own; they must depend on the goodwill of their

---

17. Most women who consent to undesired sex, and who passively acquiesce in unwanted pregnancies, undergo a destruction of selfhood. *See* ROBIN WEST, CARING FOR JUSTICE 107 (1977).

18. Interview with widows in Dar es Salaam, Tanzania (Dec. 1996). The data gathered from the interview shows that causes of widowhood include HIV/AIDS, accidents, and other natural diseases. AIDS seems to be the greatest cause of widowhood and other causes are just supplementary.

children or other heirs. In addition, immediately after the death of her husband, a widow often experiences harassment from her deceased husband's relatives, who believe that she is responsible for her husband's death. The relatives often feel they can no longer tolerate living with her. This belief may be rooted in superstitions that some women are witches or in a fear of AIDS. The following story is an illustration of one widow's harassment:

> The night my husband died, his brothers…came into the house and ransacked it to find the money….They took away all our household possessions…Even the blanket and the bed. They left nothing. When I tried to stop them they beat me and the children, and threw us out of the door….Now I have no where to live and my children are ill and have no education. They accused me of having poisoned him, using witchcraft.[19]

Such allegations may cause widows to be depressed, commit suicide, or flee to another territory. Widows whose husbands died of HIV/AIDS are particularly vulnerable to depression and suicide.

Most tribes do not regard a widow as a member of the deceased husband's family. This exclusion from the husband's family can lead to the widow's expulsion from the matrimonial home, rendering her propertyless and sometimes childless.[20] These widows suffer the additional emotional harm of separation from their children. The only option open to them is to return to their own clan-land operated by their brothers. Generally, their brothers do not welcome these returnees. The returnee is regarded as trying to "reap where she has not sown," especially in situations in which the widow has been married for a long time. Conflicts and economic problems, such as lack of shelter, food, clothes, and social support, are inevitable.[21]

A widow may also be secluded within her brother-in-law's household to become a victim of exploitation or a domestic slave. Some widows resort to prostitution to solve their economic problems.[22] In some tribes in Tanzania, women are also subjected to arduous widowhood rites that purport to afford

---

19. This is the account of a widow in Kenya, but similar situations face Tanzanian widows. *See* Margaret Owen, The World of the Widow, 3(2) People & the Planet 19 (1994).

20. Discussion with Mrs. Flora Sanga, a victim of such circumstances. (Dec. 1996).

21. Anna Tibaijuka et al., Poverty and Social Exclusion in Tanzania 100 (1996). Some widows move to towns, and they find little support from their relatives and must struggle on their own.

22. *Id.* at 101.

them spiritual purification after their spouse's death and do not apply to men in similar circumstances.[23] One of the most shocking practices is widow cleansing, in which the widow is forced to have sex with a stranger.[24] Widow cleansing, widow inheritance, and prostitution lead to other problems, such as HIV/AIDS, that are detrimental to a widow's health.

Employers are also involved in the process of harassing widows. When a husband dies of AIDS, everyone assumes the widow has the disease. In cases in which the husband leased a house from the employer, the house is taken away. If she was an employee, her employer will repudiate the employment contract ostensibly because she can no longer perform her duties properly since she is believed to have AIDS.

Moreover, lack of support from lawyers, judges, and law enforcement prevents women from discovering the rights they may have under other, non-customary systems of law. Widows have difficulty seeking legal redress for harassment and discrimination because of a lack of information as well as lack of resources to pay legal fees. They also face endemic corruption within the judicial and law enforcement systems.[23] Police sometimes demand bribes or sexual favors before they will deal with matters pertaining to widows and often refuse to be involved in widow harassment on the grounds that it is a family matter.

As a result of these forms of harassment and degradation, many widows suffer mental and physical harms. Overall, the neglect of widows and daughters causes great misery, not just for the specific targets but for society as a whole.

Erosion of the Historical Underpinnings of Customary Inheritance Laws

The historical justification for discriminating against women in inheritance, namely that widows and daughters are being cared for by the male clan members, is no longer viable in Tanzania. As a result, it is unjust to deny widows and daughters the right to inherit property using the Customary Rules when reciprocal systems of care by the community no longer exist.

The Rules were founded in a communal economy based on communal ownership and values that have now been mixed with a capitalist cash econ-

---

23. For example, the Kerewe.
24. Discussion with Mrs. Esther Mahushi (Dec. 1996).
23. *See* Tibaijuka, *supra* note 21, at 174.

omy built around individualism.[26] At the same time, the pressures of poverty, structural adjustment programs, and foreign debt have drastically affected the poor widow's access to essential services.[27] The law must change to provide women the economic and legal protection that custom no longer affords them.

Guardian Rules

Guardian rules have become obsolete. Male relatives acting as guardians often distort tradition and defraud widows and orphans of their inheritance rights. On the pretense that the clan will care for the children in accordance with custom, guardians have evicted many widows from clan land. Some widows have even been evicted from privately owned land that the deceased and his wife have acquired outside the clan system.[28]

Wife Inheritance

There is a growing belief that wife inheritance is one of the factors contributing to the spread of HIV/AIDS.[29] With the scourge of AIDS, wife inheritance is often the equivalent of committing suicide. If the deceased husband died of AIDS, the potential for the widow to infect the new husband is quite high. Similarly, the widow is at risk of infection in widow inheritance; the pressure of dependency on a clan exposes widows to high risk situations.[30] Also, in a polygamous marriage, wife inheritance exposes the wives in the new marriage to HIV if the widow's own husband died of AIDS.

Clan land

An even more fundamental question concerns the validity of the concept of clan land in contemporary Tanzania. Some statistics suggest that clan land

---

26. *See* Regina Rweyemamu, Judicial Activism and Gender Rights in Tanzania: The Task Ahead, at 3 (Unpublished LL.M. graduate paper, Georgetown University Law Center, May 1996).

27. Anna Tibaijuka et al., Land Policy in Tanzania: Issues for Policy Consideration 16 (Paper prepared for the National Conference on Land Policy organized by the Ministry of Lands, Arusha, 1995).

28. F.J. Kaijage, *AIDS Control and the Burden of History in Northwestern Tanzania*, 14(3) POPULATION & THE ENV'T 279–300.

29. Mtanzania Newspaper, Tuesday, July 9, 1996, at 4.

30. The practice of widow inheritance is, however, gradually dying out, although it is still being practiced in a few scattered rural communities. One of the reasons for the decline of the practice is the AIDS epidemic.

may have lost its significance with the advent of villagization.[31] The decline of clan land as a tenure system should result in a corresponding decline in application of the Customary Rules. Recent household land use and sociological surveys show that in some cases, land supposedly under customary communal tenure is sold as private property.[32] For instance, the 1991–92 Land Commission received complaints concerning clan leaders in the Arumeru district who had authorized land sales that resulted in the dispossession of widows as well as orphans.[33]

A combination of attitudes, customs, laws, and courts have proved to be formidable obstacles to achieving equality in women's inheritance rights. But a cry is rising from women in Tanzania, and their voices are beginning to be heeded.

Reform Strategies

Non-governmental organizations (NGOs) should aim to change the nation's mindset and alter the policies that lead to human rights abuses. First, education plays a key role in promoting change. The lack of sufficient information and communication are among the formidable challenges to improving women's social status. One possible strategy to alleviate the impoverished situation of widows and daughters is a massive information and communication campaign. By helping women become better informed, activists may instill in them a sense of self-confidence and an ability to use the choices available to them to enforce their rights. Also, activists should offer this education to members of the Parliament and law enforcement. Widows and daughters should act as agents for change by providing education on gender issues within the family to ensure eradication of gender-based discrimination. They should spearhead the change of attitudes so that more egalitarian ideologies slowly replace existing cultural beliefs; this is particularly important given the changes in the country's economic and social setup.

Activists must use empowerment as a strategy to achieve women's equality. This entails deliberate mobilization of the community in general, and widows

---

31. Roger Yeager, Tanzania an African Experiment 64 (1982). In 1977, an estimated 79% of the dwellers—more than 13 million people—were living in 7,300 villages with an average membership of about 1,849.

32. Tibaijuka, *supra* note 27, at 18.

33. *Id.* at 144. Widows and orphans are especially vulnerable to loss of access to family land through sales by family patriarchs.

and daughters in particular, to challenge the status quo on gender-based inheritance laws. To oppose inheritance discrimination based on gender, women must collaborate in local struggles by sharing their experiences and resources and by coordinating their strategies for maximum impact.[34]

Activists should lobby for changes in the Customary Rules and press for legislation that incorporates human rights standards. A new law should provide equal protection and opportunity to both genders. The uniform law, which would apply to everyone regardless of custom or tradition, should comply with the provisions of the Law of Marriage Act with regard to ownership and distribution of property between spouses. The law should also conform to Constitutional and human rights norms of gender equality.

Another way to facilitate change is through strategic litigation. The role of an activist is to encourage the court to conclude that there is a gap between the law on the books and the reality in the field.[35] Activists must bring test cases challenging the Customary Rules as a violation of the Constitution and international treaties.

An alternative to domestic reform is enforcement through international supervisory bodies. Activists should report violations to the United Nations Committee on the Elimination of all forms of Discrimination Against Women (CEDAW Committee), in order to remind Tanzanian officials of the government's legal accountability for violations of women's rights and its obligation to eliminate private discriminatory behavior.[36]

Economic development efforts to improve the economic status of widows and daughters are vital.[37] Since inheritance disparities are only a part of a larger system that impoverishes women, it is important that activists explore general strategies for women's economic development.

A human rights data bank on inheritance issues should be established. Widows and daughters who are unjustly denied inheritance or harassed could communicate with activists who will record the abuses properly for use in legal

---

34. "Empowerment poses the most serious political challenges to the state." *See* Claude E. Welch, Jr., Protecting Human Rights in Africa 55 (1995).

35. Rweyemamu, *supra* note 26, at 40.

36. CEDAW's effectiveness in monitoring state compliance is greatly enhanced by NGOs that provide them with alternative reports about violations of women's rights in reporting countries. *See* Sharon Ladin, IWRAW to CEDAW: Country Reports, International Women's Rights Action Watch (1992).

37. Cultural barriers interact with low levels of economic development. Raising women's incomes is a good way to strengthen women's status.

test cases, educational literature, and events. Documenting the plight of victims and pressing the government for corrective action are crucial tasks.

Conclusion

Tanzanian customary law discriminates against women. Under customary law, the Rules bar widows from inheriting land from their deceased husbands and subject widows to harmful customary practices, such as being inherited by the male relatives of the deceased. The Rules favor sons by allowing them to inherit more than daughters and by preventing daughters and widows from being administrators of estates. The customary Rules undermine the fundamental principles of equality enshrined in the Constitution and in international human rights law. Securing inheritance rights for women is critical not only to the advancement of women, but also to the development of the Tanzanian nation. As the former President of Tanzania Mwalimu Nyerere said, "it can be done; play your part."

CHAPTER FOUR

Reproductive Health, Women's Subordination, and HIV/AIDS

Chapter Introduction, *Johanna Bond*

Women's bodies have historically been and continue to be the site for struggles over individual autonomy and community identity and culture. In Africa, as in all parts of the world, women's rights activists have been fighting to improve women's ability to make autonomous decisions that affect their health and reproductive freedom. This effort includes not only improving access to health care facilities but also eliminating the social forces that perpetuate women's subordination and contribute to women's lack of control over their own bodies. To that end, the essays in this chapter examine many of the cultural practices in Ghana, Uganda, and Tanzania that limit women's reproductive autonomy and expose them to the risk of HIV/AIDS.

Customary Practices that Contribute to the Spread of HIV/AIDS: Before Marriage, During Marriage, and After Marriage

Before Marriage

Female genital mutilation (FGM), which is common in parts of Africa, refers to "several traditional practices which involve the cutting and removal

267

of female sexual organs."[1] Although the specific procedure and its symbolic meaning varies among communities, FGM reflects the community's efforts to control a woman's (or a girl's) sexuality, leaving her susceptible to a myriad of devastating health problems, including HIV infection. In describing FGM as practiced by the Sabiny community in Uganda, Emma Namuli writes, "It is further believed that FGM is necessary to 'tame' a girl's morality, and that a girl who is not 'cut' may disgrace her family and clan by turning wild and engaging in rampant sexual activity."[2] Fitnat Adjetey explicitly links FGM to women's sexual autonomy, saying, "[T]he basis of FGM is the belief that women are considered incapable of thinking for themselves and therefore need society's help to make basic decisions regarding their own bodies."[3]

Too often, FGM involves the use of razors, glass, or other cutting instruments that have not been sterilized. In many cases, the person performing FGM will perform the ritual on a number of girls at the same time, increasing the risk of infection.[4] As a result of this and other serious health concerns associated with FGM, some communities in Africa have begun to experiment with alternative rites of passage that do not involve genital mutilation but preserve the positive aspects of marking the transition to adulthood.[5]

During Marriage

Namuli characterizes polygamy as high-risk sexual behavior that contributes to the spread of HIV/AIDS in Uganda. According to Namuli, every community in Uganda practices polygamy; even purportedly monogynous marriages often involve informal "second wives."[6] The fact that many men have multiple sex partners, whether officially married to them or not, substantially increases women's risk of contracting HIV/AIDS. Namuli notes that because polygamy is legal and women often lack the economic means to leave a polyg-

---

1. Fitnat Adjetey, *Religious and Cultural Rights: Reclaiming the African Woman's Individuality, infra* p. 278.

2. Emma Namuli, *Women and HIV/AIDS in Uganda, infra* p. 292.

3. Fitnat Adjetey, *Religious and Cultural Rights: Reclaiming the African Woman's Individuality, infra* p. 279.

4. Fitnat Adjetey, *Female Genital Mutilation: Tradition or Torture?, infra* p. 169.

5. Molly Melching, *Abandoning Female Genital Cutting in Africa, in* EYE TO EYE: WOMEN PRACTISING DEVELOPMENT ACROSS CULTURES 156 (Susan Perry & Celeste Schenck eds., 2001).

6. Emma Namuli, Women and HIV/AIDS in Uganda, infra pp. 291–92.

amous marriage, many women find it difficult—if not impossible—to limit their exposure to HIV/AIDS.

Domestic violence, and marital rape in particular, also contributes to women's risk of contracting HIV/AIDS. Domestic violence creates a power imbalance within a relationship such that a woman cannot effectively object to or resist her partner's unsafe sexual practices. Marital rape is an extreme manifestation of that power imbalance. As Adjetey observes in her essay, "[T]he conceptual idea that a woman in a customary marriage can be raped by her husband does not even exist because all sex within a customary marriage is considered 'consensual,' whether or not the woman consents."[7] A 2003 Human Rights Watch report indicates that, in Uganda, "thirty-four out of fifty women expressly confirmed that their husbands physically forced them to have sex against their will."[8] In Uganda, as in many parts of the world, the societal expectation that women will submit—without exception—to the sexual demands of their husbands or partners means that men often do not need to force sex.[9] In either case, women's powerlessness to negotiate safe sex, which is exacerbated in situations involving domestic violence, contributes to the rising HIV infection rate among women in Uganda.[10]

Maria Tungaraza also describes the practice of "dry sex" in Tanzania, in which women "use moisture-absorbing agents to absorb vaginal fluids and tighten the vagina, creating a 'virgin-like state' and thereby enhancing sexual pleasure for men."[11] According to Tungaraza, dry sex increases women's risk of HIV transmission by killing natural, infection-fighting bacteria. She also notes that a Zimbabwean study suggests that polygamy may increase the incidence of dry sex by forcing women to compete for the affection and support of their husbands.[12]

After Marriage

When a woman's husband dies, she may face an increased risk of HIV transmission as a result of two customary practices: widow inheritance and

---

7. Fitnat Adjetey, *Religious and Cultural Rights: Reclaiming the African Woman's Individuality, infra* p. 277.

8. Lisa Karanja, Human Rights Watch, *Just Die Quietly: Domestic Violence and Women's Vulnerability to HIV in Uganda*, August 2003, at 25.

9. *Id.* at 23.

10. *See generally, id.*

11. Maria Tungaraza, "Women's Rights and the AIDS Epidemic in Tanzania," in this chapter at p. 305.

12. Maria Tungaraza, "Women's Rights and the AIDS Epidemic in Tanzania," in this chapter at p. 305.

widow cleansing. Namuli, Tungaraza, and Adjetey all describe the practice of widow inheritance or "leviratic marriage," in which a woman is "inherited" by and forced to marry the brother or other male relative of her deceased husband. Some argue that, traditionally, widow inheritance protected the woman and her children by ensuring that they remained affiliated with the husband's family. Adjetey maintains that the custom treats women as chattel and results in "forced marriages and forced sex within marriage."[13] Women risk exposure to HIV transmission as a result of the practice. In addition, a woman whose husband died of AIDS risks infecting the man who "inherits" her and any additional wives or girlfriends he may have.

The custom of widow cleansing requires that a recently widowed woman undergo certain rituals to purify her. In some communities, the ritual includes sexual intercourse. Tungaraza explains, "To be cleansed, a widow must have sexual intercourse with another or others, depending on the specific practices of the tribe concerned."[14] Because the practice forces the widow to have sex with one or more partners, it exposes her to HIV transmission, particularly in communities in which there is one person who "cleanses" many widows.

Relevant International Human Rights Law

In the past decade, the international human rights community has made great progress toward the recognition of and respect for women's reproductive rights, including women's human rights related to HIV/AIDS. The 1994 United Nations International Conference on Population and Development in Cairo was instrumental in increasing awareness of women's health rights among governments around the world. The Cairo Programme of Action, the document that came out of the Cairo Conference, represents a significant shift in human rights advocacy from an emphasis on demographic trends to an emphasis on the rights and needs of individuals.[15] However, despite the progress made at

---

13. Fitnat Adjetey, *Religious and Cultural Rights: Reclaiming the African Woman's Individuality infra* p. 278.

14. Maria Tungaraza, *Women's Rights and the AIDS Epidemic in Tanzania, infra* p. 304.

15. Rebecca J. Cook & Mahmoud F. Fathalla, *Advancing Reproductive Rights Beyond Cairo and Beijing, in* WOMEN AND INTERNATIONAL HUMAN RIGHTS LAW 73 (Kelly Askin & Doerean M. Koenig eds., 1999).

Cairo and at the United Nations Fourth World Conference on Women in Beijing a year later, the struggle for women's reproductive rights is far from over.

Many of the human rights related to health are "already recognized in…international human rights documents…."[16] They include, for example, the rights to life, liberty, security, education, equality in marriage, privacy, freedom from discrimination, and freedom from violence and the right to enjoy scientific progress. The International Covenant on Economic, Social, and Cultural Rights and the Convention on the Elimination of All Forms of Discrimination Against Women (CEDAW) both explicitly recognize the right to the highest attainable standard of health.[17] Although not binding legal documents, the Cairo Programme of Action and the Beijing Platform for Action include specific recommendations for governments concerning their efforts to improve women's health, increase women's autonomy in matters related to health, and prevent HIV transmission to women.[18]

The specific rights that are relevant to a particular health problem will vary depending on the nature of the problem. For example, women's human rights activists might invoke the rights to liberty, security,[19] and the rights related to freedom from violence (as described in chapter two) to combat FGM and domestic violence. Alternatively, activists may focus on the right to the highest attainable standard of health[20] in an effort to increase access to health care facilities. In the case of HIV/AIDS prevention and treatment, activists might rely on a number of rights specifically enshrined in international treaties. The right to be free from violence could support advocates' arguments for enact-

---

16. *Beijing Declaration and Platform for Action,* Fourth World Conference on Women, Sept. 15, 1995, ¶¶ 95, 223, U.N. Doc. A/CONF.177/20 (1995)[hereinafter Beijing PFA].

17. International Covenant on Economic, Social and Cultural Rights, Dec. 16, 1966, art. 12, 993 U.N.T.S. 3, 8 [hereinafter ICESCR]; Convention on the Elimination of All Forms of Discrimination Against Women, Dec. 18, 1979, art. 12, 1249 U.N.T.S. 13, 19 [hereinafter CEDAW].

18. *See generally* Beijing PFA, ¶¶ 91–110; Report of the International Conference on Population and Development, Cairo, ¶ 7.6, U.N. Doc. A/Conf.171/13/Rev.1 (1994).

19. *Universal Declaration of Human Rights*, art. 3, G.A. Res. 217A (III), at 71, U.N. Doc. A/810 (1948) [hereinafter UDHR]; International Covenant on Civil and Political Rights, Dec. 16, 1966, art. 9, 999 U.N.T.S. 171, 175 [hereinafter ICCPR]; African Charter on Humans and People's Rights, June 27, 1981, art. 6, 1520 U.N.T.S. 246, 247 [hereinafter African Charter].

20. UDHR, *supra* note 18, art. 25, at 73; CEDAW, *supra* note 16, art. 11(1)(f), 12, 14(2)(b), 1249 U.N.T.S. at 18–19; ICESCR, *supra* note 16, art. 12, 993 U.N.T.S. at 8; African Charter, *supra* note 18, art. 16, 1520 U.N.T.S. at 248.

ment and enforcement of laws prohibiting marital rape, while rights related to equality within marriage[21] might be used to combat polygamy, widow inheritance, and other customary practices that contribute to HIV/AIDS transmission.

In addition, the Committee on Economic, Social, and Cultural Rights issued a general recommendation on the right to health, in which it recognizes that the failure of governments to "prosecute perpetrators of domestic violence, to discourage harmful traditional practices both in law and in fact, and to adopt a gender-sensitive approach to health, amount to violations of a state's obligations under CEDAW."[22] Similarly, the CEDAW Committee has issued General Recommendation No. 15, entitled *Avoidance of Discrimination Against Women in National Strategies for the Prevention and Control of Acquired Immunodeficiency Syndrome (AIDS)*.[23] Among other things, General Recommendation No. 15 recommends that programs to combat AIDS "give special attention to the rights and needs of women, and to the factors relating to the reproductive role of women and their subordinate position in some societies which make them especially vulnerable to HIV infection."[24]

The Protocol to the African Charter on Human and Peoples' Rights on the Rights of Women in Africa also addresses human rights related to health and reproduction. Article 14 of the Protocol specifically recognizes the "right to self protection and to be protected against sexually transmitted infections, including HIV, and the right to be informed of one's health status and on the health status of one's partner...in accordance with internationally recognised standards and best practices."[25] The Protocol also protects rights that may be helpful in eradicating some of the discriminatory traditional practices that contribute to the spread of HIV/AIDS, such as widow cleansing. Article 20 of

---

21. CEDAW, *supra* note 16, art. 16, 1249 U.N.T.S. at 20; UDHR, *supra* note 18, art. 16, at 72; ICCPR, *supra* note 18, art. 23, 999 U.N.T.S. at 179.; Committee on the Elimination of Discrimination Against Women, General Recommendation 21, U.N. Doc. HRI/GEN/1/Rev.1 at 91 (1994).

22. Karanja, *supra* note 7, at 71 (summarizing ESCR Committee, General Comment No. 14, para. 51, 52).

23. Committee on the Elimination of Discrimination Against Women, General Recommendation No. 15, U.N. Doc. HRI/GEN/1/Rev.1 at 81 (1994).

24. *Id.* ¶(c) at 81 (1994).

25. Protocol to the African Charter on Human and Peoples' Rights on the Rights of Women in Africa, Art. 14, *at* http://www.africa-union.org/Official_documents/Treaties_%20Conventions_%20Protocols/Protocol%20on%20the%20Rights%20of%20Women.pdf (July 11, 2003).

the Protocol requires states to ensure that widows "are not subjected to inhuman, humiliating, or degrading treatment."[26]

Conclusion

Uganda has been the focus of expansive local, national, and international advocacy to reduce its rates of HIV infection. Those efforts have been successful in reducing the rate of infection in adults from 18.5 percent in 1995 to 8.3 percent in 1999.[27] Activists and policy makers in Uganda, however, have begun to realize that the success of these efforts depends in large part upon involving women in education, prevention, and treatment solutions. In Ghana, Uganda, and Tanzania, there is a growing recognition that improving women's legal, social, and economic status will contribute greatly to the struggle to reduce the prevalence of HIV transmission. In each of the essays in this chapter, authors emphasize the importance of eliminating stereotypes and harmful traditional practices that limit women's autonomy and make them particularly susceptible to HIV infection.

---

26. *Id.* Art. 20.
27. Karanja, *supra* note 7, at 15.

Religious and Cultural Rights: Reclaiming the African Woman's Individuality — The Struggle Between Women's Reproductive Autonomy and African Society and Culture

44 Am. U.L. Rev. 1351 (Spring 1995)*

Fitnat N-A. Adjetey

Overview

African culture and custom,[1] as they exist today, are a blend of African customs, imported colonial common and civil law notions, and religious concepts from Christianity, Islam, and traditional African religions. The application of these laws within the plural legal systems, which are the legacy of the colonial era, has left women socially and politically in a very subordinate position. The result is the inability of women to protect and ensure their reproductive rights, which include their reproductive autonomy and their reproductive health.

---

* This article originally appeared in a 1995 edition of the American University Law Review. It is reprinted here (in an excerpted form) with permission. Footnotes have been renumbered from the original to run consecutively. *Ed.*

1. African culture and custom are used in this Paper to mean the totality of African traditional practices as applied by African peoples.

Reproductive rights are defined in terms of the legal notions generally used to express the principle that women, and men as well, are entitled to control their reproductive lives.[2] A woman's right to control her reproductive life is inextricably connected to other rights in civil, political, economic, and social areas. To be able to control her reproductive life, a woman requires reproductive autonomy.

Reproductive autonomy involves an individual's ability to make decisions with respect to sexuality, pregnancy, childbearing, and formation of families....

The principle of reproductive autonomy has different significance for women than it does for men. The biological characteristics of women and their socially prescribed roles as childbearers and caretakers of families require women to bear reproductive responsibilities.... Women's reproduction in most parts of the world is controlled by male partners, families, and society in general. Reproductive autonomy and reproductive health are inextricably linked because reproductive autonomy is required by women to enable them to ensure their reproductive health.

Reproductive health, therefore, implies that people have the ability to reproduce, to regulate their fertility, and to practice and enjoy sexual relationships. It further implies that reproduction is carried to a successful outcome through infant and child survival, growth, and healthy development. It finally implies that women can go safely through pregnancy and childbirth, that fertility regulation can be achieved without health hazards, and that people are safe in having sex.[3]

In light of these definitions, the African woman's reproductive autonomy, reproductive health, and her ability to exercise her rights in these areas, are closely linked to the customary laws and traditional practices that are applied in her community....

This Paper looks at several specific African customs and traditional practices that impede a woman's exercise of her reproductive rights. These customs must be observed in the context of the evolution of customary law[4] and the notions and concepts that are valued within this system. The Paper traces the development of customary law from the pre-colonial period to the pres-

---

2. Lynn Freedman & Stephen Isaacs, *Human Rights and Reproductive Choice*, 24 STUD. FAM. PLAN. 19 (1993).

3. Mahmoud F. Fathalla, *Reproductive Health: A Global Overview*, 626 ANNALS N.Y. ACAD. SCI. 1, 1 (1991).

4. Customary law has evolved in different ways in different parts of Africa. This is because there is no homogenous African culture or customary law and customary law differs from tribe to tribe and from ethnic group to ethnic group within the same tribe. Due to time and space limitations, however, I shall limit myself to generally applicable facts and give brief specific examples where possible.

ent in an effort to highlight the bases and dynamics of these customs and traditions that affect women's autonomy in general.

Finally, this Paper suggests...response[s] to the problems that women face with regard to their reproductive autonomy....

African Customs and Norms that Impede Women's Reproductive Autonomy

Because traditional African institutions are very diverse, women's rights vary from one society to another. Gender bias in its various forms is often hard to detect because it is so embedded in these traditional institutions....For the African woman, the most severe violations of her human rights are "rooted deeply within the family system, bolstered by community norms of male privilege and frequently justified by religious doctrines or appeals to custom or tradition."[5] Thus, the reproductive decisions of the African woman are usually made under "enormous pressures from family, community, and society to comply with the prevailing gender and reproductive norms, as well as internalized commitments to act responsibly towards others."[6] Male dominated societies employ customary law to hold women captive to their reproductive functions.[7] An examination of some African traditional practices and norms will show the reasons why African women lack reproductive autonomy.[8]

General Traditional Rules

...African female children are taught from a very early age that the man is the head of the household, and are advised by their mothers to remain in com-

---

5. Sonia Correa & Rosalind Petchesky, Reproductive and Sexual Rights: A Feminist Perspective, in Population Policies Reconsidered: Health, Empowerment, and Right 107, 110 (Gita Sen et al. eds., 1994).

6. Id. at 111.

7. Rebecca J. Cook, International Protection of Women's Reproductive Rights, 24 N.Y.U. J. Int'l L. & Pol. 645, 655 (1992).

8. This is just a short sampling of some of the practices in Africa that contravene the reproductive rights of women. Some others, not discussed, include child marriage, polygamy, female religious bondage, brideprice, and spousal veto on reproductive medical care. For a complete discussion of the religious bondage of young girls in Ghana see Hilary Amesika Gbedemah, Trikosi: Twentieth Century Female Bondage – A Ghanaian Case Study, Chapter Two of this Volume, infra. pp. xx-xx. Ed.

plete subjugation to their husbands.... There are no such corresponding values imposed on male children, who therefore grow up believing that they are free to behave as they please, and that women have to shape their behavior to suit their desires and whims. Prior to marriage, a girl is taught to be ready for sex with her husband at all times and never to refuse his advances.[9] Boys also receive instruction from their fathers and are told that it is their absolute privilege to have sex. Thus, to the African male, a woman's refusal to have sex is irrelevant.[10] Consequently, an African woman has sex when her husband so desires, and the decisions as to when to have sex, and how often, are dictated by her husband's desires and needs....

Rape within Marriage

The law of customary marriages allows a man to rape his wife with impunity. Indeed, the conceptual idea that a wife in a customary marriage can be raped by her husband does not even exist because all sex within a customary marriage is considered "consensual," whether or not the woman consents.[11] This is true because in some parts of Africa marriage results in a woman's physical person and her sexuality becom[ing] part of her husband's property.[12] In other parts of Africa, even though customary law did not, in theory, incorporate the very existence of a woman into that of a man's property upon marriage, in practice women are treated as though this were the case.[13] ... Moreover, it is a general rule all over Africa that a man can never be said to rape his own wife. As such, forced sex within marriage does not constitute an offense either under customary or statutory law. A woman is therefore not in a position to protect herself from sexually transmitted diseases by ceasing to have sex with her husband or seeking to have safe sex, even though she may suspect, or even know for a fact, that her husband or one of her co-wives has a sexually transmitted disease.

---

9. Beatrice Akua Duncan, Marital Rape as a Form of Domestic Violence and the Need for Law Reform in Ghana (1994) (unpublished LL.M. dissertation, Georgetown University Law Center).

10. *Id.*

11. *See generally* Duncan, *supra* note 9.

12. *See* Duncan, *supra* note 9, at 14.

13. *Id.*

Leviratic Marriage or Widow Inheritance [and Sororate Marriage]

The leviratic marriage, or widow inheritance, is a custom in which a man is obliged to marry his brother's widow.[14] This system perpetually restrains the widow from marrying any other person except the customary successor of her dead husband or a member of his family. The effect of this custom is to thrust many women into unwanted marriages and results in forced marriages and forced sex within marriage. Widow inheritance treats women as chattel, instead of human beings who have rights equal to those of a man.[15] A widow who resists being inherited will most likely be evicted from her home by her in-laws, particularly if she is living on what is regarded as family land.[16] Because most rural women are dependent on their husbands for their livelihood, the threat of eviction forces women to comply with the traditional practice....

In the sororate marriage, a wife who fled her marriage or died before giving birth is replaced by her sister. This is the result of the idea that a woman has been purchased by the payment of brideprice or bridewealth and is valued mainly for her reproductive labor which constituted an important part of the purchase. The second wives are just as vulnerable as their sisters before them, having no reproductive autonomy whatsoever. This practice also results in forced marriages and forced sex within marriage....

Female Genital Mutilation

A discussion of the particular reproductive health problems faced by women in Africa would not be complete without mentioning FGM. Female Genital Mutilation (FGM) is the name given to several traditional practices which involve the cutting and removal of female sexual organs.[17]

---

14. The Oxford Encyclopedic English Dictionary 826 (1st ed. 1991).

15. *See Akorninga v. Akawagre*, 1987–88 Ghana L. Rep. Dig. 101, 247 (June 23, 1988) (holding that widow inheritance was clearly against the general law of the land because it sought to treat the woman as a chattel instead of a human being—*Ed.*).

16. Esther Mayambala, Women and HIV Transmission in Uganda: An Evaluation of Safer Sex Strategies, (1994) (unpublished manuscript, Georgetown University Law Center). *Ed.*

17. For a complete discussion of female genital mutilation, including the extensive dangerous physical effects, see Fitnat N-A Adjetey, *Female Genital Mutilation: Tradition or Torture?*, Chapter Two of this Volume, *infra*. pxx–xx. *Ed.*

There are three different types of FGM: clitoridectomy,[18] excision,[19] and infibulation or "pharaonic circumcision." Infibulation or "pharaonic" circumcision is the most extreme of these operations and involves the removal of the clitoris, labia minora, and parts of the labia majora. The remaining skin of the labia majora is then scraped to form raw surfaces and stitched together with thorns. The wound is further kept together by binding the woman with pieces of cloth made into a rope, from thigh to ankle for several weeks to enable scar tissue to form, covering the urethra and most of the vagina. A small aperture, the size of the head of a match stick or the tip of a finger, is left open for the flow of urine and menstrual blood.[20] Approximately eighty-five percent of all women who undergo FGM have the clitoridectomy or excision procedure and the remaining fifteen percent have undergone infibulation.[21]...

FGM is practiced by communities that exploit the social value of virginity. Proponents of FGM view it as the community's way of protecting women from rape and sexual assault and preventing women from having sex before marriage. This practice is tied to the traditional purpose for virginity, that is, securing the family honor and promoting religious doctrines. Thus, the basis of FGM is the belief that women are considered incapable of thinking for themselves and therefore need society's help to make basic decisions regarding their own bodies....

Rites de Passage

Rites de passage, or puberty rites, are ceremonies performed by young adolescents to signify their development into adulthood. Puberty rites are also used to keep women in subjugation in traditional societies. For example, according to custom of the Krobo people of Ghana, a female who reaches puberty must undergo a customary rite called dipo before becoming pregnant.[22] If she conceives before undergoing this ceremony she is not only ostracized but is liable to be banished from home and disowned by her parents.[23]

---

18. Clitoridectomy is the removal of the clitoral prepuce or tip of the clitoris. Note, *What's Culture Got to Do With It? Excising the Harmful Tradition of Female Circumcision*, 106 HARV. L. REV. 1944, 1946 (1993). *Ed.*

19. Excision is the removal of the clitoris and the inner lips of the female external genitalia or labia minora. *Id. Ed.*

20. Nahid Toubia, FEMALE GENITAL MUTILATION: A CALL FOR GLOBAL ACTION 10 (Gloria Jacobs ed., 1993).

21. *Id.*

22. *Tanor v. Akosua Koko*, 1974 Ghana L. Rep. 451, 453 (dictum of Apaloo, J.A.).

23. *Id.*

According to societal view, the moral objective of the custom cannot be faulted in that it is designed to oblige women to maintain their purity of sexual life until they are married.[24] Accordingly, the decision as to when to have sex is not made by the woman. Thus, she is forced to comply with societal norms of when she should have sex or risk ostracism. Therefore, although it may seem to be a personal and freely made decision, the African woman lacks the sexual self-determination to make her own choices. Puberty rites are another way of forcing a woman not to have sex. FGM is also conducted as a significant part of puberty rites in some African countries such as Kenya and Mali.[25]...

The Evolution of Customary Law and the Position of Women in African Society

A combination of the above customs and traditional rules puts women in a very low bargaining position with regards to marriage and family life. It also gives them very little, if any, control over their reproductive lives and thus their reproductive health. It often denies them a choice as to the most fundamental question of whether or not to have sex....To fully understand the basis of the traditional practices and norms that exist in relation to African women, one has to consider the evolution of customary law in Africa and realize that it is mainly a male concept of customary law.[26] With that background, it will be possible to confront custom and make progress toward eradicating these practices....

Today's African legal institutions, which include customary law, are a combination of indigenous and imported institutions. African customary law is a blend of African customs, imported colonial common and civil law notions, and religious concepts from Christianity, Islam, and traditional African religions. In some parts of pre-colonial Africa, women had a reasonable amount of power and autonomy. This autonomy, however, was eroded by the colonial

---

24. *See generally id.* (discussing dipo custom in Ghana).

25. *See* Robyn Cerny Smith, *Female Circumcision: Bringing Women's Perspectives into the International Debate*, 65 S. Cal. L. Rev. 2449, 2459 (1992); *see also* Assitan Diallo, L'Excision en Milieu Bambara (unpublished thesis), cited in Efua Dorkenoo & Scilla Elworthy, Female Genital Mutilation: Proposals for Change 8–9 (3d ed. 1992).

26. Custom is an established usage or practice of society, The Concise Oxford Dictionary of Current English 252 (6th ed. 1977). For a custom to carry the force of law, it must satisfy the conditions of common adoption and acquiescence, longevity, and compulsion for the place and time in question. Contrary to common belief, custom is not static but develops to meet the changing needs of society. *Ed.*

ideas concerning the inferiority of women, which figured greatly in the evolution of customary law in the colonial and post-colonial eras....

The historic interpretation of customary law also contributed to the way in which it developed. Customary law was not written and was interpreted solely by males during the colonial era. Thus, the needs and opinions of females were completely ignored in the interpretation of custom. The geographical boundaries of judicial bodies set up by the colonial administrations sometimes cut across tribal lines. Thus, the interpretation of custom as it existed in those jurisdictions was not always consistent with the customary practices of all the tribes within that jurisdiction. This is because African societies are not homogeneous. The customary law that evolved in the post-colonial era was, therefore, devoid of women's needs, greatly discriminatory against women, and often contrary to the practices of some ethnic groups....

Religious beliefs also played an important part in the development of African customary law. One of the results of religious intervention on the legal status of women has been to subject women to the control of their husbands and families and to isolate them in the private spheres of life.[27] The laws of Rome and religious principles of Christianity were premised on the inferiority of women and contained rules that subordinated women.[28]...In these societies, there was the additional system of the Islamic qadi courts that applied Sharia Law. Sharia law prescribes rules regarding family relations, inheritance, divorce, dress, diet, and hygiene. Sharia law reinforced the tenets of natural female domesticity and incapacity by emphasizing the need for men to serve as guardians over women.[29]...

Addressing the Reproductive Health Needs of African Women Through the Use of International Human Rights Norms

...To achieve reproductive autonomy for women, specific legislation must be passed banning traditional practices that affect the health of women. Leg-

27. O.F. Robinson, THE HISTORICAL BACKGROUND, IN THE LEGAL RELEVANCE OF GENDER: SOME ASPECTS OF SEX-BASED DISCRIMINATION 40, 49–51 (Sheila McClean & Noreen Burrows eds., 1988).

28. Id.

29. Doris M. Martin & Fatuma O. Hashi, World Bank, Gender, the Evolution of Legal Institutions and Economic Development in Sub-Saharan Africa 23–24 (June 1992) (Working Paper No. 3), at 14–15.

islation recognizing that a problem exists can be a helpful starting point....In Abdullahi An-Na'im's view, the constructive approach to this problem of negative customs is to enhance the supportive elements and redress the antithetical or problematic elements in ways that are consistent with the integrity of the cultural tradition.[30] An example of such an approach is seen in the Ghanaian context. Section 88A(1) of the Criminal Code of Ghana states that whoever compels a bereaved spouse or a relative of a bereaved spouse to undergo any custom or practice that is cruel in nature shall be guilty of a misdemeanor.[31] To remove any uncertainty that might exist as to the definition of a cruel custom, the Criminal Code goes on to state that a custom or practice shall be deemed to be cruel in nature if it constitutes an assault, an assault with battery, or imprisonment within the meaning of the Criminal Code.[32] This amendment to the Criminal Code is designed to do away with the problematic aspects of widowhood rites, but stops short of doing away with the tradition of widowhood rites altogether. Although the amendment is couched in language that makes it applicable to any spouse of either sex, it is targeted toward the infringement of women's rights through the practice of widowhood rites.[33]...

Domestic courts can serve as a missing link between promulgation and realization of international human rights norms to the benefit of both international and domestic law.[34] An example comes from the Ghanaian case of *Akorninga v. Akawagre*,[35] [which rejected awarding damages to a man when his dead brother's widow refused to marry him]....The Court of Appeals of Ghana...stated that the claim was clearly against the general law of the land because it sought to treat the woman as a chattel instead of a human being.[36]

---

30. *See* Abdullahi A. An-Na'im, STATE RESPONSIBILITY UNDER INTERNATIONAL HUMAN RIGHTS LAW TO CHANGE RELIGIOUS AND CUSTOMARY LAW, IN HUMAN RIGHTS OF WOMEN: NATIONAL AND INTERNATIONAL PERSPECTIVES 167, 361 (Rebecca J. Cook ed., 1994) [hereinafter An-Na'im, State Responsibility].

31. Ghana Crim. Code 88A(1) (1960) (as amended by PNDCL 90).

32. *Id.* 88A(2).

33. In Ghana, women have hot pepper put in their eyes, their heads shaven, are confined to rooms alone for long periods of time, made to walk barefoot, and have to hold onto the large digit of their dead husband's foot while the corpse of the deceased is being prepared for burial. In practice no similar rites exist for the spouses of deceased women.

34. Anne F. Bayefsky, *General Approaches to Domestic Application of International Law*, in HUMAN RIGHTS OF WOMEN: NATIONAL AND INTERNATIONAL PERSPECTIVES at 351.

35. 1987–88 Ghana L. Rep. Dig. 101 (June 23, 1988).

36. *Id.*

The court went on to say that because [the man's] stance was blatantly discriminatory against women, it could not under modern conditions be considered part of the customary law of the country.[37]...This decision effectively outlaws the practice of the leviratic form of marriage in Ghana. Women's rights activists should therefore bring test cases in the local courts, opposing traditional practices that impinge on women's rights, in order to obtain court declarations that would effectively outlaw these practices....

Where local laws do not permit the pursuit of women's rights, international human rights norms should be used....[38] [Rights such as the right to the highest attainable standard of physical and mental health,[39] the right to life, liberty, and security,[40] the right to marry and found a family,[41] the right to freedom from customs that discriminate against women,[42] and the right of sexual nondiscrimination[43] are all violated by African customs and traditions that seek to keep women in subjugation.]...[T]o give international human rights norms credibility within African communities, they should be linked with the African Charter, which Africans would not regard as foreign.

The African Charter is unique because it "expounds an African conception of human rights taking cognizance of African culture, but at the same time it incorporates other conventional norms of human rights that are not typically

---

37. Accordingly, the respondent's claim was contrary to section 1(1)(b) of PNDCL 42, which commands respect for human rights and the dignity of the human person, and would for that reason be dismissed. [Note originally in text. *Ed.*]

38. This Paper will focus on the use of the African Charter. For a complete discussion on the international human rights law governing women's reproductive rights, please see *Introduction to Reproductive Rights under International Human Rights Law* pp. xx–xx *infra*. African [Banjul] Charter on Human and Peoples' Rights, adopted June 27, 1981, OAU Doc. CAB/LEG/67/3 rev. 5, 21 I.L.M. 58 (1982), *entered into force* Oct. 21, 1986. *Ed.*

39. International Covenant on Economic, Social and Cultural rights, 993 U.N.T.S. 3, 6 I.L.M. 360 (entered into force Jan. 3, 1976) [hereinafter ICESCR] art. 12(1); Convention on the Elimination of all forms of Discrimination Against Women, Dec. 18, 1979, 1249 U.N.T.S. 13 [hereinafter CEDAW] arts. 10, 12(1), 14(2), 16(1); African Charter on Human and Peoples Rights of 1981 [hereinafter African Charter], art. 16(1). *Ed.*

40. International Convenant on Civil and Political Rights, Dec. 16, 1966, 999 U.N.T.S. 171, 6 I.L.M. 368 [hereinafter ICCPR], arts. 6(1), 9(1); Universal Declaration of Human Rights, art. 3; African Charter, arts. 4, 6. *Ed.*

41. Universal Declaration of Human Rights, art. 16(1); CEDAW art. 16(1); ICESCR, art. 10(1); ICCPR, arts. 23(2), 23(3); African Charter, infra doc. biblio., arts. 2, 18(3). *Ed.*

42. CEDAW arts. 2, 5; African Charter, arts. 2, 18(3). *Ed.*

43. CEDAW, art. 2; Universal Declaration of Human Rights, art. 2; ICCPR, art. 2(1); ICESCR, art. 2(2); African Charter, arts. 2, 18(3). *Ed.*

or exclusively African."[44] The Charter also provides in one document a core of economic, social and cultural rights on one hand, and civil and political rights on the other. I believe that the use of this document will be the most effective means of countering the arguments of cultural relativists.[45]...

...Women's rights activists could seek a declaration that the provisions of the African Charter that relate to traditional practices ensure women's rights. They will, however, have to overcome some obstacles. Although the African Charter provides for the elimination of all discrimination against women, in the same breath it leaves substantial room for ambiguity in the interpretation of what constitutes prohibited discrimination.[46]...The case of FGM could serve as an illustration of the uncertainty created by the provisions of the Charter. FGM is a form of violence and a manifestation of men's control over women's sexuality and freedom of choice. Women's rights activists could bring an influx of complaints to show that FGM is a massive violation of women's rights, which should be brought to the attention of the AHSG.

The African Charter provides that a woman shall have the right to respect for the integrity of her person. The right to respect of the dignity inherent in human beings, the right to freedom from all forms of degradation and ex-

---

44. Ebow Bondzie-Simpson, *A Critique of the African Charter on Human and People's Rights*, 31 How. L.J. 643, 645 (1988).

45. Cultural relativists assert that an observer cannot adequately judge a society's cultural practices from outside that culture because he or she is not capable of fully understanding the significance of those practices, *id*. This is the prevailing philosophy among governments of nonwestern nations that resist the imposition of international human rights norms. According to one scholar, cultural relativists claim that the Charter and the Universal Declaration of Human Rights "give priority to individual civil and political rights over economic rights — an ideological preference that originates from Western Liberal thought," Admantia Pollis & Peter Schwab, *Human Rights: A Western Construct with Limited Applicability*, in HUMAN RIGHTS: CULTURAL AND IDEOLOGICAL PERSPECTIVES 4 (Admantia Pollis & Peter Schwab eds., 1979), cited in Nancy Kim, *Towards a Feminist Theory of Human Rights: Straddling the Fence Between Western Imperialism and Uncritical Absolutism*, 25 COLUM. HUM. RTS L. REV. 49, 57 (1993). Relativists maintain that an interpretation of human rights that gives civil and political rights priority over social, economic, and cultural rights is western-biased. *Ed.*

46. The Charter provides that "the promotion and protection of the morals and traditional values recognized by the community shall be the duty of the State," African Charter, art. 17(3). The Charter also states that the individual shall have the duty to strengthen positive African cultural values in his relations with other members of the society, African Charter, art. 29(7). The reference to cultural values requires definition and the questions of which traditional values are recognized by the community and who makes that determination leave a lot of uncertainty in the interpretation of the rights in the Charter. *Ed.*

ploitation, the right to freedom from cruel, inhuman and degrading treatment, the right to the highest attainable standard of health, and the right to equal protection of the law are all provided for in the Charter. FGM is seen by its proponents, however, as a means of ensuring the virginity and moral values of their young girls, and accordingly as a moral and traditional value that the community must keep. NGOs must urge the African Commission to declare FGM a custom that has no positive cultural value.

In addition to seeking change through law, it is imperative to seek change through education.[47] ... [The African woman must be educated] to a level at which she can feel confident enough to assert her rights. Education is one of the most important means of empowering women with the knowledge, skills, and self confidence necessary to participate fully in a development process.[48] As a member of FIDA (Ghana) working at our legal aid clinic, I have experienced the frustration of trying to convince an illiterate woman that she can assert her rights when she cannot understand or believe she has these rights. Rights activists should embark on a massive education effort that stresses international human rights norms in relation to local laws and re-orients the societies' thinking on socio-cultural issues relating to women's autonomy. NGOs must also begin a dialogue with indigent women to break the myths and barriers about the discussion of sex-related matters, so that they can be easily discussed by women with a view to solution of related problems.

General education in localities on international human rights norms in relation to local laws will go a long way toward acclimatizing African society to the idea that females have a right to reproductive autonomy. Special efforts should be made to emphasize men's shared responsibility, and promote their active involvement in sexual and reproductive behavior, family planning, prenatal and maternal and child health. It should be stressed that men should also share responsibilities in the prevention of sexually transmitted diseases, including HIV,[49] the prevention of unwanted and high-risk pregnancies, and the recognition and promotion of the equal value of children of both sexes.[50]

---

47. African women have only fifty-seven percent of the educational opportunities of males. *Ed.*

48. ICPD Programme of Action, infra doc. biblio., P11.2.

49. For a discussion on the inability of African women to protect themselves from contracting the AIDS virus because of traditional practices, see Esther Mayambala, Women and HIV Transmission in Uganda: An Evaluation of Safer Sex Strategies, (1994) (unpublished manuscript, Georgetown University Law Center).

50. ICPD Programme of Action, P4.27.

Male responsibilities in family life must be included in the education of children from the earliest ages.[51]...

An effort to change religious and customary laws in accordance with international human rights law should seek to persuade people of the validity and utility of the change.[52] For instance, WiLDAF[53] Ghana and its associate member organizations[54] have embarked on a rights-awareness program for grassroots women leaders on leadership skills and legal education on four laws that are of particular interest to women in Ghana: Intestate Succession Law; Wills Act; Marriage Laws; and Maintenance of Children Act.[55] As a result of the legal education carried out by these participants in their various communities, women have identified the need for an information office in various district capitals where women can go to seek information and advice on all issues relating to them, including law, health, and family planning. The realization of the need for change now emerges from within the communities after the introduction of the concept from outside the communities....

Conclusion

African culture and custom, as they exist today, are a blend of African customs, imported colonial common and civil law notions, and religious concepts from Christianity, Islam, and African traditional religions. The application of [customary] laws within the plural legal systems which are the legacy of the colonial era, and the unauthentic interpretation of customary law through this period, have left women in a very subordinate position, both socially and politically. The result is the inability of women to protect their re-

---

51. ICPD Programme of Action, P4.29.

52. An-Na'im, State Responsibility, *supra* note 38, at 347; Abdullahi A. An-Na'im, *Problems of Universal Cultural Legitimacy for Human Rights*, in Wiredu, *supra* note 10, at 331, 347–49.

53. Women in Law and Development in Africa (WiLDAF) is an NGO which promotes networking among women's organizations and activists in Africa, and collaborates with other human rights organizations and networks outside Africa. Its headquarters is situated in Harare, Zimbabwe.

54. One such organization is FIDA Ghana, which is the Ghana chapter of the International Federation of Women Lawyers. This organization has been in the forefront of advocacy for women's rights in Ghana. Among its projects are a legal literacy program and a legal aid clinic for indigent women.

55. Country Report of WiLDAF Ghana, WiLDAF General Assembly (June 27–30, 1994).

productive autonomy and ensure their reproductive health. Whole communities have to be educated on women's rights in order to re-orient the thinking of society in general....Culture and custom are such a mixture of concepts that they cannot be changed without a concerted effort to attack the problem on many fronts. Simultaneous massive action for change on legal, educational, and other fronts will help us make progress in the right direction and towards women's reproductive autonomy.

Women and HIV/AIDS in Uganda

Emma Ssali Namuli

Introduction

The AIDS epidemic has dramatically affected Uganda. Although the National Resistance Movement Government of Uganda initiated a number of AIDS control and prevention programs,[1] women continue to be at particular risk for exposure.[2] Women's economic dependence on men deprives them of the ability to refuse sexual practices that expose them to AIDS.[3] Cultural attitudes that subordinate women lead to widespread practices like polygamy and female genital mutilation, which increase women's likelihood of contracting the disease.[4] Ugandan laws discriminate against women and government health policies that do not adequately serve women's needs[5] only exacerbate the problem. Uganda must improve the situation for women because women are essential to the well-being of their families and the economy,[6] and because their right to live a healthy and productive life is a basic human right.

---

1. In 1986 the national government established a subdivision of the Ministry of Health, the Uganda AIDS Commission, to combat the epidemic. UGANDA AIDS COMMISSION SECRETARIAT, UGANDA NATIONAL OPERATIONAL PLAN FOR HIV/AIDS/STD PREVENTION, CARE AND SUPPORT 1994–98, 3 (1993) [hereinafter Uganda National Operation Plan].

2. *Id.* at 5.

3. EDWARD A. KIRUMIRA, UNDO RAPID ASSESSMENT STUDY SOCIO-CULTURAL FACTORS RELATING TO HIV/AIDS—SUSTAINING SEXUAL BEHAVIORAL PATTERNS 18–19, 21, 29–30 (1992).

4. CHRISTOPHER IZAMA, THE PROBLEM HIV/AIDS: A DISCOURSE ON LAWS, MARRIAGE, AND THE SUBORDINATE STATUS OF WOMEN IN UGANDA 21 (Uganda Law Books Ltd. 2003) (1997).

5. TOM BARTON & GIMONO WAMAI, NATIONAL COUNCIL FOR CHILDREN (UGANDA) AND UNICEF, EQUITY AND VULNERABILITY: A SITUATIONAL ANALYSIS ON WOMEN, ADOLESCENTS, AND CHILDREN IN UGANDA 40 (1994).

6. The United Nations Development Programme estimates that 60–80 percent of the labor for food and cash crops is done by women. *See* UNDP, STUDY PAPER #2: THE SOCIO-

HIV/AIDS In Uganda

HIV/AIDS is the most serious health problem presently facing Uganda and also the leading cause of death. The Uganda AIDS Commission estimated that by 1998 roughly 1.5 million people—10 percent of the total population and 20 percent of sexually active men and women—would be infected with the HIV virus.[7] Nearly 80 percent of those infected with HIV are between 15 and 45 years of age,[8] and are often both the breadwinners and the parents of families with an average of seven children.[9] As of 2002, 880,000 Ugandan children have been orphaned by AIDS.[10]

Despite an aggressive education campaign, 2002 estimates reveal that 5 percent of the population is currently infected with HIV.[11] According to the Uganda AIDS Commission, rates of infection increase rapidly between the ages of 11 to 19 years, especially among girls of 15 to 19 years, who are five times more likely to be infected than boys.[12] Girls between the ages of 20 to 24 are twice as likely to be infected as boys.[13] The vast majority of new infections occur as a result of sexual transmission (84 percent) followed by perinatal transmission (14 percent); other routes of transmission account for only 2 percent of new infections.[14]

Economic Impact of HIV/AIDS on Rural Families in Uganda: an Emphasis on Youth 1 (1994), *available at* http://www.undp.org/hiv/publications/study/english/sp2ech1.htm (last visited on July 27, 2003).

7. *Id.* at 4.

8. *Id.* at tbl. 1.

9. *Id.* at 5.

10. This statistic was introduced at the 2002 UN Conference on AIDS in Barcelona. *See* Sub-Saharan Africa Fact Sheet 2002 2, *available at* http://www.unaids.org/barcelona/presskit/factsheets.html (last visited on June 26, 2003).

11. Current estimated figures on HIV/AIDS in Uganda are available at http://www.unaids.org/hivaidsinfo/statistics/fact_sheets/pdfs/Uganda_en.pdf. (last visited on June 26, 2003).

12. Ministry of Gender, Labor and Social Dev., National Action Plan on Women 10 (1999).

13. UNICEF, SYFA, New Phase of UNICEF Support for AIDS Control in Uganda (1992).

14. Uganda National Operation Plan, *supra* note 1, at 4.

Cultural Practices and how They Have Exposed Women to HIV/AIDS

Position of Women in Society

Ugandan society is patriarchal and women are considered inferior.[15] Cultural attitudes regard women as subordinates who must obey their husbands.[16] Society values women only as homemakers and family caretakers.[17] When women do not conform to these expectations—for example, some women do not get married, others get separated or divorced—society considers them to be disgraces to their families and failures in life.[18]

Because girls are supposed to get married and become homemakers, families are often reluctant to educate girls beyond the free primary education offered by the government.[19] When parents must make a choice between educating a girl or boy, they often prioritize the boy's education. This lack of education leaves women in a position in which they cannot defend their rights due to illiteracy[20] and lack of economic independence.

---

15. HEATHER LYNN GUENTZEL, THE AVAILABILITY AND SUITABILITY OF HEALTH CARE FOR WOMEN WITH HIV/AIDS IN KAMPALA, UGANDA 30 (1998) (unpublished manuscript on file with UMI).

16. Indeed, any attempt by women to assert themselves, or to shift the power structures, is generally viewed as a threat to the order of society and met with physical and psychological violence. *See* MINISTRY OF GENDER, LABOR, AND SOCIAL DEV. [Uganda], REPORT ON DOMESTIC VIOLENCE IN UGANDA 4 (1999).

17. MINISTRY OF GENDER, LABOR, AND SOCIAL DEV. [Uganda], BALANCING THE SCALES: ADDRESSING GENDER CONCERNS IN NATIONAL DEVELOPMENT PROGRAMMES 22 (1999).

18. Izama, *supra* note 4, at 68–75; moreover, women who do not conform to these social expectations may find themselves without any support from their family, denied access or use of land, and potentially loose their children for lack of means to support them. *See generally* Winnie Bikaako & John Ssenkumba, *Gender, Land and Rights: Contemporary Constestations in Law, Policy and Practice in Uganda, in* WOMEN AND LAND IN AFRICA: CULTURE, RELIGION, AND REALIZING WOMEN'S RIGHTS 232, 250–53 (L. Muthoni Wanyeki ed. 2003).

19. Guentzel, *supra* note 15, at 6.

20. The illiteracy rate for women is 55.1 percent and for men it is 36.5 percent, *see* MINISTRY OF GENDER, LABOR AND SOCIAL DEV. [Uganda], *supra* note 17, at 8.

Cultural Practices

Brideprice

Brideprice, paid by the groom's family to the bride's family[21], is a symbol of gratitude from the husband and his family to the woman's parents for raising her. The determination of how much brideprice the groom's family must pay depends on whether the woman is a virgin, her age, tribe, family background and, until recently, her level of education.[22] The wealth of the family the woman is marrying into may also determine how much is to be paid.[23]

If a woman decides to separate or divorce, her family must refund the brideprice.[24] If the woman's family cannot refund the money, which is common because parents often use the brideprice to pay the brideprice for a son or school fees for younger siblings, the woman must remain in the marriage.[25] This practice can increase HIV/AIDS exposure when a woman is aware that her husband is engaging in high-risk sexual behavior but is unable to leave because she is unable to repay the bride price.[26]

Polygamy

All communities in Uganda still practice polygamy.[27] Even in Christian marriages that are supposed to be monogamous,[28] men often have second

---

21. *See* Esther M. Kisaakye, *Women, Culture and Human Rights: Female Genital Mutilation, Polygamy and Bride Price, in* Human Rights of Women: International Instruments and African Experiences 268, 280–81 (Benedek, Kisaakye, and Oberleitner, eds. 2002).

22. *Id.*

23. *Id.*

24. Hussaina Abdullah & Ibrahim Hamza, *Women and Land in Northern Nigeria: The Need for Independent Ownership Rights, in* Women and Land in Africa: Culture, Religion, and Realizing Women's Rights 133, 159 (L. Muthoni Wanyeki ed., 2003).

25. Kisaakye, *supra* note 21, at 281; Izama, *supra* note 4, at 65–66.

26. Kisaakye, *supra* note 21, at 282.

27. Indeed, when the question is brought up in Uganda, most people questioned do not see a problem with the institution. *See id.* at 277.

28. The Marriage Act, Cap. 211 [Uganda] §§ 43–53 (1904). This rule exists only for Christians, and a number of different statutes control the customary, Islamic, or Hindu marriages. *See* The Marriage of Africans Act, Cap. 212 [Uganda] (1904); The Marriage and Divorce of Mohammedans Act, Cap. 213 [Uganda] (1906); The Hindu Marriage and Divorce Act [Uganda] (1961); however, because 83.7 percent of the population is some form of Christian it is the controlling statute. *See generally* Bikaako & Ssenkumba, *supra* note 18, at 233.

wives. The number of wives a man has depends on whether he can pay bride price for each wife. Although tradition holds that he should be able to financially maintain multiple wives, this is not usually the case. Wives are thus forced to fend for themselves and their children.[29]

There are various reasons why polygamy is practiced. Muslims say they practice polygamy because their religion permits them to marry up to four wives.[30] Some men practice it for prestige, since it is assumed that the more women a man has, the wealthier he is. Other men practice polygamy to have more children, particularly if a wife is not willing to have the number of children a husband wants, is barren, or has given birth only to girls.[31]

Regardless of the justification, there is no doubt that polygamy exposes women to HIV/AIDS because multiple partners are involved in the relationship.[32] Since many women are powerless to end these relationships,[33] a husband's risky behavior inevitably exposes them to the deadly risk of contracting AIDS.[34]

Female Genital Mutilation (FGM)[35]

The Sabiny community, in eastern Uganda, practices female genital mutilation (hereinafter FGM).[36] FGM marks entry into membership in the tribal community, and it serves as a puberty and maturity rite.[37] The Sabiny believe that an uncircumcised girl is not fit for marriage and that no man would ever want to marry such a girl.[38] It is further believed that FGM is necessary to "tame" a girl's morality, and that a girl who is not "cut" may disgrace her family and clan by turning wild and engaging in rampant sexual activity. Thus, in order to avoid such disgrace, the most sensitive organs, those deemed "responsible" for making girls "stubborn," must be removed.[39]

---

29. Izama, *supra* note 4, at 77.

30. Kisaakye, *supra* note 21, at 277.

31. Izama, *supra* note 4, at 78–79.

32. *Id.*

33. *Id* at 79–80.

34. *Id* at 77–80.

35. It is estimated that half a million women in Uganda have undergone female genital mutilation. L Muthoni Wanyeki, *Uganda: The Search for Secure Land Tenure, in* WOMEN AND LAND IN AFRICA: CULTURE, RELIGION, AND REALIZING WOMEN'S RIGHTS 306 (L. Muthoni Wanyeki ed., 2003).

36. Kisaakye, *supra* note 21, at 273.

37. MINISTRY OF GENDER, LABOR, AND SOCIAL DEV., 8(1) GENDER BULLETIN 8 (1999).

38. Kisaakye, *supra* note 21, at 272–73.

39. MINISTRY OF GENDER, LABOR AND SOCIAL DEV., *supra* note 37, at 8.

According to the Sabiny, the custom was handed down to them by their ancestors and therefore must be upheld.[40] The Sabiny also view FGM as a symbol of cultural unity and tribal identity.[41] The circumcised women feel a strong cultural bond through the practice.[42] Consequently, the strongest advocates for the practice are women, who feel that those arguing against the practice are eroding Sabiny culture.[43]

Despite opposition to reform, the prevalence rate for FGM within the Sabiny community has declined from over 90 percent to 50 percent. This has been attributed to the efforts of some Sabiny elders, the Ugandan government, and local and international non-governmental organizations (NGOs), all of whom have worked to highlight the medical problems associated with the practice.

Widow Inheritance

Widow inheritance is a practice in which a widow is "inherited" by one of the brothers of her deceased husband.[44] The Itesot in northeastern Uganda argue that this tradition ensured that widows and their children remained in the family and thus were provided for on the death of a husband or father.[45] Others argue that since the husband's family paid bride price for the woman, she "belongs" to the clan, and even on the death of her husband she must remain within the family unless she can refund the bride price.[46]

Widow inheritance is extremely dangerous for women because the brother-in-law who "inherits" the widow may be HIV positive and pass on the disease.[47] This is also true for the widow who could pass on HIV to her brother-

---

40. *Id.*

41. The Sabiny responded to attempts to legally ban FMG by drafting and ratifying a Resolution that declared all girls who had not undergone FMG to be social outcastes; the resolution was later rescinded. Kisaakye, *supra* note 21, at 273, 283 n.27.

42. *Id.* at 273–74.

43. *Id.*

44. Such practice is also called "levirate marriage," and is often used as a method to keep women from inheriting full rights to property. *See* L. Muthoni Wanyeki, *Introduction, in* WOMEN AND LAND IN AFRICA: CULTURE, RELIGION, AND REALIZING WOMEN'S RIGHTS 1, 17 (L. Muthoni Wanyeki ed., 2003).

45. Such logic stems from the patriarchal belief that the children of a marriage belong to the father and his clan; therefore, widow inheritance ensures that the children are not separated from the mother, but still remain within the male line. *See* Izama, *supra* note 4, at 162–69.

46. Bikaako & Ssenkumba, *supra* note 18, at 261.

47. Izama, *supra* note 4, at 167–69.

in-law.[48] It is crucial to take action on behalf of women since they do not have the bargaining power to refuse this practice.[49] Those who refuse to be inherited are chased away from their homes and their children are forcefully removed from them.[50] Other women are seriously beaten for refusing to be inherited.[51]

How the Laws of Marriage and Inheritance Have Exposed Women to HIV/AIDS

Laws on Marriage

Both polygamous and monogamous marriages are recognized under Ugandan law, but are governed by different laws. The Marriage Act governs civil and Christian marriages, which are supposed to be monogamous in nature.[52] Grounds for divorce require a woman to prove that her husband committed adultery coupled with another offense.[53]

The burden of proof for the party seeking the divorce is extremely high, and many women are not willing to go through the process, especially since

---

48. *Id.*

49. *Id.*

50. Bikaako & Ssenkumba, *supra* note 18, at 261.

51. This is something within my personal knowledge, from conducting rural legal awareness sessions in the district of Kumi (northeastern Uganda) with widows who had gone through widow inheritance—and had formed a support group for widows to support those who were not willing to be "inherited."

52. *Id.*

53. Under the Divorce Act, a wife may apply by petition to the court for the dissolution of her marriage on the ground that since the solemnization of their marriage:

(a) her husband has changed his profession of Christianity for the profession of some other religion, and gone through a form of marriage with another woman; or

(b) has been guilty of:

(i) incestuous adultery; or

(ii) bigamy with adultery; or

(iii) marriage with another woman with adultery; or

(iv) rape, sodomy, or bestiality; or

(v) adultery coupled with cruelty; or

(vi) adultery coupled with desertion, without reasonable excuse, for two years or more.

The Divorce Act, Cap. 215 [Uganda] §§ 5(2) (1967)

their behavior during the marriage is likely to become an issue.[54] If a woman is found to have had an extramarital affair, she may lose her right to alimony,[55] and if she is not employed she will not be able to support herself.[56] Moreover, divorce is expensive and time consuming, and many women lack the money to go through with the process.[57] As a result, many women choose to remain in a marriage that exposes them to AIDS rather than pursue a divorce that will leave them in a poor economic situation.[58]

The threat of losing custody of her children may also discourage a woman from seeking a divorce.[59] Courts place great weight on the ability of a parent to financially support the children when making custody determinations.[60] Since women are often financially dependent on their husbands, they are less likely to be granted custody. [61] Many women may choose to remain in a relationship that exposes them to AIDS because they are not willing to be separated from their children.

The Marriage and Divorce of Mohammedans Act governs Islamic marriages.[62] Islamic marriages may be polygamous; a man may marry up to four

---

54. Unlike the husband, the wife must prove adultery and one other ground before the court can grant her a divorce, moreover, the court is not only allowed, but obligated to investigate the petitioner's behavior, and deny a plea for divorce if "during the marriage [the petitioner has] been guilty of adultery, or been guilty of unreasonable delay in presenting or prosecuting the petition, or of cruelty to the respondent, or of having deserted or willfully separated himself or herself from the respondent before the adultery complained of, and without reasonable excuse, or of such willful neglect of or misconduct towards the respondent as has conduced to the adultery." *See id.* §9.

55. *Id.* at 27.

56. Furthermore, because women's land rights are dependent on their relationships with men, divorced or widowed women are particularly vulnerable and economically unable to fend for themselves. *See* L. Muthoni Wanyeki, *supra* note 35, at 2.

57. On average a divorce case takes about two years because there is a separation period of one year during which the parties are given a chance to reconcile. Appearing before a judge may take about four to six months.

58. Izama, *supra* note 4, at 162–67.

59. This threat is a serious one because, traditionally, children are viewed a property of the man. *See id.*; Dorota Gierycz, *Human Rights of Women at the Fiftieth Anniversary of the United Nations, in* HUMAN RIGHTS OF WOMEN 30, 39–40 (Rebecca Cook ed., 2002).

60. The Divorce Act, Cap. 215 [Uganda] §§28–32 (1967).

61. The Children Statute No. 6 of 1996 [Uganda]. Section 6 states that it shall be the duty of a parent having custody of a child to maintain the child. This duty gives the child a right to education and guidance, immunization, adequate diet, clothing, shelter, and medical attention.

62. *Id.*

wives.[63] A man does not need to consult his wife before marrying another, and a second marriage is not grounds for divorce.[64] Since polygamy necessarily increases women's exposure to AIDS, their lack of bargaining power leaves them at a disadvantage and puts their health at risk.

The Customary Marriage (Registration) Decree governs marriage under customary law.[65] Customary marriages are also potentially polygamous in nature, and a man may marry as many women as he pleases as long as he fulfills all the customary requirements.[66] As in Islamic marriages, a wife in a customary marriage has no say as to how many wives her husband may marry, and marriage to another wife is not a ground for divorce.[67] Under customary law, children belong to the man, and upon divorce they remain with their father unless a child is still breast-feeding.[68] Therefore, if a wife wishes to leave the marriage, she may not receive custody of her children or may not be able to financially support them.

Thus, as a result of marriage and divorce law, many women opt to remain in marriages that expose them to AIDS; their only hope is that their husband and co-wives will exercise caution in their sexual behavior.[69]

Law on Succession

Many communities follow customary inheritance law.[70] According to most customs, women do not inherit any property on the death of their husbands.[71] Property is usually distributed among the deceased's male relatives.[72] If a woman is completely financially dependent on the deceased husband,[73] she is

---

63. *Id.* §3.

64. The Divorce Act, Cap. 215 [Uganda] §5 (1967).

65. *Id.*

66. These requirements include the payment of bride price, and the ability to adequately maintain all wives and children. *See* Kisaakye, *supra* note 21, at 280.

67. The Divorce Act, Cap. 215 [Uganda] §5 (1967).

68. Although the Children Statute No. 6 of 1996 [Uganda] states that children belong to both parents and that a child is entitled to live with both parents, *see id.*, §5(1), the mentality that children belong to the man still persists.

69. Izama, *supra* note 4, at 75–82.

70. Bikaako & Ssenkumba, *supra* note 18, at 232–76.

71. *Id.* at 248–49.

72. *Id.*

73. Women are only able to own land if the men in their family's approve; once a woman moves into her husband's home she is dependent upon him for access to land, and this does not change unless her father accepts her back into her childhood home upon her husband's death. *See id.* at 232–76.

either coerced into marriage with one of her brothers-in-law[74] or forced to resort to prostitution in order to maintain her children. The latter choice leaves women even more vulnerable to AIDS than the former.

Steps for Reform

There are presently no laws in Uganda that address AIDS. This leaves women at the mercy of their husbands or boyfriends, who continue to infect them with AIDS. It is estimated that 60 percent of HIV-positive women in Uganda are married and monogamous.[75] It is critical to protect women in light of this reality.

Law Reform

Regulate the Practice of Polygamy

Although the ideal situation would be to completely outlaw polygamy, this is not practical.[76] Because polygamy remains entrenched in and supported by society, enforcing a prohibition would be difficult.[77] Banning polygamy would also fail to address the underlying reasons that cause women to enter into polygamous marriages. Therefore, it would be more useful to impose conditions on men in polygamous marriages while discouraging the practice at the same time.

The Uganda Law Reform Commission has recommended several measures that would promote this goal. First, there should be a requirement of spousal consent, made before a court, to any subsequent marriage. Although wives may be coerced into giving this consent, other measures should be established to prevent this type of coercion. Additionally, a man should be required to show reasonable cause before a magistrate court in order to marry another wife.[78] He should also satisfy the court that he has the capacity to financially maintain his wives and the children at the same standard.

---

74. *Id.* at 261.

75. Mark Schoofs, *The Deadly Gender Gap: Fighting AIDS in Africa*, The Village Voice, Jan. 5,1999, at 34.

76. *See* Lara Santoro, *First Wives' Club Unites in Africa*, Christian Science Monitor, Jan. 23, 1992, at 1.

77. Essentially one would have to do away with the entire system of customary marriages. *See* Kisaakye, *supra* note 21, at 268–82.

78. *See* Lilian Ekkirikubinza-Tibatemwa, Gender and Human Rights: A Case Study of Polygamy Among the Basoga of Uganda 48–49 (Ctr. for Basic Research, Working Paper No. 81, 2003), *available at* http://www.cbr-ug.org/WorkingPaper81.pdf (last

Consent of the Parties

The practice of widow inheritance should be outlawed immediately. The Uganda Law Reform Commission has recommended that widow inheritance should be made an offense punishable with imprisonment or a fine if the essential and formal requirements for marriage under the law are not met.[79] Additionally, when a clansman of a deceased man wishes to marry a widow, the parties must observe all requirements for entering a valid marriage as set out by the law, including valid consent.[80]

Payment of Bride Price

Because the practice of bride price is deeply entrenched in society, abolishing it may not have any meaningful impact.[81] Instead, laws should be put in place to strictly regulate its practice. The Uganda Law Reform Commission has recommended that payment of marriage gifts should not be essential to the establishment of a valid marriage; instead, the validity of customary marriages must depend on agreement of the parties intending to marry. Also, the legal requirement of return of bride price upon divorce must be eradicated.

Female Genital Mutilation (FGM)

The aggressive education campaign against FGM must continue. Because this practice is deeply entrenched in the Sabiny cultural tradition, outlawing it would only drive the practice underground.[82] It is therefore extremely important that the communities are made aware that the practice has severe adverse medical consequences for women. Courses on the effects of FGM should

visited on July 30, 2003); *see also A Husband Cannot Be Divided Equally*, IRISH TIMES, Mar. 31, 1998, *available at* http://www.polygamyinfo.com/intnalmedia%20plyg%206it.htm (last visited on July 29, 2003).

79. Uganda Law Reform Commision, Report on the Law of Domestic Relations (on file with the author).

80. *Id.*

81. Indeed, most communities believe that if bride price has not been paid then the marriage is not valid. *See* Kisaakye, *supra* note 21, at 280–82; Izama, *supra* note 4, at 49–60, 63–66.

82. The Sabiny have already proven to be very resistant to the eradication of this tradition. *See* Kisaakye, *supra* note 21, at 273, 283 n.27.

be included in training programs for medical personnel and traditional birth attendants. Advocates should also target traditional elders because of the influence the elders wield in traditional communities.

Law on Divorce

Uganda must amend the law on divorce in order to protect women. The Uganda Law Reform Commission has recommended that there should be no-fault divorce for all forms of marriage. A person seeking divorce would only need to establish evidence that the marriage broke down irretrievably and that the relationship could not be saved.[83] This will enable women to leave a marriage that exposes them to HIV/AIDS without having to prove any other ground for divorce.

The law should also take into consideration the contribution of the wife(s) when dividing property on divorce, even when a woman is a housewife. This will enable women to seek divorce when they believe that they are at risk of contracting HIV.[84]

Policy Implementation

Without economic empowerment, women will continue to find themselves forced into polygamous marriages in order to survive and will continue to be exposed to HIV/AIDS. It is thus important to continue with adult literacy, bookkeeping, and management programs to improve how women run their businesses. Women must have access to loans, mortgages, and other forms of financial credit so they will be less dependent on their husbands and, over

---

83. *See* Anne Akia Fiedler, *The Laws of Love*, Orbit, vol. 72 (Spring 1999), *available at* http://www.vso.org.uk/publications/orbit/72/love.htm (last visited on July 28, 2003).

84. The Uganda Law Reform Commission has recommended that contribution shall constitute both monetary and non-monetary contribution made to the maintenance of the family. The value of the non-monetary contribution shall be determined by court and in so doing the court shall consider and assign a value to the following:

(a) domestic work and management of the home;
(b) provision of child care;
(c) the duration of the marriage;
(d) companionship; and
(e) any other matter deemed relevant at the court's discretion. UGANDA LAW REFORM COMMISSION, DOMESTIC RELATIONS PROJECT, EXECUTIVE SUMMARY AND RECOMMENDATIONS ON REFORM OF THE LAW OF DOMESTIC RELATIONS, at 43.

time, have more choice, including whether they would like to contract or stay in polygamous marriages.

It is also crucial to improve women's access to health care.[85] The government of Uganda should ensure that medical personnel and medicine are. equally distributed all over the country and should increase the quality and quantity of facilities for safe motherhood. Improved access to health care will help women understand the risks associated with HIV/AIDS.

Education will also improve girls' chances of being independent from men later in life by increasing employment options outside of the home. This will ensure that by the time children leave primary school, they will be aware of the dangers of AIDS and will be in a better position to protect themselves, both physically and economically.

Conclusion

Given the factors that have enhanced the spread of HIV/AIDS to women in Uganda, it is important to alleviate the plight of Ugandan women by enacting and implementing laws to improve their position in society.

AIDS is unique in its devastating impact on women. Because women are key figures in Ugandan families as well as in the social and economic development of the country, Uganda must improve the status of women and ameliorate the serious consequences of the AIDS epidemic on Ugandan women. The country cannot afford to do anything less. An ever-growing AIDS epidemic is not inevitable, but unless the government takes decisive action against the epidemic, the damage already done will seem minor compared with what lies ahead.

---

85. Guentzel, *supra* note 15, at 34–57.

Women's Rights and the AIDS Epidemic in Tanzania

Maria Tungaraza

Introduction

The AIDS epidemic has been spreading at an alarming rate in Tanzania.[1] It is estimated that about 71,000 AIDS cases occurred in the year 2001 alone, and a cumulative total of 772,490 AIDS cases exist since the beginning of the epidemic in the country.[2] Although the reported AIDS cases appear to be equally distributed between the sexes, women, especially younger women, are currently more at risk of contracting HIV than men.[3] Seroprevalence rates from blood donor screening indicate that 13.7 percent of women are HIV positive compared to 10.4 percent of men.[4] Data collected from high transmission areas of truck stops indicate that HIV seroprevalence in women is almost double that in men, 55.7 percent and 31.0 percent respectively.[5]

Many factors are responsible for this age and sex difference in HIV infection. To a large extent, women are disproportionately affected by the epidemic because of their cultural and sexual subordination through long-standing customary sexual practices. Customary sexual practices such as mokamona marriage, polygamy, widow cleansing, widow inheritance, wife exchange, female genital mutilation, and dry sex are among the factors contributing to the spread of HIV. These cultural practices impede behavior change, which is necessary for AIDS prevention and mitigation. If AIDS prevention is to be effective, AIDS educators must realize that AIDS prevention and mitigation strate-

---

1. The United Republic of Tanzania, Ministry of Health, National AIDS Control Programme, *HIV/AIDS/STD Surveillance, Report No.9*, at 5 (Dec. 1995).
2. The United Republic of Tanzania, Ministry of Health, National AIDS Control Programme, *HIV/AIDS/STD Surveillance, Report No.16*, at v (Dec. 2001).
3. *Id.* at 12.
4. *Id.* at v.
5. *Id.*

gies must move beyond merely teaching facts about AIDS. Activists and educators must now focus on securing women's rights and changing behavior with respect to dangerous sexual practices, including those practices entrenched in the culture. Generally, Tanzania has not explored legal reform as a way to change AIDS-related behavior and to eliminate many of the cultural practices that help spread the disease. Tanzanian laws have not addressed HIV/AIDS issues. The only comprehensive document responding to the AIDS epidemic is the National Policy on HIV/AIDS, 2001.

This essay is divided into four sections. Section one examines how customary sexual practices expose women to HIV infection. Section two focuses on women's economic status and the risk of HIV transmission. Section three examines current government efforts to address HIV/AIDS and the impact of gender-biased laws on HIV transmission. Section four gives recommendations on how Tanzania can promote women's rights and protect women from HIV infection.

Customary Sexual Practices and HIV Transmission

The spread of HIV infection in Tanzania is not random. Rather, it follows the paths laid down by customary laws and sexual practices. These practices make women especially vulnerable to AIDS by depriving them of the will or ability to protect themselves against the spread of AIDS. Although many cultural practices increase women's vulnerability to HIV infection,[6] this section focuses specifically on the practices of polygamy, mokamona marriage (marriage for the purpose of getting a surrogate mother), widow inheritance, widow cleansing, and dry sex.

Polygamy

Polygamy is the practice of men marrying more than one spouse at a time in purported exercise of the right of plural marriage.[7] One out of every three married women aged forty years and over has a polygamous husband, and one out of every three married men are polygamous by the time they are forty

---

6. Other relevant practices may include female genital mutilation and wife exchange. AFRICAN WOMEN'S HEALTH 76 (Meredeth Turshen ed., Africa World Press, Inc. 2000).

7. Fitnat Naa-Asjeley Adjetey, *Reclaiming the African Woman's Individuality: The Struggle Between Women's Reproductive Autonomy and African Society and Culture*, 42 AM. U. L. REV. 1351, 1357 (1995).

years old.[8] Because polygamy involves multiple sexual partners, female spouses in this practice have a higher risk of HIV infection.[9] As wives and care givers, women bear the burden of caring for sick and dying spouses, co-wives, and children in attempting to hold the family unit together. [10]

Mokamona

Mokamona or nyumba ntobu is a practice of marriage between a married woman, called the mother-in-law, of a sonless house and a woman, usually a girl, called the daughter-in-law, who is used as a surrogate mother to procure a son.[11] In Tanzania, sons are considered more valuable than daughters because, under inheritance laws, sons are the main heir of the family's property and therefore provide security for aged parents.[12] Thus, a sonless house pays bride price to the parents of the daughter-in-law, and the latter becomes the

---

8. Pelad Paschal Mamfua, Polygamy in Tanzania, its Determinants and Effects on Fertility 38 (1982) (unpublished dissertation).

9. For example, Asha was in a polygamous marriage of four wives. Her husband, Mitala, had married seven times before Asha was married to him, but by the time he married Asha he had divorced some of his wives. Mitala was in a process of marrying Zogo, unaware of her HIV status. Asha and the other wives objected to Mitala's relationship with Zogo fearing the risk of contracting HIV. But Mitala assured them of their safety, claiming Zogo did not have HIV. Zogo transmitted HIV to Mitala who in turn infected Asha. Soon after, Asha conceived and transmitted HIV vertically to her infant. I visited Mitala in the process of drafting a will. Aware that he infected his young wife, Asha, and his youngest son who was then six years of age, this is what Mitala stated to me: "My daughter, in my lifetime I loved two things, good times and women. I married eight wives in my lifetime and had thirty-two children. It is women now who are removing me from the world. Life in this world is like a stormy sea, and a ship needs a good captain otherwise it will sink. The same applied to me. I was not a good captain so my wives, my youngest son, and I are now sinking." AIDS Programme, Comprehensive Community Rehabilitation in Tanzania (1995).

10. An example of this situation is Suzana, whose husband Kombo, had two wives and infected them both with HIV. The first wife, Kibibi, was the first to die leaving behind two children. Along with her own six children, Suzana had to care for Kibibi and Kombo until they died, and for Kibibi's two children after she died. Suzana was left alone to care for the eight children (Kibibi's two and the six of her own) with no help from relatives. The only assistance she received came from NGOs until she died of AIDS a few years later. *Id.*

11. Balthazar Aloyse Rwezaura, Traditional Family Law and Change in Tanzania: A Study of the Kuria Social System 143 (Institut für Internationale Angelegenheiten der Universität Hamburg 1985).

12. *Id.* at 145.

wife who has to conceive by having sex with a chosen suitor, usually someone in the lineage of the husband of the mother-in-law.[13] The child then belongs to the house that paid the bride price.[14] This practice increases their vulnerability to HIV infection.

Widow Inheritance

Widow inheritance, or levirate, connotes a customary practice in which, upon the death of her husband, the widow is inherited by one of the deceased's brothers or male relatives.[15] This practice, done to perpetuate the family of the dead brother,[16] is widespread in Tanzania and, in the wake of HIV, is risky to the widow. By the same token, widow inheritance is risky to the widow inheritor and his wives, because the widow's deceased husband may have died of AIDS, meaning that the widow may also be HIV positive.

Widow Cleansing

Widow cleansing is a sexual ritual aimed at cleansing a widow from a bad omen following her husband's death. To be cleansed, a widow must have sexual intercourse with one or more men, depending on the specific practices of the tribe concerned. Among the Kerewe, for instance, a widow is cleansed twice. A widower cleanses the widow sexually four days after her husband's burial. Two to three months later, the widow has to be cleansed by a stranger by having sexual intercourse with him only once in her lifetime. In order to have sex with a stranger, a widow must go to a village where she is not known. There she generally goes to a tavern and entices a man into having sexual intercourse with her. After the cleansing ritual, a widow is considered to be free from the evil spirits and is eligible to be inherited by the deceased husband's brother. The two acts of cleansing put the widow at risk for contracting HIV or infecting the cleansers if she had previously contracted HIV. Since a widower cleanses widows, he too may be infected and may infect other widows in that village. Finally, if the infected widows are inherited then her new co-wives in the case of a polygamous marriage will also be infected.

---

13. *Id.*

14. *Id.*

15. Adjetey, *supra* note 7, at 1360.

16. M.C. Mukoyogo, Lead Paper on Legal and Ethical Issues at the National AIDS Policy Workshop 27 (July 1995) (unpublished).

Dry Sex

Dry sex is a practice in which women use moisture-absorbing agents to absorb vaginal fluids and tighten the vagina, creating a "virgin-like state" and thereby enhancing sexual pleasure for men.[17] According to a Zimbabwe study, "[a] preference for a dry, tight vagina during sexual intercourse [...] has been identified in several Central and Southern African countries including Zaire, Zambia, Malawi, South Africa, and Zimbabwe."[18] This practice is also found in Tanzania, although there are no specific data on the percentage of the population exercising this practice. Most drying agents are powders made from pounded plants and stones that women insert directly into their vaginas to absorb moisture.[19] Baboon urine, which is inserted in the vagina, is another drying agent.[20] Women sometimes mix other agents with porridge and take them orally; also, women administer still other drying agents "by making cuts on the inner thighs or other parts of the body and rubbing powder onto these cuts."[21] A study done in Zimbabwe suggests that women practice dry sex as a result of economic and cultural subordination, which puts several wives or potential wives in competition for the love of one man.[22]

The use of herbs to enhance men's sexual pleasure has existed since time immemorial; but in the wake of AIDS, women who insert moisture-absorbing herbs into their vaginas, believing this increases male sexual pleasure, expose themselves not only to the risk of cervical cancer but also to increased risk of HIV infection. Vaginal drying herbs kill certain vaginal bacteria known as lactobacilli.[23] Lactobacilli are known to fight infections, including HIV. Studies have shown that women with less lactobacilli are at higher risk of HIV

---

17. Diane Civic & David Wilson, *Dry Sex in Zimbabwe and Implications for Condom Use*, 42 Soc. Sci. & Med. 91, 91 (Jan.–Feb. 1996).

18. *Id.*

19. *Id.* at 93.

20. *Id.*

21. *Id.*

22. Gathered from Civic and Wilson's Zimbabwe study, the following are quotes from women explaining why they practice dry sex:
" 'If a man goes away, he'll come home – even if he has other girlfriends while he is away'... ; 'The man will experience character changes. He will show you his salary and how he spent it and expressing his love for you'...; 'If a man goes out drinking beer, he won't think of anyone but you.' " *Id.*

23. Ahmad Latig, *Vaginal Herbs Increases Risk of AIDS and Cancer*, PAN AFRICAN NEWS AGENCY, October 16, 1996.

infection and risk becoming infertile.[24] Vaginal drying agents have a negative effect for women who want to practice safe sex because they cause condoms to break.[25] Also, the cuts made in the body to insert herbs allow HIV to pass directly into the woman's blood stream.

Women's Economic Status and HIV Transmission

It is widely recognized that HIV is a "disease of poverty."[26] Female vulnerability to HIV infection arises from impoverished conditions resulting, in part, from discriminatory laws of inheritance[27] and division of matrimonial property.[28] These laws, which restrict women's ownership of and access to property generally, and land, in particular, render women dependent upon men for their economic well-being. Under these laws, when a woman's husband dies or she divorces, she is deprived of her home and income, which in turn may lead her to engage in risky sexual practices to make a living, putting her at risk for HIV infection.[29] Fear of facing such a decision keeps women in relationships that

---

24. *Id.*

25. Civic, *supra* note 17, at 95.

26. Martha Ainsworth & Mead Over, *AIDS and African Development*, 9 THE WORLD BANK RES. OBSERVER 203, 208 (1994).

27. *See generally* Salma Maoulidi, Rethinking Property: Women and Matrimonial Property Rights in Tanzania (1995) (unpublished L.L.M. paper, Georgetown University Law Center) (on file with the Georgetown University Law Center).

28. *See generally* Monica E. Magoke-Mhoja, Impact of Customary Inheritance Law on (The Status of) Widows and Daughters in Tanzania: A Challenge to Human Rights Activists (1997) (unpublished L.L.M. paper, Georgetown University Law Center) (on file at Georgetown University Law Center).

29. An example of this situation is illustrated by the story of a widow, Maua. Maua was referred to the Comprehensive Community Based Rehabilitation for orphan support. She had suffered from syphilis which she contracted through prostitution. She was forced to prostitute herself because her husband died of AIDS leaving her with five children, and she had no other means to support them. Her husband's relatives had taken her property and left her alone to raise her children. Maua is not well educated and could not find employment. According to Maua's statement, she decided to engage in prostitution in order to feed her children and protect her daughters from prostitution and HIV infection. The fact that Maua contracted syphilis and was later on diagnosed to have AIDS demonstrates that she was not practicing safe sex and many male clients, married and unmarried, may have contracted HIV. After Maua was treated she reported to me that she was no longer working as a prostitute but had found one faithful partner whom she was intending to marry.

they know place them at risk for infection. Likewise, the practice of bride price and the rule that bride price must be refunded if the wife fails in certain ways keeps women in risky relationships.[30] For young girls, economic considerations lure them into giving sexual favors to older well to-do-men.[31]

Education is a key to economic success. Lack of education traps women in the cycle of poverty. As a result of cultural factors, such as the pressure to marry young and a preference for educating male children, and economic factors, such as a family's ability to educate only one child, girls have a lower enrollment rate than boys at the secondary school level.[32] Women are even less likely to pursue University education. [33] Women's limited education level undermines their bargaining power in negotiations over sex, even when they realize it will put them at risk.

Law and Policy Affecting Women and HIV/AIDS

The Constitution of the United Republic of Tanzania

The Constitution of the United Republic of Tanzania is not facially discriminatory towards women, but the country's laws and customs are discriminatory

---

The groom-to-be was married and she was to be a second wife. Thus, due to the economic situation she found herself in after her husband's death, she may have contracted HIV and infected many clients as well as her husband-to-be and his wife.

30. If a wife refuses sex without protection because of fear of AIDS, it appears that the husband could divorce her and seek refund of bride price. If the wife's family refuses or cannot repay bride price, the wife is trapped either into sex or poverty. The prospect can lead wives to desperate measures. For example, in Mwajuma Marwa and Kwirege Bega, v. R,, Criminal Appeal No. 30 of 1982 (Mwanza Registry), the Court of Appeal of Tanzania upheld a conviction of two women who murdered their polygamous husband. Both were the wives of the deceased, Mashauri Ubwage. The deceased was an elderly man, aged sixty, who had married a total of eight wives. Ubwage kept the two wives, Mwajuma and Kwirege, aged twenty-four years and nineteen years respectively, under his control because their parents were unable to refund him bride price. The fate of these two desperate women illustrates the injustice that is caused by the laws that are oppressive to women.

31. AFRICAN WOMEN'S HEALTH xiii, 69, 77 (Meredeth Turshen ed., Africa World Press, Inc. 2000).

32. *Id.* at 44.

33. In 1992–93, the total number of students enrolled at the University of Dar es Salaam was 2,676, only 451 were female students. THE UNITED REPUBLIC OF TANZANIA, MINISTRY OF HEALTH, NATIONAL AIDS CONTROL PROGRAMME, *HIV/AIDS/STD Surveillance, Report No.15*, at 57 (Dec. 2000).

in practice. Articles 12 and 13 provide for the right to equality,[34] with article 13 specifically prohibiting gender discrimination. Laws that discriminate against women and force them into socioeconomic positions and customary practices that expose them to HIV should be held unconstitutional. The customary laws and practices of Tanzania discussed in this paper are inconsistent with its Constitutional guarantee of equality.[35] As long as gender discriminatory laws prevail over the Bill of Rights, AIDS prevention and mitigation strategies will be futile. We must therefore prioritize the prevention of HIV through law reform that promotes equality for women and eliminates discriminatory laws and practices.

National Policy on HIV/AIDS, 2001

There have been various national efforts to control the spread of HIV. The National Policy on HIV/AIDS, 2001, currently in force, was created to widen and strengthen the national response.[36] The policy intends for all actors en-

---

34. "12. –   (1) All human beings are born free, and are all equal.

(2) Every person is entitled to recognition and respect for his dignity.

13. –   (1) All persons are equal before the law and are entitled, without any discrimination, to protection and equality before the law.

(2) No law enacted by any authority in the United Republic shall make any provision that is discriminatory either of itself or in its effect." TANZ. CONST. chap. 1, part III, §§ 12, 13.

35. As the former Tanzanian President J. K. Nyerere stated, "Equality and polygamy could not go together because if a person is allowed to marry more than one woman, those women cannot by any stretch of logic or imagination claim to be equal to him. He actually becomes a master in a real sense of the word." Barbara Mitchell, *Improving the Status of Women Through Family Law Reform: The Tanzanian Experience*, 8 THE MELANESIAN LAW JOURNAL 54, 66 n. 51 (1980).

36. "Specific Objectives of the Policy [include]

[1] Prevention of transmission of HIV/AIDS…[by] creat[ing] and sustain[ing] an increased awareness of HIV/AIDS through targeted advocacy, information, education, and communication for behaviour change at all levels by all sectors… [Also, t]o prevent further transmission of HIV/AIDS through : (a) making blood and blood products safe, and (b) promoting safer sex practices…[and] (c) early and effective treatment of STIs…[2] HIV [t]esting…[by] promot[ing] early diagnosis of HIV infection through voluntary testing with pre-and-post test counselling.…[Also,] to plan for counselling training and accreditation of training programs in Tanzania to ensure that counselling in HIV/AIDS abides by a common code of practice.…[3] Care of [people living with HIV/AIDS.]…[4] Sectoral [r]oles and [f]inancing [through] strengthen[ing] the role of all the sectors, [including] public [and] private…to ensure that all stake holders are actively involved in HIV/AIDS work and to provide a framework of coordination and col-

gaged in national multi-sectoral efforts to prevent further transmission of HIV and to mitigate the disease's socioeconomic effects. Although the National Policy on HIV/AIDS/STDs of 2001 (hereafter referred to as the Policy) is not a legally enforceable document, it may be highly persuasive in judicial decisions because Tanzania has a tradition of adopting policy documents in enacting new legislation.

Inadequacy of the Laws and Policies in Safeguarding Women Against HIV/AIDS

National Policy on HIV/AIDS, 2001

Although the Policy appears to be exhaustive, it does not adequately protect women's rights.[37] The Policy does not explicitly prohibit customary sexual practices that expose women to HIV infection. Rather, it states in general terms that, "[p]ower relations in traditional and customary practices that inhibit equal participation of men and women in preventing the spread of HIV/AIDS shall be addressed by all sectors."[38] Further, the Policy states that

---

laboration.... [5] To participate in HIV/AIDS research, nationally and internationally, and to establish a system to disseminate scientific information resulting from this research while upholding ethics that govern interventions in HIV/AIDS.... [6] To create a legal framework by enacting a law on HIV/AIDS with a view to establishing multisectoral response to HIV/AIDS and to address legal and ethical issues in HIV/AIDS and to revise the legal situation of families affected by HIV/AIDS in order to give them access to family property after death of their parent(s).... [7] To monitor the efforts towards community mobilization for living positively with HIV/AIDS in order to cope with the impact of the epidemic while safeguarding the rights of those infected or affected directly by HIV/AIDS in the community.... [Also, t]o identify human rights abuses in HIV/AIDS and to protect PLHAs and everyone else in society against all forms of discrimination and social injustice." National Policy on AIDS, §3.2 (2001) (Tanz.).

37. There are some essential issues, which have not been addressed by the Policy, therefore impeding a mechanism for protection of vulnerable groups of women such as prisoners, refugees, and disabled women. This group of women is quite often exposed to sexual violence due to the environment they live in. For instance, disabled women such as the blind and the deaf require special educational aid and an enabling environment for protection against HIV/AIDS. Along the same view, people with mental disabilities should also be provided with a kind environment and protection against sexual exploitation.

38. National Policy on AIDS, §5.15(a) (2001) (Tanz.).

customary practices and cultural institutions should be used to raise public awareness and to encourage empowerment and dissemination of information on reproductive health and HIV/AIDS. Under the Policy, community programs should address the dangers of multiple sex partnership and the impact of gender equality and reproductive rights on the transmission of HIV/AIDS. The Policy reflects an understanding that existing inheritance laws must be reviewed and harmonized. The Policy also recognizes that customary laws and practices must be reformed to become gender sensitive. Most importantly, the Policy articulates that unless harmful traditional practices are explicitly denounced, the Policy will have no effect.

Other National Policies Concerning Women and Reproductive Health

The Policy on Women, Development and Gender provides guidelines to promote gender equality in Tanzania and encourages communities to refrain from harmful traditional practices, such as female genital mutilation. The Policy, however, falls short of condemning such practices. According to the 2003 National Policy Guidelines for Reproductive and Child Health, all women and girls have the right to be protected against all forms of discrimination, exploitation, and abuse, including practices that adversely affect their reproductive health. The National Policy Guidelines for Reproductive and Child Health are more effective than the Policy on Women, Development and Gender, because they address community education and the vital role of the community in combating harmful traditional practices that have a deleterious effect on women's reproductive health.

The Penal Code Cap. 16

When AIDS was first discovered in Tanzania, the only existing provision that dealt directly with the spread of an infectious disease was Section 179 of the Tanzania Penal Code, Chapter 16 of the Laws (Revised), which provides that any person who negligently or willfully transmits an infectious disease dangerous to life commits a misdemeanor offense. Through this existing law, the Penal Code deems the negligent or willful spread of HIV/AIDS a criminal offense. If enforced against AIDS transmitters, however, women will be the primary targets of criminalization because sexual practices in Tanzania place women in the situation of infecting both their partners and their babies.

Although this seems like an effective deterrent to the spread of HIV, it may have adverse effects. It will only apply to a small minority of people who access hospitals for medical care and who agree to be tested for HIV. As such, this may scare people from going to the hospital and impede HIV surveillance by the National AIDS Control program.

The Sexual Offences Special Provisions Act, 1998

The Sexual Offences Special Provisions Act, 1998 (hereafter referred to as the Sexual Offences Act) aims to protect women and children against rape[39] and sexual exploitation by providing general deterrents that prevent HIV transmission. The offense of rape includes circumstances in which a person in a position of authority, management or on the staff of a remand home, management or staff of a hospital, or a traditional healer or religious leader takes advantage of his position and sexually exploits a girl or woman.[40] The Act has some shortcomings, including its failure to criminalize marital rape. The Act is also silent on the protection of disabled women, who may be particularly vulnerable to sexual abuse due to their disability.

The Act also protects sex workers, including children, from coercion and trafficking. Aside from trafficking, however, the Act does little to protect the health rights of women and girls engaged in prostitution. Tanzania has many brothels that employ young girls and protection of these young girls against HIV infection is doubtful.

The Act has amended the Penal Code by adding section 169A (1), a provision that prohibits female genital mutilation.[41] Enforcement of this section, however, has been weak and female genital mutilation is still practiced. With the advent of the AIDS epidemic, FGM poses a serious threat to the lives of young girls.

Recommendations

Law is a critical intervention strategy for AIDS prevention and mitigation. The reform of laws on inheritance, bride price, division of matrimonial assets, and custody of children may promote women's rights. The Law of Mar-

---

39. The Sexual Offences Special Provisions Act, §§ 5,6 (1998) (Tanz.).
40. *Id.* at § 5.3.
41. *Id.* at § 21.

riage Act, for example, must be amended to raise the minimum age of marriage for girls to eighteen, reducing the reproductive health complications of childbirth and increasing the bargaining power of young wives. This will, in turn, enable women to negotiate safe sex from a stronger bargaining position and reduce women's vulnerability to HIV infection. The government must simultaneously reform the laws and the National Policy on HIV/AIDS. Law reform that eliminates traditional practices will promote women's human rights, particularly the right to life, the right to self-determination, and the right to equality.

Gender Sensitization

Legal reform must be accompanied by large scale public awareness campaigns concerning gender equality. To achieve this, human rights lawyers must work with respected members of the society, such as progressive politicians, members of parliament, religious leaders, and traditional healers and judges, to sensitize and educate people. Tanzanians must be aware that women's rights are human rights, and these rights must be enforced to ensure true democracy.

Taking a community based approach is the most effective way to disseminate information on sexual behavior change and women's rights. In order to reach people of all walks of life, paralegals must be trained to work in community based programs. Paralegals may reinforce dissemination of education materials on women's rights as human rights and assist affected women by providing access to various legal aid organizations. Peer educators and peer counselors are needed to promote changes in customary sexual practices. If men and women are educated and counseled on the benefits of behavior change, it may be more effective than imposing a top-down requirement that the community adopt the cultural changes.

Decriminalization of Willful Transmission of HIV Policy

Criminalizing the willful spread of HIV is not an effective strategy to combat HIV. As long as gender discriminatory laws continue to exist, HIV will continue to spread. Punishing women who have no freedom to control their sexual behavior will have no deterrent effect. Activists for women's rights must argue against the criminalization of women's willful transmission of HIV. Because women are sometimes compelled to engage in risky sex by cultural and socioeconomic circumstances, they cannot willfully spread the disease. They are likely, however, to be the targets of prosecution. If the criminalization strategy continues, women will continue to be blamed for the entire AIDS epidemic, revictimizing them when the culture and the existing laws force them to be exposed to and pass on the AIDS virus. In order to save lives, efforts must be directed towards abolishing gender discriminatory laws and customs that force women to engage in high risk sexual behavior.

Best Practices

For legal reform to be successful in this area, legislation must be enacted encouraging the replacement of dangerous sexual practices with beneficial practices. For example, mokamona marriage may be replaced by the law of adoption so that a sonless family may adopt an orphan without endangering women's lives. Widow cleansing may be replaced by scientific counseling or counseling by traditional healers, who are respected by the community. Thus, a widow may be counseled to cope with grief and to rid her of evil spirits without being sexually cleansed and exposed to HIV infection. Widow inheritance may be eradicated through the economic and educational empowerment of women. If women are empowered intellectually and economically, they will not need the security provided by the widow inheritor. Information, education, and communication concerning safe sexual practices may help to find and encourage alternatives to dangerous practices. Legislation must follow and reflect thorough research regarding how communities may modify sexual practices to protect women and others from HIV infection. Legislation encouraging these best practices must involve active community participation so that people embrace both the law reform and the safer sexual practices.

Other Recommendations

1. Law makers, judges, and other law enforcement officials must be trained as to the gender dimensions of the HIV/AIDS epidemic, human rights, women's rights, the Constitution as a tool for stemming the AIDS epidemic and for promoting human rights, and Tanzania's obligations under international human rights law.

2. The government must comply with international instruments, including reporting requirements. Non-governmental organizations (NGOs) should play

the lead role in monitoring and supplementing any submissions the state might wish to make to members of international human rights committees, such as the Committee on Elimination of Discrimination Against Women.

3. Women must be politically empowered. The government must implement affirmative action programs to increase women's representation in all branches of the government.

4. Women must be economically empowered. Women must have equal access to land, inheritance, credit,[42] and job training.

5. The government and NGOs must conduct widespread education on human rights, gender sensitization, and health education to prevent STDs and HIV.

6. Girls must have access to education. The girl child, in particular, must be protected from all forms of sexual exploitation and be equipped with sex education to strengthen her negotiation skills and assert herself in safe sexual practices.

7. Research on women's rights and publications must be encouraged.

Conclusion

Gender discriminatory laws and customs have played a major role in HIV transmission to women. Eradication of these discriminatory laws and practices is necessary to improve women's health and status. If women are oppressed, HIV will continue to be transmitted. Gender discrimination perpetuates women's poverty, powerlessness, and lack of literacy, all of which contribute to women's vulnerability to HIV infection. Women's rights are human rights, and law, if used genuinely and effectively for promoting women's equality, will be an essential intervention strategy in the fight against HIV/AIDS.

---

42. Many widows living with AIDS, other women living with AIDS, and AIDS-related female orphans, often seek microcredits once husbands or fathers die in order to be independent and avoid resorting to prostitution. One such example is Sunna's story. Sunna consulted me for microcredit to start running a food stall. Her efforts to obtain credit elsewhere failed, and she started working in a tavern as a barmaid. Working as a barmaid did not pay well, and she resorted to prostitution after work hours with some of the customers who came to the tavern. Sunna contracted HIV. Because it was difficult for her to continue with prostitution, she decided to continue seeking credit. If Sunna had access to credit when she first made the initiative to obtain it, she would not have resorted to prostitution and would not have contracted HIV. Women's lack of access to credit was a factor that led to Sunna's HIV infection. There are many more women in Sunna's situation.

CHAPTER FIVE

WOMEN'S ECONOMIC EMPOWERMENT

Chapter Introduction, *Johanna Bond*

Women constitute 70 percent of the world's 1.3 billion people living in absolute poverty.[1] Although women in Africa are responsible for 80 percent of that continent's agricultural labor,[2] the vast majority struggle to feed themselves and their families. The effects of poverty touch almost every aspect of African women's lives, including, for example, their education, their health, their exposure to violence, and their reproduction. Therefore, poverty reduction and, more specifically, economic empowerment is critical to African women's enjoyment of basic human rights.

As the authors in this chapter illustrate, traditional conceptions of women's roles in African society often serve to exclude them from the formal labor market, forcing women into the informal employment sector and compounding their economic dependence on men. Even when women are able to enter the formal labor market, there they face sexual harassment and other forms of gender discrimination. Women's rights activists in many parts of the world, including Ghana, Uganda, and Tanzania, have begun to explore the use of national constitutions and international human rights treaties to protect women's employment rights in the formal sector.

In this chapter, Evelyn Nassuna explores the effect of gender stereotyping on hiring practices in Uganda. According to Nassuna, those responsible

---

1. Virginia Ofosu-Amaah, *Linkage Between Development and the Implementation of the Cairo/Beijing Agenda for Women's Empowerment*, 2 ILSA J. Int'l & Comp. L. 709, 710 (1996).
2. Gwendolyn Mikell, *African Structural Adjustment: Women and Legal Challenges*, 69 St. John's L. Rev. 7, 9 (1995).

for hiring decisions often assume that married women will be distracted by family obligations and that single women will marry and eventually have children, compromising their commitment to the job.[3] These and other stereotypes about women's competence and ability to juggle multiple roles lead to discriminatory hiring practices in Uganda. Nassuna also describes the problem of sexual harassment and the dearth of Ugandan laws addressing it, noting that "[t]he Government of Uganda has acknowledged that 'working women widely report sexual harassment at their work places'" to no avail.[4]

However, the formal labor market represents only one form of income generation for African women. In Ghana, Uganda, and Tanzania, land ownership is another significant source of wealth. Under customary law, women do not enjoy the same rights to land ownership as men. For example, according to Ugandan custom, a woman marries into her husband's clan, and the clan traditionally allocates customary land to the man upon marriage.[5] A woman's right to use the land extends to her by virtue of the marriage alone; when the husband dies, the ownership of the land reverts goes back to the clan.[6] As Jacqueline Asiimwe observes, "[S]ince women are seen as belonging to neither their families nor marital clans, they are denied by both sources the opportunity to own land."[7]

In this chapter, Naome Kabanda describes how the British colonization of Uganda changed that country's rules of customary land ownership, creating obstacles to women's ownership and use of land. Kabanda notes, "The British introduced leasehold, freehold, and *Mailo* (private estates), which were deeply rooted in individual and predominantly male ownership and indirectly abolished traditional communal land holding."[8] In addition, as land became more commercialized, cash crops came increasingly under male control,[9] and women were forced into subsistence farming on smaller and smaller plots of

---

3. Evelyn Nassuna, Women and Employment Discrimination in Uganda in the Formal Sector: Facing Challenges and Forging Change, *infra* p. ___.

4. Evelyn Nassuna, Women and Employment Discrimination in Uganda in the Formal Sector: Facing Challenges and Forging Change, *infra* p. ___.

5. Jacqueline Asiimwe, *Making Women's Land Rights A Reality in Uganda: Advocacy for Co-Ownership by Spouses*, 4 YALE HUM. RTS. & DEV. L.J. 171, 175 (2001).

6. *Id.*

7. *Id.*

8. Naome Kabanda, Women's Access to and Control Over Land in Uganda: A Tool for Economic Empowerment, (internal citations omitted) *infra* p. ___.

9. Naome Kabanda, Women's Access to and Control Over Land in Uganda: A Tool for Economic Empowerment, (internal citations omitted) *infra* p. ___.

land.[10] Kabanda also details continuing barriers to women's land ownership in postcolonial Uganda, including the system of "land titling," the widespread reliance on customary law that denies inheritance rights to women, and the inability to acquire land through direct purchase.

Because land is a significant form of collateral, women's lack of land ownership often makes it difficult for them to obtain loans and credit. Without access to credit, many women are unable to establish small businesses or petty trade activities. Similar to Kabanda's observations on this problem in Uganda, Gloria Ofori-Boadu argues that Ghanaian women's difficulty in obtaining credit is attributable to shortsighted colonial policies that underestimated the centrality of women's precolonial economic activities.[11] Sarah Lubega also describes a constellation of contemporary gender stereotypes in Uganda that consistently thwart women's efforts to obtain credit, establish and operate viable businesses, own land, and secure lucrative employment.[12]

Sex discrimination in the formal labor market, difficulties in obtaining loans and credit, and discrimination against women in land ownership constitute major hurdles for women seeking economic independence in Ghana, Uganda, and Tanzania. As the authors in this chapter demonstrate, their governments must take action to eliminate these barriers to women's economic empowerment. International human rights law compels such action, and the beneficiaries will not be women alone. With adequate women's rights reform, the entirety of the next generation born in these countries will be better fed, healthier, more educated, and better able to contribute to the long-term development needs of their societies.

Relevant International Human Rights Law

As described in chapter one, economic, social, and cultural rights have not traditionally enjoyed the same level of respect as civil and political rights, with some commentators even arguing that the former are nonjusticiable.[13] In the

---

10. *See* Nadia H. Youssef, *Women's Access to Productive Resources: The Need for Legal Instruments to Protect Women's Development Rights, in* WOMEN'S RIGHTS, HUMAN RIGHTS: INTERNATIONAL FEMINIST PERSPECTIVES 279, 281 (Julie Peters & Andrea Wolper eds., 1995).

11. Gloria Ofori-Baodu, Ghanaian Women, the Law and Economic Power, *infra* p. ___.

12. Sarah Lubega, Law Reform and Effective Implementation as the Means to Economically Empower Ugandan Women, *infra* p.___.

13. Shadrack B.O. Gutto, *Beyond Justiciability: Challenges of Implementing/Enforcing Socio-Economic Rights in South Africa,* 4 BUFF. HUM. RTS. L. REV. 79, 87 (1998) (describ-

past decade, however, human rights activists have emphasized the indivisibility and interdependence of the two types of rights,[14] elevating the status of economic, social, and cultural rights. In particular, women's human rights activists, recognizing the high percentage of women among the world's poor, have explored the human rights implications of severe poverty. In so doing, these activists have begun the difficult task of providing normative content to vaguely defined economic rights, such as the right to development.

Nowhere are the human rights dimensions of poverty more acute than in rural sub-Saharan Africa. The authors in this chapter explore many of the historical, social, and cultural forces that conspire against sub-Saharan women, excluding them from economic pursuits that might allow them to escape crippling poverty such as formal employment, land acquisition, and entrepreneurship. Although the international human rights law concerning economic, social, and cultural rights is, in many ways, less developed than other areas of human rights law, it does offer some hope for raising the standard of living for women and for ensuring that women reap the benefits of progress and development alongside their male counterparts.

Formal Employment

Many international treaties generally protect women's employment rights and women's right to nondiscrimination. This section merely offers a glimpse at some of the international human rights provisions that are relevant to the employment-related abuses that Nassuna and others identify in this chapter. Under a number of international treaties—including the International Covenant on Civil and Political Rights (ICCPR),[15] International Covenant on Economic, Social and Cultural Rights (ICESCR),[16] Convention on the Elimination of All Forms of Discrimination Against Women (CEDAW),[17] and the African (Banjul) Charter on Human and Peoples' Rights

---

ing the justiciability debate).

14. *See, e.g., Vienna Declaration and Programme of Action,* World Conference on Human Rights, U.N. Doc. A/CONF.157/23 (1993).

15. International Covenant on Civil and Political Rights, Dec. 16, 1966, art. 3 & 26, 999 U.N.T.S. 171, 174 [hereinafter ICCPR].

16. International Covenant on Economic, Social and Cultural Rights, Dec. 16, 1966, art. 3, 993 U.N.T.S. 3, 5 [hereinafter ICESCR].

17. Convention on the Elimination of All Forms of Discrimination Against Women, Dec. 18, 1979, art 1 & 2, 1249 U.N.T.S. 13, 16 [hereinafter CEDAW].

(African Charter),[18]—women have the right not to be discriminated against in the enjoyment of their rights. Because the ICESCR, for example, protects the right to work,[19] women must be permitted to enjoy the right to work without discrimination. Accordingly, governments must ensure that women are not subject to the employment practices that Nassuna describes as occurring in Uganda, such as the discrimination in hiring evidenced by the government itself and the rampant sexual harassment in public and private sector employment.

CEDAW also enshrines a range of employment-related rights, including the right to "the application of the same criteria [for men and women] for selection in matters of employment."[20] Women's human rights activists are exploring ways to use CEDAW to challenge discriminatory employment practices such as the Ugandan government's civil service hiring practices. CEDAW's prohibition against discrimination in employment and the ICESCR's requirement of "just and favourable conditions of work" provide additional ammunition to be used against sexual harassment in the African workplace. The CEDAW's Committee's General Recommendation No. 19 and the United Nations Declaration on the Elimination of Violence Against Women, both of which are discussed in the introduction to chapter two, condemn sexual harassment as a form of gender-based violence and an egregious form of discrimination against women.[21]

Activists may also draw upon the extensive work of the International Labour Organisation (ILO) to challenge discrimination against women in formal employment. The ILO has a long-standing commitment to the elimination of discrimination in employment, as embodied in its 1960 Discrimination (Employment and Occupation) Convention (ILO Convention 111).[22] In addition to having become parties to CEDAW, the ICCPR, the ICESCR, and the African Charter, Ghana and Tanzania have ratified ILO Convention 111,[23] making it applicable in both of those countries.

---

18. African Charter on Human and Peoples' Rights, June 27, 1981, art. 2 & 18(3), 1520 U.N.T.S. 246 [hereinafter African Charter].

19. ICESCR, *supra* note 16, art. 6 & 7, 993 U.N.T.S. at 6.

20. CEDAW *supra* note 17, art. 11 (1)(b), 1249 U.N.T.S. at 18.

21. Committee on the Elimination of Discrimination Against Women, General Recommendation No. 19 ¶¶ 22–23, U.N. Doc. HRI/GEN/1/Rev.1 at 87 (1994); Declaration on the Elimination of Violence Against Women, G.A. Res 48/104, U.N. GAOR, 48th Sess., 85th mtg. art. 2(d), U.N. Doc. A/RES/48/104 (1993).

22. Discrimination (Employment and Occupation) Convention (ILO 111), June 25, 1958, 362 U.N.T.S. 31 (entered into force June 15, 1960).

23. Ghana ratified ILO Convention 111 on April 4, 1961; Tanzania ratified it on Feb-

Land

The African Charter guarantees the right to property[24] and the enjoyment of that right "without distinction [based on]…sex."[25] Activists may use such guarantees in challenging laws that discriminate against women in the acquisition of land. CEDAW also protects women's rights in the "ownership, acquisition, management, administration, enjoyment, and disposition of property"[26] and requires states to ensure that rural women enjoy "equal treatment in land and agrarian reform."[27]

The general nondiscrimination principles embodied in the Universal Declaration of Human Rights, the ICCPR, the ICESCR, CEDAW, and the African Charter also provide support for challenges to discriminatory land acquisition policies ranging from systematized land allocation practices such as titling to customary inheritance practices that prohibit women from inheriting land. CEDAW, for example, requires states to eliminate discrimination against women "through all appropriate measures, including legislation, to modify or abolish existing laws, regulations, customs and practices…."[28] This broad obligation requires states not only to amend laws that are facially discriminatory toward women but also to strive to change cultural patterns that amount to discrimination.[29] The example of Ghana is illustrative here. Ghana's Constitution protects spousal property rights,[30] and its intestate succession law is gender neutral, referring to the inheritance rights of "spouses" without distinction between women and men.[31] In practice, however, widespread polygamy in Ghana undermines the gender-neutral application of the law, effectively discriminating against women, who must fight for what will ultimately be a

---

ruary 26, 2002.

24. African Charter, *supra* note 18, art. 14, 1520 U.N.T.S. at 248.

25. African Charter, *supra* note 18, art. 2, 1520 U.N.T.S. at 246.

26. CEDAW *supra* note 17, art. 16(1)(h), 1259 U.N.T.S. at 20.

27. CEDAW *supra* note 17, art. 14(g), 1249 U.N.T.S. at 20.

28. CEDAW, *supra* note 17, art. 2(f), 1259 U.N.T.S. at 16.

29. Article 5 of CEDAW provides further support for this, stating the following: "States Parties shall take all appropriate measures to modify the social and cultural patterns of conduct of men and women, with a view to achieving the elimination of prejudices and customary and all other practices which are based on the idea of the inferiority or the superiority of either of the sexes or on stereotyped roles for men and women…." CEDAW *supra* note 17, art. 5(a), 1249 U.N.T.S. at 17.

30. GHANA CONST. art. 22.

31. Intestate Succession Law, P.N.D.C.L. 111 (1985) (Ghana).

diminished share of "spousal" property.[32] CEDAW, among other conventions, therefore requires that Ghana remedy the de facto discrimination resulting from its polygamous inheritance scheme, which has a detrimental impact on women's ability to inherit self-acquired land along with other property.[33]

Credit and Lending

The freestanding nondiscrimination clause in the ICCPR, which is not limited in application to the specific rights acknowledged in that covenant, may be used to compel governments to eliminate discrimination against women in lending and credit schemes.[34] Similarly, CEDAW specifically obligates states parties to ensure that women enjoy—on an equal basis with men—"access to agricultural credit and loans."[35] Discussing the limitations African women face within formal lending structures, Nadia Youseff observes, "These constraints include high levels of illiteracy, lack of information about the availability of loans, and the unwillingness of many credit institutions to deal with new and small-scale borrowers who, in most cases, are women."[36] CEDAW's far-reaching obligation to use all appropriate measures, including legislation, to eliminate discrimination requires states parties to make lending and credit schemes nondiscriminatory in purpose *and* effect.[37] The Protocol to the African Charter on Human and Peoples' Rights on the Rights of Women in Africa, which is not yet in force, will also offer protection of women's right to equality in employment,[38] women's right to access and control over "productive resources

---

32. Jeanmarie Fenrich and Tracy E. Higgins, *Promise Unfulfilled: Law, Culture, and Women's Inheritance Rights in Ghana*, 25 FORDHAM INT'L L. J. 259, 288–89 (2001).

33. The scope of Ghana's 1985 Intestate Succession Law is limited to the deceased's "self-acquired" property rather than "lineage" property. Although land is often considered lineage property, to be managed by the village or clan elders, it may also be self-acquired property. *See id* at 288.

34. ICCPR, *supra* note 15, art. 26, 999 U.N.T.S. at 179.

35. CEDAW *supra* note 17, art. 14(g), 1249 U.N.T.S. at 20.

36. Youssef, *supra* note 10, at 284.

37. Article 1 of CEDAW defines discrimination as "any distinction, exclusion or restriction made on the basis of sex which has the effect or purpose of impairing or nullifying the recognition, enjoyment or exercise by women...on a basis of equality of men and women...." CEDAW, *supra* note 17, art. 1, 1249 U.N.T.S. at 16.

38. Protocol to the African Charter on Human and Peoples' Rights on the Rights of Women in Africa, art. 13, *at* http://www.africa-union.org/Official_documents/Treaties_%20Conventions_%20Protocols/Protocol%20on%20the%20Rights%20of%20Women.pdf (July 11, 2003).

such as land,"[39] women's right to inherit on an equal basis with men,[40] and women's right to equal access to credit.[41]

Conclusion

Human rights activists increasingly recognize the critical links between different types of human rights. Many women's human rights activists have identified women's economic rights, for example, as being essential to women's enjoyment of other fundamental human rights. Activists now understand that without resources for basic necessities such as food and clean water, most women will not concern themselves with the right to political participation. Activists understand that women with economic resources will have more options for escaping a violent family situation or greater opportunity to access basic health care. In this sense, economic rights are indivisible and interdependent with, among others, the right to be free from violence and the right to the highest attainable standard of physical health.

As the authors in this chapter demonstrate, gender stereotypes often operate to systematically exclude women from resource-generating activities. Several international human rights treaties require the governments that have ratified them to protect women's ability to engage in formal employment without discrimination, to acquire and control land, and to obtain credit for entrepreneurial activities. Through these financial opportunities, women will be able to meaningfully participate in their countries' developmental processes and contribute to the well-being of their families.

---

39. *Id.* at art. 19(c).
40. *Id.* at art. 21.
41. *Id.* at art. 19(d).

WOMEN AND EMPLOYMENT DISCRIMINATION IN UGANDA'S FORMAL SECTOR: FACING CHALLENGES AND FORGING CHANGE

Evelyn Nassuna

Introduction

By custom and circumstance, women are both the most vulnerable and the center of Uganda's social and economic development. Heavy responsibilities fall disproportionately on women, who have assumed new roles as wage earners in addition to their traditional role of taking care of the family. Much of women's service to the family and the community, however, is not quantified or given economic value. Their struggle for equal opportunities in the employment area is viewed by some, especially men, as an equality joke. Women's influence is not felt in policy. They do not enjoy equal opportunities with men. The persistent devaluation of women as workers permeates every corner of Ugandan society.[1]

---

1. In a staff meeting, employees asked an employer to explain the disparity in salary between a male employee and his female colleagues of similar qualifications and replied that, unlike the women, the man had a family to support. (This is the writer's personal experience.) A young woman was fired from her job with the World Bank in Uganda for becoming pregnant within three months of employment. She is currently unemployed and a single mother. THE NEW VISION (UGANDA), February 1, 2000. It was also reported that it is the bank's policy to fire female employees who become pregnant before serving two years. Moreover, most women are not informed about this policy until they become victims to this discriminatory policy. *Id.* Another pregnant woman was fired from an international bank, when management became aware of her condition during the bank's routine medical checkups. *Id.* These incidents represent only a small picture of the disparity

Employment Status of Women[2]

Women's Rates of Participation[3]

In Uganda, over 60 percent of men are in the labor force, and 53 percent of women are in the labor force.[4] The lower participation rates for females can, in part, be attributed to the underreporting of women's predominant economic activities because they are mainly confined to the domestic sphere with no direct monetary value accruing to them. In addition, women's low education levels and literacy rates prevent them from entering into formal, paid employment,[5] especially at higher levels. Employment participation rates for females below the age of twenty are slightly higher than those for men, attributed to and contributing to the higher school dropout rate for girls than boys.[6] In their twenties and thirties, women's marital roles inhibit their entry into and retention in the labor force.[7] Older women, by contrast, feel both freer and more compelled to work for income.[8]

In every field, women form the bulk of the least skilled and least well-paid workers.[9] Women were only 20 percent of the formal sector employees, of

---

in treatment of Ugandan women in the workplace on the basis of gender, irrespective of individual capabilities and responsibilities

2. Although this paper focuses on problems of women in the formal sector, it is important to acknowledge that no law establishes or outlines the rights of women in the informal sector and serious discrimination issues arise there that also warrant study and action. By the informal sector, the writer refers to women engaged in petty trade as well as the service sector. The law frequently criminalizes their work in the informal sector simply because it falls outside the established state and city regulations. Their work is rarely recognized in law and custom as valuable work.

3. Although gender disaggregated data is available, gaps still exist in information on many aspects of women's work. The last survey of employees in Uganda was conducted in 1968 and only covered current employees in the formal sector and hence could not technically be called a labor force survey. Since then, several attempts have been made to study the labor force, but they have not provided a proper analysis. Further study of women's circumstances is needed to best address the widespread problems they face.

4. GOVERNMENT OF UGANDA, WOMEN AND MEN IN UGANDA: FACTS AND FIGURES 41 (1998) [hereinafter WOMEN AND MEN IN UGANDA]. The term "labor force" can be defined to refer to individuals employed and unemployed.

5. *Id.* at 42

6. *Id.* at 42–43.

7. *Id.* at 42.

8. *Id.* at 42–43.

9. ANITA KELLES-VIITANEN, EMPLOYMENT PROMOTION OF WOMEN IN UGANDA: FROM

these only 26 percent were skilled workers.[10] Women in Uganda have lower educational levels than men and have been trained for gender-stereotyped careers, such as typing, and are therefore concentrated in the lower end of salary scale hierarchies.[11] For example, in the non-governmental sector, women were clustered in low-level occupations as agricultural workers (81.8 percent), clerks (.71 percent) and service and sales workers (6.4 percent).[12] Very few women made it to managerial positions (only one twentieth of a percent).[13] In management, there is silent resistance to women in positions of power because they are considered inferior and subordinate to men. Studies have indicated that negative attitudes toward women by those who hire constitute the major barrier to female advancement in management.[14]

Gender Stereotyping

There were even fewer managers and administrators (5.8 percent) in the public sector.[15] This has been attributed to the recruitment methods in the civil service that deliberately emphasize gender roles. Among other things, the application form requires the applicant to specify marital status and number of children. For men, a large number of children may be considered indicative of organizational and managerial skills, while in the case of the woman, a large family may be believed to demonstrate ineffectiveness.[16] Married women are not considered good candidates for training or promotion because it is assumed that their family obligations will interfere with work. Single women are not considered good candidates either as it is assumed that they may eventually marry and have children.

DISABLING TO ENABLING ENVIRONMENT, REPORT ON ILO/UNDP TSSI MISSION ON WOMEN'S EMPLOYMENT PROMOTION, at 11.

10. National Manpower Survey was conducted from 1988 to 1989 to study the characteristics and circumstances of skilled workers. Formal sector refers to women who take up paid employment in both the government and non-government sector. This does not include women employed in the informal sector, which includes women engaged in petty trade, agriculture, the service sector, and domestic workers.

11. KELLES-VIITANEN, supra note 9, at 19.

12. WOMEN AND MEN IN UGANDA, supra note 4, at 47.

13. Id. at 47.

14. P.B.M. Sezi, A Paper on Gender and Management, presented at Makerere University, 3.

15. KELLES-VIITANEN, supra note 9, at 19.

16. See Sezi, supra note 14.

Married working women are almost single-handedly responsible for child-care and domestic work. In this regard, Uganda is no different from other African countries. Child care facilities are nonexistent at the work place, and most working parents cannot afford private child care.[17] The Constitution guarantees maternity leave for most women in salaried employment, but the majority of working women are not aware of this constitutional right.[18] Even if they are aware of this right, women often lose their jobs when they get pregnant or give birth, and a new mother is torn between keeping her job and looking after a newborn.[19] Due to increased economic pressure, some new mothers choose to forego maternity leave.[20] Women are also coerced into forfeiting part of their meager salary each time they go for antenatal care in order to keep their jobs.[21]

Even when women's educational levels are similar to men's, women tend to be concentrated in jobs like teaching, nursing, and community development. In one study, the professional category (doctors, lawyers, engineers) included only 16.2 percent women compared to 79.9 percent men.[22] The Ministry of Education was the biggest employer of women civil servants, followed by the Ministry of Health.[23] The second largest female occupational category was in the elementary school teaching. These kinds of jobs—teaching, nursing, secretarial, support staff, and the like—offer limited opportunities to move to management levels. Jobs that have rapid career mobility, high status, weighty responsibilities, and more pay are dominated by men.

In the Uganda Public Service, men and women who occupy the same jobs get paid the same salary. When jobs are segregated by sex, however, "men's" jobs are routinely higher paying than "women's" jobs, reflecting the fact that the work of women is still less valued than that of men. Moreover, women are clustered in the lower level jobs, while men dominate the top management level positions.[24]

---

17. Bonnie Keller, Uganda Country Gender Profile 19–20 (1996).

18. Uganda National Council for Children, Equity and Vulnerability: A Situation Analysis of Women, Adolescents and Children In Uganda 171 (1994).

19. It is common for women to take maternity leave, only to return and be told that the job has been taken by somebody else, or if "lucky," return to a lower position than the one held prior to taking leave. See id. at 171.

20. Id. at 171.

21. The New Vision (Uganda), May 9, 2000, at 17.

22. See Kelles-Viitanen, supra note 9, at 15 (quoting Sylvia Tereka, Employment of Women in the Civil Service 148 (1988)).

23. 1987 Census of Civil Servants (Uganda).

24. Sezi, supra note 14, at 6.

Sexual Harassment

The Government of Uganda has acknowledged that "working women widely report sexual harassment at their work places."[25] Although it is a criminal offense to sexually assault someone, there is no law defining what sexual harassment is or providing a civil remedy for it.[26] Victims of sexual harassment are mostly young women; managers often pressure them for sex in return for employment or promotion.[27] "Horizontal segregation, vertical stratification, and income inequality of women compared with men in the workforce" make them more vulnerable to experiencing harassment.[28] Fear of losing a job makes workers vulnerable to abusive language, harassment, exploitation, and arrogance from employers.[29] Robin Phillips details the conditions these women face:

> Women often fear retaliation if they report inappropriate conduct and, as a result, rarely report sexual harassment. They are sometimes ashamed or embarrassed about their experiences or do not feel that their claims will be taken seriously. Even if a woman does report sexual harassment, it is often difficult to prove, because there are not always witnesses willing to provide information. Either the conduct oc-

----

25. MINISTRY OF GENDER, LABOR AND SOCIAL DEV'T OF UGANDA, THIRD COUNTRY STATUS REPORT ON THE CONVENTION ON THE ELIMINATION OF ALL FORMS OF DISCRIMINATION AGAINST WOMEN 43 (1999).

26. A report by the International Labor Organization has caused concern among MPs that a law prohibiting sexual harassment is necessary. No information on the creation of such a bill is currently available. *See Employers Lead in Sexual Harassment,* NEW VISION, (Kampala, Uganda), Dec. 31, 2002, *available at* http://allafrica.com/stories/200212310358 .html; *MPs Call for Law On Sexual Harassment,* THE MONITOR (Kampala, Uganda), Dec. 11, 2002, *available at* http://allafrica.com/stories/200212110310.html.

27. THE NEW VISION (Kampala, Uganda), Mar. 2, 2000, at 19.

28. CARLA SUTHERLAND, PREVENTION IS BETTER THAN CURE: SOME COMMENTS ON THE LAW OF SEXUAL HARASSMENT IN THE WORKPLACE IN SOUTH AFRICA, quoting CATHERINE MACKINNON, SEXUAL HARASSMENT OF WORKING WOMEN 9 (1979). "Horizontal Segregation" means that most women perform the jobs they do because of their gender, with the elements of sexuality pervasively implicit… "Vertical Stratification" means that women tend to be in low ranking positions, dependent upon the approval and goodwill of male superordinates for hiring, retention, and advancement. Being at the mercy of male superiors adds direct economic clout to male sexual demands. Low pay is an index to the foregoing two dimensions. It also deprives women of material security and independence, which could help make resistance to unreasonable job pressures practical.

29. THE NEW VISION (Kampala, Uganda), March 2, 2000, at 19.

curs when the two parties are alone or other employees are afraid that they will jeopardize their own jobs if they testify.[30]

Current Laws on Women's Employment

In theory, there is no legal impediment to the equal opportunity of women to employment: the Constitution itself prohibits discrimination on the basis of sex. In practice, however, various forms of gender discrimination persist.[31] The laws do not adequately address women's work-related problems in the formal sector. Current labor legislation has been designed to safeguard women's family and social roles by ensuring pregnancy protection and restricting women from employment in certain sectors of production considered incompatible with society's perception of women. None of this legislation addresses women's equality in the workplace.

Both the Employment Decree[32] and the Constitution[33] provide measures to protect pregnant workers. The Decree provides four weeks leave for a pregnancy-related disability without providing similar protection to a pregnant woman working for a family business.[34] The Constitution states "the employer of every worker shall accord her protection during pregnancy and after birth, in accordance with the law."[35] Men, however, are not similarly protected if they leave work in order to look after a wife recovering from childbirth or to provide child care.

Although sexual harassment violates the right to protection against sex discrimination[36] and is closely linked to the inequality that women face in the workplace, there is no law directly addressing the issue of sexual harassment. Sexual harassment degrades women and contravenes the Constitution, which provides that "no person shall be subjected to any form of torture, cruel and inhuman or degrading treatment or punishment,"[37] and it guarantees women "full and equal dignity of the person with men."[38] Furthermore, Parliament is

---

30. Robin Phillips, *Violence in the Work Place: Sexual Harassment, in* 1 WOMEN AND INTERNATIONAL HUMAN RIGHTS LAW, 260 (Kelly Askin & Dorean Koenig eds., 1998).

31. THIRD COUNTRY STATUS REPORT ON CEDAW, *supra* note 25, at 64.

32. Employment Decree (Decree no. 4 of 1975) (Uganda).

33. UGANDA CONST.

34. *See* Employment Decree (Decree no. 4 of 1975) (Uganda) §46.

35. UGANDA CONST. art. XL §4.

36. *See* Phillips, *supra* note 30 at 261.

37. UGANDA CONST. art. XXIV.

38. UGANDA CONST. art. XXXIII §1.

permitted to make laws to ensure the "right of persons to work under satisfactory, safe and healthy conditions."[39] Not only is women's equality jeopardized by harassment, but their mental and physical health and safety are jeopardized as well.

The lack of laws aimed at discrimination violate the government's obligations under the Constitution. More specifically, Article 40 provides that the state is obliged to guarantee to all its citizens the right to social justice and economic development and to "ensure that all Ugandans enjoy rights and opportunities including work and retirement benefits."[40] Similarly, the right to equality, including economic equality, is a critical part of the right to protection from sex discrimination.[41] The state is also mandated to enact laws to implement "policies and programs aimed at redressing imbalances in society" including those in the economic sphere,[42] and women are entitled to equal treatment with men, including equal opportunities in economic activities.[43] In addition, the state is to provide facilities and opportunities to "enhance the welfare of women to enable them to realize their potential and advancement"[44] and to ensure that their unique status and maternal functions are protected.[45]

The constitutional guarantee of equal opportunities in economic activities reaches situations in which women's wages are systematically discounted and women are denied equal pay for jobs of equal value (sometimes called "comparable worth"). The principle that women and men should receive "equal pay for equal work" without discrimination, provided for under Article 40(1)(b), has been read too narrowly to mean that only where a woman is doing precisely the same job as a man must she be paid the same salary.[46] The narrow

---

39. UGANDA CONST. art. XL.

40. UGANDA CONST. objective XIV.

41. UGANDA CONST. art. XXI §3. (defining discrimination to mean giving " different treatment to different persons attributable only or mainly to their respective descriptions of sex.").

42. UGANDA CONST. art. XXI §3. Discrimination under this article has been defined to mean giving " different treatment to different persons attributable only or mainly to their respective descriptions of sex."

43. UGANDA CONST. art. XXXIII §4.

44. UGANDA CONST. art. XXXIII §2.

45. UGANDA CONST. art. XXXIII §3.

46. An example is the U.S. Equal Pay Act, 29 U.S.C. §206(d), which has been narrowly interpreted by the Supreme Court. *See, e.g.,* Corning Glass Works v. Brennan, 417 U.S. 188 (1974); *see also* Shultz v. Wheaton Glass Co., 421 F.2d 259 (3d Cir. 1970), *cert denied,* 398 U.S. 905 (1970) (while "equal" work need not be identical, it must be "substantially equal").

interpretation fails to address the pay inequity suffered by women who are doing the jobs that are comparable to, or that involve the same skills as, jobs held primarily by men.

Models and Mandates for Change

A Basic Antidiscrimination Provision

Discrimination against women in the workplace takes many forms, from discriminatory hiring and firing to failure to promote women workers. Accordingly, a broad non-discrimination provision is a necessary foundation for protecting women's employment rights. Uganda should draw on the example of the International Labor Organization (ILO) Discrimination (Employment and Occupation) Convention,[47] which aims to promote equality of opportunity and treatment with respect to employment and occupation.[48] Other ILO instruments refer to groups or bases of discrimination in addition to gender or sex that may affect women, such as older workers, workers with family responsibilities, and married workers.[49] This Convention prohibits discrimination in access to vocational training, employment, and particular occupations, and in terms and conditions of employment.[50] Article 5 provides that special measures, protection, or assistance, such as affirmative action programs, provided for in other ILO conventions or recommendations shall not be deemed to be discrimination. By excluding affirmative action programs from the def-

---

Compare Corning and *Shultz with* Washington County v. Gunther, 452 U.S. 161 (1981) (Title VII's prohibition of compensation discrimination must be interpreted in light of the Bennett Amendment to Title VII (42 U.S.C. §703(h)) establishing the relationship between Title VII and the Equal Pay Act; Title VII is not limited to equal pay for the same work, as in the Equal Pay Act, in that it covers situations where there is "direct evidence" that women's wages were depressed because of intentional sex discrimination. At the same time, it does not go so far as to require equal pay for jobs of comparable worth in the absence of discriminatory intent.).

47. Convention No. 111 of 1958.

48. Article 1(a) of the convention defines discrimination as "distinction, exclusion or preference made on the basis of race, colour, sex, religion, political opinion, national extraction or social origin, which has the effect of nullifying or impairing equality of opportunity or treatment in employment or occupation."

49. Recommendation 162 of 1980, Older Workers Convention No. 156 of 1981, Workers with Family Responsibilities, and Convention No. 158.

50. Convention No. 111 of 1958, article 1(3).

inition of discrimination, the ILO specifically allows for programs designed to increase women's representation in the work force.

Sexual Harassment

Two types of conduct in the workplace have generally been prohibited in countries that offer legal protection against sexual harassment:[51] quid pro quo sexual harassment[52] and harassment that generates a hostile work environment.[53] In the United States,[54] sexual harassment is not expressly prohibited by a specific legislative provision, but rather, the Equal Employment Opportunity Commission (EEOC)[55] published guidelines identifying harassment on the basis of sex as a violation of the basic non-discrimination provision, Title VII.[56]

---

51. Countries that offer legal protection against sexual harassment did not recognize this cause of action until the 1980s and early 1990s. *See* Phillips, *supra* note 30, at 259.

52. The most commonly recognized form of sexual harassment is quid pro quo. It normally arises where an employer conditions a benefit or term of employment, such as continued employment, promotion, or increased compensation on participation in some sexual activity. Quid pro quo harassment arises where "submission to or rejection of such conduct by an individual is used as the basis for employment decisions affecting the individual." *EEOC Policy Guidance on Current Issues of Sexual Harassment*, Daily Lab. Rep., March 28, 1990, at E-1. Thus if a manager makes sexual favors a condition of a woman's continuing employment he has committed quid pro harassment.

53. Sexual harassment also occurs when an individual experiences unwelcome sexual advances, requests for sexual favors, or other verbal or physical conduct of a sexual nature where such conduct has the purpose or effect of unreasonably interfering with that individual's work performance or creating an intimidating, hostile, or offensive working environment. 29 C.F.R. § 1604.11 (a).

54. I will primarily be using the United States as an example in this section because this country has the most developed case law. While other countries have adopted statutes, either civil or criminal, to prohibit sexual harassment, they have not yet decided cases under these statutes. Phillips, *supra* note 30, at 260.

55. The EEOC was created by the Congress of the United States to enforce the Civil Rights Act of 1964. *See generally* 42 U.S.C. §2000e (1999).

56. The Guidelines defined sexual harassment as "unwelcome sexual advances, requests for sexual favors, and other verbal or physical conduct of a sexual nature," where:

1) submission to such conduct is made either explicitly or implicitly a term or condition of an individual's employment;

2) submission to or rejection of such conduct by an individual is used as the basis for employment decisions affecting such individual; or

3) such conduct has the purpose or effect of unreasonably interfering with an individual's work performance or creating an intimidating, hostile or offensive working environ-

In the United States, many suits have revolved around the question of whether the conduct was welcome[57] and whether harassment was sufficiently severe and pervasive that it affected the terms of employment.[58] In determining whether sexual harassment is actionable, it is important to acknowledge the power differential in the relationship between employee and employers or supervisors. The power differential causes employees to feel forced or coerced to engage in conduct in which they would not otherwise participate.[59] Fur-

---

ment.

See 29 C.F.R. § 1604.11 (a) (1990).

57. *See* Phillips, *supra* note 30, at 263. Phillips includes the details of Meritor Savings Bank v. Vinson, 477 U. S. 57 (1986): "The plaintiff in Meritor, Michelle Vinson, worked in a bank and rose through the ranks from teller trainee to assistant branch manager. Shortly after her probationary period as a teller-trainee, Vinson's supervisor invited her to dinner and asked her to have sexual relations with him at a motel. Initially, Vinson refused his advances but eventually agreed because she was afraid she would lose her job. Over the next three years, the supervisor demanded sexual relations numerous times. He touched her and fondled Vinson in front of other employees, followed her into the women's restroom, exposed himself to her, and forcibly raped her on several occasions. (*Id.* at 60–61.) Vinson notified the supervisor that she was taking sick leave for an indefinite period of time. The bank eventually fired her. Vinson sued both the bank and the supervisor claiming that she had "constantly been subjected to sexual harassment" by the supervisor during her four years of employment. The court ruled that the fact Vinson had voluntarily engaged in a sexual act does not preclude a finding that the supervisors conduct was "unwelcome" and thus, sexual harassment. The court stated, "the correct inquiry is whether Vinson by her conduct indicated that the alleged sexual advances were unwelcome, not whether her actual participation in sexual intercourse was voluntary."

58. *See* Phillips, *supra* note 30, at 263. The issue whether harassment that creates a hostile environment is actionable as sexual harassment was discussed for the first time by the United States Supreme Court in 1986, in the case of Meritor Savings Bank v. Vinson, 477 U. S. 57 (1986). (Harassment rising to the level of creating a hostile work environment affects a "term or condition of employment" based on the employee's sex and thus violates the law's general prohibition of sex discrimination.) In addition, the United States Supreme Court in 1993 developed standards for determining whether the harasser's conduct is severe as to affect a term, condition, or privilege of employment. In Harris v. Forklift Systems, Inc., 510 U.S. 17 (1993), the Supreme Court held "that the offensive conduct need not have caused serious physical or emotional injury to the plaintiff. Therefore evidence of psychological injury is not necessary to establish a claim for sexual harassment based on a hostile and abusive work environment. "Title VII comes into play before harassing conduct leads to a nervous breakdown. A discriminatory abusive work environment, even one that does not seriously affect employees' psychological well-being, can and often will detract from employees' job performance, discourage employees from remaining on the job, or keep them from advancing in their careers…." Phillips, *supra* note 30, at 265.

59. *See* Phillips, *supra* note 30, at 264.

thermore, as some intermediate courts in the United States have recognized, the average man and the average women may not respond the same way to certain conduct and a realistic standard to evaluate whether a work environment is hostile or abusive for a female plaintiff in a sexual harassment case should be developed.[60]

Equal Pay and Non-Discrimination Standards

The Equal Remuneration Convention and its supplementary Recommendation No. 90 adopt standards governing equal pay for work of equal value without discrimination on the basis of sex. This principle applies to all aspects of an employee's remuneration, not only wages or salaries, but also any additional emoluments whatsoever,[61] intended to include cases where men and

---

60. Phillips includes the following discussion: "*Ellison v. Brady,* 924 F.2d 872, 879 (9th Cir. 1991). In *Ellison,* the Ninth Circuit Court of Appeals rejected the reasonable man standard and adopted a reasonable woman standard for sexual harassment cases, stating that "a sex blind reasonable person tends to be male biased and tends to systematically ignore the experiences of women." *Id.* at 872. The court in *Ellison* recognized that the average woman may be offended by conduct that the average man does not find objectionable. The court explained as follows:

We realize that there is a broad range of viewpoints among women as a group, but we believe that many women share common concerns which men do not necessarily share. For example, because women are disproportionately victims of rape and assault, women who are victims of mild forms of sexual harassment may understandably worry whether a harasser's conduct is merely a prelude to violent sexual assault. Men who are rarely victims of sexual assault, may view sexual conduct in a vacuum without full appreciation of the social setting or the underlying threat of violence that women may perceive...

In order to shield employers from having to accommodate the idiosyncratic concerns of the rare hypersensitive employee, we hold that a female plaintiff states a prima facie case of hostile environment sexual harassment when she alleges conduct which a reasonable woman would consider sufficiently severe and pervasive to alter the conditions of employment of employment and create an abusive working environment. *Id.* at 878–79.

The U.S. Supreme Court later articulated the following formulation: "...the objective severity of harassment should be judged from the perspective of a reasonable person in the plaintiff's position, considering all circumstances." *See* Oncale v. Sundowner Offshore Services, Inc., 523 U.S. 75 (1998).

See Phillips, *supra* note 30, at 266–67.

61. Art. I §a of Convention No. 100 provides: "the term 'remuneration' includes the ordinary, basic or minimum wage or salary and any additional emoluments whatsoever payable directly or indirectly, whether in cash or in kind, by the employer to the worker and arising out of the worker's employment."

women are paid the same pay but other benefits are unfairly given to men alone.[62] This definition is wider than that offered by the Constitution of Uganda, which only refers to "equal pay for equal work."[63] This language has sometimes been taken to mean only that a woman doing the same job as a man must be paid at the same rate. This interpretation is too narrow and fails to address the lower pay of women who are doing jobs that are comparable to, or that involve the same skills as, jobs held primarily by men. The notion of "work of equal value" as opposed to "equal work" avoids indirect limitations in the implementation of the equity principle by allowing work to be evaluated based on, for example, the tasks and duties involved and energy expended.[64] Although determining work of equal value may raise difficult questions as to how to compare different types of work, the Convention and Recommendation recommend that each state party adopt an objective appraisal system on the basis of work to be performed.[65]

Balancing Work and the Family

Maternity rights are very important for women balancing work and family, and Uganda has recognized this by providing for maternity leave,[66] and ratifying the 1919 Maternity Protection Convention.[67] This Convention applies to women working in a wide variety of settings: industrial, non-industrial, and agricultural. The Convention also applies to women working at home.[68] Twelve weeks of maternity leave are provided for under Convention No. 103 and the entire leave may be taken after the birth of the child.[69] A compulsory leave of six weeks is provided for after birth.[70]

---

62. *See* Valerie Oosterveld, *Women and Employment, in* WOMEN AND INTERNATIONAL HUMAN RIGHTS LAW, *supra* note 30, at 376.

63. UGANDA CONST. art. XL § 1(a).

64. NICOLAS VALTICOS & GERALDO W. VON POTOBSKY, INTERNATIONAL LABOR 210 (1995).

65. Convention No. 100 of 1951, art. III (I), and ¶ 5 of Recommendation No. 90 of 1951.

66. UGANDA CONST. art. XL § 4.

67. This was revised in 1952 by Convention No.103.

68. Convention No. 103 of 1952, Maternity Protection, art. I § 1. The scope of this convention is wider than its predecessor, because the 1919 Convention did not include women wage earners employed at home or in domestic work in private households.

69. *Id.* at art. III §§ 2 and 3.

70. *Id.* at art. III § 3. In addition, the EEOC in its guidelines on sex discrimination, has recognized discrimination on the basis of pregnancy and childbirth as sex discrimination.

Workers with Family Responsibilities, Convention No. 156 of 1981, aims to create equality of opportunity and treatment for men and women with family responsibilities where such responsibilities restrict the possibilities of participating or advancing in economic activity.[71] The Family Responsibilities Convention not only applies to men and women with child care responsibilities but also to workers with "responsibilities in relation to other members of their immediate family who clearly need their care or support."[72] Under the Family Responsibilities Convention, the state is to enable persons with family responsibilities to engage in employment without being subject to discrimination and, to the extent possible, without conflict between their employment and family responsibilities.[73] States are obligated to take all measures compatible with national conditions; to enable workers with family responsibilities to exercise their right to free choice of employment; to take account of their needs in terms and conditions of employment and in social security; to take account of the needs of these workers in community planning; and to develop and promote community services, such as child care and family facilities.[74]

Finally, the employment of a worker must not be based on the sex of the employee, pregnancy, family responsibilities, or absence from work during maternity leave.[75]

Conclusion: Strategies for Change

Constitutional guarantees and international labor standards, found primarily in the ILO conventions and recommendations and the Women's Convention, create a fairly comprehensive web of protective and nondiscrimination rights for women. Applying these standards, the government should put in place laws and policies that define how women's rights should be interpreted

---

See 29 C.F.R. § 1604.10 (a) (1999). Similarly, under § 1604.10(b), the EEOC has included "disabilities caused or contributed to by pregnancy and childbirth" in its definition of employment-related disabilities. Moreover, Title VII itself was amended in 1978 to clarify that discrimination on the basis of sex included discrimination on the basis of pregnancy. 42 U.S.C. §2000e(k) (1994).

71. Convention No. 156 of 1981, Workers with Family Responsibilities, art. I § 1.

72. *Id.* at art. I § 2.

73. *Id.* at art. III § 1.

74. *Id.* at art. IV § a, b and art. V § a, b.

75. *See* Convention No. 158 of 1982, Termination of Employment, art. V § d, e, and Convention No. 103 of 1952, Maternity Protection, art. VIII.

and establish institutions at the national level charged with upholding these rights.

Uganda should recognize sexual harassment as a form of violence against women and should work toward its reduction or elimination by providing various avenues of legal redress. Legal remedies should be accompanied by policies promoting awareness and public education to assist in preventing the occurrence of the problem.[76] As Phillips points out:

> The remedy most women prefer is simply for offensive conduct in the workplace to stop. A well constructed and implemented plan within the company may prevent sexual harassment or stop offensive conduct before it rises to the level of actionable sexual harassment. By treating the problem fairly and directly, a company may avoid costly, destructive litigation and maintain a healthier, more productive work environment.[77]

The government, private industry, and organizations must work together to implement strategies to protect victims, punish the perpetrators, and prevent the problem.

NGOs, particularly women's organizations and others committed to solving this problem, have a key political role to play. Women's efforts in cooperation with men must continue, in policy bodies and agencies at the national level and at the grassroots level, to influence government action to ensure the right to work without discrimination. In addition, women must realize that discrimination will likely continue until they are equally represented in the decision making process. Unless women are able to have their voices heard in discussions concerning the national budget development and implementation, women's needs and priorities will not be realized. Women must play an integral role in this effort to launch a new historical process, a more humane culture, and an economy that makes sense for all.

---

76. For information about preventing sexual harassment, *see* Mark I. Schickman, *Sexual Harassment: The Employer's Role in Prevention*, THE COMPLEAT LAWYER, Winter 1996, at 24.

77. Phillips, *supra* note 30, at 285.

WOMEN'S ACCESS TO AND CONTROL OVER LAND IN UGANDA: A TOOL FOR ECONOMIC EMPOWERMENT

Naome Kabanda

Introduction

Land remains one of the main sources of livelihood for the majority of Ugandans who live in rural areas and use their land for farming, grazing, hunting, picking, and selling wild fruits; brick making; and using and selling firewood. Because land may be loaned, rented, or sold in times of hardship, it provides a measure of financial security. Land is also an inheritable asset, serving as a basis for wealth and security for future generations. Like most developing countries, agriculture is the backbone of Uganda's economy accounting for 44 percent of the Gross Domestic Product (GDP) in 2002.[1] Most of Uganda's agriculture involves small farms, which depend on family labor, primarily that of women and children.[2] Despite the fact that women play such a central role in agriculture, only 7 percent of women own land.[3]

---

1. U.S. CENT. INTELLIGENCE AGENCY, THE WORLD FACTBOOK 2002, at 530 (2002), *available at* http://www.cia.gov/cia/publications/factbook/geos/ug.html (last visited July 10, 2003). Most of Uganda's export earnings come from the agriculture sector, with coffee alone accounting for 21 percent of all exports in 2001. COUNTRIES OF THE WORLD AND THEIR LEADERS YEARBOOK 2004, at 1727 (Karen Ellicott ed., 2003). Agricultural products also provide food for subsistence, and internal sale, as well as raw materials for local and foreign industries. UGANDA LAND ALLIANCE, CO-OWNERSHIP OF LAND BY SPOUSES 22 (2000).

2. Women contribute more than 70 percent of labor in agricultural production and work between 12–18 hours per day. UGANDA MINISTRY OF GENDER, LABOR AND SOCIAL DEV., THE NATIONAL ACTION PLAN ON WOMEN 5 (1999). Women who head households face even greater responsibilities in terms of workload. ABBEY J. SEBINA-ZZIWA, GENDER PERSPECTIVES ON LAND OWNERSHIP AND INHERITANCE IN UGANDA 6 (1995).

Because land underpins the economic, social, cultural, and political lives of the people in Uganda, ensuring that women have access to this major resource is necessary for sustainable development. Economic studies have shown that inequitable distribution of wealth may negatively impact on a country's economic growth. [4] Therefore, some argue, that reducing land concentration and providing for the more equitable distribution of wealth may be more effective in promoting economic prosperity than relying solely on agricultural growth.[5] The benefits from such measures will not only reduce poverty among women but also greatly benefit children through better education, nutrition, food security, and living standards for the whole family. Women, in particular, will likely enjoy other benefits, such as a reduction in their economic dependence on men, more stable homes, and less domestic violence—or at minimum—greater opportunities to escape violent relationships.

Status of Women and Land in Uganda

Land Tenure System in Uganda's Pre-Colonial Period

In pre-colonial Africa, land was generally held under customary land tenure. The early traditional society in Uganda was socially organized based on clans,[6] and everyone had access to land providing water, firewood, salt licks for their animals, and pastures.[7] Because land was the primary means of livelihood and an asset for everyone's use, it was collectively owned, but apportioned to family units under the authority of the male head of family. Land under communal ownership would never be transferred.

Under this system of customary land holding in pre-colonial Africa, everyone, including women, had exclusive rights to land use and control. By and

---

3. UGANDA MINISTRY OF GENDER, LABOR AND SOCIAL DEV., *supra* note 2, at 5.

4. Julian Quan, *Land Tenure, Economic Growth and Poverty in Sub-Saharan Africa, in* EVOLVING LAND RIGHTS, POLICY AND TENURE IN AFRICA 31, 40 (Camilla Toulmin & Julian Quan eds., 2000).

5. *Id.*

6. SEBINA-ZZIWA, *supra* note 2, at 3. Clans were comprised of single families headed by a male. A clan would consist of people who traced their origin from a common ancestor.

7. JENNIFER OKUMU WENGI, WEEDING THE MILLET FIELD: WOMEN'S LAW AND GRASSROOTS JUSTICE IN UGANDA 100 (1997).

large, women's land rights in pre-colonial Africa were better protected than today. For example, community values that protected women demanded that, upon marriage a woman would be allotted land for her exclusive use, together with fruits that came from her labor.[8] Such land remained under the woman's use and control until her death.[9]

Land Tenure System during the Uganda Colonial Period

The British policy was intended to develop the country into a peasant economy, producing cheap agricultural raw materials for export to the European markets.[10] The British introduced leasehold,[11] freehold,[12] and *Mailo* (private estates),[13] which were deeply rooted in individual, predominantly male ownership and indirectly abolished traditional communal land holding. As the customary system was the main system through which women accessed land, with its demise, women's land rights also vanished.

8. SEBINA-ZZIWA, *supra* note 2, at 7.

9. *Id.*

10. H.F. MORRIS & JAMES S. READ, UGANDA: THE DEVELOPMENT OF ITS LAWS AND CONSTITUTION 26 (1966). Uganda was not intended for European settlement as was proposed for Kenya.

11. The Crown Lands Ordinance in 1903 established a framework for allocation of Crown land by the Governor. *Id.* at 45; *see also id.* at 338–39.

12. Freehold land tenure under the new Land Act, 1998 (Tanz.) is still one of the land tenure systems recognized in Uganda. It is defined as the holding of registered land in perpetuity subject to statutory and common-law qualifications. The Land Act, 1998, pt. I, §2 (Tanz.). It is amazing to note that although African natives could not lease land for more than 99 years, the white settlers were given an unlimited period to hold land, and were exempted from payment of rent and other fees.

13. " *Mailo*," deriving from the English word "mile," is a local term used to describe a particular form of land owning. Mailo land was the land allotted to the then-chiefs and other gentry in Buganda (Central Region) at the time of colonization under the famous Uganda Agreement of 1900. *See* SEBINA-ZZIWA, *supra* note 2, at 8 n.2. "Mailo land" as defined today in the Land Act, 1998 (Tanz.) means the holding of registered land in perpetuity and having roots in the allotment of land pursuant to the 1900 Uganda Agreement and subject to statutory qualifications. The Land Act, 1998, pt. I, §2 (Tanz.). Mailo land consisted of private estates allotted in the central region and some areas in Eastern Uganda to the king of Buganda, chiefs, royals, and British agents who helped in the colonization process under the famous Uganda Agreement of 1900. These grants lasted until 1916 when they were stopped because; (i) the colonialists had finalized their settlement in the country, and (ii) due to the fact that many groups came up thereafter contesting such grants.

The new system meant that land was no longer freely accessible. As a result, struggles for land started, not only between colonialists and nationals, but also between higher and lower chiefs and other interest groups. The new system demanded that tenants on *Mailo* land pay rent to their landlords, a system that was expensive for many people and comparable to feudalism in England. The colonial system of land administration created a class of rich land owners; those who could afford land titling through the purchase and lease of land. The poor farmers who were unable to pay for land titling became secondary land users who could not claim ownership, making it more difficult for women to have access to land.

With the introduction of new systems of land ownership came the introduction of cash crops such as coffee and cotton and a wage economy with taxation and employment. Commercialization of land increased and the price of land became more and more prohibitive. While women were left to produce food crops to meet the subsistence and survival needs of the family, men gained more control over cash crop production. Women, therefore, were deprived of any disposable income.[14] As land titling increased, men, as heads of households, became the property owners and women were left without any land.[15] Government leases stipulated that landowners could only keep leased land if they abided by the lease agreements, including using land for defined purposes. Landowners became more responsive to government demands by growing cash crops in order to keep the land, further diminishing women's traditional use rights. Because women had no control over cash crops, everything, including their labor, became dictated by men.

Land Tenure System in Uganda during the Post-Colonial Period

Uganda's post-colonial period did not see any major changes in land administration. The plural legal system created by the British allowed custom-

---

14. UGANDA WOMEN'S NETWORK, WOMEN AND LAND RIGHTS IN UGANDA: A DOCUMENTATION OF WOMEN'S VIEWS AND SUGGESTION'S ON LAND ISSUES IN UGANDA AND THE PROPOSED LAND BILL 10 (1997).

15. The most recognized beneficiaries for land under the British Government were royals and notables (wives and mothers of royals) who received land titles (deeds), on large portions of land, which they later kept selling to the landless at a prevailing market rate. In Uganda, there were a few women notables who benefited under that system and to date, they are the well-known landowners in society. However, in accordance with the customs of the time, the notables never transferred land to their daughters.

ary laws to coexist with statutory land law, resulting in many conflicts. Through enactment of the Land Reform Decree in 1975, the government sought to abolish all feudal and private tenure by converting these properties into public land owned by the government.[16] The result, however, was to create more confusion than before, and to make the position of customary tenants even worse. Under the Land Reform Decree, customary tenants became "tenants at the will of the state."[17] Unlike before, when customary tenants could remain on land with minimal rights, the Decree allowed a lessor to give sixty days notice to a customary tenant to quit his land, regardless of what investments had been made on the land.

Women also faced challenges relating to the new system of land management. One major challenge was the new system's focus on titling. Because women had only secondary rights as land users, they risked eviction by title holders. Land managers would often surface without notice to make sure the land was being used according to the lease terms.[18] These surprise inspections meant that women could not grow income generating crops as they had in the past.

As the bureaucracy in land matters became entrenched, corruption became a factor. As one commentator notes, "[c]onflicts and contradictions became endemic in land use decision-making," resulting in insensitivity to the ordinary land using public.[19] Land managers, not courts, were solving most disputes over land. As a result, the substantive rights of land users most often ended up unresolved or unrealized.

---

16. *See* HWO Okoth-Ogendo, *Legislative Approach to Customary Tenure and Tenure Reform in East Africa, in* EVOLVING LAND RIGHTS, POLICY AND TENURE IN AFRICA, *supra* note 4, at 123–24.

17. *Id.* at 126. Under this law, any person occupying land as a customary land tenant faced the risk of being evicted by the Government or individuals holding a leasehold title from the state when the land was leased. *Id.* Ugandans became "tenants at will" of the state since the state was the owner of all former crown land—a position that was considered worse than that during the colonial period.

18. Women under this system were more disadvantaged, because the terms of the lease included a requirement that the land be used for the specific use as defined in the lease agreement for a specific period of time. Land managers had to inspect the developments on the land to confirm that the lessee was in compliance with the lease before the lease could be extended to a further term. Where the lessee was found in breach of the terms, the lease would be withdrawn. Women could not, therefore, be seen growing private crops on the land (just in case the land managers surfaced without notice to inspect the lease and found unacceptable developments), as they could originally do under the customary system.

19. *See* Okoth-Ogendo, *supra* note 16, at 128.

The legislation had been designed to protect landowners and not land users.[20] Many women did not have enough education to understand how the new system of land management worked. As commercialization of land increased and individualization became more entrenched in the system, other communal rights such as the right to collect firewood, fruits, and forest products were similarly diminished. Women had to walk further distances to fend for the family. The colonial period resulted in the concentration of land in the hands of a few powerful people, and brought an end to many of the collective user rights, most of which benefited women. The post-colonial governments did not revive these rights.

Cultural Factors that Determine a Woman's Access to and Control over Land in Uganda

Uganda's statutory laws do not bar women from holding land. In fact, the Constitution guarantees women the right to property.[21] Although statutory laws tend to provide more protection to women, Uganda's pluralistic legal system allows customary law and statutory law to apply alongside each other and rural communities are more likely to apply customary law. Under customary law, land is acquired, belongs to, and is managed by a patrilineal (male) group.[22] Women's rights to access and use land depend on their social ties to men, either as daughters, sisters, wives, widows, or mothers resulting in loss of land rights upon termination of these social relationships, for example

---

20. The colonial land administration put up new systems at various levels to govern and administer land in Districts. However, most of these officers lacked training and were influenced by political functionaries, all of whom had different interests in land. The end result was corruption and inefficiency. *Id.* Titles ended up in the hands of only the rich, who could force their way through all of the bureaucracy.

21. UGANDA CONST. ch. 4, art. 26 (1), *available at* http://www.government.go.ug/constitution/index.php (last visited July 10, 2003).

22. Land in a family transfer takes three forms, however in all these three forms, girls are not considered as beneficiaries. The first instance is where a father transfers land to his son upon reaching the age of marriage. This is done by mere showing of the son his portion of the land, customarily done with no paper transfers. The second way is usually where a woman is shown her piece of land upon divorce by her husband. Although this is very rare, it may happen where the woman has older children, especially boys, who press for a share of their mother's contribution. The third way of land transfer is through inheritance—the deceased's parcel of land is transferred to his children or heirs. Florence Butegwa, *Using the African Charter on Human and Peoples' Rights to Secure Women's Access to Land in Africa, in* HUMAN RIGHTS OF WOMEN 495, 496–97 (Rebecca J. Cook ed., 1995).

upon divorce, death, or marriage.[23] Women primarily access land through marriage.[24] A married woman has access to land only so long as her relationship with her husband is good. Where a polygamous husband marries another wife, land must be shared among all the wives.[25] When a woman's husband divorces her or dies intestate, she often loses access to the land.

Inheritance could provide another route of access to land for women, but statutory protection is limited,[26] and under customary law, women have no legally recognized land inheritance rights. The clan-appointed male heir[27] inherits the property, including the land and matrimonial home. Although the heir is supposed to take care of the family, including the widow, the widow is left in an extremely vulnerable position since she must rely on the good will of the heir and other male family members.[28] In polygamous marriages, the distribution of family land is highly influenced by marriage and birth order and often only the widow whose son is the heir retains user rights. In cultures in which wife inheritance is predominant and bride price is high,[29] a widow

---

23. Camilla Toulmin and Julian Quan, *Evolving Land Rights, Tenure and Policy in Sub-Saharan Africa, in* EVOLVING LAND RIGHTS, POLICY AND TENURE IN AFRICA, *supra* note 4, at 1, 24. Under the customary land tenure system, women's access to land is attained mostly through marriage, or through their relationship to a male person, for example, the father, son, uncle, or brother of the husband where one is a widow.

24. Customarily, a married woman is expected to fulfill gendered roles of sustaining the household; consequently, her land use rights are increased but without necessarily increasing her rights of control or ownership. *See, e.g.,* Maria Nassali Ssemakula, Co-ownership of Land by Spouses 3, Presentation at the Public Dialogue on Co-Ownership by Uganda Land Alliance, Grand Imperial Hotel, Kampala, Uganda (Sept. 1999).

25. UGANDA WOMEN'S NETWORK, *supra* note 14, at 9.

26. The Succession (Amendment) Decree 1972, § 28(1) (Uganda) provides for widows to inherit 15 percent of their husbands' estate where there are lineal descendants, and 50 percent of the estate where there are no lineal descendants. However, these provisions only apply to non-customary land and only if the husband dies without leaving a will.

27. Usually the eldest son of the deceased.

28. Denying girls the right to inherit land stems from the notion that girls are "visitors to the home" who are on their way to marriage, and thus their rights to land lie with their husbands' families. The culture presumes that every woman has to marry and leaves no room for single women or for those whose marriages fail.

29. For example, the Iteso, Kiga, Ankole, Alurs, Karamajong, Acholis, and Langis tribes demand a large bride price of over Uganda Shillings 10,000,000 or U.S. Dollars 5000 (equivalent to 100–200 cows, goats, and precious clothes), and a woman cannot leave her new family unless her parents can return the bride price. In such communities, a woman is treated as a chattel because of the amount of money paid to marry her. As a result of this, all her rights are extinguished. For example, she looses complete control over her body and

may be kept by the deceased's family.[30] If she refuses to be "inherited," her land rights are automatically revoked. In other communities, widowhood results in total dispossession of land and the matrimonial home, as widows are expected to go back to their parents' home.

Direct purchase is one way women may acquire land despite cultural norms. The law of contract governs acquisition of land under this system and contractual capacity is based on age alone.[31] Theoretically, women have access to land on equal footing with men.[32] Women remain at a significant disadvantage, however, because most women live in rural areas, with little or no income, and land at market prices is often prohibitively expensive. Men and boys may freely acquire family land through inheritance and can dispose of it through sale. In contrast, girls and women are expected to buy land they would have been entitled to under a fair system of inheritance. In exceptional cases when women are able to purchase land, sexist stereotypes sometimes cause women to register land in male names (e.g., a son or brother). When married women have independently purchased land, they are often forced to register it in their husband's names or to hold it in secret, to save their homes from instability or even abandonment.[33] In some areas of the country, it is taboo for women to own land.[34]

The Current Laws Relating to Land in Uganda

The 1995 Uganda Constitution

The land tenure system inherited during the colonial period prevailed until 1995 when Uganda adopted a new Constitution that vested land in the people.[35] The categories of land tenure as introduced by the colonial administra-

---

the right to decide on reproductive matters. She cannot decide on the number of children she will have or even when to have children. Where such a woman is "unfortunate" and produces only girls, she has to continue producing until she gets a son.

30. Typically the widow is taken in as a wife by the husband's brother, cousin, or father.

31. Butegwa, *supra* note 22, at 495, 498–99.

32. *Id.*

33. *See* UGANDA WOMEN'S NETWORK, *supra* note 14, at 10–11.

34. *Id.* at 8 (giving Lira, in the Northern part of Uganda, as an example of one such community).

35. Art. 237(1) of the 1995 Ugandan Constitution provides that "[l]and in Uganda belongs to the citizens of Uganda and shall vest in them in accordance with the land tenure systems provided for in this Constitution." *See* note 21.

tion, however, were retained.[36] Although the tenure system remains the same, the government was able to reinstitute customary land holding under the Constitution.[37]

The Ugandan Constitution recognizes the equality of all persons.[38] In order to engender equality, the Government is authorized to use affirmative action.[39] Article 26(1) of the Constitution provides that every person has the right to own property individually or in association with others. Article 31(2) further provides that parliament shall make appropriate laws for the protection of the rights of widows and widowers to inherit the property of their deceased spouses.

The Land Act 1998: A Decentralization Tool for Land Management

For the first time since independence, the Government realized the need to correct the imbalances in land ownership between men and women and enacted a new land law.[40] The Land Act of 1998 was enacted pursuant to Article 237(9) of the 1995 Constitution and sought to provide for a sound land management system through decentralization.[41] The 1998 Land Act established

---

36. *Id.* at art. 237(3) (providing that "[l]and in Uganda shall be owned in accordance with the following land tenure systems- (a) customary; (b) freehold; (c) mailo and; (d) leasehold").

37. *Id.* at art. 237(4) providing that citizens owning land under customary tenure may acquire certificates of ownership in a manner prescribed by Parliament, and that land under customary tenure may be converted to freehold land ownership by registration).

38. *Id.* at art. 21(1) (acknowledging equality between the sexes before the law, in all spheres of political, economic, social, and cultural life); *id.* at art. 21(2) (providing that no person shall be discriminated against on grounds of sex); *id.* at art. 31(1) (providing equal rights between men and women have during and after a marriage).

39. *Id.* at art. 32(1) (providing that the state shall take affirmative action in favor of groups marginalized on the basis of gender or any other reason created by history, tradition, or custom, for the purpose of redressing imbalances, which exists against them); *see also id.* at art. 33(4) (mandating provision of facilities and opportunities necessary to enhance women's welfare to enable them to realize their full potential); and *id.* at art. 33(6) (prohibiting any laws, cultures, customs, or traditions which are against the dignity, welfare, or interest of women are prohibited).

40. Hon. Baguma Isoke, Minister of State for Lands, Presentation at the Public Debate on Co-Ownership of Land by Spouses 2, Sheraton Hotel (April 11, 2000).

41. *Id.*

new land management institutions with required levels of female representation.[42] The Land Act was intended to be a tool for strengthening security of tenure and redressing the historical imbalances in land ownership between privileged and marginalized groups.[43] To the extent that women are already customary tenants on the land, their rights are subject to recognition and may be registered under the new land law. Women's land rights as newcomers, however, are likely to remain at risk, because the new law does not in any way change the land holding systems for family land and clan land.

In 2002, Parliament introduced a bill to amend the Land Act.[44] The Parliament finally passed this Bill in July 2003, but it remains to be seen whether the President will sign it into law.[45] If enacted, the amendments will be helpful to women because they recognize traditional rights to use land.[46] More importantly, the Bill includes a clause on "security of occupancy on family land"

---

42. Institutions include the Uganda Land Commission, comprised of five people, one of whom must be a woman. The Land Act, 1998, §§ 47–48 (Uganda); District Land Boards, comprised of not less than five people, one-third of whom must be women. *Id.* §§ 57–58; Parish Land Committees, compromised of four people, one of whom must be a woman. *Id.* §§ 65–66; and district, sub-county, and urban land tribunals. *Id.* §§ 77, 81–82. At the sub-county level, these tribunals must include a woman as one of their three members. *Id.* § 81(2). This is a significant development because it gives women the opportunity to hear and intervene in land disputes. However, land disputes are always very technical, and sometimes require a lot of expertise even for the lawyers themselves. The challenge, therefore, lies in the ability to find fair, educated women to sit on these tribunals.

43. Isoke, *supra* note 40.

44. The Land (Amendment) Bill, 2002 (Uganda), introduced on July 16, 2002, sponsored by the Hon. Richard Nduhuura (Minister of State for Trade and Industry), *available at* http://www.parliament.go.ug/billtrack/ (last visited July 16, 2003).

45. Mercy Nalugo, *House Passes New Land Bill*, THE MONITOR (Kampala, Uganda), June 19, 2003, http://allafrica.com/stories/200306190457.html (last visited July 16, 2003).

46. Part 3(e) of the Bill (as introduced) defines a "third party right" as:

A right, interest, privilege or liberty which a person has or possesses, either indefinitely or for life or for a lesser period under customary law, common law or equity to use or occupy for a specific purpose or for a specific period all or part of the land of a landowner or to prevent a landowner from exercising any right, interest, privilege or liberty in, on, under or over his or her land, and includes but is not limited to, an easement, a profit a prendre, a usufructuary right, a restrictive covenant, a right arising out of a share-cropping agreement, a right of a person as a member of a group to go on to and to gather and use the fruits of communally owned land and a right to use land which a spouse may acquire by virtue of marriage, but does not include a lease or sub-lease.

The Land (Amendment) Bill, 2002, pt. 3(e) (Uganda).

which grants each spouse the right to have access to and to live on family land, and requires the consent of both spouses before the land can be sold or transferred.[47] Although this does not go so far as to grant women co-ownership of family property, it is an important achievement for women's rights advocates.

Recommendations

Only a multi-dimensional approach can achieve progressive change. The following recommendations provide only a skeletal outline of an approach to increase women's land rights in Uganda:

- The Land Bill, as originally drafted, incorporated a co-ownership clause whereby women would co-own the land on which they resided and from which the family derived their living.[48] The co-ownership provision, however, was inexplicably omitted from the final version of the Act. Co-ownership of family land would ensure protection of women's inheritance rights, as it would guarantee women a share in the property, thereby reducing the economic dependency of wives. As we have seen, in June 2003 the Parliament passed an amendment granting women security of occupancy on family land. The President should assent to this law immediately and the government should work towards its swift implementation. Meanwhile, efforts must continue to ensure incorporation of a full co-ownership provision into the law.

---

47. *See* Gerald Businge, *Did Women Activists Tactfully Sneak Co-Ownership into the New Land Bill?*, New Vision (Kampala, Uganda), July 1, 2003, *available at* http://allafrica.com/stories/printable/200307010228.html (last visited July 16, 2003).

48. When the Uganda Land Bill was first drafted, a broad coalition of NGOs advocated for the inclusion of provisions which would strengthen women's land ownership rights, including an explicit provision for co-ownership of land by married couples. Although such an amendment was introduced and passed in Parliament, the amendment was left out of the final act due to technical revisions, becoming known as the "lost clause." Advocates have been active on the issue ever since. For example, on International Women's Day 2000 (March 8), hundreds of Ugandan women marched to demand the reinstatement of the "lost clause." *See* EQUALITY NOW, UGANDA: EXCLUSION OF WOMEN FROM LAND OWNERSHIP—THE "LOST CLAUSE" (2000), *available at* http://www.equalitynow.org/english/navigation/hub_ph01_en.html (last visited July 16, 2003); UGANDA LAND ALLIANCE, PRESS BRIEF ON CO-OWNERSHIP, Dec. 12, 2000, *available at* http://www.oxfam.org.uk/landrights/ULAco-own.rtf (last visited July 16, 2003).

- Advocates should bring test cases in the Constitutional Court arguing that discriminatory property laws and practices violate the Constitution and violate women's human rights more generally.[49]
- Activists should engage in open discussions with customary and religious authorities to encourage the gradual adaptation of customary rules. Rather than seeking to override, dismantle, or ignore customary law, activists should work to gradually modify customs. Education and understanding at the rural level, where customary law continues to play an important role, is necessary to ensure the implementation of modern statutory law and to improve the overall status of women.[50]
- It is necessary to make people, especially public and judicial officials, aware of the new laws through awareness campaigns, public education, seminars, and aggressive use of the media.
- Women need initiatives to increase the access to credit, to train them in modern methods of farming, and to provide them with technical advice on the preservation of the environment. Women need a nationwide program that guarantees them access to information and education on all issues concerning their lives and development. Women must be given sufficient support to assert their rights and must resist strong societal pressure to relinquish them. Only through a comprehensive law reform, public education, and empowerment program will women begin to truly enjoy their rights to the land and reap the benefits that stem there from.

---

49. This is one of the techniques that has helped American women reach where they are today. Ugandan Advocates and women activists need to prepare more often for such cases, as part of public campaign and sensitization. Even if the judgment comes out against women, advocates could appeal to international bodies using relevant international instruments including, African Charter, ICCPR, ICESCR, or CEDAW to which Uganda is a party.

50. Thea Hilhorst, *Women's Land Rights: Current Developments in Sub-Saharan Africa*, *in* EVOLVING LAND RIGHTS, POLICY AND TENURE IN AFRICA, *supra* note 4, 182, 195–96.

GHANAIAN WOMEN, THE LAW AND ECONOMIC POWER

Gloria Ofori-Baodu

Introduction

Economic empowerment of women enhances the economic stability of families, increases women's self-esteem, enables them to take advantage of legal rights and participate in the political sphere, and contributes significantly to the economic strength of countries. For an individual woman, economic independence forms the basis for enjoying all her other fundamental liberties: "Money may not buy happiness, but it can certainly help to buy freedom. The ability to earn money means the ability to say no. It's an ability that does more than give financial freedom—it gives you self-respect."[1] Women's economic empowerment, however, is hampered by a lack of access to capital resources. The Deputy Governor of the Bank of Ghana, Nana Amma Yeboaa, Obaapanyin of Akuapem, said that women should aim to enhance their economic well-being, but women's ability to participate effectively in sociopolitical and economic development is "hampered by poor or no access to financial resources in the form of formal credit."[2]

Economic Empowerment of Women in Ghana: Background and Current Developments

History of Women's Economic Independence

Historically, women in most cultures in Africa have been economically independent from their male counterparts, even enjoying great economic pres-

---

1. Dr. Sonya Friedman, *Decide Your Way to Adulthood: 7 Goals for The Grown-Up Woman*, WOMAN'S OWN February, 1996, at 36–37.
2. Eleanor Pratt, *Exhibition on Women in Development*, GHANAIAN TIMES, June 21st, 1995, at 1.

tige. Generally, grasslands peoples rely on crops raised and controlled by women. Specific examples of women's economic independence abound. Ghana market women along the southeastern coast of Ghana hold an extremely important customary right to make contracts independent of men.[3] Asante women are independent even in marriage.[4] Because they see the bond between themselves and their children as more binding and lasting than any marriage covenant, these women usually maintain households separate from their husbands and tend to depend on themselves as the source of their families' survival.[5] Wealthy Yoruba women rejected all forms of subordination and spent their wealth in ways similar to male chiefs, "by acquiring followers, showing generosity to a large number of people and obtaining titles for themselves and their supporters."[6] They also received grandiose oriki (great eulogies).[7]

As a native of West Africa and akan-speaking peoples, I must emphasize that women in my culture have enjoyed status in society equal with their men. Women in their personal capacity, without the need for consent and concurrence of their husbands, can acquire and own property, both movable and immovable, and upon their death bequeath their property to their matrilineal family or whomsoever they will. Women may also inherit the property of both males and females in their family. Due to the matrilineal succession of most Akan cultures, lineages in families are traced from women ancestors.

---

3. Claire Robertson, *Comparative Advantage: Women in Trade in Accra, Ghana And Nairobi, Kenya, in* African Market Women and Economic Power: The Role of Women in African Economic Development 106 (Bessie House-Midamba & Felix K. Ekechi, eds., 1995).

4. *See generally* Gracia Clark, Onions Are My Husband: Survival and Accumulation by West African Market Women (1994).

5. *See generally id.*

6. House-Midamba & Ekechi, *supra* note 3, at 35 (1995).

7. House-Midamba & Ekechi, *supra* note 3, at 35–36 (1995). Part of the oriki of Efunsetan, a rich lady of Ibadan, Nigeria who died in 1874 illustrates the respect and even awe with which such women were regarded: "Efunsetan, Iyalode. One who has horses and rides them not. The child who walks in a graceful fashion. Adekemi Ogunrin! The great hefty woman who adorns her legs with beads Whose possessions surpass those of the Aare…One who has bullets and gunpowder, Who has the gunpowder as well as guns, And spends money like a conjurer, The Iyalode who instills fear into her equals." *Id.*

British Colonial Policy

The British, unfamiliar with the role of women in African societies, under-estimated women's importance when colonizing the Ashantis in Ghana. In 1900, hoping to suppress rebellion, the British deported King Prempeh I of the Ashanti Kingdom to the Seychelles Islands with all male Royals. Yaa Asantewaa, the Queen Mother, immediately declared war on the British, leading her army into battle. The British forces were shocked to discover a female leading the Ashanti army. Yaa Asantewaa was playing her traditional role, for in the Ashanti and Akan-speaking areas the Queen mother's role is on par with, if not superceding, that of the chief.[8]

Similarly, the colonial government failed to notice or appreciate the economic autonomy women enjoyed and from which they contributed to the welfare of their families and society in general. In Ghana, for example, the colonial government failed to understand that women formed a sizeable majority of farmers, providing a large quantity of the country's food, and that women processed and distributed foodstuffs across the country. Because of this grave oversight, the colonial administration did not support and enhance the activities of these women, which had a detrimental effect on the overall economic development of Ghana. While the colonial government granted agricultural credits and training schemes to their male counterparts, women farmers were relegated to the informal sector and starved of the requisite resources for expansion. Although women had historically formed the majority of traders, banking institutions directed access to credit for expansion of businesses to expatriate trading companies and male-owned businesses. Women, thus deprived of resources, were limited to the small-scale sectors of the economy.

In the field of education, the policies of colonization hampered the existing equality between men and women. British colonial policy favored the formal education of boys in areas like economics and the sciences, training them for well-paid jobs and top management positions in the formal colonial structure. Women, on the other hand, were encouraged to enter the low-income fields of elementary school teaching, cookery, needlework, nursing, and secretarial work.

---

8. DAVID SWEETMAN, WOMEN LEADERS IN AFRICAN HISTORY 41 (1984).

The Marketplace

Despite colonization, women continued with their traditional economic pursuits in the areas of trading and retailing of imported goods, and cultivating, processing, and marketing of farm produce. The economic ventures that women undertook, included but were not limited to, the following: soap-making; gari (cassava-granules) processing; coconut processing; extraction and processing of groundnut, palm and kernel oils; pottery; tie-dyeing and designing cotton fabrics; dress-making; hair-dressing; basketry weaving; beads-making and designing; pito (local gin) brewing; decorating calabashes; poultry-keeping; vegetable gardening; fish-smoking; bread-making; kenkey (corn-dough balls) making, and other food processing activities.

The marketplace was and continues to be the domain of women. Traditionally, the market was the central place where people bought and exchanged goods and services. It served as the society's grocery store, shopping center, and the base for every service in the society including the pharmacy, educational, and cultural exchange center, and the travel port. The women are referred to as "market women."

Urban centers developed with the advent of colonialism. Some of the women who moved from the rural areas took up petty-trading. They branched out from petty trading to retailing, buying goods such as cloth, groceries, and other consumer items from the European and Lebanese merchant companies. These women often made a substantial profit and used it to supplement the household income and support the education of their children. Some of the women were the sole breadwinners for their families.[9]

Women's economic activities, though grossly overlooked by the colonial government, were of such importance that in the struggle for independence, women were the major players in the organized boycotts of Syrian and European stores that led to the riots of 1948 and sped up the process of independence. The Convention Peoples Party, which won the pre-independence elections, saw the importance of harnessing the power of women, particularly the market women. The party established a women's wing, made up of these economically independent women, to canvass and campaign for the party and win the votes of their families and the mass of the Ghanaian people.

9. Takyiwaa Manu, Law and the Status of Women in Ghana 8–9 (1984).

The Post-Colonial Experience

The Legacy of Colonialism

The post-colonial government continued the colonial policy of overlooking the role that Ghanaian women's economic activities had played and could play in increasing the country's economic development. There were no streamlined laws to formally define and enhance women's economic participation. Credit sources continued to elude these women since the financial institutions, dominated by male and British trained management, continued to pursue male-oriented policies in their lending activities. In addition, most women had no acceptable forms of security. Although some had properties, often their title had not been perfected in compliance with the provisions of land title registration, which was based on the common law and was a legacy of British colonial rule. Financial institutions saw these women, despite their successful economic activities, to be high-risk borrowers.

Denied credit and other forms of financial assistance, many women found it difficult to inject new capital into and expand their businesses. Gradually, women's active participation in the economic domain, which had been cultural and historic, became relegated to the informal sector. There were no policy provisions made for them in the formal banking and finance sector. They instead had to rely on informal sources of credit such as individual moneylenders, their friends and relatives, and their own personal savings. Their businesses, unable to expand, remained in the ambit of sole proprietorship and small-scale entrepreneurship. Economic legislation, which necessarily affected women's economic activities, failed to address such issues, ignoring the women who were major actors in the market place.

Problems with Existing Economic Legislation

Some economic legislation that could have had a favorable impact on Ghanaian women's economic activity has been passed. It has fallen short, however, because the government failed to consult with women in the drafting processes, employed only men to carryout schemes, and underfunded potentially helpful programs.

The Wholesale Fish Marketing Act,[10] which received Presidential assent on January 3, 1963, deals with demarcation of fish marketing zones. The fish industry in Ghana is governed by gender roles: the men go fishing, but once they reach the shores their role ends and the women take over. Women sell and preserve fish and other sea species and handle distribution to the hinterlands. Because women play the dominant role in fish mongering, an act demarcating zones for wholesale fish marketing should have incorporated and reflected women's input. Generally, the Act provides for demarcation of specified fish marketing zones, creation of regulations for the establishment, organization, management, and operation of any wholesale fish market, and the imposition of charges for fish sold, transferred, or stored in the market. All duties are charged to the Minister. Since women market and distribute fish, the law should have expressly provided for the Minister to consult with the leaders of the women fish sellers associations in making any regulations for establishing and managing wholesale fish markets.

The Agricultural Credit and Co-operative Bank Act[11] was passed to provide credit for developing farms, renting materials for agricultural business, purchasing equipment and services, and providing warehousing facilities on favorable terms and conditions to farmers. The statute recognized the previous lack of credit resources for farmers and recognized that farmers had to rely on borrowing from moneylenders at cutthroat interest rates. It sought to review and regulate moneylenders' credit terms to farmers and to provide for a moratorium on interest payments on prior loans to the agricultural sector. The government showed its commitment to agriculture by including on the Bank's board membership two representatives of the United Ghana Farmer's Co-operatives. The Bank was also mandated to conduct training and research, including research on agricultural credit, marketing of agricultural produce, and agricultural credit cooperative societies. The Bank, however, was male-oriented in its outlook, despite the fact that women constituted the majority of farmers.[12] The Agricultural Credit Officers, who were mostly male, selected mostly male farmers as beneficiaries of the bank's credit and training resources. In addition, the requirement of security restricted women's access to credit because women usually did not have the forms of security acceptable to the bank (landed property with registered title).

Since 1992, the Bank, renamed the Agricultural Development Bank (ADB), has, with the assistance of the International Fund for Agricultural Development (IFAD), embarked on a form of affirmative action to give an increased

---

10. Wholesale Fish Marketing Act (Act No. 156 of 1963) (Ghana).

11. The Agricultural Credit and Co-operative Bank Act (Act No. 286 of 1965) (Ghana).

12. EMBASSY OF THE REPUBLIC OF GHANA, THE PROBLEMS OF WOMEN, 31ST DECEMBER WOMEN'S MOVEMENT REPORT (1995). In Ghana, women produce 90 percent of food crops, and approximately 70 percent of the various raw materials for agro-industry.

percentage (60 percent) of loans to women farmers.[13] The ADB has recognized that women head about 35 percent of households and that most processing and marketing of agricultural produce, which the fund supports, are traditionally undertaken by women. In addition, ADB and IFAD have increased recruitment of female credit and technical officers to assist women farmers because the women farmers tend to identify closely with other women. This is a remarkable step in recognizing the traditional role of women in farming communities and an effort to economically empower them, even though such a policy was embarked upon after twenty-seven years after the bank's establishment.

The Co-operative Societies Decree,[14] like the Act establishing the ADB, was designed to provide more credit and other assistance for local businesses. The decree establishes Registered Business groups to assist each other financially. It provides for loans to be granted to members of registered cooperative societies from a common source of funding to which registered societies contribute. In addition, the Act provides for shares and deposits of members to be charged as security for loans, with security requirements less stringent than those of banks. The government showed its commitment to creating avenues for credit to businesses by giving a right to appeal to the Commissioner for Labor and Social Welfare for any cooperative society whose registration under the provisions of this statute was refused.[15] Activities of Business groups registered as members and financed by the cooperative societies include disposal and sale of agricultural produce, animal husbandry, handicraft, and fishing, most of which are performed by women.

The small size of the credit operations of the cooperatives societies, however, prevent the statute from having a wide impact on the economic activities of women, even after a 1986 amendment permitted cooperative societies to operate as banks.[16] Moreover, credit grant functions of cooperative soci-

---

13. The report by the ADB/IFAD credit coordinator indicates that since the commencement of the rural credit scheme in 1992, ADB had as of June 30, 1994, disbursed a total of 1,802.7 million cedis to 1220 groups comprising 13,322 beneficiaries of which number 8,183 or 61.4 percent were women farmers. Their share of the total amount was 1,105.7 million cedis (*i.e.*, 61.3 percent). J.K. DEBRAH, THE IFAD RURAL CREDIT SCHEMES IN GHANA 8 (1994).

14. The Co-operative Societies Decree, 1968, N.L.C.D. 252 (Ghana).

15. The Co-operative Societies (Amendment) Decree 1968, N.L.C.D. 292 (Ghana), empowered any co-operative society whose registration under the provisions of this statute was refused, to appeal to the Commissioner for Labor and Social Welfare.

16. The Co-operative Societies (Amendment) Law, 1986, P.N.D.C.L. 158, brought these

eties were not streamlined until the 1986 amendment (eighteen years later), undoubtedly limiting the statute's effectiveness for all of its members, including women. If the credit functions had been streamlined earlier, co-operative society operations would have had an increasing impact on members over the years and an affirmative policy to benefit women entrepreneurs could have been established in the process.

Government Recognition of Women's Entrepreneurial Efforts

Although successive governments and donor agencies have made efforts to promote women's entrepreneurial development through various forms of economic legislation, capital investment, and technical assistance, much still needs to be done to affect the majority of Ghanaian women, who still struggle to sustain their traditional role in the country's economy.

In 1970, the Progress Party[17] established the Small Business Credit Scheme to provide organized credit on reasonable terms to operators in the informal sector.[18] Because a large percentage of Ghanaian women entrepreneurs work in the informal sector, this scheme, unlike earlier ones, enhanced women's economic independence. The government of the National Redemption Council (NRC)[19] continued this positive trend and enacted the Ghanaian Enterprises Development Decree,[20] establishing the Ghana Enterprise Development Commission (GEDC). The GEDC, which offered financial assistance and technical support to the small business sector, benefited women entrepreneurs. In recognition of the United Nation's International Year of the Woman, the NRC promulgated the National Council on Women and Development (NCWD) Decree.[21] The statute, which came into effect on April 8th, 1975, established a council consisting of twenty persons (fifteen of whom had to be women) to advise the government on matters relating to the full integration of women in national development at all levels; to examine and evaluate the

---

banks under the rules of the Banking Act of 1970 (Act 339 of 1970) (Ghana).

17. The Progress Party governed from 1969 to 1972.

18. KWAME NINSIN, THE INFORMAL SECTOR IN GHANA'S POLITICAL ECONOMY 75 (1991).

19. The National Redemption Council governed from 1972 to 1976.

20. Ghanaian Enterprises Development Decree, 1975, N.R.C.D. 330 (Ghana).

21. National Council on Women and Development Decree, 1975, N.R.C.D. 322 (Ghana).

contribution of women in the economic, social, and cultural fields; to advise the government on specific areas where participation by women might be strengthened or initiated; and to devise a program for the continuous review and evaluation of women's integration in the total development effort at local, regional, and national levels. To show the government's commitment to advancing women's issues, the statute also provided that representatives of major government ministries in the country would serve on the Board.[22] Since coming into effect, the NCWD has had a favorable impact on the economic prospects of Ghanaian women. The Council has stressed income-generating projects for women such as the Gari Processing Factory at Mafi-Kumase and the Potash Processing Factory at Kwamoso.[23] It has also organized research and training seminars on women's economic issues. In performing its advisory role to government, the NCWD has compiled many reports, the most significant being the Women's World Banking Report that led to the incorporation of the Women's World Banking Ghana Ltd.[24] The Bank had "as its major objective to act as a catalyst to facilitate access of women to organized credit through the offer of guarantees to lending institutions on behalf of women entrepreneurs seeking financial assistance."[25] The Women's World Banking Report now provides technical assistance to its clientele and, through its subsidiary Mutual Assistance Susu Limited (MASU), grants micro-loans to small-scale business owners.

When the government of the People's National Party (PNP)[26] came to power, small businesses continued to receive attention. The National Board for Small Scale Industries Act[27] established the National Board for Small Scale Industries (NBSSI), which had goals similar to the defunct Small Business Credit Scheme and GEDC. The NBSSI was mandated to identify types of small-scale industries in the country; to assist the Minister responsible for In-

---

22. These ministries included Education, Health, Labor, Social Welfare & Co-operatives, Agriculture, Economic Planning, Foreign Affairs, Information, Finance, Attorney-General's Dept., and the Public Services Commission. A subsequent amendment to this Statute substituted the membership of the Establishment Secretariat for the Public Services Commission.

23. Both projects funded by the United States Agency for International Development.

24. The WWBG was formed on January 27th, 1983.

25. NATIONAL COUNCIL ON WOMEN AND DEVELOPMENT, ANNUAL REPORT 70–71 (1980–84).

26. The People's National Party governed from 1979 to 81.

27. The National Bond for Small Scale Industries Act (Act No. 434 of 1981) (Ghana).

dustries in the development and support of small-scale industries; to implement policies in relation to small-scale industries duly approved by the government; to monitor utilization of funds, to control inflow and outflow of foreign aid and foreign loans granted to small-scale industries; and to identify constraints imposed on small-scale industries respecting high taxation, lack of credit, lack of borrowing facilities, and high rates of interest. The PNP lost power shortly after the National Board for Small Scale Industries Act passed, but the succeeding government of the Provisional National Defence Council (PNDC)[28] saw to the setting up of the NBSSI in 1985. The Board, having identified finance as a persistent problem facing small-scale industries in Ghana, established a revolving fund valued at 80 million cedis to assist small-scale business operators obtain raw materials for their businesses. Presently the Board administers its own credit schemes and has formulated a policy that at least 40 percent of its available credit should be directed to women. This measure is in response to various studies and statistics on women's participation in economic activity in Ghana, the importance of which can no longer be overlooked. So far about 42 percent of the total clientele of the Board are women and their repayment performance has been good.[29]

Other Efforts at Enhancing Women's Economic Activity

Not all of the efforts to enhance women's economic activities are government initiated. One private effort is the World Bank initiative "Ghana: Private Small and Medium-Size Enterprise Development (fiscal 1989);" the project's principal objective is to support private small and medium-size enterprise development. The project's achievements include the channeling of resources through the Women's World Banking (WWB) to provide more technical assistance and entrepreneurial training for women and also to improve their access to institutional credit.[30] The Danish International Development Agency (DANIDA) has also been supportive by providing capital to the WWB to assist the entrepreneurial development and expansion of women owned businesses.[31] The enactment of the Non-Banking Financial Institution Law[32] has

---

28. The Provisional National Defence Council governed from 1981 to 1992.
29. Laurencia Tetteh, Address at the Center for National Culture (June 23, 1995).
30. WOMEN IN DEVELOPMENT, CREDIT AND ENTREPRENEURSHIP 22 (1990).
31. Kwesi Biney, *Women's World Banking Steps Up Activities*, BUSINESS CHRONICLE, Apr. 22 – May 5, 1996, at 6.
32. Non-Banking Financial Institution Law, 1993, P.N.D.C. Law 328 (Ghana).

enabled the establishment of non-bank financial institutions to assist women in mobilizing and saving their cash deposits, obtaining credit resources, leasing facilities, and providing technical and entrepreneurial training. These institutions include the Citi Savings & Loans Co. Ltd. Ghana, and MASU, the subsidiary company of the WWB. Their operations, however, are still young and limited and thus have not yet had a widespread effect on women in Ghana.

Another significant effort for women throughout the African continent is in the planning stages. The African woman's access to adequate resources to maintain her historical economic autonomy has been elusive. For this reason, a group of women bankers and economists from countries on the continent met in Kampala, Uganda, in August of 1994. The purpose of this meeting was to develop the modalities for the establishment of an African Bank for Women. Obaapanyin Nana Amma Yeboaa, Deputy Governor of the Bank of Ghana, was named Chairperson.[33] The proposal involves the establishment of a woman-owned Commercial Bank with branches in all African countries. Although the Bank's services would be open to the general public, its primary purpose is to finance women's economic activity on the African continent. The proposal, however, is in its formative stages. How soon it will materialize and how effectively it will contribute to the economic empowerment of women on the continent remains to be seen.

Economic Empowerment of Women in Ghana: Legal Mandates

Constitution of the Republic of Ghana

Ghana prohibits all forms of discrimination under Article 17(2) of the Constitution of the Republic of Ghana, 1992.[34] The Constitution also permits Par-

---

33. At the meeting, the following executives were appointed:

Obaapanyin Nana Amma Yeboaa, the Deputy Governor of the Bank of Ghana, as chairperson; Mrs. Bernadetter Yadi Sukho of the Departmente Credit, Bank of Africa, Mali, as Vice-Chairperson; Mrs. Christine Guwatudde of the Ministry of Women in Development, Culture and Youth, Uganda, as Rapporteur.

34. The prohibition on discrimination on the basis of sex is consistent with Ghana's obligations under the Convention on the Elimination of Discrimination Against Women. On July 17, 1980, Ghana became one of the fifty-seven signatory countries.

liament to enact laws to implement policies and programs aimed at redressing social, economic, or educational imbalance.[35] It is therefore appropriate for Parliament to pass laws to ensure that women and men are given equal attention and support in generating income, accessing credit, and participating in entrepreneurial skills training programs. The Constitution specifically supports working mothers, providing for paid maternity leave and day care for preschool children.[36] Women entrepreneurs need to ensure the care and safety of their children while they conduct business. Likewise, they are equally entitled to training in entrepreneurial skills, technical assistance, and other forms of training that will help them improve their economic position.[37]

Draft African Platform for Action

In preparation for the 1995 United Nations Fourth World Conference on Women, the Draft African Platform for Action was adopted by African countries that attended the 5th African Regional Conference in November 1994 at Dakar, Senegal. One of the objectives of the Draft African Platform for Action is "[t]o ensure the full participation and empowerment of women and girls in society in order to make full use of all human resources in the struggle against poverty" through equal access by women to economic opportunities.[38] This provision has persuasive force that can also serve as a basis for urging further action by the Ghanaian government.

Beijing Proposals

At the Fourth World Conference on Women in Beijing in September 1995, government commitments presented in plenary speeches showed that many countries were committed to creating an enabling environment for the economic empowerment of women. The proposals included:

---

35. GHANA CONST. art. XVII §4(a).

36. "(1) Special care shall be accorded to mothers during reasonable period before and after child-birth; and during those periods, working mothers shall be accorded paid leave.

(2) Facilities shall be provided for the care of children below school-going age to enable women, who have the traditional care for children, realize their full potential." GHANA CONST. Art. XXVIII.

37. "(3) Women shall be guaranteed equal rights to training and promotion without any impediments from any person." GHANA CONST. Art. XXVIII.

38. Draft African Platform for Action Vol. 3 ¶83(c). adopted at the 5th African Regional Conference on Women, Nov. 16–23 , 1994, at Dakar, Senegal.

Eliminating all laws that discriminate against women in economic activities; guaranteeing loans for women; implementing employment programs targeting women; creating a women's bank to increase women's access to credit; creating a special development fund to finance women's projects in agriculture and business; establishing financial credit institutions for women's small businesses; expanding existing credit supplies and income generation programs for women; intensifying training of rural women and giving them more access to credit; involving NGO financial intermediaries to increase women's access to credit and reducing the poverty and powerlessness of women.[39]

Ghana was among the governments that pledged their commitment to the above proposals. Considering that Ghana ratified the Convention on the Elimination of All Forms of Discrimination Against Women (CEDAW), incorporated CEDAW provisions in its Constitution, and pledged its commitment to advancing women's economic rights, the Ghanaian government should take all appropriate measures to ensure that the above goals are achieved.

Recommendations

Recognizing the Importance of Women's Economic Role

Women's economic activity must become a priority for policy makers. Since women play a dominant role in agricultural production, food processing, and the sale and distribution of goods and services, economic measures that address their needs will not only enable them to perform their traditional role in the formal sector, but also enhance the performance of the Ghanaian economy as a whole. In order to avoid repeating the mistakes of its predecessors, the Parliament of Ghana should consider the input of women when enacting economic legislation as women are the major economic practitioners in the Ghanaian market. The legislature should solicit women's input when passing laws that affect an area dominated by women. In particular, any bill affecting agriculture in Ghana must have the input of women at the drafting stage as women are the bulk producers of agricultural produce in the country.

---

39. Government Commitments Presented in Plenary Speeches At the Fourth World Conference on Women.

Increasing Women's Access to Credit

Women's access to credit from formal credit institutions remains a problem. The Ghanaian government should provide specialized banks to meet women's credit needs. These banks should not require any stringent pre-loan criteria such as a good credit history. The government may also require the commercial banks to set up a specialized package for lending to these women at subsidized interest rates below the market value. The government can reimburse the banks for the subsidies. The package can also include a moratorium on interest payments for these women.[40] A Women's Business Assistance Agency can also undertake studies and prepare feasibility reports for these women to enhance their opportunities to obtain credit from the formal sector.

The government should also implement affirmative action programs to enhance women's access to credit. Parliament should amend the Co-operatives Societies Decree,[41] establishing more credit-oriented cooperative societies to meet the specific needs of women in Ghana since they form a sizable majority of the country's entrepreneurs yet lack access to viable credit alternatives. The government should also educate lenders, such as banks, on the creditworthiness of women entrepreneurs. Contrary to the expectations of the commercial banks, the repayment rate of women is highly encouraging. The Women's World Banking in Ghana has a repayment rate of 95 percent. The Grameen Bank of Bangladesh, known for giving micro-loans to women at low interest rates, has a repayment rate of 97 percent.[42]

Women must be educated on the importance of perfecting title to any securities they may have. Women should seek legal assistance, and, if they are unable to pay, women's NGOs should set up legal aid branches to assist women. In the alternative, banks could do away with the requirement of collateral security. Christine Dadson, Executive Secretary of the Citi Savings and Loan Co., Ltd. in Ghana, stated that her company's target is to grant credit and lease facilities to small-scale microentrepreneurs, usually market women, without requiring collateral. The only security required of customers is that they have both a checking and a savings account with the bank. The checking account would be the working and lending account

---

40. The Government of Ghana, in an effort to increase agricultural production, had a ten-year moratorium on interest for borrowing for agricultural purposes.

41. Co-operative Societies Decree, 1968, N.L.C.D. 252 (Ghana).

42. Connie Morella, *Giving Credit Where Credit's Due*, THE WASHINGTON POST, advertising supp., Tuesday, Oct. 17, 1995, at A27.

while the savings account would be the security account. The savings account should have a balance of about 30 percent to 50 percent of the borrowing capital. Women may borrow amounts as low as 50,000 cedis (approximately $50).[43] MASU has a similar arrangement for granting loans to their customers without requiring any form of collateral security. The securities required are the savings deposits of the customers (that must at all time, be a percentage of the borrowed amount) and a guarantee from three clients of the Company's fund. In order to encourage increase in the savings of its customers, deposits as low as 500 cedis (approximately 50 cents) are acceptable.[44]

Women may also form credit cooperatives to assist themselves in obtaining credit. The Country Women's Association of Nigeria (COWAN) pools together the savings of its members and lends from such savings.[45] Such organizations should be encouraged and supported in Ghana.

Implementing and Enforcing Constitutional Provisions

Although Article 17(2) of the Constitution protects against gender discrimination, women have not typically brought lawsuits to challenge violation of their rights under the Constitution. In addition to its public education of women on their family law rights, the International Federation of Women Lawyers (FIDA Ghana) should also educate Ghanaian women on their constitutional rights not to be discriminated against and explore ways that the anti-discrimination principle can be used to enhance women's economic opportunities.

With respect to Article 17(4), which mandates that Parliament enact laws necessary for the implementation of policies and programs aimed at addressing the economic imbalance, activists should lobby and educate Parliamentarians (and, particularly, the women, who constitute 10 percent of the present total) to ensure that they move Parliament to pass the appropriate legislation to increase women's access to credit. In addition, more women should be encouraged to run for political office in an effort to advance the interests, economic and otherwise, of Ghanaian women. Politically oriented NGOs including the United Women Front (UNIWAF), can assist on this drive.

---

43. Christine Dadson, address at the Photo Exhibition of Ghanaian Women in Development, June 23, 1995.

44. Interview with Aba Amissah-Quainoo, Manager, Women's World Banking (July 1995).

45. Interview with Chief Bisi, Country Women Association of Nigeria (Mar. 20, 1996).

To implement Article 27 of the Constitution, Parliament should approve budget funding to establish more government-run day care centers. To encourage private initiative for establishing day care centers in the country, special packages like annual prize awards should be made available to private day care owners. Women's groups and the government must help formulate policies and programs to assist women in balancing work, family, and child care to reduce women's stress so that they may concentrate on their jobs and economic activities.

To give effect to Article 27(3), management in Ghana, both in the public and private sectors, should be mandated to specifically uphold the Constitution's equality guarantees in the terms and conditions of their service. Civil remedies at low legal fees should be available for victims of discrimination. FIDA Ghana may, with the support of donors, extend the ambit of legal aid to cover women who are discriminated against in the form of equal opportunity to training and promotion.

Looking to International Standards

The Beijing Platform for Action and the African Draft Platform for Action may provide guidelines for government, women's NGOs, and women's economic rights advocates in Ghana to assist in the promotion of the economic advancement of Ghanaian women. Similarly, advocates can point to Ghana's obligations under CEDAW and other relevant human rights instruments to urge the government to economically empower women.[46]

Conclusion

Ghanaian women in the traditional culture exercised significant economic autonomy. Unfortunately, the British who colonized Ghana failed to appreciate women's roles, particularly their economic role. No accommodation was made in the formal sector for the development of the powerful market women and the women farmers who formed the majority of agricultural producers. These women, ignored and starved of the necessary credit, training, and technical assistance in the modern world, found themselves relegated to the in-

---

46. *See* Introduction to Chapter 5, International Law and the Economic Empowerment of Women in Africa, *infra* p xx–xx.

formal sector with restricted access to the means for expanding their businesses. Post-colonial governments maintained the status quo. Economic legislation failed to consider the input of women. Efforts have since been made, however, through the enactment of statutes to support small businesses in areas that women dominate. All these efforts, however, have not affected a large majority of Ghanaian women. Since the economic growth of the country depends on the recognition and promotion of women's economic efforts, the Government, Parliament, the Courts, FIDA Ghana, and Women's NGOs must enforce the Constitution's guarantee of equal rights for women.

Shattering the Glass Ceiling: What Women in Uganda Need to Make it to the Top

Harriet Diana Musoke

Introduction

Since the National Resistance Movement government came to power in 1985, the role of women in Ugandan society has undergone a change for the better. This was the result of, among other things, the government's open recognition of the equal potential of men and women to contribute to society and women's right to equal treatment. Women became more aware of their personal needs and rights and demanded greater equality both inside and outside of the home.

Professional women were at the forefront of this change. As a result of this change in women's consciousness and opportunities, more and more women have joined the labor force, Parliament, and higher institutions of learning. At the same time, professional women have been relegated to subordinate roles without regard to their managerial capabilities. Women in top decision-making and management positions remain a tiny minority.[1] Working women remain limited to the so-called "women's ghetto,"[2] despite national and inter-

---

1. Women's participation in top decision-making is highest in the political sector, where they constitute 44 percent of the political leaders. This is compared to 12 percent of the non-political decision-makers at the national level. Ministry of Gender, Labour, and Social Development, *Sectoral Series: Decision Making, in* Women and Men in Uganda: Facts and Figures 10 (2000). Although these statistics do not provide for women in top management in corporations, they reflect the tiny minority of women in top decision-making positions at all levels.

2. The women's ghetto or the pink collar sector refers to the low-paid jobs traditionally filled by women such as teaching, secretarial work and nursing. Steven L. Winter, *The "Power" Thing*, 82 Va. L. Rev. 722, 817 (1996).

national declarations affirming the legal rights of women and equality of the sexes. This subordination creates an invisible but virtually impenetrable barrier to women's ability to reach the top management in both private and public sector corporations. This invisible barrier is referred to as the "glass ceiling." [3]

The glass ceiling concept is straightforward: women in corporations experience barriers to upward mobility that are unrelated to their intellect and abilities.[4] The glass ceiling may not act as a barrier to each individual woman, but it operates against women as a group. It keeps them from advancing because they are women. It is a simple case of discrimination based on sex. The glass ceiling is not only a total denial of social justice to women but also a significant regression in the advancement of the country's economy because the country does not utilize all of its human capital resources.[5]

Legal Framework

The Constitution of Uganda, 1995

The Constitution states: "Women shall have the right to equal treatment with men and that right shall include equal opportunities in political, economic, and social activities."[6] The Constitution further provides for the establishment of an Equal Opportunities Commission to ensure equality between women and men.[7] Unfortunately, six years after the promulgation of the Constitution Parliament has yet to discuss the issue. Because no Commission exists to police equality in appointments or opportunities and because sexist stereotypes still prevail, women continue to lag behind.

---

3. The term glass ceiling was popularized in the mid-1980s after an article in the *Wall Street Journal's* "Corporate Women" column identified and described what seemed to be an invisible and impenetrable barrier that confronted women as they moved nearer to management. FEDERAL GLASS CEILING COMM'N, GOOD FOR BUSINESS: MAKING FULL USE OF THE NATION'S HUMAN CAPITAL iii, iv (1995).

4. *Id.* at iii.

5. *Id.* at iv.

6. UGANDA CONST. art. XXXIII, §4.

7. "Parliament shall make relevant laws, including laws for the establishment of an equal opportunities commission, for the purpose of giving full effect to clause (1) of this article." UGANDA CONST. art. XXXII, §2.

The Employment Decree Number 4 of 1975

The Employment Decree addresses women's employment and includes a provision prohibiting women from working underground with some exceptions; a provision concerning maternity leave; and a provision prohibiting the dismissal of a woman during maternity leave.[8] The Decree, however, is silent regarding equal opportunities between women and men and fails to provide for employment protection within the government, the largest employer in the country, or within private corporations. This failure to provide for equal opportunities gives the government and large private and public corporations leeway to discriminate against women without fear of breaking the law.

The Companies Act

The Companies Act of 1965 regulates corporations in Uganda.[9] A result of colonization, the Act was a direct transplant from the United Kingdom's company law. To date, the law has not been amended. The law provides for two types of companies: private and public. The law does not specifically provide for the duties of the directors or the method of their appointment. The company's Articles of Association, required to legally incorporate a company, stipulate both duties and appointment methods.[10] Nothing in the law provides for gender equality in the appointment of either directors or top managers of a company. The content requirements for the Articles of Association are also silent on gender equality.[11]

Despite the absence of legislation that provides equal opportunities, it is unwritten government policy that at least one woman must be appointed to the boards of directors. The shortfalls of this are twofold: first, this policy applies only to government corporations, which are all being privatized so the policy will become moot; and second, the appointment is for only one woman, so the policy is not very helpful and might even be harmful to the extent it is interpreted as a maximum quota not a minimum requirement. Furthermore, the policy applies to boards of directors and provides no protection with respect to chief executive officers or managing directors.

---

8. The Employment Decree, §§ 45–47 (1975) (Uganda).
9. The Companies Act (1965) (Uganda).
10. *Id.*
11. L.C.B. GOWER, GOWER'S PRINCIPLES OF MODERN COMPANY LAW 273 (5th ed. 1992).

Causes of the Glass Ceiling in Uganda

The glass ceiling is contrary to international instruments and the Uganda Constitution, which provides for equality for all without discrimination on the basis of sex. The glass ceiling is discriminatory, and it hampers the international and Ugandan effort to bring about equality between men and women. Despite women's advancement and capabilities, improved educational qualifications, and improved equality policies, both worldwide and in Uganda, the glass ceiling still affects the advancement of women to top decision-making positions.

Society's Lack of Confidence in Women

Society considers women to be second-class citizens, lacking skills for leadership and decision-making. This attitude has roots in the assumption that women are inferior and the societal dominance of men over women.[12] Society has the mentality that women cannot be good managers nor can they make wise decisions; and therefore, women are not recommended for promotion to or appointment as top managers when male alternatives have the same qualifications.[13] Society also perceives women as "delicate roses" that need protection from the withering effects of the outside world. Because society lacks confidence in women, policy makers do not deem it necessary or appropriate to enact positive affirmative action legislation and policies in the field of top management employment.[14]

Families raise girls to be wives and mothers. Because kitchen chores do not require education, girls are excluded from training that would prepare them for public affairs, the labor force, or other career paths. [15] Socialization teaches girls not to be aggressive as it is "unladylike," not to answer back when a male speaks (however meaningless it may be), to be satisfied with what one has, and never to be ambitious.[16] Any woman who acts contrary to the set standards is considered a misfit and her mother is shunned for failure to properly raise her daughter. As a result, many women conform to the standards society has established.[17]

---

12. Maria Nzomo, Women in Top Management in Kenya 30 (1995).
13. *Id.*
14. *Id.* at 39, 41.
15. Victoria N. Nwaka, Women in Top Management in Uganda 50 (1995).
16. *Id.*
17. *Id.*

Some women internalize pervasive negative stereotypes, causing them to lack confidence.[18] Women have negative attitudes toward top management jobs, viewing these jobs as very time consuming, competitive, manly, and not the type of work done by a "lady."[19] They lack confidence in their capabilities and do not assert themselves when opportunities arise. This lack of self-confidence drives women to be defensive, submissive, and unnecessarily quiet, all of which may breed hostility and further erode self-respect.[20]

Multiple Role Conflict

Women's "parental, conjugal, domestic, kin, community and individual roles conflict with occupational roles," and this conflict weighs heavily on women's shoulders.[21] A woman's socially mandated domestic responsibilities are extensive and include, among other things: preparing her husband's meals, having a warm bath ready for her spouse when he returns from a night out, and providing a warm bed and sexual satisfaction at night. As the saying goes, a woman in Uganda is a "beast of burden." Forced to choose, many women opt to focus on what society deems their primary role and neglect their occupational roles.[22] In addition to society's expectations, lack of support and demanding behavior by spouses lead women to neglect their public role, thus reducing the chances of promotion or appointment to top positions.[23]

The few women who have made it to the top are good at setting priorities and balancing roles.[24] One would think that single women, be they single mothers or separated, are in a better position to penetrate the glass ceiling due to reduced role conflict. Society in Uganda, however, measures a woman's capabilities by the success of her marriage and child rearing and explains a woman's single status by assuming she must be difficult and unmanageable, discouraging possible suitors. This treatment of single women as unfit affects women's confidence in themselves and hinders their advancement. Therefore, instead of women concentrating on their careers, they spend time searching for a husband.

---

18. *Id.* at 67.
19. *Id.*
20. Nwaka, *supra* note 15, at 70.
21. *Id.* at 84.
22. *Id.*
23. *Id.*
24. Nzomo, *supra* note 12, at 32.

The societal view that women's primary role is that of wife and mother affects not only women's choices but those of employers as well. Many employers do not want to hire women, especially those of child-bearing age,[25] because even when women are better qualified, employers regard the required forty-five days of maternity leave as a setback to the companies' progress.[26] If employed, women who take maternity leave miss out on promotions. Thus, a woman has to choose between getting pregnant and keeping her job. Not surprisingly, many women prefer pregnancy to their jobs.[27]

Education and Training

Despite the introduction of Universal Primary Education[28] by the government, the enrollment of girls at the primary level is only 47 percent compared to 53 percent for boys.[29] This percentage decreases at the secondary school level to 41 percent for girls compared to 59 percent for boys.[30] This is as a result of many factors including the preference to educate boys, early marriages of girls, and early pregnancy. Even where girls are admitted to institutions of higher education, they are admitted to stereotypical studies for women, such as nursing, secretarial work, and teaching.[31] Institutions of higher education admit very few women for studies in statistics, medicine, engineering, and other science courses, because these courses are considered too masculine and

---

25. This reluctance by corporations to employ women because of the maternity leave may be one of the reasons why in Uganda men do not have paternity leave. When paternity leave was brought up for debate in Parliament, men strongly opposed it. Their argument was that they have no business with babies, and that it is a job for women. Their only job, they argued was to ensure that a woman gets pregnant.

26. NWAKA, *supra* note 15, at 85.

27. *Id.*

28. Universal Primary Education was introduced in 1997 and it provided that four children from each family will be educated free of charge for the primary level, that is, from primary one to primary seven. Susanne Arbeiter & Sally Hartley, *Teachers' and Pupils' Experiences of Integrated Education in Uganda*, 49 INT'L J. OF DISABILITY, DEV., AND EDUC. 61, 63 (2002).

29. MINISTRY OF GENDER, LABOUR, AND SOCIAL DEVELOPMENT, *Sectoral Series: Education, in* WOMEN AND MEN IN UGANDA: FACTS AND FIGURES 2 (2000).

30. *Id.* at 7.

31. In 1998–99, women's enrollment for Bachelor of Arts courses was 51% in Education, 62% in Mass Communication , 51% in Social Work Social Administration, and 54% in Tourism Management. *Id.* at 31–32.

not fit for "ladies."[32] This lost opportunity contributes to women's lack of confidence in themselves. In the field, women are not given training opportunities, because husbands will not grant permission or because a woman's supervisor will decide that she does not need any further training. Despite the lack of training opportunities, women are still expected to work harder and perform better than their male colleagues to prove their worth.[33]

Corporate Culture

Women encountering the glass ceiling confront intimidation, sexual harassment, ridicule, and pressure to settle for less. The culture of "the old boys club," the norm in corporate culture that embraces the belief that only the men who had been in management for so long are capable of management,[34] is predominant. These old boys fear getting orders and instructions from women, and they consider it demeaning because of their sense of superiority over women. Other old boys consider the leadership roles to be very taxing, aggressive, and manly; many assume that women, being delicate, cannot manage it. The appointing boards are also reluctant to appoint women to top management because they fear that women will face negative attitudes both inside and outside of the business, which will negatively affect profits.

Effects of the Glass Ceiling

The glass ceiling creates a concentration of women in low-level occupations that offer no opportunity for promotion.[35] This discourages women from working hard to reach higher positions and generates low morale. Lack of ambition, in turn, encourages women not to assert their rights or prove their capabilities. Low morale also affects productivity levels, which in turn affects the country's economy.[36]

---

32. In 1998–99, women's enrollment for Bachelor of Science courses was 31% in Statistics, 32% in Medicine, 18% in Engineering, and 17% in Veterinary Medicine. *Id.* at 30–31.

33. NWAKA, *supra* note 15, at 69.

34. Ronald Burke, *Women Directors: selection, acceptance and benefits of board membership*, 5 CORP. GOVERNANCE: AN INT'L REV. 118 (1997).

35. GOOD FOR BUSINESS: MAKING FULL USE OF THE NATION'S HUMAN CAPITAL, *supra* note 3, at 155.

36. Interview with Nsubuga Vincent Musoke, Principal Statistician, Uganda Bureau of Statistics, Kampala, Uganda.

Because women are denied opportunities to serve in top management positions, corporations lose out on the benefits of diversity. Women in top management positions "bring new sensitivities and raise issues of greater relevance to women in board deliberations."[37] They also serve as mentors for other women working in corporations.[38] This has "an effect on the level and tone of board discussions as well as the approaches used to raise and discuss issues."[39] Not drawing on the talent of over half of the population, by definition, limits the talent pool to the corporation's detriment. This is not a wise business practice for corporations especially given the increase in competition and the globalization of the marketplace.

The Way Forward

There is, unfortunately, no straight and golden path through, over, or around the glass ceiling but efforts such as policy formation, litigation, and education can help dismantle the glass ceiling over time.

Lobby Government to Enact and/or Amend Employment Non-Discrimination Laws

The Employment Decree of 1975 does not provide for equality in appointments at the top employment tier.[40] Similarly, the Companies Act, 1965 does not provide for the mode of appointment at the top.[41] Apart from the Constitution's general provision for equality between men and women, no labor laws provide for equality either at the top management level or non-discrimination in the modes of appointment. It is insufficient for the government to claim that it has non-discrimination provisions in the Constitution; it must enact specific policies to provide for equal employment. Such policies will be a commitment by the government to "engage in employment practices and procedures which do not discriminate, and which provide equality be-

---

37. Ronald J. Burke, *Do Women on Corporate Boards Make a Difference? Views of Women Directors*, 3 CORP. GOVERNANCE: AN INT'L REV. 138, 138 (1995).
38. *Id.* at 143.
39. *Id.* at 138.
40. The Employment Decree (1975) (Uganda).
41. The Companies Act (1965) (Uganda).

tween individuals of different groups or sex to achieve full, productive and freely chosen employment."[42]

Activists should lobby Parliament to enact and enforce labor policies that provide for equality in appointment at the top of the management ladder. The Ministry of Labor should enforce these policies through its labor inspectors and officials of the labor advisory who have been sensitized on gender issues.[43] The government should also amend the Employment Decree to ensure that employment regulations exist in all corporations to provide for equal opportunity and treatment in training and promotion for all workers. The employment laws should promote objective procedures that reduce or eliminate discrimination and sexual harassment in employment.

The Companies Act is outdated and in dire need of amendment, including specific provisions on the mode of appointments to boards of directors and quotas for women. Women on the boards of directors will have a ripple effect, leading to more women appointed as chief executive officers.

Activists should also lobby to appoint the Equal Employment Opportunities Commission as stipulated in the 1995 Constitution.[44] The Commission should be an independent agency charged with the responsibility for eliminating employment discrimination based on gender, religion, race, age, disability, and national origin. It should be able to receive complaints and investigate the complaints of employment discrimination.[45] The government should also create a Commission or Higher Council to supervise the implementation of measures designed to ensure equality of opportunity in employment throughout Uganda.[46]

The government should be reminded that it must set an exemplary standard for other employers by ensuring equality for women within government institutions. As a model employer, the government must ensure that the civil service, public agencies, and state-owned enterprises implement "non-dis-

---

42. LIN LEAN LIM, MORE AND BETTER JOBS FOR WOMEN: AN ACTION GUIDE 109 (1996).

43. International Labour Organization, *Note on the Proceedings: Breaking Through the Glass Ceiling: Women in Management* ¶ 39 (Dec. 1997), http://www.ilo.org/public/english/dialogue/sector/techmeet/tmwm97/tmwmnote.htm.

44. UGANDA CONST. art. XXXII, § 2.

45. The proposals made for the Ugandan Equal Employment Opportunities Commission were modeled after the provisions that govern the United States Equal Employment Opportunity Commission. *See* 29 C.F.R. § 1601 (2003).

46. GERMAINE BORCELLE, JOBS FOR WOMEN: A PLEA FOR EQUALITY OF OPPORTUNITY 60 (1985).

crimination and transparent procedures in recruitment, training and promo-tions" and achieve equal "representation of women in senior decision-making positions."[47]

Challenge Discrimination in Courts of Law

Advocates should consider filing law suits challenging the government's failure to protect its citizens from discrimination. According to the Consti-tution,[48] any person whose rights have been violated may file a claim. Using this provision, litigation might force the government to provide remedies in the form of specific measures to reduce or totally eliminate discrimination against women in employment. Another remedy might require the govern-ment to ensure equal opportunity during the privatization of its corpora-tions. Although it may be difficult to enforce such judgments against the ex-ecutive branch, these issues will nonetheless have been brought to the attention of the government.

Change Societal Attitudes

Societal attitudes toward women change by revisiting the culture and ed-ucating society about the capabilities of women.[49] Mothers need this educa-tion first. Mothers teach their daughters about stereotypical behavior and set examples for them. Once mothers become aware that leadership and competition is not unladylike, then they will impart leadership skills to their daughters and encourage them to develop a desire to be competitive. Fa-thers, or men in general, should encourage both boys and girls to manage the hard tasks of business and leadership. This education, which begins in the home, will have a great impact on society as it filters from one home to another.

Apart from changing society's attitudes as a whole, activists need to edu-cate and sensitize men that domestic chores are not for women alone but are a shared responsibility. Once men start participating in domestic chores,

47. Lim, *supra* note 42, at 119.
48. "Any person who claims that a fundamental or other right or freedom guaranteed under this Constitution has been infringed or threatened, is entitled to apply to a compe-tent court for redress which may include compensation." Uganda Const. art. L, §1.
49. International Labour Organization, *supra* note 43, ¶40.

women will have time to concentrate on their professional or working lives. Men should also be educated about the need to take paternity leave soon after the birth of a baby.[50] This public education should be accomplished through the use of media, radio, newspapers, and open communication between women and their husbands.[51]

The community must devise ways to reconcile the demands of job and family for all workers. To this end, activists should encourage the creation of part-time jobs, to allow employees to work in shifts, and the creation of day care and elder care centers. Employers should also recognize the value of flexibility in working hours so family members can best handle their responsibilities.[52] Activists should also educate corporate boards about the value of diversity, the advantages of the different perspectives that women may bring, the benefits of large applicant pools, and the importance of having women in leadership roles to motivate women in lower ranks.

Prepare Women for Leadership Positions

Women are not appointed to top management, in part, because they are not prepared for leadership positions. Employers must include women in leadership skills training to increase their self-confidence. Inclusion of leadership skills training in the education curriculum for men and women could help create a new concept of power, one that is gender-neutral and that does not perpetuate the notion that being a leader is unladylike. Such training should eschew sexist stereotypes, focus less on hierarchical aspects, and be more open to women generally.[53] The educational system should encourage women to balance their training in human relations with technological and scientific skills. The curriculum should include "tailored courses such as assertiveness training and public speaking skills."[54] Educational institutions should build

---

50. Proponents of paternity leave argue that it allows the father to know the baby better, cement a bond with the child right from the beginning, and gives the new mother time to recover quickly from the birth hardships she has endured. Corporations should be required to make paternity leave mandatory for all their male employees in the case of a newborn baby.

51. Telephone Interview with Victoria Balwana, Secretary, Sidpra Consulting Engineers, Kampala, Uganda (Jan. 20, 2001). (The introduction of paternity leave has met with resistance because men argue that they do not know its purpose).

52. International Labour Organization, *supra* note 43, ¶ 6.

53. *Id.* ¶ 14.

54. *Id.* ¶ 17.

up a critical mass of women who have taken on traditionally male jobs.[55] These women would be role models, teachers, and friends to the girls. Mentoring is critical to improving personal skills and knowledge that, in the long run, will benefit both corporations and society as a whole.[56] In addition, non-governmental organizations should develop "training programmes for women in conflict resolution, managing hostility, and assertiveness."[57]

Affirmative Action

Instituting affirmative action[58] means taking steps "whereby male privileges are phased out and equality for both sexes ensured."[59] The first step is to eliminate stereotypes that suggest that an occupation is either a man's job or a woman's job.[60] The notion of sex will become irrelevant when discussing occupations, which should be open to men and women alike according to their ability.[61] Mentoring, career guidance, and employment agencies for girls and women may encourage them to enter non-traditional careers. Employers should recruit candidates through the mass media (newspapers, radio, and television) to attract "women to occupations in which they are still in the minority."[62] Also, the government should be encouraged to award contracts only to those corporations that can demonstrate adherence to equal opportunity laws.[63] Finally, legislation that provides for quotas in appointment should be enacted.[64] Over time, this will ensure that employers appoint women to the top management positions.

---

55. *Id.*

56. *Id.* ¶ 32.

57. International Labour Organization, *supra* note 43, ¶ 48.

58. As a matter of caution, affirmative action should be used in such a way that it will not spoon-feed the women and promote them without merit but help build confidence in themselves.

59. BORCELLE, *supra* note 46, at 126.

60. *Id.* at 95.

61. *Id.*

62. *Id.* at 126.

63. Interview with Mary Hartnett, Executive Director, Women Law and Public Policy Fellowship Program, Georgetown University Law Center, in Washington, D.C. (Mar. 28, 2001).

64. International Labour Organization, *Note on the Proceedings: Breaking Through the Glass Ceiling: Women in Management*, Affirmative/positive action: Clarification and different approaches. Quotas or targets? (Dec. 1997), http://www.ilo.org/public/english/dialogue/sector/techmeet/tmwm97/tmwmnote.htm.

Conclusion

Discriminatory attitudes and practices prevent women's progress to top management positions. Employers still use outmoded and illegitimate reasons to justify blocking women from advancement, despite a pool of qualified women. Although the Ugandan government has committed itself to policies and programs to advance women, there has been almost no progress in the employment sector. The government, corporations, organizations, and society need to commit themselves fully to ensuring women equal opportunities and treatment in employment. Uganda must increase opportunities for women and must provide more catalysts for change if it hopes to cope with global economic changes. The government must implement affirmative action and other positive legislation for women in order to create a level playing field in corporate governance in which, "[t]he the theme of the future must be inclusion, not exclusion- inclusion not at the expense of any group, but to the benefit of all."[65]

---

65. GOOD FOR BUSINESS: MAKING FULL USE OF THE NATION'S HUMAN CAPITAL, *supra* note 3, at 38.

Law Reform and Effective Implementation as the Means to Economically Empower the Ugandan Woman

Sarah B. Lubega

Introduction

To increase economic development, Uganda must take a fresh look at the laws that affect women and amend them to give women real access to resources. Without women's full emancipation, Uganda will be underutilizing over half of its population[1] and will not be able to maximize its economic potential. Why does the Ugandan woman lack economic independence? The traditional concepts of women in Uganda place women in an inferior position in relation to men, and Uganda's economic empowerment programs to date have not been effective. Women's poverty is directly related to the absence of economic and educational opportunities, the lack of access to resources including credit, the barriers to land ownership and inheritance, the limited access to education and legal remedies, and minimal participation in decision-making.

A new model that would encompass the cultures and values of Ugandan society and involve men in the struggle is more likely to be acceptable as well as successful. Ugandans will not view this model as completely new and foreign but, rather, as an improvement to the existing way of life.

---

1. *Consideration of Reports, Submitted by State Parties Under Article 18 of the Convention on the Elimination of All Forms of Discrimination Against Women, Third Periodic Reports of State Parties, Uganda*, U.N. CEDAW, Extraordinary Sess., U.N. Doc. CEDAW/c/UGA/3, at 5 (2002) [hereinafter Uganda's Third Periodic Report to CEDAW].

The Traditional Concept of a Ugandan Woman

Uganda is a country of many tribes and each tribe has its own proverbs and sayings. Proverbs such as these demonstrate societal attitudes toward women: [2]

Ezenkanankana nebisiki tezaaka —Luganda
(Small pieces of firewood that seek to equate themselves to the big ones do not light)

Omukazi asa oburo tamanyire eraabaagwe —Runyankore/Rukiga
(The woman grinds the flour but does not decide which ox shall be slaughtered)

Ahu abashaija batari, abakazi bacwa emanja —Runyankole/Rukiga
(Where there are no men, women become judges)

Nyumba ya mwanamuke hukaribisha bweha —Kiswahili
(When a woman assumes power in the house, the house is as good as destroyed because all sorts of people will seize the opportunity to confuse it)

Nyako dhi do
(A woman is a cook)

Enyamwonyo ku ekura eriibwa, omwishiki aku kurashwera —Runyankore/Rukiga
(Just as a ripe banana is eaten, so a girl is married at puberty)

Omwami kyakobye, zeena kyenkoba —Lusoga
(What my husband says is what I say)

These proverbs are used in the context of gender relations. The first clearly indicates that women should not equate themselves to men, and when they attempt to do so, nothing works. According to these proverbs, a woman may not decide anything, even in her own kitchen. Her family may force her into marriage at the first sign of puberty. She is not supposed to speak in public or express her own views. These proverbs demonstrate why many women lack self-esteem and confidence. They also reveal that power and decision-making are expected to be in the hands of men. Because the majority of lawmakers are

---

2. MINISTRY OF GENDER, LABOUR & SOCIAL DEV. [Uganda], BALANCING THE SCALES: ADDRESSING GENDER CONCERNS IN NATIONAL DEVELOPMENT PROGRAMMES, PARTICIPANTS' MANUAL 7 (1999).

men and have traditionally been men,[3] they made sure that the laws and rules favor men. Some of the rules included prohibiting women from inheriting land or heading a household, meddling in politics or aspiring for high offices of leadership, working outside the home, and eating certain foods. These proverbs are not merely traditional sayings but the embodiment of common traditional perceptions that govern the lives of many Ugandan men and women.

The Economic and Political Marginalization of Women in Uganda

Political Incapacity

Women in political and decision-making positions have the opportunity to ensure that women's gender-specific concerns are included in mainstream development issues. Women's participation in decision-making is not only a demand for simple fairness or democracy but also a necessity for the country's progress. There is a cultural belief, however, that decision-making is the domain of men in Uganda.

Since 1986, the Ugandan government has taken measures to enhance the participation of women in politics through affirmative action in favor of women.[4] At the local level, women are encouraged to participate in the local councils and committees.[5] At every level, one post of Secretary for Women is reserved for a woman. In addition, women may compete for the remaining eight positions on the committee. The Uganda Constitution requires that one-third of the councilor seats in local government be reserved for women.[6] The constitution also provides for the election of women councilors by universal and adult suffrage,[7] unlike the 1993 law under which women had to rely on the votes of a male dominated electoral college. The 1997 Local Government Act seeks to institute a higher degree of political independence for women candidates by having them elected directly by the population at large.[8] In 1989 (dur-

---

3. Uganda's Third Periodic Report to CEDAW, *supra* note 1, at 31.

4. *Id.*

5. The local council court is an informal court system that starts at the village level. It consists of between five and nine members and is given limited powers to try some specified cases, such as domestic matters and petty thefts.

6. Uganda Const. art. 180(2)(b).

7. Uganda Const. art. 176(3).

8. The Local Government Act, Act 1 of 1997, §118 [Uganda].

ing the expansion of Parliament), the electoral law was amended so that each district was required to elect one woman as a representative to Parliament.[9] In addition, women could compete on equal footing at the county level with men. Affirmative action played a major role in boosting the proportion of women in Parliament. To a certain extent, this has given women the confidence to articulate women's issues and to participate in policy and decision-making.

Although positive changes are taking place at the national and local government levels, women still number significantly fewer than men in decision-making positions, largely due to the patriarchal view that men are the natural leaders. Few women take up or even contemplate taking up such challenges because of this negative attitude. A striking example is the 1996 parliamentary elections. Of the 896 candidates vying for the 214 direct county seats in Uganda, only 32 candidates were women and only 8 of the women made it to Parliament.[10] The majority of the women in Parliament are there through affirmative action. The government and women's rights non-governmental organizations (NGOs) are making efforts to encourage women to compete for elected offices at local, regional, and national levels, and to help them understand the power of the vote and the importance of women holding elective office.[11]

Despite the progress in increasing women's participation in public decision-making, the balance of power within the family has changed little. The majority of Ugandan women have little or no access to information relating to politics and the law. In rural areas, where the majority of Ugandans live,[12] men who control and own the wealth and property usually make the decisions. Rural women see women's increased political participation and power as a myth, because traditional norms still dictate the conditions of their lives. Uganda must increase women's leadership skills, education, and economic emancipation in order to empower more women to assume decision-making roles, not only in the political sphere, but in the private sphere of the family as well. The government and activists must take steps to transform societal attitudes; these steps must be carefully constructed to gradually challenge cul-

---

9. Now this requirement is provided for in the Uganda Constitution. Uganda Const. art. 78(1)(b).

10. Uganda's Third Periodic Report to CEDAW, *supra* note 1, at 31.

11. *See, e.g.,* Mary Kaddu, Women Emerging in Uganda's Democracy: A Documentation of Women's Experiences in Uganda's Local Council and Local Government Elections, 1998, 5 (Sheila Kawamara ed., 1998).

12. In 1999, only about 14.2% of Uganda's population lived in urban areas. Uganda's Third Periodic Report to CEDAW, *supra* note 1, at 5.

tural norms. A more aggressive, radical transformation could create a negative backlash.

Although the future looks brighter, traditional family norms and Ugandan cultural values still hinder women's efforts. The majority of women must seek permission from their husbands to participate in these activities. If the husband refuses, the woman must choose between either participating in these activities, thereby creating discord in the family, and not participating, thereby sustaining their place as inferior to men.[13] In most cases, women choose family peace, forfeiting the chance of becoming politically active, or achieving some degree of economic independence. The vicious cycle thus continues. Politics and economic empowerment run hand in hand because access to and control of property, credit, and cash play a key role in political participation. Because it is very expensive to run for elective offices, many women are discouraged by their poverty[14] while others are forced to rely on propertied sponsors who may compromise their principles.

Economic Disadvantage

Distortions in resource allocation, a result of discrimination against women, have a negative impact on Uganda's development that must be addressed in economic development strategies. The government has introduced a range of measures to address widespread poverty and the social concerns of the most vulnerable groups.[15] It is unclear whether and how these initiatives will address gender disparities and contribute to the economic empowerment of Ugandan women.

For women specifically, efforts have been made to access credit through non-traditional financial institutions.[16] Women's rights NGOs, together with

---

13. *See, e.g.,* Kaddu, *supra* note 11, at 24.

14. *Id.* at 39–40, 52.

15. Initiatives include the Program for the Alleviation of Poverty and Social Cost Adjustment, the Poverty Alleviation Program, and the Entandikwa and Youth Enterprises (YES) schemes. *See* Uganda's Third Periodic Report to CEDAW, *supra* note 1, at 53–54. These programs have been complemented by the national Poverty Eradication Action Plan (PEAP), designed to "remove mass poverty by the year 2017 by increasing household incomes" which would in turn result in improvement in "the quality of life of the poor through the provision of basic services." *See* MINISTRY OF GENDER, LABOUR & SOCIAL DEV. [Uganda], THE NATIONAL ACTION PLAN ON WOMEN 6 (1999).

16. Women's NGOs like the National Strategy for the Advancement of Rural Women in Uganda (NSARWU), Uganda Women Entrepreneurs Association (UWEAL), and the

the Ministry of Gender, Labor and Social Development (MGLSD), are trying to improve women's quality of life, especially for those in the informal sector.[17] The MSGLD has made it a priority to raise public awareness that women are creditworthy.[18] There are also efforts to build financial institutions for women and to make existing institutions more accepting of women. Women are accessing credit both individually and in groups, while undertaking training in business management and entrepreneurial skills. The beneficiaries of most of these efforts, however, have been primarily educated and urban women. Traditional norms continue to negatively impact the efforts to empower uneducated and rural women. For example, cultural norms restricting women's ownership of land is a significant hindrance to women who attempt to access credit from financial institutions.

Land is a key factor of production, the mainstay of the Ugandan economy, and an important status symbol. The agricultural sector is responsible for more than 50 percent of Uganda's gross domestic product (GDP) and nearly all export earnings and it produces cash crops for export, food for subsistence, and raw materials for industry.[19] Although they constitute 70 to 80 percent of the agricultural labor force and account for 80 percent of food production,[20] women lack meaningful control over productive resources and the crops they produce.[21] Only 8 percent of Ugandan women have leaseholds, and only 7 percent own land.[22] Men control both land allocation in rural and urban areas and decisions affecting land development. If a woman divorces or is widowed, she must return to her father's home area and become dependent on a male relative for use rights to the land. It is thus very rare for women to inherit

---

Council for Economic Empowerment of Women of Africa (CEEWA)-Uganda Chapter were all inspired to work on promoting women's economic empowerment.

17. Uganda's Third Periodic Report to CEDAW, *supra* note 1, at 22.

18. A striking example is the MGLSD support that extended to a two-day workshop (August 24-25, 2000) on the study of micro-finance institutions in Uganda organized by The Africa Rural and Agricultural Credit Association (AFRACA) with the theme "The promotion of financial services to women." *See* workshop notes, *available at* http://www.afraca.org/html/ugandareport.htm (last visited on July 9, 2003). At this workshop, the minister of the MGLSD said that institutional barriers have often excluded women from formal banking institutions, yet women are creditworthy and there is evidence that women have demonstrated high levels of repayment for loans. *Id.* at §§2, 5.3(4).

19. Uganda's Third Periodic Report to CEDAW, *supra* note 1, at 6.

20. *Id.*

21. *Id.* at 57.

22. MINISTRY OF GENDER, LABOUR & SOCIAL DEV. [Uganda], THE NATIONAL ACTION PLAN ON WOMEN 5 (1999).

land.[23] For example, when my father died, his land was automatically divided between my brothers. My sisters and I received nothing because the clan members feared that if we were given land, the land might fall into the hands of a different clan when we married. Although I was young then, I do not remember anyone arguing on our behalf; it was simply the order of the day. Women's lack of land ownership reinforces their low social and economic status. Land and other economic resources such as credit, information, and skills are crucial to providing options to women by reducing undue dependence on marital partners and male relatives.

Economic Empowerment of Women and the Law

In Uganda, women's low legal status and general lack of power is widespread. Institutions from the household to the government sustain this inequality. Legal constraints range from the immediate, such as the foreign language of the court system, to the structural, such as institutional bias in the administration of justice.[24] A critical look at the legal system shows inequalities resulting from discriminatory laws, although some existing legislation appears to be gender neutral on its face. Such gender neutral laws, in particular property and land laws, enable de facto discrimination against females to continue by failing to address women's realities and experiences. The government fails to enforce the few existing laws that benefit women. Poor implementation of the law is a result of negative attitudes and gender bias, stemming from socio-cultural norms and beliefs.[25]

The 1995 Uganda Constitution

The Uganda Constitution is highly beneficial to women as it protects gender equality through numerous provisions. Article 21 protects the equality of all persons and prohibits discrimination based on sex.[26] Article 33 provides for the rights of women and the duty of the State to respect, protect, and pro-

---

23. Ugandan society being patrilineal, property ownership passes on through the male line. *See* Jacqueline Asiimwe, *Making Women's Land Rights a Reality in Uganda: Advocacy for Co-Ownership by Spouses*, 4 YALE HUM. RTS. & DEV. L.J. 171, 175 (2001).

24. Uganda's Third Periodic Report to CEDAW, *supra* note 1, at 62.

25. *Id.*

26. Uganda Const. art. 21(1).

mote those rights;[27] it also prohibits laws, cultures, and customs or traditions that undermine women's welfare, interest, or status.[28] Article 32 establishes the rights of marginalized groups, including women, to affirmative action as a general human rights principle.[29] The Constitution also provides for affirmative action in leadership at the national level, by providing reserved seats for women representatives in Parliament[30] and in local government.[31] The appointment of a female Vice President,[32] more female cabinet ministers, and senior civil servants reflects the government's commitment to improve and increase representation of women in decision-making.[33] In most senior political appointments, including diplomatic representation and presidential advisors, however, gender gaps still exist.[34] No women have been elected as local chairpersons at the district or sub-county level, a concern because changes at the grassroots or most local levels often indicate whether there has been a genuine attitudinal shift in contrast to a top-down directive that is unlikely to change behaviors or attitudes toward women.

The 1998 Land Act

The Land Act, passed in 1998,[35] is a good step toward legislation that implements the constitutional principle of gender equality. It provides that any decision that prohibits women, children, or persons with disability access to

---

27. Uganda Const. art. 33.

28. Uganda Const. art. 33(6). This is an important prohibition because female subordination often stems from religious or cultural norms and practice.

29. Uganda Const. art. 32.

30. Uganda Const. art. 78(1)(b).

31. Uganda Const. art. 180.

32. Uganda's female Vice-President, Specioza Kazibwe, resigned on May 21, 2003. Emily Wax, *Africa's Women Beginning to See Progress in Politics*, WASH. POST, June 6, 2003, at A14.

33. In 2003, women held several major ministry positions, among them Minister of Gender, Labour and Social Development (Zoe Bakoko-Bakoru), Minister of State—Luwero Triangle (Ruth Nakabirwa), Minister of Justice and Constitutional Affairs (Janat Mukwaya), and Minister of State—Entandikwa (Grace Akello). *See* THE WORLDWIDE GOVERNMENT DIRECTORY 2003, 1395–1401 (2003); *see also* http://www.government.go.ug/ministries/index.php (last visited on July 9, 2003). Margaret Sekaggya heads the Human Rights Commission. *See* http://www.hrw.org/reports/2001/africa/uganda/uganda2.html (last visited on July 9, 2003).

34. Uganda's Third Periodic Report to CEDAW, *supra* note 1, at 31–32.

35. The Land Act, Act 16 of 1998 [Uganda].

ownership, occupation, or use of land, or that otherwise violates constitutional principles, shall be invalid. The term "disability," however, is not defined. Communities must determine equitable provisions for land allocation, and courts must then determine if these provisions treat men and women equally. The Uganda Constitution also requires that at least one member out of a total of four or five of each land management institution be female.[36] The constitution further stipulates that women form at least one-third of local councils at every level.[37] These steps ensure at least token representation for women, but the representation may be too minimal to provide real decision-making authority. In addition, the land tribunals that adjudicate land disputes have no gender balance requirement; women may have only minimal representation in these important institutional bodies.

Access to the Law

Uganda must also address the issue of women's lack of access to the legal system.[38] Constraints of distance, time, cost, and procedural formalities serve to alienate women from legal institutions. Most women do not know their legal rights and do not make as much use of legal services as do men.[39] Unless women are made aware of their legal rights, progressive laws will not be useful to, and may in fact be used against, women. For example, a husband may decide to mortgage a matrimonial home without seeking his wife's consent. [40] The wife is no doubt unaware that her consent is required before the transaction can take place. In all likelihood, the husband will proceed and the wife will remain unaware until the couple divorces or the house is taken over by creditors. Moreover, women must be economically empowered to be able to access the courts, which is very costly. Because the majority of women have no reasonable income or property, they often cannot pursue their claims. For rural women in particular, geographic distance from the courts, the time re-

---

36. Uganda Const. art. 48(4); *see also* Asiimwe, *supra* note 23, at 177.

37. Uganda Const. art. 180(2)(b).

38. *See* Asiimwe, *supra* note 23, at 176.

39. *Consideration of Reports, Submitted by State Parties Under Article 18 of the Convention on the Elimination of All Forms of Discrimination Against Women, Initial and Second Periodic Reports of State Parties, Uganda,* U.N. CEDAW, 14th Sess., U.N. Doc. CEDAW/c/ UGA/1-2, at 72 (1995).

40. The Land Act, Act 16 of 1998 §40(1) [Uganda]; *see also* Uganda's Third Periodic Report to CEDAW, *supra* note 1, at 17.

quired to get to and participate in legal proceedings, and the alienating for-
mality of the courtroom are impediments that prevent women from accessing the legal system.

Creating Change: A Critical Look at the 1999 National Action Plan and Other Recommendations

The Legal System

One of the objectives of the 1999 National Action Plan on Women in
Uganda is to ensure sustained, comprehensive reform of the laws and the legal
system in Uganda.[41] The Plan aims to identify gender gaps, amend discriminatory legislation, enact affirmative action legislation, and reform gender-neutral laws to make them gender-specific where necessary to promote equality.[42]
Ideally, the National Action Plan would instigate reform of all legal processes
to improve access to justice for women. The government must not only reform the law but also engage in extensive campaigns to raise awareness about
the changes and to ensure women's access to the legal systems. This public education would also involve educating the relevant authorities on how to implement or interpret the law in a manner consistent with equality and the intent of the law.

The Uganda Constitution requires the state to promote public awareness
of the Constitution's provisions by disseminating it as widely as possible.[43] Although the law requires that new statutes, bylaws, ordinances, and other enactments be published in a gazette, Uganda gazettes are primarily intended
for lawyers, politicians, and judges. Very few ordinary Ugandans have access
to gazettes, and the majority of women live in villages where no one has heard
of—let alone seen—a gazette.[44] Instead of relying on the gazette, the government and activists should use the media to announce new laws and to ensure that the public understands the content, spirit, and intent of such laws.

---

41. Ministry of Gender, Labour & Social Dev. [Uganda], The National Action
Plan on Women 20 (1999).

42. Id.

43. Uganda Const. art. 4.

44. In 1999, only about 14.2% of Uganda's population lived in urban areas. Uganda's
Third Periodic Report to CEDAW, supra note 1, at 5.

This type of education is particularly beneficial when the law embodies concepts and values that run counter to the traditional values and culture in the community.

The law has been used as an instrument of control by restricting women's access to economic and social resources and by supporting attitudes and behaviors that are oppressive to women. The law, however, may also serve as a powerful instrument of social transformation to eradicate discrimination. Transformation of the law must go hand in hand with a change in societal attitude and behavior. In order to achieve this, law reform should not attempt to sweep away existing customary laws wholesale. Customary law has governed the country for centuries, and a change cannot be expected with the stroke of a pen. Rather, reform efforts should focus on changing those aspects of customary law that are discriminatory or harmful to women. To that end, activists should work to secure popular support for these changes within the population at large.

Economic Empowerment

Legal reform should be conducted together with the fostering of economic and political empowerment of women since the value of the law is largely dependent on the political context in which it must operate. Similarly, the value of law reform is subject to women's ability to access the legal system. The first strategic objective under the Poverty, Income Generation and Economic Empowerment section of the 1999 National Action Plan on Women is to improve the economic status of women.[45] The Action Plan further provides that there is a need to improve women's access to financial services by encouraging a culture of saving.[46] The culture of saving is almost nonexistent in Uganda today. Prevailing economic conditions are not conducive to saving. The local banks are collapsing one by one, and the international banks require a large balance to open and maintain an account. The majority of Ugandans, especially women, cannot afford this. Most Ugandans live from hand to mouth. If they try to save, it is often only for a short time before they need to use the money. Although some group-saving schemes have recently been introduced, the amount of money that can be loaned to the members is too small to start a viable business. The National

---

45. Ministry of Gender, Labour & Social Dev. [Uganda], The National Action Plan on Women 6 (1999).

46. *Id.* at 8.

Action Plan also promotes training women in the use of credit.[47] Obtaining credit without collateral, however, is next to impossible in Uganda, and women do not have access to collateral since the majority of women do not own land.[48] There is an urgent need to convince society that giving women the right to own land does not in any way degrade men, but that instead improves the family in particular and society in general by improving women's quality of life.

Activists must work with cultural chiefs, who will, in turn, educate society about the benefits of extending land rights and credit to women. Most Ugandans still place a great deal of trust in their cultural leaders. As a result, a cultural change presented and explained to them by the chief will stand a better chance of survival. Involving men in women's organizations may help to educate men about the importance of gender equality. This will also result in men being invested in the change and therefore ensuring that it works.

Conclusion

As women continue to run from the darkness to the light, they must remember that they cannot afford to run with only their daughters on their backs, for their sons also look up to them for a safe direction. Moreover, Uganda must strike a balance to ensure that culture is not sacrificed on the altar of development and emancipation. Reforming the laws to ensure gender equality would be a positive step forward, but enforcement and proper implementation should immediately follow suit. A new development model that would recognize the positive, non-discriminatory aspects of Ugandan culture and that would specifically involve men and traditional Chiefs in the struggle will stand a better chance of acceptance by Ugandan society.

---

47. *Id.*

48. Women comprise more than half of Uganda's population, *see* Uganda's Third Periodic Report to CEDAW, *supra* note 1, at 5, but they own only 7% of the land. *Id.* at 52.

CONCLUSION

NATIONAL HUMAN RIGHTS COMMISSIONS: GHANA, UGANDA, AND TANZANIA

Vanessa Brocato

Introduction

Although international and, often, national law set forth essential human rights, these rights are not useful to individuals absent adequate recognition and enforcement by the state. State-sponsored human rights institutions represent one way in which the state may act on that responsibility.[1] Institutions such as government human rights commissions, however, have an inherent tension in their work. By definition, human rights violations result from state action or inaction.[2] As a government entity with the sole purpose of preventing and addressing such violations, national human rights institutions continuously threaten to bite the hand that feeds them.

Part of the government, national human rights institutions (NHRIs) typically extend from the administrative branch. Enabling legislation or decree de-

---

1. According to the United Nations, "the effective enjoyment of human rights calls for the establishment of national infrastructures for their protection and promotion." Office of the High Commissioner for Human Rights, Fact Sheet No.19, *National Institutions for the Promotion and Protection of Human Rights* (April 1993) [hereinafter Fact Sheet No. 19] *available at* http://www.unhchr.ch/html/menu6/2/fs19.htm.

2. As many of the articles in this book demonstrate, state action is now defined quite broadly, and the actions of private individuals constitute human rights violations when the state fails to appropriately intervene.

lineates each institution's particular functions, powers, and jurisdiction.[3] Their power resides primarily in education and persuasion, and sometimes extends to referring cases to court, bringing suit, or, less frequently, performing quasi-judicial operations. Most NHRIs consider complaints brought by individuals or groups, and many are authorized to investigate areas of concern even without a specific complaint.[4]

Human rights commissions, such as those found in Ghana, Uganda, and Tanzania, typically serve three functions: hearing and investigating complaints; monitoring government policy and action; and communicating with and educating the public, government, and the international community.[5] Some commissions perform arbitration or mediation to resolve disputes, but very few commissions actually hold authority to generate legally binding resolutions to complaints.[6] A commission's decision may carry some weight with the judiciary if the case is referred to court. Commissions may appear as amicus curiae or as a party before the courts on important human rights cases.

In addition to addressing specific complaints or concerns, a commission serves as an advisor to the government. Commissions conduct on-going analysis of current law and policy for compliance with human rights norms and advise lawmakers and administrators on appropriate legislative changes or other measures.[7] Commissions often play a significant role in the state's reporting to international bodies on the status of human rights throughout the country.

---

3. The term "national human rights institution" refers to any of a group of state-based institutions that are explicitly mandated to protect and promote human rights. Most common are the human rights commissions and ombudsmen. Some nations create specialized national institutions to protect the rights of a particular vulnerable group such as women, ethnic and linguistic minorities, or indigenous populations. This article focuses on national human rights commissions because Ghana, Uganda, and Tanzania have this type of NHRI. For a detailed discussion of the differences and similarities among the various forms, please see generally Linda Reif, *Building Democratic Institutions: The Role of National Human Rights Institutions in Good Governance and Human Rights Protection*, 13 Harv. Hum. Rts. J. 1 (2000).

4. Fact Sheet No. 19, *supra* note 1.

5. *See* U.N. Centre for Human Rights, *National Human Rights Institutions: A Handbook on the Establishment and Strengthening of National Institutions for the Promotion and Protection of Human Rights*, at para. 46–52, U.N. Doc HR/P/PT/4 (1995).

6. *See id* at para. 49. For a more general discussion of the "task of investigating alleged human rights violations" and NHRI's powers to address individual complaints, *see id* para. 216–97.

7. *Id* at para. 181–215.

In the role of educator, commissions conduct community out-reach, informing people of their rights and of avenues for redress should they believe their rights have been violated.[8] This includes publicizing the work of the commission itself and publishing opinions, recommendations, proposals, and reports. Commissions also educate their governments by alerting the government to possible human rights violations across the country and proposing interventions or other solutions.

The Increase of National Human Rights Commissions in Africa in the Past Decade

Between 1989 and 2000, Africa saw a veritable boom in NHRIs, increasing from one country to twenty-four providing for such an institution in their laws in just over ten years.[9] The democratization of many African states has lead to the development of myriad institutions and systems, especially those intended to safeguard democracy and human rights. At the regional level, the African Commission on Human and Peoples' Rights calls national human rights institutions "essential partner[s]" in realizing the rights described in African Charter on Human and Peoples' Rights.[10]

The international community has generally responded enthusiastically to the creation of NHRIs in Africa: many NHRIs are the current pet projects of multilateral bodies and donor countries. The Office of the U.N. High Commissioner on Human Rights has appointed a special advisor to provide technical advice and material assistance to governments with NHRIs. Krzysztof Jakubowski, Chairperson of the Commission on Human Rights, "emphasized the important role and contribution which national institutions played with regard to the promotion and protection of human rights." He called them "in-

---

8. *See id* at para. 139–80.

9. Mary Ellen Tsekos, *Human Rights Institutions in Africa*, 9 Hum. Rts. Br. 21, 21 (2002). As of 2000, the following countries has provisions in their laws for a national human rights institution: Algeria, Benin, Cameroon, Central African Republic, Chad, Ethiopia, Ghana, Kenya, Liberia, Malawi, Mali, Mauritania, Morocco, Niger, Nigeria, Rwanda, Senegal, Sierra Leone, South Africa, Sudan, Togo, Tunisia, Uganda, and Zambia. *Id.*

10. The African Commission on Human and Peoples' Rights, *Resolution Granting Observer Status to National Human Rights Institutions in Africa*, 24th Ordinary Session (Oct. 31, 1998).

valuable partners in the translation of international human rights norms and standards into deeds at the national level."[11]

The international community views NHRIs as an integral part of a much broader system of human rights promotion, monitoring, and enforcement.[12] Beyond the fanfare, many human rights activists have been pragmatic and skeptical about NHRIs and the international eagerness for them. According to Human Rights Watch, "the enthusiasm for their establishment has not been accompanied by a corresponding vigilance by the U.N. for the role that they play following their creation."[13]

Evaluating National Human Rights Commissions

General Strengths of National Human Rights Institutions

Although the general framework and norms of human rights law have been set at the international level, the national human rights institution has several strengths in realizing human rights for individuals. NHRIs probably function best as institutions of prevention. Their very presence and active education and monitoring may stop problems before they escalate into human rights violations.

Located within a specific country, a national human rights institution will be likely to approach human rights education in a culturally relevant matter. An NHRI has a vantage point that allows it to prioritize human rights matters of particular urgency to its country. Decisions and opinions from an "insider" entity are often more palatable to the government and population of a country alike. More concretely, NHRIs have a significant role to play in facilitating immediate individual and community enjoyment of human rights given the remoteness of international enforcement mechanisms. Because NHRIs are part of the government, they carve out a space for official human rights discourse and lend legitimacy to the human rights agenda. Their status as a government entity also offers these institutions access to restricted places

---

11. U.N. Press Release, *Commission on Human Rights Hears Statements by Regional Human Rights Commissions, Non-Governmental Organizations*, Commission on Human Rights 58th session, (18 April 2002), *available at* http://www.unhchr.ch/huricane/huricane.nsf/view01/AF35BF403355AFFAC1256BA00025D60A?opendocument.

12. U.N. Centre for Human Rights, supra note 5, para. 9.

13. Human Rights Watch, *Protectors or Pretenders? Government Human Rights Commissions in Africa* (2001) [hereinafter HRW Report] *available at* http://hrw.org/reports/2001/africa/contents.html.

and information and makes their recommendations politically difficult for the executive to dismiss out of hand.

General Weakness of National Human Rights Institutions

For all the apparent advantages NHRIs have in protecting and promoting human rights, there are weaknesses inherent in their position and potential difficulties in their operations. Created by government, NHRIs are at risk of deliberately narrow mandates, under-funding, and bureaucratic staffing. As part of the government, NHRIs may be "pressured into silence by the executive branch, or manipulated to serve as a mouthpiece for the government."[14] Even where direct governmental control or coercion is absent, some NHRIs may nevertheless shy away from politically or culturally sensitive issues, which often include human rights violations disproportionately affecting women. Countries with questionable human rights records may set up NHRIs to curry favor with the international community and donor countries without any real change in the human rights situation.[15] Some academics propose making funding and technical support conditional on likelihood of success.[16]

Because NHRIs often have broad mandates, the institutions are likely to suffer from inadequate resources, under-staffing, and lack of expertise. In situations of scant resources and over-worked staff, human rights violations specific to women may be overlooked, or women's unique experiences with a more general human rights violation may go unacknowledged. It almost goes without saying that institutions in Africa are under-funded, and NHRIs are no exception.

In a 2002 hearing by the U.N. Commission on Human Rights, Komi Gnondoli, Chairperson of the Togo Human Rights Commission, on behalf of the African Group of National Human Rights Institutions, noted that national human rights institutions in Africa were crippled by "severe lack of resources."[17] Human Rights Watch, however, notes, "The more credible and active human rights commissions, while also mentioning being constrained by finances, never used the lack of funding as an excuse for inactivity."[18]

---

14. HRW Report, *supra* note 13, at 2.
15. Tsekos, *supra* note 9, 21.
16. *Id.*
17. U.N. Press Release, *supra* note 11.
18. HRW Report, *supra* note 13, at Overview of Factors, 5.

Standards for Maximum Effectiveness of National Human Rights Institutions

The strengths of the NHRI can be maximized if governments ensure the independence of the institutions. In the early nineties, representatives of national institutions, states, the United Nations, its specialized agencies, intergovernmental and non-governmental organizations generated a set of standards for the operation of NHRIs, called the Paris Principles.[19] The Paris Principles provide comprehensive criteria for the success of any NHRI, including the following: (1) a broad mandate specified in founding legislative or constitutional statute; (2) an independent appointment process for commission members with fixed terms of office; (3) a pluralistic and representative composition from related fields; (4) regular and effective functioning; and (5) adequate resources, including infrastructure, staff, and funding.[20] Each of these factors contributes to the actual and perceived independence of a national human rights institution, arguably the most important indicator of a NHRI's success. Independence allows the NHRI to criticize its government and gives the institution credibility with the people whose rights it is charged with protecting.

In addition to the elements set forth in the Paris Principles, "many of which set a high standard," a NHRI requires committed, creative leadership and members to be successful. This critical factor is difficult to legislate or even predict when examining candidates for office. Human Rights Watch calls for commissioners "who are committed to making respect for human rights a reality and are willing to stand firm in the face of inevitable resistance from other government departments."[21]

Analysis of Uganda, Ghana, and Tanzania

The human rights commissions in Uganda and Ghana are highly respected African NHRIs. In its 2001 report, Human Rights Watch named both as

---

19. The Paris Principles arose out of an international workshop convened by the Center for Human Rights convened October 1991. They were endorsed by the Commission on Human Rights in March 1992 (Resolution 1992/54) and by the General Assembly in December 1993 (GA Resolution A/RES/48/134 of 20 December 1993). Fact Sheet No.19, *supra* note 1.

20. *See* The Paris Principles, Fact Sheet No.19, *supra* note 1 at appendix.

21. HRW Report, *supra note 13*, at International Standards: The Paris Principles, 2.

among "the most promising" national human rights commissions "in their willingness to actively speak out strongly against government abuses and to exhibit their independence in the interest of protecting the rights of their citizens," calling their work "a testament to the integrity of those commissions' members."[22] Tanzania, still a young commission, is struggling under a restrictive mandate but seems promising.

The Uganda Human Rights Commission

The 1995 Constitution establishes the Uganda Human Rights Commission (UHRC) and defines its functions, powers, and structure.[23] The UHRC's powers include the ability to initiate investigations of human rights violations, monitor detention conditions, conduct educational and other activities to promote human rights awareness, and monitor and make recommendations for government compliance with its international obligations.[24] The UHRC can subpoena any witness or document, order the release of any detained person, and recommend payment or compensation, or any other possible legal remedy after it finds the existence of a human rights abuse.[25] The UHRC is comprised of a Chair, who must be a Judge of the High Court, and no less than three additional persons appointed by the President and subject to approval by Parliament, who serve for a fixed term of six years.[26] The Uganda Human Rights Commission Act No. 4 of 1997 implements the powers, functions, and structure of the UHRC in greater detail.

Three limits in the UHRC mandate only minimally impinge on the Commission's freedom to investigate. To avoid redundancy, the UHRC cannot undertake "a matter which is pending before a court or tribunal."[27] The UHRC also cannot question "a matter relating to the exercise of prerogative of mercy."[28] The last restriction is the most troubling from a human rights perspective; the UHRC is prohibited from looking into "a matter involving the

---

22. *Id.*, at Summary, 3.

23. THE CONSTITUTION OF UGANDA, chap. 4, art. 51–59 (1995) *available at* http://www.government.go.ug/constitution/detail.php?myId=4.

24. *Id.* at art. 52.

25. *Id.* at art. 53.

26. *Id.* at art. 51.

27. The Uganda Human Rights Commission, *About Us: What the Commission is Barred From at* http://www.uhrc.org/aboutus.php (last visited Dec. 6, 2003).

28. *Id.*

relations or dealings between the government and any other government or international organization."[29]

In the past, the UHRC has not devoted significant energy to women's human rights issues. In the highlights of its annual report, mediations involving women's rights, including domestic violence situations, receive only passing mention.[30] Similarly, in a section discussing visits to refugee camps, women are mentioned only in that they (along with children) are at particular risk for violation of rights.[31] The UHRC is not completely insensitive to women's plight. Chair Margaret Sekaggya delivered the keynote address, "Civic Education: Implications for Women in Uganda," at a workshop designed to identify issues affecting women in Uganda.[32]

Ghana's Commission on Human Rights and Administrative Justice

Established by the Constitution as part of the transition from single-party authoritarian rule to a constitutional democracy in the early nineties, the Commission on Human Rights and Administrative Justice (CHRAJ) has a broad mandate, including the ability to investigate complaints of human rights violations by state and non-state actors and allegations of corruption by state officials. It has the power to issue subpoenas "requiring the attendance of any person before the Commission and the production of any document or record relevant to any investigation," to bring contempt charges against any person failing to obey, and refer matters to court.[33] CHRAJ shares the limitations of the UHCR and cannot investigate any matters pending before a court of law, relating to Ghana's dealings with other countries or international organizations, or concerning the prerogative of mercy.[34]

CHRAJ also has one of the most extensive networks of offices among the NHRIs of Africa, currently working through ten regional offices and ninety-

---

29. *Id.*

30. The Uganda Human Rights Commission, *Highlights of the Commission's Annual Report* (Jan. 2001 – Sept. 2002) *available at* http://www.uhrc.org/publications.php.

31. *Id.*

32. Margaret Sekaggya, keynote address at the NAWOU-FES workshop to identify the women and gender issues of concern and strategizing for transition in Uganda (November 2003) at Kampala Regency Hotel *available at* http://www.uhrc.org/publications.php.

33. The Commission on Human Rights and Administrative Justice Ghana *at* http://www.chrajghana.org/AboutCHRAJ.jsp (last visited October 8, 2003).

34. *Id.*

nine district offices.[35] In order to ensure that the services of the Commission are accessible to the widest possible number of Ghanaians, Article 220 of the Constitution requires the Commission to establish offices in all 10 regions and 110 districts of the country.

The Commission is comprised of a Commissioner and two deputy commissioners, and it is actively lobbying for more members.[36] The Commissioner has security of tenure until the age of retirement but is a direct presidential appointee. Institutionally, the political appointment of the commissioner is a problem, but, for now, direct presidential appointee Commissioner Emile Short "has created one of the most credible human rights commissions" in Africa.[37]

The CHRAJ has confronted some particularly sensitive human rights abuses, including violence against women. Commissioner Short said, "The high incidence of violence against women should be a matter of concern for anyone who believes in human dignity and national development."[38] CHRAJ has been working to end the banishment of and other violence against women accused of being witches, after a 1997 investigation found hundreds of elderly women living in camps.[39]

Most recently, CHRAJ published "State of Human Rights 2002," which included a section on women's rights.[40] The Commission noted Ghanaian women's contributions to the good of the nation and called for the elimination of on-going violations of their human rights, including domestic violence, the banishment of elderly women as witches, and harmful cultural practices such as widowhood rites, trokosi, and female genital mutilation.[41] The Commission also noted "with satisfaction" the increased active participation of women in politics, although it did not discuss enduring barriers to this participation.[42]

---

35. *Id.*

36. HRW Report, *supra* note 13, at *Ghana: Staffing and Appointment Procedures.*

37. HRW Report, *supra* note 13, Overview of Factors, 3.

38. Francis Asamoah Tuffour, *Let's Campaign Against Violence*, THE DAILY GRAPHIC (Ghanaian newspaper), June 16, 2003, at 20.

39. HRW Report, *supra* note 13, at *Ghana: Activities.*

40. Commission on Human Rights and Administrative Justice, *State of Human Rights 2002*, (Dec. 10, 2002) *available at* http://www.chrajghana.org/PressReleasePage.jsp.

41. *Id.*

42. *Id.*

The Human Rights Commission and
Good Governance in Tanzania

Required by the Constitution,[43] enacted by the Commission for Human Rights and Good Governance Act 2001, the Human Rights Commission and Good Governance was inaugurated in March 2002. The Commission replaced an ombudsman that human rights activists criticized as limited in its capacity to address human rights abuses.[44] Headed by an Appeal Court judge, the new Commission is charged with promoting human rights through civic education and investigating human rights violations. The Commission conducts its work through public hearings, showcasing human rights issues for the public.

Unfortunately, the legislature granted the President significant powers over the Commission, including determining salaries of the Commissioner and appointing the Executive Secretary of the Commission.[45] Most significantly, the President has discretion to bar the commission from investigating any matter.[46] These ties to the President may compromise the independence, innovativeness, and financial security of the Commission. As a result, five NGOs independently screened applicants for posts of chairman, vice chairman, and five commissioners, creating a report that was submitted to the appointing committee, which made appointments subject to the president's approval.[47]

The individual members of a national human rights institution often determine whether it will be a real catalyst for change or ineffective bureaucracy. The Commission inherited the bulk of its staff from the former office of the ombudsman; human rights advocates are concerned that this staff is not adequately familiar with the new, broader mandate.[48] Some of the Commissioners are political retirees, who may have or appear to have an allegiance to the government. Some human rights activists complain that the commissioners are "too busy attending human rights conferences" to pursue effective pro-

43. TANZANIAN CONSTITUTION, chap. VI, part 1, art. 129–31.

44. The Tanzanian ombudsman, and ombudsmen in general, was limited to investigating complaints against civil servants. Given the variety of perpetrators of human rights violations this is an inadequate scope of office. Projectus Rwehumbiza for the Southern Africa Human Rights NGOS Network, Tanzania, *Human Rights Monthly Reports* (Dec.–Nov. 1999).

45. Commission for Human Rights and Good Governance Act 2001.

46. *Id.*

47. *Id.*

48. E-mail from Vincent Shauri, Ag. Executive Director, Lawyers' Environmental Action Team (LEAT) (Tanzania) (Nov. 2003) (on file with author).

tection and promotion on the ground.[49] Human rights activists agree that for the Tanzanian Commission, hampered by reliance on the government for funding and for approval of its investigations, success "will ultimately depend on the commitment of the commissioners."[50]

Conclusion: Hope for Women's Human Rights in Africa

The human rights commissions in Ghana, Tanzania, and Uganda are working under limited mandates, resource constraints, and staffing shortages to address dire and complex human rights situations. Despite the difficulties, even the most modest of national human rights commissions represents hope for the women living in these countries. This optimism, however, does not stem from the existence of these commissions per se but from the thoughtful and tenacious women's human rights activists working to forge policy, case law, and popular dialogue. In Ghana, Tanzania, and Uganda, human rights activists push their national human rights commissions to do the best work possible under the circumstances.

---

49. *Id.*
50. Projectus Rwehumbiza for the Southern Africa Human Rights NGOS Network, Tanzania, *Human Rights Monthly Reports* (May–June 2001).

CONTRIBUTORS

FITNAT ADJETEY

B.A., University of Ghana; B.L., Ghana School of Law; L.L.M., Georgetown University Law Center.

Ms Adjetey is currently principal counsel with the Legal Department of the Volta River Authority, a power utility corporation. While in Washington, D.C. to pursue her L.L.M. and during her internship with the Women's Rights Project of Human Rights Watch, Ms. Adjetey analyzed how traditional practices such as polygyny, brideprice, child and forced marriages, and female genital mutilation prevent African women from making choices about their reproductive lives. Ms. Adjetey is a former Co-Director of Leadership and Advocacy for Women in Africa – Ghana (LAWA Ghana), an organization that works to improve women's legal status. Ms. Adjetey has co-authored a handbook on domestic violence and several training manuals for training police officers, health workers, and the judiciary on domestic violence. She also authored a 1995 American University Law Review article addressing African women's reproductive autonomy.

NYANJAGI HADIJA ALLY

L.L.B.; University of Dar es Salaam; L.L.M., Georgetown University Law Center.

Prior to joining the Leadership and Advocacy for Women in Africa (LAWA) program at Georgetown University Law Center, Washington D.C., in 1995, she worked as a State Attorney in Mwanza, Tanzania. While she was in the LAWA Program, she focused on the issue of refugees, an important issue in Western Tanzania bordering Rwanda, Burundi, and the DRC. During the LAWA program, her work placement was with the Women's Commission for Refugee Women and Children, where she assessed the impact of the U.S. Immigration and Naturalization Service Gender Guidelines.

In March 1999, Ms. Ally joined the United Nations High Commissioner for Refugees at the Branch Office, Dar es Salaam, in the Protection/Legal Unit as an Assistant Protection Officer. She quickly established her expertise in issues affecting refugee women and coordinated UNHCR's Sexual and Gender-Based Violence (SGBV) reports. She participated in the review of the Tanzania Refugees Act, 1998, a task initiated by UNHCR in 2000 to recommend editorial and substantive amendments to the law. From October to November 2001, Hadija carried out a protection/legal review of the 1995 UNHCR Guidelines on Sexual Violence and submitted a draft to UNHCR headquarters in Geneva. In 2002, she was promoted to a Protection Officer and re-assigned to UNHCR's Sub-Office in Peshawar, Pakistan.

Jacqueline Asiimwe

L.L.B., Makerere University; Post Graduate Diploma in Legal Practice, Law Development Center, Uganda; L.L.M., Georgetown University Law Center.

Ms. Asiimwe, whom the Monitor Daily, a major Ugandan newspaper, selected as one of the "Leaders of Tomorrow," is an experienced women's rights advocate. Ms. Asiimwe began her legal career at the Uganda Association of Women Lawyers (FIDA) where she promoted women's rights in the areas of property ownership, violence against women, family law, and sexual harassment. Ms. Asiimwe also served as FIDA's Program Officer in Charge of Information and Publicity, where she conducted an education campaign for women and children and served as a media contact, both by writing newspaper articles and appearing on radio and television shows. After leaving FIDA, Ms. Asiimwe began working as a human rights lawyer at Action for Development, a role that enabled her to continue her work on women's rights. Ms. Asiimwe, who is Chairperson of the Uganda chapter of Women in Law and Development in Africa, has also served on several committees, including the Uganda Women's Network and the Coalition on the Domestic Relations Bill. In 2001, she published *Making Women's Land Rights a Reality in Uganda: Advocacy for Co-ownership by Spouses*, 4 Yale Hum. Rts. & Dev. L.J. 171 (2001). Ms. Asiimwe is currently the Coordinator of the Uganda Women's Network, one of the leading women's rights advocacy coalitions in Uganda.

Vanessa Rae Brocato

J.D., Georgetown University Law Center; B.S., Bradley University

Ms. Brocato has had a unique opportunity to work with several generations of Leadership and Advocacy for Women in Africa ("LAWA") fellows while working at the Women's Law and Public Policy Fellowship Program. In the summer of 2003, she lived in Ghana and developed a training manual on the interrelatedness of violence against women and the HIV/AIDS pandemic. As a student in the Georgetown University Law Center's International

Women's Human Rights Clinic, she participated in a fact-finding mission to Tanzania on domestic violence and helped to write the resulting human rights report. As a legal intern with the Sexuality Information and Education Council of the United States (SIECUS), Ms. Brocato analyzed U.S. policy affecting sexuality education and reproductive health abroad. Ms. Brocato has also written *Profitable Proposals: Explaining and Addressing the Mail-Order Bride Industry through International Human Rights Law,* which is forthcoming in the 2004 San Diego International Law Journal.

Dora C. Kanabahita Byamukama

L.L.B., Makerere University; Post Graduate Diploma in Legal Practice, Law Development Center, Uganda; L.L.M., Georgetown University Law Center.

Ms. Kanabahita Byamukama, an Honorable Member of the Ugandan Parliament, has advocated for women's human rights both throughout Uganda and in over thirty countries worldwide. Most recently, Ms. Kanabahita Byamukama has been the Managing Director of Paradigm Consult Ltd., a firm specializing in gender, legal, financial, and environmental issues. In this capacity, she has utilized a women's human rights framework to analyze women's economic and property rights under the Ugandan Domestic Relations Bill and has completed a project entitled "Customary and Religious Constraints to Women's Access to Social Justice in Decentralized Arrangements" for the World Bank. Ms. Kanabahita Byamukama is a co-founder and active member of Law and Advocacy for the Women of Uganda, a non-governmental organization dedicated to using the law to improve women's lives, the Human Rights Network, and the Uganda Women's Network.

Ms. Kanabahita Byamukama is the Chairperson of the Parliamentary Committee on Equal Opportunities, which was established in August 2002. She is also the Chairperson of the Parliamentary Committee on Legal and Parliamentary Affairs, the Committee responsible for 80 percent of the Bills of Parliament and for ensuring respect for the rule of law. Ms. Kanabahita Byamukama is the Vice Chairperson of the Uganda Women Parliamentary Association, which is composed of seventy-five women members of Parliament.

Anne Daugherty Leiter

J.D., Georgetown University Law Center; B.A. Mary Washington College.

Although primarily a fiction author, Ms. Daugherty Leiter enjoys using her love of writing to draw attention to the continued need for equality between the sexes. As a 2002–03 recipient of a Women's Law and Public Policy Fellow in the Program on Women's Employment Rights at the DC Employment Justice Center, she represented victims of sexual harassment and employment discrimination. Ms. Daugherty Leiter previously focused on these issues in an international context, having participated in fact-finding in Poland in 2001 to document that nation's legal and social responses to domestic violence and sex-based employment discrimination. As a result of this experience, Ms. Daugherty Leiter served as a contributing author of a report entitled *Domestic Violence in Poland*. While at Georgetown University Law Center, where she was a Public Interest Law Scholar, she also authored the overview of Hate Crimes legislation published in the *Georgetown Journal of Gender and the Law's* 2001 Annual Review. Ms. Daugherty Leiter, who is grateful for all that she has learned from the Leadership and Advocacy for Women in Africa ("LAWA") fellows, currently lives in Madison, Wisconsin.

BEATRICE DUNCAN

L.L.B., University of Ghana; B.L., Ghana School of Law; L.L.M., Georgetown University Law Center.

Ms. Duncan has utilized her talents as a lawyer, filmmaker, and author to advocate for women's rights. She has worked at the International Human Rights Law Group, where she focused on land reform efforts in Ghana and in Zimbabwe. She also worked for the Ghana National Commission on Children, where she completed a thorough analysis of Ghanaian laws affecting children and proposed new legislation to improve children's legal protection. In 1995, Ms. Duncan produced a film that explored Ghanaian market women's reactions to their government's structural adjustment programs. In 1997, Ms. Duncan established Gender-Child Development Consultancy Ltd.; since the company's founding, Ms. Duncan has written and published *Women in Agriculture in Ghana* and, in June 1997, addressed the Second World Congress on Children in San Francisco. Currently, Ms. Duncan is the head of the Rights Protection and Promotion Section of the United Nations Children's Fund in Accra, Ghana where, among other activities, she helps women and adolescent girls to develop income-generating skills.

Angela Dwamena Aboagye

L.L.B., University of Ghana; B.L., Ghana School of Law; L.L.M., Georgetown University Law Center.

Ms. Aboagye is a tireless and innovative advocate for women's rights. She founded the Ark Foundation in 1995 while pursuing her LL.M. degree at Georgetown University Law Center. The Ark Foundation is an advocacy-based human rights organization working to protect women's and children's rights. The Ark Foundation has established two cutting edge programs in Ghana, including the first shelter for abused women and children in the country and a program designed to identify and cultivate young women leaders from Ghanaian tertiary institutions. While in Washington, D.C., working on her graduate law degree, Ms. Aboagye While worked at the Women's Rights Project of Human Rights Watch. She has written several articles on women's rights that were published in major Ghanaian newspapers. Ms. Aboagye has also collaborated with other leaders in the field to establish a number of networks and coalitions, including the Gender Violence Survivors Support Network and Network for Women's Rights. She has won recognition for her work from the Rotary Club, the African Women's Development Fund, and UNICEF.

Hilary Gbedemah

L.L.B., University of Ghana; B.L., Ghana School of Law; L.L.M., Georgetown University Law Center.

Ms. Gbedemah specializes in the intersection of human rights and public health. While in Washington, D.C., she completed an advocacy internship with the ACLU's National Prison Project. Specifically, Ms. Gbedemah provided legal assistance to lawyers representing people infected with AIDS. In addition to this work, Ms. Gbedemah spent two semesters lecturing at a Florida University on the status of women in Ghana. Her time in the United States also enabled her to research an advocacy paper against Trokosi, a practice of sexual slavery for young girls that is common in her home district in the Volta region of Ghana. Upon her return to Ghana in 1996, Ms. Gbedemah continued in private legal practice, where she specialized in female adolescent health. She now directs the Volta Region's Legal Awareness Programme, which engages in legal literacy campaigns, advocacy, lobbying, and pro bono representation.

Sheila Gyimah

B.A. (Hons), University of Ghana, Legon; B.L., Ghana School of Law; L.L.M., Georgetown University Law Center.

Ms. Gyimah developed an expertise in women's rights through her work with Women, Law and Development International. Ms. Gyimah completed a thorough analysis of the types of domestic violence legislation that exist worldwide, a project that the UN Special Rapporteur on Violence Against Women requested. She also developed a manual to train women's human rights advocates regarding the process for reporting human rights violations. Ms. Gyimah presented results of these projects at the United Nations Fourth World Conference on Women in Beijing in 1995, where she also spoke as part of a domestic violence panel. After Beijing, Ms. Gyimah returned to Ghana, where she took over a private law practice. Ms. Gyimah has presented papers at various conferences, including the African Society of International and Comparative Law Conference in the late 1990s. She is currently a co-director of LAWA-Ghana, a women's human rights organization in Accra.

Scholastica Jullu

L.L.B., University of Dar es Salaam; L.L.M., Georgetown University Law Center.

Ms. Jullu is currently the Executive Director of the Women's Legal Aid Centre (WLAC) in Tanzania. Ms. Jullu's activism in the area of women's human rights has achieved important results for the Tanzanian women that she serves. As a provider of direct legal services to women through WLAC, Ms. Jullu raises awareness among Tanzanian women about their legal rights. She has analyzed the government's methods of addressing crimes committed by women in the hopes of identifying ways to reduce the number of these crimes. Ms. Jullu also documented cases of domestic violence fatalities that led to a march in memory of the victims. In addition to these experiences, Ms. Jullu has conducted educational seminars designed to abolish female genital mutilation and domestic violence.

Naome Kabanda

L.L.B., Makerere University; Post Graduate Diploma in Legal Practice, Law Development Center, Uganda; L.L.M., Georgetown University Law Center.

Before studying women's rights in Washington, D.C., Ms. Kabanda served as the Senior Land Management Officer for the Mukono District Council in

Uganda. This position, in which her duties included educating individuals about their land rights, enabled her to assist women who wished to assert their property rights. She also was able to advise Mukono women on how to lease and purchase land, receive credit, and use their land for development. Ms. Kabanda also volunteered at Uganda Human Rights Activists, where she provided counseling services and legal advice to victims of human rights violations.

After completing her LL.M. degree program at Georgetown, Ms. Kabanda became the Prinicipal Land Officer focused on governance issues in the Ministry of Water, Lands and Environment. She is in charge of policy related to the decentralized institutions established under the 1998 Land Act. She is also responsible for governance issues within the Ministry including issues related to gender and the law and land reforms. Ms. Kabanda also continues to work toward the economic empowerment of women through microfinance programs with non-governmental organizations.

Mande Limbu

L.L.B., University of Dar es Salaam; L.L.M., Georgetown University Law Center.

Ms. Limbu is currently a doctoral candidate at Cornell Law School in New York. She participated in the Women's Law and Public Policy Fellowship Program's Leadership and Advocacy for Women (LAWA) program and graduated with an LL.M. from Georgetown University Law Center in Washington, D.C. in 2001. After graduating from Georgetown, Ms. Limbu interned at the Washington, D.C. offices of Amnesty International and the United Nations High Commissioner for Refugees [UNHCR], where she conducted research on women, children, and refugee rights. While at Cornell, Ms. Limbu is focusing her graduate research on Equal Access to Justice and her dissertation is entitled "Improving Access to Justice: Law School Clinics and Women's Access to Legal Aid and Human Rights Protection: A Comparative Study of Tanzania, South Africa, and the United States." After completing her doctoral program, she hopes to be both an academic researcher and a human rights activist.

Sarah Babirye Lubega

L.L.B., Makerere University; Post Graduate Diploma in Legal Practice, Law Development Center, Uganda; L.L.M., Georgetown University Law Center.

Ms. Babirye Lubega has participated in numerous community-based activities designed to empower women, including offering free legal advice to members of the Uganda Women Entrepreneurs Association and counseling women on their rights under property ownership, succession, and marriage law for the Federation of Women Lawyers Uganda Chapter (FIDA –U). Ms. Babirye Lubega has won several awards for her work on behalf of women entrepreneurs, and she has attended numerous international conferences focusing on businesswomen. Most notably, she presented a paper entitled "The Impact of Technology and Communication on Women Entrepreneurs in the Global Economy" at the 1998 IFWE/WASME Sixth International Women's Conference in Accra Ghana and a paper entitled "The Contribution of Women Entrepreneurs to Economic Development" at the 1997 Asia Africa Forum on Economic Empowerment Women in Bangkok, Thailand. Ms. Babirye Lubega also worked as a Consultant for the World Bank and as a Banking Officer for the Legal Central Bank of Uganda. She is currently a partner at Frederick, Francis and Associates Advocates in Kampala, Uganda, and a Board Member of the Uganda Women Entrepreneurs Association. She is also a Board Member of Pride Uganda, one of the largest micro-finance institutions in Uganda.

JANE MAGIGITA

L.L.B., University of Dar es Salaam; L.L.M., Georgetown University Law Center.
Ms. Magigita's work at Tanzania's Women's Legal Aid Center, both as a law student and as a practicing attorney, has enabled her to work on many women's and children's rights issues. Ms. Magigita began as a volunteer at the Center in 1996, at which time she simultaneously interned at the Tanzanian Ministry of Justice. Ms. Magigita later became a legal officer at the Center, where she has worked to educate women about their legal rights. By the time Ms. Magigita left the Center in 2000 for Washington, D.C., she had become the co-head of the outreach department. As part of her work, Ms. Magigita has contributed to the establishment of nine paralegal units that specialize in women's and children's rights. These units, which Ms. Magigita also monitored, are located across Tanzania. Ms. Magigita also works with a number of coalitions that campaign for legal reform. These efforts led to two major reforms, the enactment of the Sexual Offences Act of 1998, which created stricter punishments for sexual offenses against women and children, and the enactment of the Land Act of 1999, which increased women's property rights.

In 2002, Ms. Magigita became a qualified facilitator for Women, Law, and Development International (WLDI), an organization based in the United States. She has conducted trainings on human rights advocacy for women from nine states in eastern Nigeria.

Monica Magoke-Mhoja

L.L.B., University of Dar es Salaam; L.L.M., University of Dar es Salaam; L.L.M., Georgetown University Law Center.

Ms. Mhoja is an experienced attorney and human rights activist who currently directs the Women's Legal Aid Centre (WLAC), an NGO that she founded to provide free legal aid to impoverished Tanzanian women and children. Ms. Mhoja left WLAC to come to Washington, D.C. where, in addition to obtaining her L.L.M. degree, she completed an advocacy internship at the International Human Rights Law Group. Her internship enabled Ms. Mhoja to conduct a comparative analysis of women's inheritance and property rights in ten African countries and to help to develop a workshop that the Law Group conducted in West Africa on the subject. While in the United States, Ms. Mhoja also served as an observer at a session of the Committee on the Elimination of All Forms of Discrimination Against Women in New York and completed a report that detailed CEDAW procedures. Upon returning to Tanzania in 1997, Ms. Mhoja returned to WLAC. In recognition of her human rights activism, the American Bar Association awarded her its 2003 International Human Rights Award. Ms. Mhoja is currently pursuing her Ph.D. in the field of human rights.

Salma Maoulidi

L.L.B., University of Dar es Salaam; L.L.M., Georgetown University Law Center.

Ms. Maoulidi is active in the gender and human rights movements in her native Tanzania and the East Africa region. While participating in the Women's Law and Public Policy Fellowship Program's Leadership and Advocacy for Women in Africa (LAWA) program in 1995, Ms. Maoulidi interned at the National Organization of Women Legal Defense Fund, where she worked on welfare reform issues and single-sex education. Since her return to Tanzania, she has applied her legal background in working with local communities and organizations to build leadership and organizational capacities. Ms. Maoulidi heads a Muslim women's development network and consults widely on human rights, organizational development, and policy issues. She has played a critical role in key policy areas including violence against women, education, children's rights, the formation of a national Human Rights Commission, land reform, and poverty reduction. Ms. Maoulidi's is currently exploring the relationship of culture and religion to women's status with a particular emphasis on Muslim women and youth.

Harriet Diana Musoke

L.L.B. (with Honors), Makerere University; Post Graduate Diploma in Legal Practice, Law Development Center, Uganda; L.L.M. (with Distinction), Georgetown University Law Center.

Since 1993, Ms. Musoke has been a partner with Messrs. Musoke and Company Advocates, where she specializes in domestic relations law. She is also a Senior Principal Lecturer at the Law Development Center in Uganda, where she teaches courses in domestic relations and human rights law. Since 1997, she has been Head of the Department of Law Reporting at the Law Development Center. While in Washington, D.C., she interned at the Center for Reproductive Law and Policy, where she worked on health and human rights issues. Ms. Musoke served as: President of the Uganda Law Society from 1998–2000, Chairperson of the Uganda Association of Women Lawyers (FIDA-U) from 1992–93, and Chairperson and Founding Member of the Uganda Consumers Protection Association.

Regina Mutyaba

L.L.B., Makerere University; Post Graduate Diploma in Legal Practice, Law Development Center, Uganda; L.L.M., Georgetown University Law Center.

Ms. Mutyaba is a former consultant to the National Task Force of the Uganda Network on Law Ethics and HIV/AIDS. In that capacity, she analyzed the laws of succession, human rights, and public health and reported her findings to the public and to the Law Reform Commission. Ms. Mutyaba spent six months as the first staff person of FOWODE, an organization dedicated to supporting women members of parliament; after her tenure at FOWODE, Ms. Mutyaba became the education officer at the Uganda Human Rights Education and Documentation Center. While in Washington, D.C., Ms. Mutyaba interned at the NAACP Legal Defense & Education Fund where she provided legal advice in ongoing litigation and attended Congressional hearings. In addition to these professional experiences, Ms. Mutyaba is active in volunteer organizations, including FIDA Uganda, where she headed the divorce and separation team's study of family law, and the Uganda Law Society, where she served on the Executive Committee as the chairperson for continuing legal education and where she became the first woman ever to hold the post of Secretary of the organization. Ms. Mutyaba is also the Second Deputy Treasurer of the East African Law Society, a member of Law and Advocacy for Women—Uganda (LAW-U), and a country representative within the alumni network of the Women's Law and Public Policy Fellowship Program.

EMMA SSALI NAMULI

L.L.B., Makerere University; Post Graduate Diploma in Legal Practice, Law Development Center, Uganda; L.L.M., Georgetown University Law Center.

Ms. Namuli is an experienced advocate who has worked on a number of women's rights issues, including the laws of marriage, succession, land and tenancy, child care, and, most recently, HIV/AIDS. Before coming to Washington, D.C. to pursue her L.L.M. degree, Ms. Namuli worked as a legal officer for the Uganda Association of Women Lawyers. This position, which she held for several years, enabled her to counsel clients and to represent them in court on a variety of issues affecting Ugandan women. While in Washington, D.C., Ms. Namuli completed an advocacy internship at Whitman-Walker Legal Clinic, an organization that serves the HIV/AIDS community. While at Whitman-Walker Clinic, Ms. Namuli specialized in counseling HIV/AIDS affected women, a role that complemented her graduate research on women and HIV/AIDS in Uganda. Ms. Namuli returned to Uganda in 2000, at which time she began work on women's legal rights at Law and Advocacy for Women - Uganda (LAW-Uganda) in Kampala. She has continued to work as a volunteer, providing legal advice to clients of the Uganda Association of Women Lawyers and the National Association of Women Living with HIV/AIDS. Ms. Namuli is currently the Project Manager of the Juvenile Justice Project of Save the Children in Uganda.

EVELYN NASSUNA

L.L.B., University of Dar es Salaam; Post Graduate Diploma in Legal Practice, Law Development Center, Uganda; L.L.M., Georgetown University Law Center.

Ms. Nassuna worked as a Program Associate at the Foundation for Human Rights Initiative, where she organized and implemented legal literacy campaigns in districts throughout Uganda, and as a Legal Intern for the Office of Legal Counsel, U.S. Equal Employment Opportunity Commission, where she researched employment law issues, including sexual harassment. Prior to these experiences, Ms. Nassuna worked as a Legal Associate for Ibanda-Nahamya and Company Advocates in Kampala, where she completed a project on the legal and sociological implications of compulsory HIV-AIDS testing of sexual offenders. Her volunteer activities include designing a training manual for women community leaders in Kampala District and conducting human rights trainings for two Ugandan community-based organizations specializing in women's rights. Ms. Nassuna is currently a Justice and Advocacy Manager for Catholic Relief Services—Uganda, where she provides technical assistance concerning policy analysis and advocacy focused on issues including debt relief, HIV/AIDs, peace, and justice.

Gloria Ofori-Boadu

B.A., University of Ghana; B.L. (Barrister-at-Law), Ghana School of Law; LL.M., Georgetown University Law Center.

After a distinguished career in the private sector, Ms. Ofori-Boadu participated in the Leadership and Advocacy for Women in Africa (LAWA) Program in 1995–96. As part of the program, she worked in the office of United States Representative Eva Clayton (1st District, North Carolina). Shortly after returning to Ghana, Ms. Ofori-Boadu became the Executive Director of the Women's Assistance and Business Agency. She later became the Executive Director of the International Federation of Women Lawyers (FIDA), a post she held for almost four years. Ms. Ofori-Boadu is currently the President of the Women's Assistance and Business Agency. In August of 2002, she was elected to the Tema Municipal Assembly (T.M.A.).

Margaret C. Oguli Oumo

L.L.B., Makerere University; Post-Graduate Diploma in Legal Practice, Law Development Center, Uganda; L.L.M., Georgetown University Law Center.

Mrs. Oguli Oumo represents Ugandan women both as a Country Representative to the Women in Law and Development in Africa (WILDAF) program and as a Senior Advisory Committee member of the Uganda Association of Women Lawyers (FIDA). In 1998, Ms. Oguli Oumo served as a UNICEF consultant to the Convention on the Elimination of all Forms of Discrimination Against Women (CEDAW). In addition to these volunteer activities, Ms. Oguli Oumo spent sixteen years at the Ugandan Ministry of Justice, a tenure that culminated in the three years she spent as Principal State Attorney. Upon leaving the Ministry of Justice in 1994, Mrs. Oguli Oumo spent four years as the Commissioner for Legal Affairs at the Ministry of Gender, Labour & Social Development. Since 1998, Mrs. Oguli Oumo has been the Director of Legal Affairs for the Movement Secretariat in Uganda.

Regina Rweyemamu

L.L.B., University of Dar es Salaam; M.B.A., University of Newcastle; L.L.M., Georgetown University Law Center.

Ms. Rweyemamu, a member of the Tanzanian judiciary, is currently working as a Labour Commissioner in the Ministry of Labour & Youth Development. She worked at the Federal Judicial Center and the International Association of Women Judges during her time in Washington, D.C., placements that enabled her to design and implement training programs on women's rights issues for African judges. Ms. Rweyemamu has presented numerous papers concerning women's rights and the Tanzanian judiciary. Most notably, in 1997, Ms. Rweyemamu made a presentation at a conference for East African judges regarding judicial bias and its negative impact on rape prosecutions. The same year, she completed a presentation at the Tanzania Gender Networking Program Annual Conference in which she identified strategic litigation as a promising tool for realizing gender equality. Ms. Rweyemamu has also presented two papers entitled "Combating Violence Against Women: International Human Rights or National Strategies," and "In Search of Women's Human Rights—How to Capture "Living" Customary Law in Tanzania."

Bernice Sam

L.L.B., University of Ghana; B.L., Ghana School of Law; L.L.M., Georgetown University Law Center.

Ms. Sam is well-known for her commitment to women's and children's rights. She co-authored a book on violence against women and children and spousal property rights. Ms. Sam has conducted human rights trainings for legal literacy volunteers and traditional Ghanaian authorities. She worked on a pilot project in three communities designed to explore community-based methods of combating violence against women. Ms. Sam also directed a legal rights education program that assisted women to use the law to improve their lives and hosted a radio talk show on women's rights. Currently, Ms. Sam is the Programme Coordinator of the Africa Office of the Commonwealth Human Rights Initiative.

Maria Tungaraza

L.L.B., University of Dar es Salaam; L.L.M., Georgetown University Law Center.

Ms. Tungaraza's area of expertise is HIV/AIDS law and policy, dispute settlement, and the impact of HIV/AIDS on women in Tanzania. She was the

Director of an AIDS program in Tanzania prior to coming to Washington, D.C. to earn her L.L.M. degree and has completed several substantive projects on that topic. While in Washington, D.C., Ms. Tungaraza worked at the World Bank, where she researched the intersection between customary sexual practices and AIDS transmission and methods that governments could use to replace skilled workers who died of AIDS. She also worked at UNAIDS in Geneva, where she evaluated the Canadian AIDS Society's Project on HIV testing and confidentiality and their report on criminal law and AIDS.

Upon her return to Tanzania, Ms. Tungaraza joined the Julius Nyerere Foundation, where she focused on peace, unity, and people-centered development, including the Burundi Peace Negotiations. She also worked as a consultant for Africare Tanzania, advising on AIDS programs before joining the POLICY Project of the Futures Group International, where she works as a Resident Advisor. She has also worked as an advisor to the Tanzania Parliamentarians AIDS Coalition and as a consultant for the Tanzania Women Lawyers Association on an assessment of the domestic laws and their affect on HIV/AIDS. Ms. Tungaraza has made numerous national and international presentations on human rights, the legal implications of HIV/AIDS, and safe motherhood.

KULSUM WAKABI

L.L.B., Makerere University; Post-Graduate Diploma in Legal Practice, Law Development Center, Uganda; L.L.M., Georgetown University Law Center.

Ms. Wakabi, who passed away unexpectedly on November 16, 2000, made numerous important contributions to women's human rights. While in Washington, D.C., Ms. Wakabi completed an advocacy internship at the Women's Rights Project of Human Rights Watch, where, among other projects, she contributed to a report concerning women and armed conflict in Rwanda. Upon her return to Uganda, Ms. Wakabi conducted research on domestic violence in Uganda. Ms. Wakabi also worked in private practice and was active in Law and Advocacy for Women in Uganda (LAW-U), a organization dedicated to Ugandan women's legal rights that she co-founded with the Honorable Dora Kanabahita Byamukama. Her passion for and dedication to women's rights continues to be a source of inspiration and pride for women's human rights attorneys in Uganda.

INDEX